The Little Seagull Handbook *with Exercises*

FOURTH EDITION

The Little Seagull Handbook *with Exercises*

Richard Bullock
WRIGHT STATE UNIVERSITY

Michal Brody

Francine Weinberg

WRITE

RESEARCH

EDIT

EXERCISE

W. W. NORTON & COMPANY
Independent Publishers Since 1923

W. W. Norton & Company has been independent since its founding in 1923, when William Warder Norton and Mary D. Herter Norton first published lectures delivered at the People's Institute, the adult education division of New York City's Cooper Union. The firm soon expanded its program beyond the Institute, publishing books by celebrated academics from America and abroad. By midcentury, the two major pillars of Norton's publishing program—trade books and college texts—were firmly established. In the 1950s, the Norton family transferred control of the company to its employees, and today—with a staff of five hundred and hundreds of trade, college, and professional titles published each year—W. W. Norton & Company stands as the largest and oldest publishing house owned wholly by its employees.

Copyright © 2021, 2017, 2014, 2011 by W. W. Norton & Company, Inc.

All rights reserved
Printed in Canada

Editor: Erica Wnek
Senior Associate Editor: Claire Wallace
Assistant Editor: Edwin Jeng
Project Editor: Christine D'Antonio
Manuscript Editor: Laurie Lieb
Production Manager: Liz Marotta
Media Editor: Joy Cranshaw
Assistant Media Editor: Katie Bolger
Media Project Editor: Cooper Wilhelm
Managing Editor, College: Marian Johnson
Managing Editor, College Digital Media: Kim Yi

Ebook Manager: Ashley van der Grinten
Marketing Manager, Composition: Michele Dobbins
Design Director: Rubina Yeh
Text Design: Lisa Buckley / Anna Palchik
Designer: Lissi Sigillo
Permissions Specialist: Josh Garvin
Photo Editor: Ted Szczepanski
Composition: Six Red Marbles
Manufacturing: TC-Transcontinental Printing

Permission to use copyrighted material is included in the Credits section of this book, which begins on page 551.

Library of Congress Cataloging-in-Publication Data

Names: Bullock, Richard H. (Richard Harvey), author. | Brody, Michal, author. | Weinberg, Francine, author.
Title: The Little Seagull handbook : with exercises / Richard Bullock, Michal Brody, Francine Weinberg.
Description: Fourth edition. | New York, NY : W. W. Norton & Company, [2021] | Includes index.
Identifiers: LCCN 2020041104 | **ISBN 9780393422917** (paperback)
Subjects: LCSH: English language--Rhetoric--Handbooks, manuals, etc. | English language--Grammar--Handbooks, manuals, etc. | Report writing--Handbooks, manuals, etc.
Classification: LCC PE1408 .B8838233 2021 | DDC 808.042--dc23
LC record available at https://lccn.loc.gov/2020041104

W. W. Norton & Company, Inc., 500 Fifth Avenue, New York, NY 10110
wwnorton.com

W. W. Norton & Company Ltd., 15 Carlisle Street, London W1D 3BS

1 2 3 4 5 6 7 8 9 0

Preface

This book began as an attempt to create a small handbook that would provide help with the specific kinds of writing college students are assigned to do, and to make it as user-friendly as possible. It's been more successful than we had hoped: much to our surprise, it's been adopted by many instructors who had been using much larger handbooks. These teachers tell us they like it because it's got "just enough detail," it's easy to use, and it costs less than half what their former books cost.

From our own experience as teachers, we've seen how much students prefer smaller books, and so, to paraphrase Elmore Leonard, we've tried to give the information college writers need—and to leave out the details they skip. We've also seen how important it is that a handbook be easy to use. To that end, the book is organized around four familiar categories of Write, Research, Edit, and Exercise, and it includes menus, directories, a glossary / index, and more to help students find the help they need.

In order to preserve the handbook for easy reference, the exercises are in the back of the book, with links in the margins to make it easy to navigate between the handbook and the exercises. To enable students to check some of their work, we've included answers to even-numbered items after the exercises. We're pleased now to offer a fourth edition, with new student model essays for five key genres; a new genre chapter on summary/response essays; updated advice on finding and evaluating sources and new guidance on fact-checking sources; expanded advice on respectful and inclusive language, including non-gendered third-person singular pronouns; improved chapters on revision and reading strategies; and updated APA and Chicago documentation guides.

Highlights

Help with the kinds of writing students are assigned, including arguments, analyses, reports, narratives, and more. Brief chapters cover ten common genres, with annotated model student essays included for the five most-assigned genres and thirty additional models offered online.

Easy to use. Menus, directories, a glossary / index, and color-coded parts help students find the information they need. A simple four-part organization—Write, Research, Edit, Exercise—makes it easy for them to know where to look. And students agree: in a survey of more than 250 students using the handbook, 93 percent say it's easy to use, and 88 percent say it's easier and more reliable than sifting through information online.

Just enough detail, but with color-coded links that refer students to the glossary / index for more information if they need it.

User-friendly documentation guidelines for MLA, APA, Chicago, and CSE styles. Documentation directories lead students to the examples they need, color-coded templates show what information to include, and documentation maps show where to find the required detail. Model papers demonstrate each style, with a complete MLA paper and brief examples of the other three styles in the book with complete papers available online.

A full chapter on paragraphs, a subject that other pocket handbooks cover in much less detail. But students write in paragraphs—and they'll find the help they need in this handbook [W-5].

A section on "Editing the Errors That Matter." Covering 14 errors that teachers identified as undermining a writer's authority and weakening an argument, this section explains why each of these errors matters, describes how to spot them in a draft, and walks students through some ways of editing them out [E-1 to E-6].

Uniquely helpful guidance for multilingual students, including chapters on idioms [L-3] and prepositions [L-5] and additional detail on articles, phrasal verbs, and modal verbs—with more resources and exercises provided online.

Customizable. Add your own materials to the book: outcomes statements, syllabi, student writing, and so on. You can even customize the title and cover to replace our little seagull with your school mascot.

What's New?

Complete, annotated student model essays. Five new student-written essays—most of them documented—model the kinds of writing most often assigned: arguments, rhetorical analyses, reports, personal narratives, and summary/response essays [W-8 to W-12].

A new genre chapter on summary/response essays. Tips, templates, and a complete model student paper help students to summarize and respond in writing to what they read, skills expected of writers at all levels [W-12].

Expanded guidance on using respectful, inclusive language. New advice encourages students to see edited academic English as just one dialect among many, address people by the terms they prefer for themselves, consider capitalizing all races and ethnicities, respectfully refer to disabilities and people living with disabilities, and much more [L-9].

A new chapter on pronouns and gender. In light of changing grammatical conventions regarding pronouns and gender, we've provided practical, adaptable advice on using non-gendered pronouns, including singular "they," when an individual's gender is unknown or when referring to a person who uses such pronouns [L-10].

Updated advice for doing research online and fact-checking sources. New advice guides writers in investigating their own biases; using popular sites and search engines responsibly; and fact-checking text, images, and videos to avoid misinformation [R-1 to R-2]. And a new InQuizitive activity helps students practice fact-checking sources.

New APA and Chicago style guides. The APA and Chicago chapters have been updated to reflect new guidelines introduced in 2020 and 2017, respectively, and to provide color-coded templates and models for documenting the kinds of sources college students most often cite [APA-a to APA-e; CMS-a to CMS-d].

New exercises on using preferred terms and singular "they" [EX. L-9b; EX. L-10b].

What's Online?

DIGITAL.WWNORTON.COM/LITTLESEAGULL4

An interactive, accessible ebook makes it easy to use the *Little Seagull* on the go. Links between chapters and tools for searching, annotating, and bookmarking information make the digital version as simple to navigate as its paper counterpart. Norton Ebooks can be viewed on—and synced among—all computers and mobile devices and can be made available for offline reading. **Four years of access** to the ebook is included with all new copies of *The Little Seagull Handbook.*

InQuizitive for Writers is an adaptive learning tool that provides students with personalized practice editing sentences and working with sources, including a new activity on "Fact-Checking Sources." Explanatory feedback and links to the *Little Seagull* ebook offer advice precisely when it's needed, and gamelike elements keep students engaged. In addition, an activity on "How to Make the Most of *The Little Seagull*" will prepare your students to use their handbook when they need it most—as they write, research, and edit on their own.

Resources for your LMS include integrated links to InQuizitive for Writers, a plagiarism tutorial, model student essays, exercise worksheets, premade quizzes, resources for multilingual students, and more.

Acknowledgments

It takes a big team to publish even a small handbook. We have benefited from the astute comments and suggestions by many reviewers: Gillian Andersen, Eastern New Mexico University; Evan Balkan, Community College of Baltimore County–Catonsville; Jason Barr, Blue Ridge Community College; Josh M. Beach, University of Texas at San Antonio; Logan Bearden, Eastern Michigan University; Cynthia Bily, Macomb Community College; William Black, Weatherford College; Nancy Rochelle Bradley, Blinn College; Nicole Branch, Santa Clara University; Carole Chapman, Ivy Tech Community College–Southwest; Thomas Chester, Ivy Tech Community College–Marion; Jesseca Cornelson, Alabama State University; Rita D. Costello, McNeese State University; Michael Cripps, University of New England; Virginia Crisco, California State University–Fresno; Syble Davis, Houston Community College; Laura Ann Dearing, Jefferson Community and Technical College; Darren DeFrain, Wichita State University; Joann K. Deiudicibus, State University of New York at New Paltz; Christie Diep, Cypress College; Allison Dieppa, Florida Gulf Coast University; Anne-Marie Dietering, Oregon State University; Amy Doty, Southeast Community College–Lincoln; Virginia P. Dow, Liberty University; Clark Draney, College of Southern Idaho; Brenna Dugan, Owens Community College; Marie Eckstrom, Rio Hondo College; Megan Egbert, Utah State University; Tara Estes, Wallace Community College Dothan; Sara A. Etlinger, Rock Valley College; Africa Fine, Palm Beach State College; Megan Fulwiler, The College of Saint Rose; Philip Garrow, United States Naval Academy; Jonathan C. Glance, Mercer University; Carey Goyette, Clinton Community College; Anissa Graham, University of North Alabama; Shonette Grant, Northern Virginia Community College; Opal Greer, Eastern New Mexico University; Kendra Griffin, Aims Community College; Clinton Hale, Blinn College; Ann C. Hall, Ohio Dominican University; Anna Hall-Zieger, Blinn College; Melody Hargraves, St. Johns River State College; Joel B. Henderson, Chattanooga State Community College; Elizabeth Shaye Hope, Delgado Community College;

Robert Hurd, Anne Arundel Community College; Geri (Geraldine) Jacobs, Jackson College; Anne Marie Johnson, Utah State University; Jo Johnson, Ivy Tech Community College–Fort Wayne; Rachel Kartz, Ivy Tech Community College; Alexandra Kay, SUNY Orange County Community College; Michael Keller, South Dakota State University; Heather King, Ivy Tech Community College; Debra S. Knutson, Shawnee State University; Brian Leingang, Edison State Community College; Joseph Lemak, Elmira College; Matthew Masucci, State College of Florida–Venice; Courtney McGraw, Broward College; Kyle McIntosh, University of Tampa; James McWard, Johnson County Community College; L. Adam Mekler, Morgan State University; Lora Meredith, Western Wyoming Community College; Jeannine Morgan, St. Johns River State College; Tracy Ann Morse, East Carolina University; Amy Nawrocki, University of Bridgeport; Luke Niiler, University of Alabama; Jenifer Paquette, Hillsborough Community College; Jessica L. Parker, Metropolitan State University of Denver; Eden Pearson, Des Moines Area Community College; Heather Pristash, Western Wyoming Community College; Glenda Pritchett, Quinnipiac University; Jonathan Purkiss, Pulaski Technical College; Paula Rash, Caldwell Community College; Nick Recktenwald, University of Oregon; Dara Regaignon, New York University; Louis Riggs, Hannibal-LaGrange University; Tony Russell, Central Oregon Community College; David Salomon, The Sage Colleges; Anthony Sams, Ivy Tech Community College; Karen Schwarze, Utah State University; Dixie A. Shaw-Tillmon, University of Texas at San Antonio; Carol Singletary, Eastern New Mexico University; Daniel Stanford, Pitt Community College; Katie Stoynoff, The University of Akron; Linda Strahan, University of California, Riverside; Hannah Sykes, Rockingham Community College; Jarrod Waetjen, Northern Virginia Community College–Alexandria; Christy Wenger, Shepherd University; Jenny Williams, Spartanburg Community College; Nancy Wilson, Texas State University.

Ana Cooke, Pennsylvania State University, offered excellent advice on reshaping the "Evaluating Sources" chapter before we revised it and then provided a thoughtful and helpful review once we did. We also want to thank Emily Suh, Texas State University, for her insightful comments that helped us revise the "Edit" section.

We are especially grateful to the more than 250 students who reviewed the third edition. They affirmed what we already suspected: *The Little Seagull Handbook* meets their needs as writers, offering comments including "a great pocket guide for writing and editing," "a valuable tool," and—our favorite—"basically a book, but it's got a teacher inside."

We owe a big thank-you to all our friends at Norton. Erica Wnek led the editorial effort on this new edition, capably assisted by Edwin Jeng. In addition, Claire Wallace improved each section with her detailed editing and guided the documentation chapter updates. Thanks to their hard work and perceptive reading of the book, this edition is arguably the best one yet. A deep bow goes to Joy Cranshaw for all her work on InQuizitive, the LMS resources, instructor materials, and the ebook—and to Katie Bolger as well. We are once again grateful to Carin Berger and Debra Morton Hoyt for yet another charming cover design. And we thank Michele Dobbins, Elizabeth Pieslor, Emily Rowin, and Kim Bowers for their work getting the word out about this book.

Little books are always more complex than they look, and we are especially grateful to Christine D'Antonio and Liz Marotta for their expertise managing and producing *The Little Seagull Handbook*. Finally, we thank Marilyn Moller, the guiding intelligence behind all our textbooks.

Rich thanks his students and colleagues at Wright State for all they've taught him about teaching and writing over the years, and the many writing teachers using the *Little Seagull* who have offered suggestions or invited him to campus: Kelly Ritter, Kristi McDuffie, and their graduate teaching assistants at the University of Illinois, Urbana–Champaign; Collie Fulford, Kathryn Wymer, and their students in ENG 3040 at North Carolina Central University; Sylvia Miller at Pikes Peak Community College; Kevin Moore at SUNY Cobleskill; and Mary S. Tuley at Fayetteville Technical Community College. Finally, he thanks his wife, Barb, for her unwavering and good-humored support. Michal thanks her *pareja* Mucuy and her families and students in the United States and Mexico for always keeping her thinking. Fran thanks Marilyn for trading places with her so many years ago and her husband, Larry Strauss, for his confidence in her at all times.

Hats off to you all.

Richard Bullock
Michal Brody
Francine Weinberg

How to Use This Book

Write. Research. Edit. Perhaps you've been assigned to write a paper arguing that parking on campus should be free. Maybe you need to find sources for a report on organic farming in your state. Or you may want to make sure that the punctuation in your cover letter is perfect. Whether you need to write, research, edit—or all three—this little handbook can help.

More than anything else, the *Little Seagull* is a reference work. Other reference works include dictionaries, encyclopedias, and telephone directories. What do all of these have in common? You wouldn't read one cover to cover; instead, you would use it to find specific information. If you know how a reference work is organized, you can go directly to the information you need. In a dictionary, for example, the organization is alphabetical; if you know that J follows I and that Q follows P, then you'll know how to find what you're looking for. This section—and the InQuizitive activity on "How to Make the Most of *The Little Seagull*"—will help you learn your way around this book so that you'll be able to quickly find the information you need.

Ways of Navigating the Book

Menus. If you are looking for a specific chapter, start with the Brief Menu on the inside front cover; if you are looking for a specific section in a chapter, start with the Detailed Menu on the inside back cover. If you're looking for a specific exercise, turn to the Menu of Exercises at the back of the book.

Glossary / index. If you're looking for definitions of key terms and concepts, turn to the combined glossary and index at the back of the book. Words highlighted in **TAN** throughout the book are defined in the glossary / index. Check the glossary / index when you aren't sure which chapter covers a topic you're looking for.

Color-coded organization. The parts of this book are color-coded for easy reference: red for WRITE, blue for RESEARCH, yellow for EDIT, and green for EXERCISE.

Guidelines for common writing assignments. Chapters W-8 to W-17 cover ten kinds of writing you'll probably be expected to do in many college classes. The front inside flap lists model student essays by genres and where to find them.

Checklist for revising and editing. On the back flap (p. 601 in the instructor edition) is a list of prompts to guide you as you revise and edit a draft—and that lead you to pages in the book where you'll find help.

Help editing common errors that matter. We all make mistakes and need to learn how to edit them out. The front flap lists some of the errors that really matter and leads you to advice for spotting them in your writing and for editing them out.

MLA, APA, Chicago, and CSE guidelines. Color-coded chapters cover each style, with directories in the back of the book that lead to the specific examples you need. Color-coded templates show what information to include, and documentation maps show you where to find the information required. You'll find an MLA-style paper on pages 192–200, an APA-style paper on pages 76–79, and papers using each of the other styles online at: **digital.wwnorton.com/littleseagull4**.

Exercise. If you're looking for an exercise on a specific topic, turn to the Menu of Exercises at the back of the book—or look for links to exercises in the margins of the Edit chapter. Find answers to even-numbered exercises on pages 529–49.

Scanning for information. Sometimes you may turn to a part of the book where you know that information you're looking for is located. You could scan the red headings where the topic is explained. Or if you just want to find an example showing you what to do, look for little red pointers (▶) that make examples easy to spot.

Write

I think I did pretty well, considering I started out with nothing but a bunch of blank paper.

—STEVE MARTIN

W-1   Rhetorical Contexts

Whenever we write, whether it's an email to a friend, a toast at a wedding, or an essay, we do so within some kind of context—a rhetorical context that helps shape our choices as writers. Whatever our topic, we have a purpose, a certain audience, a particular stance, a genre, and a medium to consider—and often as not, a design. This chapter discusses each of these elements and provides some questions that can help you think about some of the choices you have to make as you write.

W-1a Purpose

All writing has a purpose. We write to explore our thoughts, express ourselves, and entertain; to record words and events; to communicate with others; to persuade others to think or behave in certain ways. Here are some questions to help you think about your purpose(s) as you write:

- What is the primary purpose of the writing task—to entertain? inform? persuade? demonstrate knowledge? something else?
- What are your own goals?
- What do you want your **AUDIENCE** to do, think, or feel? How will they use what you tell them?
- What does this writing task call on you to do? Do you have an assignment that specifies a certain **GENRE** or strategy—to argue a position? report on an event? compare two texts?
- What are the best ways to achieve your purpose? Should you take a particular **STANCE**? write in a particular **MEDIUM**? use certain **DESIGN** elements?

W-1b Audience

What you write, how much you write, and how you phrase it are all influenced by the audience you envision. For example, as a student writing an essay for an instructor, you will be expected to produce a text with few or no errors, something you may worry less about in a text to a friend.

- What audience do you want to reach? What expectations do they have from you? What's your relationship with them, and how does it affect your **TONE**?

- What is your audience's background — their education and life experiences?

- What are their interests? What motivates them? Do they have any political attitudes or interests that may affect the way they read your piece?

- Is there any demographic information that you should keep in mind, such as race, gender, sexual orientation, religious beliefs, or economic status?

- What does your audience already know—or believe—about your topic? What do you need to tell them?

- What kind of response do you want from your audience? Do you want them to do or believe something? accept what you say? something else?

- How can you best appeal to your audience? What kind of information will they find interesting or persuasive? Are there any design elements that will appeal to them?

W-1c Genre

Genres are kinds of writing. Reports, position papers, poems, letters, instructions—even jokes—are genres. Each one has certain features and follows particular conventions of style and presentation. Academic assignments generally specify the genre, but if it isn't clear, ask your instructor. Then consider these issues:

- What are the key elements and conventions of your genre? How do they affect the type of content you should include?

- Does your genre require a certain organization or **MEDIUM**? Does it have any **DESIGN** requirements?
- How does your genre affect your **TONE**, if at all?
- Does the genre require formal (or informal) language?

W-1d Topic

An important part of any writing context is the topic—what you are writing about. As you choose a topic, keep in mind your rhetorical situation and any requirements specified by your assignments.

- If your topic is assigned, what do the verbs in the assignment ask you to do: **ANALYZE**? **COMPARE**? **SUMMARIZE**? Something else?
- Does the assignment offer a broad subject area (such as the environment) that allows you to choose a limited topic within it (such as a particular environmental issue)?
- What do you need to do to complete the assignment? Do you need to do research? find illustrations?
- If you can choose a topic, think about what you are interested in. What do you want to learn more about? What topics from your courses have you found intriguing? What local, national, or global issues do you care about?
- Do you need to limit your topic to fit a specified time or length?

W-1e Stance and Tone

Whenever you write, you have a certain stance, an attitude toward your topic. For example, you might be objective, critical, passionate, or indifferent. You express (or downplay) that stance through your tone—the words you use and the other ways your text conveys an attitude toward your subject and audience. Just as you are likely to alter what you say depending on whether you're speaking to a boss or a good friend, you need to make similar adjustments as a writer, too. Ask yourself these questions:

- What is your stance, and how can you best present it to achieve your purpose?

- How should your stance be reflected in your tone? Do you want to be seen as reasonable? angry? thoughtful? ironic? something else? Be sure that your language—and even your font—conveys that tone.

- How is your stance likely to be received by your **AUDIENCE**? Should you openly reveal it, or would it be better to tone it down?

W-1f Media/Design

We might communicate through many media, both verbal and nonverbal: our bodies (we wink), our voices (we shout), and various technologies (we write with a pen, send email, tweet). No matter what the medium, a text's design affects the way it is received and understood. Consider these questions:

- Does your assignment call for a certain medium or media—a printed essay? an oral report with visual aids? a website?

- How does your medium affect the way you write and organize your text? For example, long paragraphs may be fine on paper, but bulleted phrases work better on slides.

- How does your medium affect your language? Do you need to be more **FORMAL** or **INFORMAL**?

- What's the appropriate look for your writing situation? Should it look serious? whimsical? personal? something else?

- What fonts and other design elements suit your writing context? Is there anything you should highlight by putting it in a box or italics?

- Would headings help you organize your material and help readers follow the text? Does your genre or medium require them?

- Will your audience expect or need any illustrations? Is there any information that would be easier to understand as a chart?

W-2   Academic Contexts

An **ARGUMENT** on a psychology exam debating whether genes or environment do more to determine people's intelligence, a **REPORT** for a science course on the environmental effects of electricity-generating windmills on wildlife, a **PROPOSAL** for a multimedia sales campaign in a marketing course—all of these are kinds of writing that you might be assigned to do in college classes. This chapter describes some of the elements expected in academic writing.

W-2a Key Elements of Academic Writing

Evidence that you've carefully considered the subject. You can use a variety of ways to show that you've thought seriously about the subject and done any necessary research, from citing authoritative sources to incorporating information you learned in class to pointing out connections among ideas.

A clear, appropriately qualified thesis. In academic writing, you're expected to state your main point explicitly, often in a **THESIS** statement, as MIT student Joanna MacKay does in an essay about selling human organs: "Governments should not ban the sale of human organs; they should regulate it."

Often you'll need to qualify your thesis statement to acknowledge exceptions or other perspectives. Here's a qualified thesis from an essay by Michaela Cullington, a student at Marywood University: "Although some believe that texting has either a positive or negative effect on writing, it in fact seems likely that texting has no significant effect on student writing." By adding **QUALIFYING WORDS** like "seems likely" and "significant," the writer indicates that she's not making a definitive claim about texting's influence on student writing.

A response to what others have said. Whatever your topic, it's likely that others have written or spoken about it. It's almost always best to present your ideas as a response to what others have said— **QUOTING**, **PARAPHRASING**, or **SUMMARIZING** their ideas and then agreeing, disagreeing, or both.

For example, in an essay arguing that the American Dream is alive and well, University of Cincinnati student Brandon King presents the views of two economists who say that because wealth is concentrated in the hands "of a rich minority," "the American Dream is no longer possible for most Americans." He then responds by disagreeing, arguing that "the American Dream . . . is based on perception, on the way someone *imagines* how to be successful."

Good reasons supported by evidence. You need to provide good **REASONS** for your thesis and **EVIDENCE** to support those reasons. Joanna MacKay offers several reasons that sales of human kidneys should be legalized: a surplus exists; the risk to the donor is not great; and legalization would enable the trade in kidneys to be regulated, thereby helping many patients and donors. For that third reason, her evidence includes statistics about death from renal failure.

Acknowledgment of multiple perspectives. In any academic writing, you need to investigate and represent fairly the range of perspectives on your topic—to avoid considering issues in an overly simple "pro/con" way and, instead, to explore multiple positions as you research and write. Brandon King, for instance, looks at the American Dream from several angles: the ways it is defined, the effects of government policies on achieving it, the role of education, and so on.

Carefully documented sources. Clearly acknowledging sources and **DOCUMENTING** them correctly both in your text and in a list of **WORKS CITED** or **REFERENCES** at the end is a basic requirement of academic writing. If your text will appear online, you can direct readers to online sources by using hyperlinks, but your instructor may want you to document them formally as well.

A confident and authoritative **STANCE**. Your **TONE** should convey confidence and establish your authority to write about your topic. To do so, use active verbs ("X claims," "Y and Z have found"), avoid such phrases as "I think," and write in a direct style. Michaela Cullington establishes an authoritative stance in her essay on texting this way: "On the basis of my own research, expert research, and personal observations, I can confidently state that texting is not interfering with students' use of standard written English and has no effect on their writing abilities in general." Her simple, declarative sentences and strong, unequivocal language ("I can confidently state," "has no effect") send the message that she knows what she's talking about.

An indication of why your topic matters. Help your readers understand why your topic is worth exploring—and why your writing is worth reading. In an essay called "Throwing Like a Girl," James Fallows explains why that topic matters, noting that his title reflects attitudes about gender that have potentially serious consequences.

Careful attention to appropriate style norms. For academic contexts, you should almost always write in complete sentences, use capitalization and punctuation as recommended in this handbook and other guides, check your spelling by consulting a dictionary—and avoid any abbreviations used in texting and other informal writing. Grammar conventions are important, and it's a good idea to follow them, especially in academic writing. Still, the primary goals of your writing are clarity and appropriateness and not simply strict adherence to convention for its own sake.

W-2b Thinking about the Writing Context

- What **GENRE** does the assignment suggest—or require?
- What is your instructor's **PURPOSE** for this assignment? What is your purpose, apart from fulfilling those expectations?
- Who is your **AUDIENCE**?
- How can you convey a confident, authoritative **STANCE**?
- What **MEDIA** are available, permitted, and appropriate? Are any required?
- What **DESIGN** issues need to be considered?

» To read the student essays cited in this chapter, go to **digital.wwnorton.com/littleseagull4**.

W-3 Reading Strategies

We read for many different purposes. We read textbooks to learn about history, biology, and other academic topics. We read social media to find out what people think of the events of the day. We read what other people write, but we also read our own drafts to make sure they say what we intend them to say. This chapter offers strategies for reading both your own and other people's texts accurately and strategically—and with a critical eye.

W-3a Reading Strategically

Academic reading can be challenging; it presents new vocabulary and new concepts, and scholarly articles and books often assume that readers already know key ideas, vocabulary, and background information. As you progress in an academic major, reading will become easier, but the following tactics will help you understand and remember what you read now—and ultimately save you time.

Adjust your reading speed. Different texts require different amounts of effort. Simple, straightforward texts can be skimmed fairly quickly, but academic texts usually require a slower, more careful reading—and may require more than one.

Look for organizational cues. As you read, look for hints that signal the way the text's ideas are organized and how each part relates to those around it. Introductory paragraphs and the **THESIS** usually offer a preview of the topics to be discussed and the order in which they will be addressed. **TRANSITIONS** guide readers in following the direction of the writer's thinking from idea to idea. And headings identify a text's major and minor sections.

Be persistent with difficult texts. For texts that are especially challenging or uninteresting, first try skimming the abstract or introduction, the headings, and the conclusion to look for something that relates to knowledge you already have. Then read through the text once just to understand what it's saying and again to look for parts that relate to other parts, to other texts or course information, or to other knowledge you have. Treat such a text as a challenge: "I'm going to keep working on this until I make sense of it."

W-3b Reading Efficiently, Annotating, and Summarizing

Following these steps can help you understand and remember what you read.

Think about what you already know about the topic—and what you want to learn. It always helps to approach new information in the context of what you already know. Before you begin reading, BRAIN-STORM what you already know about the topic. List any terms or phrases that come to mind, and group them into categories. Then read the first few paragraphs, list any questions that you expect or hope to be answered as you read, and number them according to their importance to you. Finally, after you read the whole text, list what you learned from it. Compare your second and third lists to see what you still want or need to know—and what you learned that you didn't expect.

Preview the text and think about your initial response. Skim the text to get its basic ideas: read the title and subtitle, any headings, the first and last paragraphs, and the first sentences of all the other paragraphs. Study any visuals. Then jot down brief notes about your initial reaction, and think about why you reacted as you did. What aspects of the text account for this reaction?

Annotate. To better understand a text, annotate it by underlining or highlighting key words and phrases, connecting ideas with lines or symbols, and writing comments and questions in the margins.

A Sample Annotated Text

Here is an excerpt from Justice: What's the Right Thing to Do?, *a book by Harvard professor Michael J. Sandel, annotated by a writer doing research for a report on the awarding of military medals:*

What Wounds Deserve the Purple Heart?

On some issues, questions of virtue and honor are too obvious to deny. Consider the recent debate over who should qualify for the Purple Heart. Since 1932, the U.S. military has <u>awarded the medal to soldiers wounded or killed in battle by enemy action.</u> In addition to the honor, the medal entitles recipients to special privileges in veterans' hospitals.

Purple Heart given for wounding or death in battle.

Since the beginning of the current wars in Iraq and Afghanistan, <u>growing numbers of veterans have been diagnosed</u> with post-traumatic stress disorder and treated for the condition. Symptoms include recurring nightmares, severe depression, and suicide. At least <u>three hundred thousand veterans reportedly suffer</u> from traumatic stress or major depression. Advocates for these veterans <u>have proposed that they, too, should qualify for the Purple Heart.</u> Since psychological injuries can be at least as debilitating as physical ones, they argue, soldiers who suffer these wounds should receive the medal.

PTSD increasingly common among veterans.

300,000! That's a lot!

Argument: Vets with PTSD should be eligible for PH because psych. injuries are as serious as physical.

After a Pentagon advisory group studied the question, the Pentagon announced, in 2009, that the Purple Heart would be reserved for soldiers with physical injuries. Veterans suffering from mental disorders and psychological trauma would not be eligible, even though they qualify for government-supported medical treatment and disability payments. The Pentagon offered two reasons for its decision: <u>traumatic stress disorders are not intentionally caused by enemy action, and they are difficult to diagnose objectively.</u>

2009: Military says no: PTSD injuries are accidental and hard to diagnose.

Annotate to help you understand the author's **PURPOSE**: if you need to follow a text that makes an argument, underline the **THESIS**, the **REASONS**, and the **EVIDENCE** that support that thesis—and restate them in your own words in the margin.

Have a conversation with the author. Assume that the author is someone you take seriously but whose words you do not accept without question. Write your part of the conversation in the margin, on sticky notes, or in your reading notebook. Respond, ask questions, talk back: "What's this mean?" "So what?" "Says who?" You might use emoji or texting shorthand—whatever allows you to respond to the text.

Summarize. As you read, restate points that you think are important in your own words in the margins. When you're done, restate the entire text's main ideas—the ideas that together are crucial to its meaning—in your own words in a single paragraph, leaving out most examples and other details. Doing this can help you understand those ideas and see the relationships among them—and help you remember the text better than rereading or trying to memorize.

W-3c Reading Analytically

Sometimes you'll need to think about a text in greater depth, engaging with it to understand not only what it says but what it means and how it works. The following strategies can help you read texts in order to analyze them.

Read rhetorically. Texts are part of ongoing conversations with other texts and respond to ideas and events. As you read, ask yourself: What is the **PURPOSE** of the text—to inform? persuade? entertain? What arguments or events are prompting the writer's response? What sources does the writer cite? Who is the intended **AUDIENCE**? If you're not a member of that group, are there terms or concepts you'll need to look up? What is the **GENRE**? a report? an analysis? something else? What do you know about the writer, and what is the writer's **STANCE**? critical? objective? something else? Is the text in print or online—and how does the **MEDIUM** affect what it says?

Identify patterns. Look for notable patterns in the text: recurring words and their synonyms, repeated phrases and metaphors, and types of sentences. Does the author rely on any particular writing strategies? Is the evidence offered more opinion than fact? nothing but statistics? Is there a predominant pattern to how sources are presented? As quotations? paraphrases? summaries? In visual texts, are there any patterns of color, shape, and line? What isn't there that you would expect to find? Is there anything that doesn't really fit in?

Play the believing and doubting game. Regardless of how you actually feel about what the writer says, **LIST** or **FREEWRITE** as many reasons as you can think of for believing it, given the writer's perspective, and then as many as you can for doubting it. This exercise helps you consider new ideas and question your current ideas—as well as clarify where you stand in relation to the ideas in the text.

Analyze how the text works. Outline the text paragraph by paragraph. If you're interested in analyzing its ideas, identify what each paragraph *says*. Are there any patterns in the topics the writer addresses? How has the writer arranged ideas, and how does that arrangement develop the topic? If, however, you're concerned with the way the ideas are presented, pay attention to what each paragraph *does*: does it introduce a topic? provide background? describe something? entice you to read further?

W-3d Analyzing an Argument

All texts make some kind of argument, claiming something and then offering reasons and evidence as support for the claim. As a critical reader, you need to look closely at the argument a text makes.

- *What is the claim?* What is the main point the writer is trying to make? Is there a clearly stated **THESIS**, or is it merely implied?

- *What support does the writer offer for the claim?* What **REASONS** are given to support the claim, and what **EVIDENCE** backs up those reasons? Are the reasons plausible and sufficient?

- *How evenhandedly does the writer present the issues?* Are the arguments appropriately qualified? Is there any mention of **COUNTER-ARGUMENTS** —and if so, how does the writer deal with them?

- *What authorities or other sources of information are cited?* How credible and current are they?

- *How does the writer address you as the reader?* Does the writer assume that you know something about what's being discussed? Does the writer's language include you, or not? (Hint: if you see the word "we," do you feel included?)

Be sure to check for **FALLACIES**, arguments that rely on faulty reasoning. Such arguments can seem plausible, and they can be persuasive —but they're misleading.

W-3e Reading Visual Texts

Photos, drawings, graphs, diagrams, and charts are frequently used to help convey important information and often make powerful arguments themselves. So learning to read and interpret visual texts is just as necessary as it is for written texts.

Take visuals seriously. Remember that **VISUALS** are texts themselves, not just decoration. When they appear as part of a written text, they may introduce information not discussed elsewhere in the text. Or they might illustrate concepts hard to grasp from words alone. In either case, it's important to pay close attention to any visuals in a written text.

Looking at any title, caption, or other written text that's part of a visual will help you understand its main idea. It might also help to think about its purpose: Why did the writer include it? What information does it add or emphasize? What argument is it making?

How to read charts and graphs. To read the information in charts and graphs, you need to look for different things depending on what type of chart or graph you're considering. A line graph, for example, usually contains certain elements: title, legend, x-axis, y-axis, and source information. Figure 1 shows one such graph taken from a sociology textbook.

Other types of charts and graphs include some of these same elements. But the specific elements vary according to the different kinds of information being presented, and some charts and graphs can be challenging to read. For example, the chart in Figure 2, from the same textbook, includes elements of both bar and line graphs

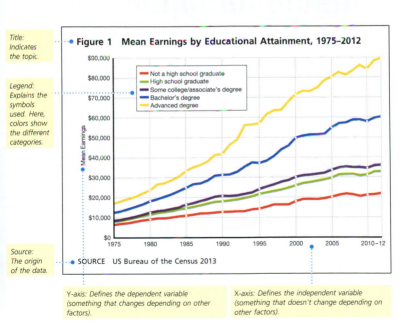

Title: Indicates the topic.

Figure 1   Mean Earnings by Educational Attainment, 1975–2012

Legend: Explains the symbols used. Here, colors show the different categories.

Legend:
- Not a high school graduate
- High school graduate
- Some college/associate's degree
- Bachelor's degree
- Advanced degree

Mean Earnings (y-axis): $0, $10,000, $20,000, $30,000, $40,000, $50,000, $60,000, $70,000, $80,000, $90,000

x-axis: 1975, 1980, 1985, 1990, 1995, 2000, 2005, 2010–12

Source: The origin of the data.

SOURCE   US Bureau of the Census 2013

Y-axis: Defines the dependent variable (something that changes depending on other factors).

X-axis: Defines the independent variable (something that doesn't change depending on other factors).

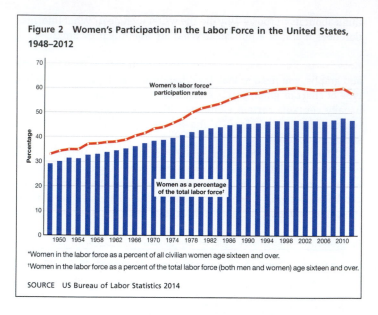

Figure 2 Women's Participation in the Labor Force in the United States, 1948–2012

*Women in the labor force as a percent of all civilian women age sixteen and over.

†Women in the labor force as a percent of the total labor force (both men and women) age sixteen and over.

SOURCE US Bureau of Labor Statistics 2014

to depict two trends at once: the red line shows the percentage of women who were in the US labor force from 1948 to 2012, and the blue bars show the percentage of US workers who were women during that same period. Both trends are shown in two-year increments. To make sense of this chart, you need to read the title, the x-axis and y-axis labels, and their definitions carefully.

W-4   Writing Processes

To create anything, we generally break the work down into a series of steps. We follow a recipe (or the directions on a box) to bake a cake; we divide a piece of music into various singing parts to arrange it for a choir. So it is when we write. We rely on various processes to get from a blank page to a finished product. This chapter offers advice on some of these processes—from generating ideas to drafting to revising and editing.

W-4a Generating Ideas

The activities that follow can help you explore a topic—what you already know about it or how you might look at it in new ways.

- *Brainstorming.* Jot down everything that comes to mind about your topic, working either alone or with others. Look over your list, and try to identify connections or patterns.

- *Freewriting.* Write as quickly as you can without stopping for five to ten minutes. Then underline interesting passages. Write more, using an underlined passage as your new topic.

- *Looping.* Write for five to ten minutes, jotting down whatever you know about your subject. Then write a one-sentence summary of the most important idea. Use this summary to start another loop. Keep looping until you have a tentative focus.

- *Clustering.* Clustering is a way of connecting ideas visually. Write your topic in the middle of a page, and write subtopics and other ideas around it. Circle each item, and draw lines to connect related ideas.

- *Questioning.* You might start by asking *What? Who? When? Where? How?* and *Why?* You could also ask questions as if the topic were a play: What happens? Who are the participants? When does the action take place? How? Where? Why does this happen?

- *Keeping a journal.* Jotting down ideas, feelings, or the events of your day in a journal is a good way to generate ideas—and a journal is a good place to explore why you think as you do.

- *Starting some research.* Depending on your topic and purpose, you might do a little preliminary research to get basic information and help you discover paths you might follow.

W-4b Developing a Tentative Thesis

A **THESIS** is a statement that indicates your main point, identifying your topic and the **CLAIM** you are making about it. Here are some steps for developing a tentative thesis statement:

1. *State your topic as a question.* You may have a topic, such as "gasoline prices." But that doesn't make a statement. To move from a topic to a thesis statement, start by turning your topic into a question: "What causes fluctuations in gasoline prices?"

2. *Then turn your question into a position.* A thesis statement is an assertion—it takes a stand or makes a claim. One way to establish a thesis is to answer your own question: "Gasoline prices fluctuate for several reasons."

3. *Narrow your thesis.* A good thesis is specific, telling your audience exactly what your essay will cover: "Gasoline prices fluctuate because of production procedures, consumer demand, international politics, and oil companies' policies."

4. *Qualify your thesis.* Though you may sometimes want to state your thesis strongly and bluntly, often you need to acknowledge that your assertion may not be unconditionally true. In such cases, consider adding **QUALIFYING WORDS** such as "may," "very," "likely," and "often" to qualify your statement: "Gasoline prices <u>very</u> <u>likely</u> fluctuate because of production procedures, consumer demand, international politics, and oil companies' policies."

Whatever tentative thesis you start with, keep in mind that you may want to modify it as you proceed.

W-4c Organizing and Drafting

Organizing. You may want to use an outline to organize your ideas before you begin to draft. You can create an informal outline by simply listing your ideas in the order in which you want to write about them.

Thesis statement

First main idea
    Supporting evidence or detail
    Supporting evidence or detail

Second main idea
    Supporting evidence or detail
    Supporting evidence or detail

An outline can help you organize your thoughts and see where more research is needed. As you draft and revise, though, stay flexible—and be ready to change direction as your topic develops.

Drafting. At some point, you need to write out a draft. As you draft, you may need to get more information, rethink your thesis, or explore some new ideas. But first, you just need to get started.

- *Write quickly in spurts.* Try to write a complete draft, or a complete section of a longer draft, in one sitting. If you need to stop in the middle, jot down some notes about where you're headed so that you can pick up your train of thought when you begin again.

- *Expect surprises.* Writing is a form of thinking; you may end up somewhere you didn't anticipate. That can be a good thing—but if not, it's OK to double back or follow a new path.

- *Expect to write more than one draft.* Parts of your first draft may not achieve your goals. That's OK—as you revise, you can fill in gaps and improve your writing.

- *Don't worry about correctness.* You can check words, dates, and spelling at a later stage. For now, just write.

W-4d Getting Response

As writers, we need to be able to look at our work with a critical eye, to see if our writing is doing what we want it to do. We also need to get feedback from other readers. Here is a list of questions for reading a draft closely and considering how it should or could be revised:

- Will the **OPENING** paragraph grab readers' attention? If so, how does it do so? If not, how else might the piece begin?

- What is the **THESIS**? Is it stated directly? If not, should it be?

- Are there good **REASONS** and sufficient **EVIDENCE** to support the thesis? Is there anywhere you'd like to have more detail?

- Is there a clear pattern of organization? Does each part relate to the thesis? Are there appropriate **TRANSITIONS** to help readers follow your train of thought? Are there headings that make the structure of the text clear—and if not, should there be?

- Will the text meet the needs and expectations of its **AUDIENCE**? Where might they need more information or guidance?

- Are all **QUOTATIONS** introduced with a **SIGNAL PHRASE** and documented? Are they accurately quoted, and have any changes and omissions been indicated with brackets and ellipses?

- Is your **STANCE** on the topic clear and consistent throughout? Is the **TONE** appropriate for your audience and purpose?

- Is the **CONCLUSION** satisfying? What does it leave readers thinking? How else might the text end?

- Is the title one that will attract interest? Does it announce your topic and give some sense of what you have to say?

- Are there any **VISUALS**—tables, charts, photos? If so, are they clearly labeled with captions? Is **ALTERNATIVE TEXT** provided for visuals in a digital text? If you did not create the visuals yourself, have you cited your sources?

W-4e Taking Stock and Revising

Once you've gotten response from others, it's time to take stock of what you've drafted and what readers have said about it. Revision may feel daunting, but it will improve your finished work. Also, knowing that you're going to revise could reduce writer's block when you sit down to write the first draft. Since you know you'll be making changes later, you can think of your first draft as a rehearsal, a warm-up.

Revising also gives you a chance to try out words and ideas and weigh different options for expressing the points that you've already written. Give yourself a little room to play and experiment. Here are some tips for taking stock of your draft and planning your next moves:

- *Summarize from memory.* Before you read any comments on your first draft made by your instructor or peers, and without looking at the draft, your notes, or any of your sources, sit down and write a brief **SUMMARY** of your whole draft. You probably won't remember everything, but it will be useful to know what sticks with you and what doesn't. Mention which parts you remember struggling with and what you thought about writing but didn't.

- *Imagine how others might understand your draft.* Imagine you're someone who knows nothing about your topic—your grandfather, perhaps, or a friend from work—and read your first draft the way they might. (Try reading out loud.) Did it read smoothly? Note any parts that didn't. What questions might your reader ask? Where might they stop and say "Wow!"? Next, read your draft again, imagining you are someone who has an *opposing* opinion on your topic. Where might they want to question or challenge you? Make a note of your imagined readers' questions or comments.

- *Consider the feedback you've received.* If you've received comments on your draft from your instructor and/or peers, trust that the feedback has been given in a spirit of helpfulness; read it calmly and in good faith. Evaluate all the comments with an open mind—which ones make the most sense, are the most important? Which ones can you disregard?

- *Put it all together.* Look again at the summary you wrote from memory, your notes about the responses of your imagined readers, and the feedback you've received. Where do they coincide? Where do they differ? Considering those three angles will give you a good idea of what to work on. Keep in mind that the goals of a revision, in general, are to sharpen and polish what you've already done. Having a grasp of the whole task ahead of you will help you focus and get it done.

Set your goals for revising. Remember what you are trying to accomplish with your revision:

- First, you want to sharpen your focus. Find your **THESIS**; does it clearly articulate your main point? Have you provided the necessary contextual information in the opening paragraph? Does your ending provide a satisfactory conclusion?

- Next, you want to strengthen your argument. Check every key idea to make sure that each one is fully explained. You may need to qualify some of your **CLAIMS** or provide more **REASONS** or **EVIDENCE** to support them.

- Third, check to make sure that everything is understandable and cohesive. Is every new or unfamiliar term defined? Does your title give readers a good sense of what your text is about?

Plan and execute. Make a realistic estimate of the time (and energy) you have available for doing the work and assess what can reasonably be accomplished in that available time. Set yourself step-by-step deadlines and try not to do it all at once.

Use your main revising tools: cut, add, and reorder. Now that you have a good idea of the scope of your revision, you can classify the tasks involved into three categories: cutting existing material that may be repetitive or unnecessary; adding new material; and reorganizing existing material. The order in which you do the tasks is a matter of preference.

- *Changing the sequence of sections or paragraphs* (or even sentences within a paragraph) can help your work flow more smoothly. Try it the old-school way: print your draft, cut the paragraphs apart with scissors, mix up the slips of paper, and arrange them in a logical order. Does everything end up in the same order as the original draft? (Hint: it often doesn't.)

- *Cutting whole paragraphs or just sentences and phrases* can sharpen your focus. Don't just delete material; save it in a separate "out-takes" document with any related notes or comments. Dropped pieces might be useful later.

- *Adding material*—details, supporting evidence, examples, etc.— can strengthen a point or clarify information. And don't forget to add good **TRANSITIONS** to tie your ideas together.

W-4f Editing and Proofreading

Your ability to produce clear, error-free writing shows something about your ability as a writer, so you should be sure to edit and proof-read your work carefully. Editing is the stage at which you work on the details of your paragraphs, sentences, language, and punctuation to make your writing as clear, precise, and appropriate as possible. The following guidelines can help you check the paragraphs, sentences, and words in your drafts.

Editing paragraphs

- Does each paragraph focus on one point and have a **TOPIC SENTENCE** that announces that point? Does every sentence in the paragraph relate to that point?

- Where is the most important information in each paragraph—at the beginning? at the end? in the middle?

- Check to see how your paragraphs fit together. Does each one follow smoothly from the one before it? Do you need to add **TRANSITIONS**?

- How does the **OPENING** paragraph catch readers' attention? How else might you begin?

- Does the **CONCLUSION** provide a satisfactory ending? How else might you conclude?

For more help with paragraphs, see **W-5**.

Editing sentences

- Check to see that each sentence is complete, with a **SUBJECT** and a **VERB**, and that it begins with a capital letter and ends with a period, question mark, or exclamation point.

- Are your sentences varied? If they all start with the subject or are all the same length, try varying them by adding **TRANSITIONS** or introductory phrases—or by combining some sentences.

- Be sure that lists or series are **PARALLEL** in form—all nouns (lions, tigers, bears), all verbs (hop, skip, jump), and so on.

- Do many of your sentences begin with "It" or "There"? Sometimes these words help introduce a topic, but often they make a text vague.

For more help with sentences, see **S-1** through **S-9**.

Editing language

- Are you sure of the meaning of every word?

- Do your words all convey the appropriate **TONE**?

- Is any of your language too general? For example, do you need to replace verbs like "be" or "do" with more specific **VERBS**?

- Check all **PRONOUNS** to see that they have clear **ANTECEDENTS**.

- Have you used any **CLICHÉS**? Academic writing in the US tends to avoid clichés.

- Double check language that refers to other people to be sure you're using preferred terms. Edit out language that might be considered **SEXIST** or would otherwise stereotype any individual or group.

- Check for "it's" and "its." Use "it's" to mean "it is" or "it has" and "its" to mean "belonging to it."

For more help with language, see *Editing the Errors That Matter* (**E-1** through **E-6**) and **L-1** through **L-11**.

Proofreading

This is the final stage of the writing process, when you check for misspelled words, mixed-up fonts, missing pages, and so on.

- Use your computer's grammar and spelling checkers, but be aware that they're not foolproof. Computer programs rely on formulas and banks of words—so what they flag (or not) as mistakes may not be accurate.

- Place a ruler or piece of paper under each line as you read. Use your finger or a pencil as a pointer.

- Focus on each sentence, one at a time, looking for anything that needs to be changed. Try beginning with the last sentence and working backward.

- Read your text out loud to yourself—or better, to others. Ask someone else to read your text aloud to you. Listen for areas that could be clearer.

W-4g Collaborating

Even if you do much of your writing alone, you probably spend a lot of time working with others, either face-to-face or online. Here are some guidelines for collaborating successfully.

Working in a group

- For face-to-face meetings, make sure everyone is facing one another and is physically part of the group.

- Be respectful and tactful. This is especially important when collaborating online. Without tone of voice, facial expressions, and other body language, your words carry all the weight. Remember also that what you write may be forwarded to others.

- When collaborating online, decide as a group how best to exchange drafts and comments. Group members may not all have access to the same equipment and software. Name files carefully.

- Each meeting needs an agenda—and careful attention to the clock. Appoint one person as timekeeper and another person as group leader; a third member should keep a record of the discussion and send around a summary afterward.

Working on a group writing project

- Define the overall project as clearly as possible, and divide the work into parts.

- Assign each group member specific tasks with deadlines.

- Try to accommodate everyone's style of working, but make sure everyone performs.

- Work for consensus, if not necessarily total agreement.

W-5 Developing Paragraphs

Paragraphs help us organize our writing for our readers. Here one writer recalls when he first understood what a paragraph does.

> I still remember the exact moment when I first understood, with a sudden clarity, the purpose of a paragraph. I didn't have the vocabulary to say "paragraph," but I realized that a paragraph was a fence that held words. The words inside a paragraph worked together for a common purpose. They had some specific reason for being inside the same fence. . . .
> —Sherman Alexie, "The Joy of Reading and Writing"

This chapter will help you build "fences" around words that work together on a common topic. It offers tips and examples for composing strong paragraphs.

W-5a Focusing on the Main Point

All the sentences in a paragraph should focus on one main idea, as they do in this paragraph from an article about the Mall of America.

> There is, of course, nothing naturally abhorrent in the human impulse to dwell in marketplaces or the urge to buy, sell, and trade. Rural Americans traditionally looked forward to the excitement and sensuality of market day; Native Americans traveled long distances to barter and trade at sprawling, festive encampments. In Persian bazaars and in the ancient Greek agoras the very soul of the community was preserved and could be seen, felt, heard, and smelled as it might be nowhere else. All over the planet the humblest of people have always gone to market with hope in their hearts and in expectation of something beyond mere goods—seeking a place where humanity is temporarily in ascendance, a palette for the senses, one another. —David Guterson, "Enclosed. Encyclopedic. Endured. One Week at the Mall of America"

Topic sentences. To help you focus a paragraph on one main point, state that point in a TOPIC SENTENCE. Often, but not always, you might start a paragraph with a topic sentence, as in this example from an essay arguing in favor of the American Electoral College.

> The Electoral College was created by our nation's founders to prevent one region from controlling the country. When the United States was founded, most of the population was concentrated within a few states, and those states would be able to dominate the country if the government were a pure democracy. Because of this population disparity, many small-population states feared that the larger ones would force them to conform to any laws and legislation that the larger states desired, creating a tyranny of the majority. So the founders put multiple measures in place to avoid this imbalance. One of those measures is the Electoral College, which gives each state a voice while also reflecting the opinion of the general population.
>
> —Gavin Reid, "The Electoral College Embodies American Ideals"

Sometimes, you may choose to put the topic sentence at the end of the paragraph. See how this strategy works in a paragraph about "high-concept pitches," brief descriptions of potential movie scripts.

> Jane Espenson, who has written for television shows such as *Buffy the Vampire Slayer*, reveals an interesting fact: Though TV writers don't use high-concept pitches for episodes—they're expected to present worked-out story ideas—the concepts that actually get picked up and turned into episodes are often not the fully worked-out ones. Instead, they're the ones based on single sentences thrown out at the end of a longer pitch. Jane sold two ideas to *Star Trek: The Next Generation* using single sentences. One was "Data is stranded on a Luddite planet," and the other was "Every time we go warp speed we're actually destroying the fabric of the universe." Jane speculates that the one-sentence pitches are bought because the writers who hear them are able to flesh them out in their own minds. They want to be able to fill in the details. In this case, there was a benefit to leaving *out* information. Clarity means finding the right level of detail for the circumstances.
>
> —Christopher Johnson, *Microstyle: The Art of Writing Little*

Occasionally, the main point is so obvious that you don't need a topic sentence. Especially in **NARRATIVE** writing, you may choose only to imply—not state—the main idea, as in this paragraph from an essay describing a young man's realization about his cousin's life choices.

> College Point, Queens. They called it "Garbage Point." I didn't agree with that for a while because it was home, but when I turned sixteen, I looked at College Point differently. Sure, it wasn't Compton or Chicago, but as in any city, it was easy to slip up if you hung out in the wrong places. I was still sixteen when a family member I'll call "T" shot up heroin right in front of me. He was driving, and I was unlucky enough to be in the passenger seat beside him; I was in for a rough ride.
> —Mohammed Masoom Shah, "One Last Ride"

Sticking to the main point. Whether or not you announce the main point in a topic sentence, be sure that every sentence in a paragraph relates to that point. Edit out any sentences that stray off topic, such as those crossed out below.

> In "Se Habla Español," Tanya Maria Barrientos notes some of the difficulties she encounters as a Latina who is not fluent in Spanish. ~~Previous generations of immigrants were encouraged to speak only English.~~ When someone poses a question to her in Spanish, she often has to respond in English. In other instances, she tries to speak Spanish but falters over the past and future tenses. Situations like these embarrass Barrientos and make her feel left out of a community she wants to be part of. ~~Native Guatemalans who are bilingual do not have such problems.~~

W-5b Developing the Main Point

A good paragraph provides enough good details to develop its main point—to fill out and support that point. Following are some common strategies for fleshing out and organizing paragraphs—and sometimes even for organizing an entire essay.

Analyzing cause and effect. Sometimes, you can develop a paragraph on a topic by analyzing what **CAUSES** it—or what its **EFFECTS**

might be. The following paragraph about air turbulence identifies some of its causes.

> A variety of factors can cause turbulence, which is essentially a disturbance in the movement of air. Thunderstorms, the jet stream, and mountains are some of the more common natural culprits, while what is known as wake turbulence is created by another plane. "Clear air turbulence" is the kind that comes up unexpectedly.
> —Susan Stellin, "The Inevitability of Bumps"

Classifying and dividing. When we CLASSIFY something, we group it with things that share similar characteristics. The following paragraph uses classification to describe the various features formed by hydrothermal vents, cracks in Earth's surface through which heated water is released.

> Under the sea, hydrothermal vents can form features called black smokers and white smokers. The colour depends on the minerals present in the water. On land these cracks form land hot springs, fumaroles (holes in a volcanic area from which hot smoke and gases escape) and geysers.
> —Peter Biro, "Questions and Answers about Hydrothermal Vents"

As a writing strategy, DIVISION is a way of separating something into parts. See how the following paragraph divides the concept of pressure into four kinds.

> I see four kinds of pressure working on college students today: economic pressure, parental pressure, peer pressure, and self-induced pressure. It is easy to look around for villains—to blame the colleges for charging too much money, the professors for assigning too much work, the parents for pushing their children too far, the students for driving themselves too hard. But there are no villains; only victims.
> —William Zinsser, "College Pressures"

Comparing and contrasting. Comparing things looks at their similarities; contrasting them focuses on their differences—though often we use the word "comparison" to refer to both strategies. You can structure a paragraph that **COMPARES AND CONTRASTS** in two ways. One is to shift back and forth between each item point by point, as in this paragraph contrasting the ways men and women "cyberloaf," or use the internet at work for non-work activities.

> Although the consequences of cyberloafing are similar across different populations, Lim and Chen's 2012 study demonstrated there are some meaningful differences based on gender. Men are more likely to cyberloaf than women, but when it comes to switching back to work, women take around eight minutes, while men take only four (pp. 346–347). There are differences, too, in how men and women think cyberloafing affects their work: men are more likely to say cyberloafing activities have a positive impact while women tend to say they have a negative impact (p. 347). However, Kim and Chen's results also show overall that many workers—men and women—believe there are some positive effects: 75% of participants say that cyberloafing increases their engagement at work, and 49% say that cyberloafing helps them to solve problems at work (p. 348). And most respondents believe it's not breaking any rules to browse the internet for personal reasons while at work (p. 346).
>
> —Rocio Celeste Mejia Avila, "Cyberloafing: Distraction or Motivation?"

Another way to compare and contrast two items is to use the "block method," covering all the details about one and then all the details about the other. See how this approach works in the following example, which contrasts photographs of Bill Clinton and Hillary Clinton on the opening day of the 1994 baseball season.

> The next day photos of the Clintons in action appeared in newspapers around the country. Many papers, including the *New York Times* and the *Washington Post*, chose the same two photos to run. The one of Bill Clinton showed him wearing an Indians cap and warm-up jacket. The President, throwing lefty, had turned his shoulders sideways to the plate in preparation for delivery. He was bringing the ball forward from behind his head in a clean-looking throwing action as the photo was snapped. Hillary Clinton was pictured wearing a dark jacket, a scarf, and an oversized Cubs hat. In preparation for her throw she was standing directly facing the plate. A right-hander, she had the elbow of her throwing arm

pointed out in front of her. Her forearm was tilted back, toward her shoulder. The ball rested on her upturned palm. As the picture was taken, she was in the middle of an action that can only be described as throwing like a girl.

—James Fallows, "Throwing Like a Girl"

Another way to make a comparison is with an **ANALOGY**, explaining something unfamiliar by comparing it with something familiar. See how one writer uses analogy to explain the way DNA encodes genetic information.

Although the complexity of cells, tissues, and whole organisms is breathtaking, the way in which the basic DNA instructions are written is astonishingly simple. Like more familiar instruction systems such as language, numbers, or computer binary code, what matters is not so much the symbols themselves but the order in which they appear. Anagrams, for example, "derail" and "redial," contain exactly the same letters but in a different order, and so the words they spell out have completely different meanings. . . . In exactly the same way the order of the four chemical symbols in DNA embodies the message. "ACGGTA" and "GACAGT" are DNA anagrams that mean completely different things to a cell, just as "derail" and "redial" have different meanings for us.

—Bryan Sykes, "So, What Is DNA and What Does It Do?"

Defining. When you **DEFINE** something, you put it in a general category and then add characteristics that distinguish it from others in that group. The following paragraph provides a definition of anhydrobiosis, one way that desert organisms stay alive during droughts.

Anhydrobiosis is dehydrated life—life shrunk down to its most primary aspects. No energy is spent on what would normally be considered to be living. The participants become sealed containers against the world, cells turning from living structures into reinforcement material. Sensitive organs are tucked away into specialized membranes, like wine glasses wrapped in newspaper for a move. Molecules, mostly a disaccharide called trehalose, are produced to shore up the shriveling internal structures. The organism's insides become crystalline, a material very similar to the liquid crystal in

digital watches. A dehydrating roundworm converts a quarter of its body weight into this trehalose material before going completely dry, coiling into a compact circle and reducing its surface area to a hardened bulb about seven percent of the original size.
— Craig Childs, *The Secret Knowledge of Water*

Describing. A DESCRIPTIVE paragraph provides specific details to show what something looks like—and perhaps how it sounds, feels, smells, and tastes. Here a paragraph weaves together details of background, appearance, and speech to create a vivid impression of Chuck Yeager, the first pilot to break the sound barrier.

Yeager grew up in Hamlin, West Virginia, a town on the Mud River. His father was a gas driller (drilling for natural gas in the coalfields), his older brother was a gas driller, and he would have been a gas driller had he not enlisted in the Army Air Force in 1941 at the age of eighteen. In 1943, at twenty, he became a flight officer and went to England to fly fighter planes over France and Germany. Even in the tumult of the war Yeager was somewhat puzzling to a lot of other pilots. He was a short, wiry, but muscular little guy with dark curly hair and a tough-looking face that seemed (to strangers) to be saying: "You best not be lookin' me in the eye, you peckerwood, or I'll put four more holes in your nose." But that wasn't what was puzzling. What was puzzling was the way Yeager talked. He seemed to talk with some older forms of English elocution, syntax, and conjugation that had been preserved uphollow in the Appalachians. There were people up there who never said they disapproved of anything, they said: "I don't hold with it." In the present tense they were willing to *help* out, like anyone else; but in the past tense they only *holped.* "H'it weren't nothin' I hold with, but I holped him out with it, anyways."
— Tom Wolfe, *The Right Stuff*

Explaining a process. Sometimes you might write a paragraph that explains a process —telling someone how to do something, such as how to parallel park—or how something is done, such as how bees make honey. Cookbooks explain many processes step-by-step, as in this explanation of how to pit a mango.

> The simplest method for pitting a mango is to hold it horizontally, then cut it in two lengthwise, slightly off-center, so the knife just misses the pit. Repeat the cut on the other side so a thin layer of flesh remains around the flat pit. Holding a half, flesh-side up, in the palm of your hand, slash the flesh into a lattice, cutting down to, but not through, the peel. Carefully push the center of the peel upward with your thumbs to turn it inside out, opening the cuts of the flesh. Then cut the mango cubes from the peel.   —Paulette Mitchell, *Vegetarian Appetizers*

Narrating. When you write a **NARRATIVE** paragraph in an essay, you tell a story to support a point. In the following paragraph, one author tells about being mistaken for a waitress and how that incident of stereotyping served "as a challenge" that provoked her to read her poetry with new confidence.

> One such incident . . . happened on the day of my first public poetry reading. It took place in Miami in a boat-restaurant where we were having lunch before the event. I was nervous and excited as I walked in with my notebook in my hand. An older woman motioned me to her table. Thinking (foolish me) that she wanted me to autograph a copy of my brand-new slender volume of verse, I went over. She ordered a cup of coffee from me, assuming that I was the waitress. Easy enough to mistake my poems for menus, I suppose. I know that it wasn't an intentional act of cruelty, yet of all the good things that happened that day, I remember that scene most clearly, because it reminded me of what I had to overcome before anyone would take me seriously. In retrospect, I understand that my anger gave my reading fire, that I have almost always taken doubts in my abilities as a challenge—and that the result is, most times, a feeling of satisfaction at having won a convert when I see the cold, appraising eyes warm to my words, the body language change, the smile that indicates that I have opened some avenue for communication.
>
> —Judith Ortiz Cofer, *The Latin Deli*

Using examples. Illustrating a point with one or more examples is a common way to develop a paragraph, like the following one, which presents several examples of country musicians whose music includes elements of pop, rock, and rap to make a point about the exclusion of "Old Town Road," a rap/country song by rapper Lil Nas X, from the Billboard Hot Country Songs chart.

> Country music gatekeepers are selective about how they use this muscle. Universal Nashville's (white) hip-pop raconteur Sam Hunt is embraced by Billboard's Hot Country Songs, and "Meant to Be," a pop-leaning ballad by Bebe Rexha with Florida Georgia Line is played ad nauseam. Taylor Swift could also lasso the country albums top spot for 16 weeks with her career-realigning pop-rock masterpiece *Red*. White country artists' rap collaborations also tend to get a pass. Jason Aldean tapped Ludacris for a remix of his country No 1 "Dirt Road Anthem"; Nelly's feature on Florida Georgia Line's bro-country classic "Cruise" helped it become country music's best selling US single of the digital era. Yet when black rappers draw from country styles . . . they are denied a seat at the table.
>
> —Owen Myers, "Fight for Your Right to Yeehaw:
> Lil Nas X and Country's Race Problem"

W-5c Making Paragraphs Flow

There are several ways to make your paragraphs **COHERENT** so that readers can follow your train of thought. Repetition, parallelism, and transitions are three strategies for making paragraphs flow.

Repetition. One way to help readers follow your train of thought is to repeat key words and phrases, as well as pronouns referring to those key words.

> Not that long ago, blogs were one of those annoying buzz words that you could safely get away with ignoring. The word "blog"—it works as both noun and verb—is short for "Web log." It was coined in 1997 to describe a website where you could post daily scribblings, journal-style, about whatever you like—mostly critiquing and linking to other articles online that may have sparked your thinking. Unlike a big media outlet, bloggers focus their efforts on narrow topics, often rising to become de facto watchdogs and self-proclaimed experts. Blogs

can be about anything: politics, sex, baseball, haiku, car repair. There are blogs about blogs.   —Lev Grossman, "Meet Joe Blog"

Instead of repeating one word, you can use synonyms.

Predictably, the love of cinema has waned. People still like going to the movies, and some people still care about and expect something special, necessary from a film. And wonderful films are still being made.... But one hardly finds anymore, at least among the young, the distinctive cinephilic love of movies, which is not simply love of but a certain *taste* in films.

—Susan Sontag, "A Century of Cinema"

Parallel structures. Putting similar items into the same grammatical structure helps readers see the connection among those elements and follow your sentences—and your thoughts.

The disease was bubonic plague, present in two forms: one that infected the bloodstream, causing the buboes and internal bleeding and was spread by contact; and a second, more virulent pneumonic type that infected the lungs and was spread by respiratory infection. The presence of both at once caused the high mortality and speed of contagion. So lethal was the disease that cases were known of persons going to bed well and dying before they woke, of doctors catching the illness at a bedside and dying before the patient. So rapidly did it spread from one to another that to a French physician, Simon de Covino, it seemed as if one sick person "could infect the whole world."

—Barbara Tuchman, "'This Is the End of the World': The Black Death"

Transitions help readers follow your train of thought—and move from sentence to sentence, paragraph to paragraph. Here are some common ones:

- *To show causes and effects:* accordingly, as a result, because, consequently, hence, so, then, therefore, thus

- *To show comparison:* along the same lines, also, in the same way, like, likewise, similarly

- *To show contrasts or exceptions:* although, but, even though, however, in contrast, instead, nevertheless, nonetheless, on the contrary, on the one hand . . . on the other hand, still, yet

- *To show examples:* for example, for instance, indeed, in fact, of course, such as

- *To show place or position:* above, adjacent to, below, beyond, elsewhere, here, inside, near, outside, there

- *To show sequence:* again, also, and, and then, besides, finally, first, furthermore, last, moreover, next, too

- *To show time:* after, as soon as, at first, at last, at the same time, before, eventually, finally, immediately, later, meanwhile, next, simultaneously, so far, soon, then, thereafter

- *To signal a summary or conclusion:* as a result, as we have seen, finally, in a word, in any event, in brief, in conclusion, in other words, in short, in the end, in the final analysis, on the whole, therefore, thus, to summarize

See how Julia Alvarez uses several transitions to show time and to move her ideas along.

> Yolanda, the third of the four girls, became a schoolteacher but not on purpose. For years after graduate school, she wrote down *poet* under profession in questionnaires and income tax forms, and later amended it to *writer*-slash-*teacher.* Finally, acknowledging that she had not written much of anything in years, she announced to her family that she was not a poet anymore.   —Julia Alvarez, *How the Garcia Girls Lost Their Accents*

Transitions can also help readers move from paragraph to paragraph and, by summing up the previous paragraph's main point, show how the paragraphs are connected. A common way to summarize is to use phrases like "this/these ____" and "such ____." Here's an example, from an anthropologist's study of American college students:

> When I asked students in interviews whether they felt they had a "community" at AnyU, most said yes. But what they meant by community were these personal networks of friends that some referred to as my "homeys." It was these small, ego-centered groups that were the backbone of most students' social experience in the university.
> On a daily basis these personal networks were easily recognizable within the dorm and on campus. "Where are you now?" says the cell phone caller walking back to the dorm from class. "I'm on

my way home, so ask Jeffrey and Mark to come, and I'll meet you at my room at 8." Such conversations are everywhere. . . .
—Rebekah Nathan, *My Freshman Year*

W-5d Starting a New Paragraph

Paragraphs may be long or short, and there are no strict rules about how many sentences are necessary for a well-developed paragraph. But while a brief, one- or two-sentence paragraph can be used to set off an idea you want to emphasize, too many short paragraphs can make your writing choppy. Here are some reasons for beginning a new paragraph:

- to introduce a new subject or idea
- to signal a new speaker (in dialogue)
- to emphasize an idea
- to give readers a needed pause

W-5e Writing Opening and Closing Paragraphs

A good opening engages readers and provides some indication of what's to come; a good closing leaves them feeling satisfied—that the story is complete, the questions have been answered, the argument has been made.

Opening paragraphs. Sometimes, you may begin with a brief anecdote or story that provides context for your topic and then proceed to state your **THESIS**. In the following opening paragraph, the writer describes a meeting of "scientific management" experts to introduce Frederick Taylor and other early efficiency experts:

Ordering people around, which used to be just a way to get things done, was elevated to a science in October 1910 when Louis Brandeis, a fifty-three-year-old lawyer from Boston, held a meeting in an apartment in New York with a bunch of experts, including Frank and Lillian Gilbreth, who, at Brandeis's urging, decided to call what they were experts at "Scientific Management." Everyone there, including Brandeis, had contracted "Tayloritis": they were enthralled by an industrial engineer from Philadelphia named Frederick Winslow Taylor, who had been ordering people around, scientifically, for years. He made work fast, and even faster. "Speedy Taylor," as he was called, had invented a whole new way to make money. He would get himself hired by some business; spend a while watching everyone work, stopwatch and slide rule in hand; write a report telling them how to do their work faster; and then submit an astronomical bill for his invaluable services. He is the "Father of Scientific Management" (at least, that's what it says on his tombstone) and, by any rational calculation, the grandfather of management consulting.

—Jill Lepore, *The Mansion of Happiness*

OTHER WAYS OF OPENING AN ESSAY

- with a quotation
- with a question
- with a startling fact or opinion

Concluding paragraphs. One approach is to conclude by summarizing the text's argument. The following paragraph reiterates the writer's main point and then issues a call for action.

The bottom line is that drastically reducing both crime rates and the number of people behind bars is technically feasible. Whether it is politically and organizationally feasible to achieve this remains an open question. It would be tragic if the politics proved prohibitive, but it would be genuinely criminal if we didn't even try.   —Mark A. R. Kleiman, "The Outpatient Prison"

OTHER WAYS OF CONCLUDING AN ESSAY

- by discussing the implications of your argument
- by asking a question
- by referring to something discussed at the beginning
- by proposing action

» SEE W-4f for help editing paragraphs.

W-6 Designing What You Write

Whether you're putting together your résumé, creating a website for your intramural soccer league, or writing a research essay for a class, you need to think about how to design what you write. Sometimes you can rely on established design conventions: in academic writing, there are specific guidelines for headings, margins, and line spacing. (This book includes guidelines for MLA, APA, Chicago, and CSE styles. If you're unsure what specific style is required for your discipline, check with your instructor.)

But often you'll have to make design decisions on your own—and not just about words and spacing but also about integrating your written text with visuals (and sometimes video and audio clips and hyperlinks) in the most attractive, effective, and accessible way. No matter what your text includes, its design will influence how your audience responds to it and therefore how well it achieves your purpose. This chapter offers advice on designing print and online texts to suit your PURPOSE, AUDIENCE, and the rest of your RHETORICAL CONTEXT.

W-6a Some Basic Principles of Design

Be consistent. To keep readers oriented as they browse multipage documents or websites, use design elements consistently. In a print academic essay, choose a single font for your main text and use boldface or italics for headings. In writing for the web, place navigation buttons and other major elements in the same place on every page. In a presentation, use the same background and font for each slide unless there's a good reason for differences.

Keep it simple. Help readers see quickly—even intuitively—what's in your text and where to find specific information. Add headings to help them see the parts, use consistent colors and fonts to help them recognize key elements, set off steps in lists, and use white space to set off blocks of text or highlight certain elements. Resist the temptation to fill pages with unnecessary graphics or animations.

Aim for balance. Create balance through the use of margins, images, headings, and spacing. **MLA**, **APA**, **Chicago**, and **CSE** styles have specific design guidelines for academic research papers that cover these elements. A website or magazine might balance a large image with a narrow column of text or use **PULL QUOTES** and illustrations to break up columns of dense vertical text.

Use color and contrast carefully. Academic readers usually expect black text on a white background, with perhaps one other color for headings. Presentation slides and webpages are most readable with dark text on a plain, light-colored background. Make sure your audience will be able to distinguish any color variations in your text well enough to grasp your meaning. Remember that an online text with several colors might be printed out and read in black and white and that not everyone can see all colors; red-green contrasts can be particularly challenging for some people.

Use available templates. To save time and simplify design decisions, take advantage of templates. In *Microsoft Word*, for example, you can customize font, spacing, indents, and other features that will automatically be applied to your document. Websites that host personal webpages and presentation software also offer templates that you can use or modify.

W-6b Some Elements of Design

Whatever your text, you have various design decisions to make. The following guidelines will help you make those decisions.

Fonts. The fonts you choose will affect how well readers can read your text. For most academic writing, you'll want to use 10- or 11- or 12-point type. It's usually a good idea to use a serif font (such as Times New Roman or Bookman) for your main text, reserving sans serif (such as Calibri, Verdana, or Century Gothic) for headings and parts you want to highlight. Decorative fonts (such as **Chiller**) should be used sparingly. If you use more than one font, use each one consistently: one for headings, one for captions, one for the main body of your text. You won't often need more than two or three fonts in any one text.

Every common font has regular, **bold,** and *italic* forms. In general, use regular for the main text, bold for major headings, and italic for titles of books and other long works. If, however, you are following a specific discipline's style, be sure you conform to its requirements.

Layout. Layout is the way text is arranged on a page. An academic essay, for example, will usually have a title centered at the top and one-inch margins all around. Items such as lists, tables, headings, and images should be arranged consistently.

Line spacing. Generally, academic writing is double-spaced, whereas letters and résumés are usually single-spaced. In addition, you'll often need to add an extra space to set off parts of a text—lists, for instance, or headings.

Paragraphs. In general, indent paragraphs five spaces when your text is double-spaced; either indent or skip a line between paragraphs that are single-spaced. When preparing a text intended for online use, single-space your document, skip a line between paragraphs, and begin each paragraph flush left (no indent).

Lists. Use a list format for information that you want to set off and make easily accessible. Number the items when the sequence matters (in instructions, for example); use bullets when the order is not important. Set off lists with an extra line of space above and below, and add extra space between the items on a list if necessary for legibility.

White space and margins. To make your text attractive and readable, use white space to separate its various parts. In general, use one-inch margins for the text of an essay or report. Unless you're following a format that has specific guidelines (such as APA), include space above headings, above and below lists, and around photos, graphs, and other visuals.

Headings. Headings make the structure of a text easier to follow and help readers find specific information. Some academic fields require standard headings—announcing a list of **WORKS CITED**, for example, to follow MLA format. Whenever you include headings, you need to decide how to phrase them, what fonts to use, and where to position them.

Phrase headings consistently. Make your headings succinct and parallel in structure. For example, you might make all the headings nouns (Mushrooms), noun phrases (Kinds of Mushrooms), gerund phrases (Recognizing Kinds of Mushrooms), or questions (How Do I Identify Mushrooms?). Whatever form you decide on, use it consistently.

Make headings visible. Consider setting headings in bold or italics, or with an underline—or in a different, or slightly larger, font. When you have several levels of headings, use capitalization, bold, and italics to distinguish among the various levels:

First-Level Head
Second-Level Head
Third-level head

Some academic fields have specific requirements about formatting headings; see the **MLA**, **APA**, **Chicago**, and **CSE** chapters for details.

Position headings appropriately. If you're following APA or MLA format, center first-level headings. If you are not following a prescribed format, you get to decide where to position the headings: centered, flush with the left margin, or even alongside the text, in a wide left-hand margin. Position each level of head consistently.

W-6c Visuals

Visuals (including video) can help make a point in ways that written words alone cannot. In print documents, you can often use photos, charts, graphs, and diagrams. Online or in spoken presentations, your options expand to include video and printed handouts. But choose carefully—and be sure that any items you incorporate contribute to your point and are appropriate for your purpose and audience.

Photographs can support an argument, illustrate events and processes, present other points of view, and help readers place your information in time and space. A discussion of the Nintendo Switch might be clearer when accompanied by this photo.

Tables are useful for displaying numerical information concisely, especially when several items are being compared. Presenting information in columns and rows permits readers to find data and identify relationships among the items.

ECONOMY WATCH
A snapshot of key figures for the world's largest economies.

COUNTRY	GDP in billions in 2010	GDP GROWTH Y/year (%)	CURRENT ACC'T/GDP in 2010 (%)	INFLATION Year over year (%)	JOBLE (%)
U.S.	$14,658	2.0‡	-3.2	3.5	8.6
Euro zone	12,474*	1.4	-0.2*	3.0	10.3
China	5,878	9.1	5.2	5.5	4.1
Japan	5,459	5.6‡	3.6	-0.1	4.5
Germany	3,316	2.5	5.3	2.8†	6.9
France	2,583	1.7	-2.1	2.5†	9.7
Britain	2,247	0.5	-2.5	5.0	8.3
Italy	2,055	0.8	-2.1*	3.7†	8.5
Brazil	1,601*	2.1	-1.5*	6.6	5.8
Canada	1,574	3.5‡	-3.1	2.9	7.4
India	1,538	6.9	-3.2	9.7	n.a.
Russia	1,222*	4.8	4.1*	6.8	6.4
Mexico	1,039	4.5	-0.7*	3.5	5.0
South Korea	833*	3.5	3.9*	4.2	3.1

* Actual figures of 2009   ** Harmonized figures   † Quarter on quarter annualized   ‡ Urban end September

Pie charts can be used to show how a whole is divided into parts or how parts of a whole relate to one another. Percentages in a pie chart should always add up to 100. Each segment should be labeled clearly, as in these two charts about English football league finances.

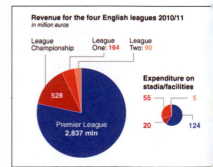

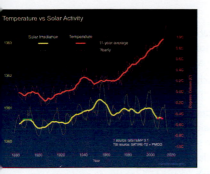

Line graphs are a good way of showing changes in data over time. One line here represents solar activity and the other temperature changes on Earth. Plotting the lines together enables readers to compare the data at different points in time. Be sure to label the x-and y-axes.

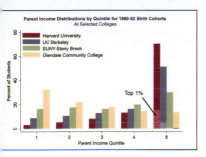

Bar graphs are useful for comparing quantitative data—measurements of how much or how many. Bars can be horizontal or vertical; this one uses vertical bars to show family income distribution at several colleges. Some software offer 3-D and other special effects, but simple graphs are often easier to read.

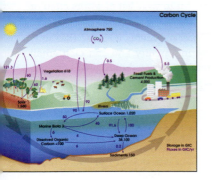

Diagrams and flowcharts are ways of showing relationships and processes. This diagram shows how carbon moves between Earth and its atmosphere. Flowcharts can be made by using widely available templates; diagrams, on the other hand, can range from simple drawings to works of art.

SOME TIPS FOR USING VISUALS

- *Choose visuals that relate directly to your subject,* support your assertions, and add information that words alone can't provide as clearly or easily. Avoid clip art.

- *In academic writing, number each image,* using separate sequences for **FIGURES** and tables: Fig. 1, Table 1.

- *Refer to the visual before it appears.* Position images as close as possible to the relevant discussion. Explain the information you're presenting—don't expect it to speak for itself: "As Table 1 shows, Italy's economic growth rate declined for thirty years."

- *Provide a title or caption for each image* to identify it and explain its significance for your text: "Table 1. Italian Economic Growth Rate, 1980–2010."

- *Label the parts of charts, graphs, and diagrams clearly*—sections of a pie chart, colors in a line graph, items in a diagram—to ensure that your audience will understand what they show.

- *Provide* **ALTERNATIVE TEXT** *for all visuals in a digital text.* This information ensures that those using screen-reader software can understand the important visual elements in your text.

- **DOCUMENT** *any visual you found or adapted from another source.* If you use data to create a graph or chart, include source information directly below and document it in your list of works cited or bibliography as you would any source.

- *Consider linking to a file rather than embedding it.* Large files may be hard to upload without altering quality and can clog email inboxes. Linking also allows readers to see the original context.

- *Integrate a video clip* by pasting its URL into your text or adding an image from the video that you've hyperlinked to the source. To include your own video, upload it to *YouTube*; choose the Unlisted setting to limit access.

- *Obtain permission* if you publish a visual in any form, including on the web. If you're in doubt about whether or not you can use an item, check "fair use" guidelines online.

If you alter a visual in some way—such as darkening a photo or cropping to include only a portion of it—tell readers what you've changed and why. Be sure to represent the original content accurately, and provide relevant information about the source. Be careful with charts and graphs as well—changing the scale on a bar graph, for example, may mislead readers.

W-6d Accessibility

As you weigh design choices, consider which features will make your text accessible to all readers—including those with differing visual, speech, auditory, physical, or cognitive abilities. The following suggestions will help you create accessible texts:

- *Consider font size in print texts.* Many readers require or prefer large type, so for printed texts, choose a font that's easy to read. When in doubt, chose a large font size or provide large-print copies. Large-print is 18 point or higher.

- *Provide* ALTERNATIVE TEXT *(alt text) for all essential images and visuals in digital texts.* Alt text describes the content or meaning of a visual. People using screen-reader software to read your text will understand visuals only if you provide alt text for the software to read out. Complex charts and graphs need not be described in detail; instead, provide alt text summarizing the main point: "A line chart shows that revenue grew incrementally from 20 percent to 60 percent between 2015 and 2020." If a visual is just decorative, you do not need to provide alt text.

- *Choose colors with high contrast.* When using multiple colors, choose ones that have a dramatic contrast (such as light blue against deep maroon) so that they are legible. And remember that some people cannot see the difference between certain colors (red and green, for example). Don't use color as the only means of conveying information. For example, underline URLs in addition to setting them in a contrasting color.

- *When giving a presentation, face the audience so lip-readers can see your face clearly, and keep your hands from blocking your face.* Provide a printout of your talk in a large font size as well as print copies of any visual aids. If your slides include important images or visuals, describe them out loud for those who may not be able to see them.

W-7 Giving Presentations

Whether in class as part of a research project, on campus in a campaign for student government, or at a wedding in a toast to the newlyweds, you may be called on to give presentations—sometimes, in combination with print and electronic media. Whatever the occasion, you need to make your points clear and memorable. This chapter offers guidelines to help you prepare and deliver effective presentations.

W-7a Key Elements of Spoken Presentations

A clear structure. Spoken texts need a clear organization so that your audience can follow you. The beginning needs to engage their interest, make clear what you will talk about, and perhaps forecast the central points of your talk. The main part should focus on a few key points—only as many as your audience can be expected to absorb. The ending should leave your audience something to remember, think about, or do.

In the Gettysburg Address, Abraham Lincoln follows a chronological structure. He begins with a reference to the past ("Four score and seven years ago"), moves to the present ("Now we are engaged in a great civil war"), looks to the future ("to the great task remaining before us"), and ends with a dramatic resolution: "that government of the people, by the people, for the people, shall not perish from the earth."

Signpost language to keep your audience on track. Provide cues, especially **TRANSITIONS** from one point to the next, to help your audience follow what you're saying. Sometimes, you'll also want to **SUMMARIZE** a complex point.

A tone to suit the occasion. Lincoln was speaking at a serious, formal event, the dedication of a national cemetery, and his **TONE**

was **FORMAL** and solemn. In a presentation to a panel of professors, you probably would want to avoid slang and speak in complete sentences. Speaking on the same topic to a neighborhood group, however, you would probably want to speak more **INFORMALLY**.

Repetition and parallel structure can lend power to a presentation, making it easy to follow—and likely to be remembered. In the Gettysburg Address, the repetition and **PARALLEL** structure in "We can not dedicate—we can not consecrate—we can not hallow" create a rhythm that engages listeners and at the same time unifies the text—one reason these words stay with us more than 150 years after they were written and delivered.

Slides and other media. Depending on the topic and occasion, you may need to use slides, video or audio clips, handouts, flip charts, whiteboards, and so on to present certain information or highlight key points.

W-7b Tips for Composing a Presentation

Budget your time. A five-minute presentation calls for about two and a half double-spaced pages of writing, and ten minutes means four or five pages. Your introduction and conclusion should each take about one-tenth of the total time available; audience responses (if the format allows), about one-fifth; and the main part of the talk, the rest.

Organize and draft your presentation. Structure and word your presentation so that your audience can easily follow it—and remember what you say.

- *Draft an introduction* that engages your audience's interest and tells them what to expect. Depending on the **RHETORICAL CONTEXT**, you may decide to begin with humor, with an **ANECDOTE**, or with a comment about the occasion for your talk. Provide any background information the audience needs, summarize your main points, and outline how you'll proceed.

- *In the main part of your talk, present your key points* in more detail, and support them with REASONS and EVIDENCE. If in drafting you find you have too many points for the time available, leave out the less important ones.

- *Let your listeners know when you're concluding.* Then restate your main points, and explain why they're important. Thank your listeners, and offer to take questions and comments if the format allows.

Consider whether to use visuals. Especially when you're presenting complex information, it helps to let your audience see it as well as hear it. Remember, though, that visuals should be a means of conveying information, not mere decoration.

- *Slides* are useful for listing main points and projecting illustrations, tables, and graphs.

- *Videos, animations, and audio* can add additional information.

- *Flip charts, whiteboards, or chalkboards* enable you to create visuals as you speak or to track audience comments.

- *Posters* can serve as the main part of a presentation, providing a summary of your points. You then offer only a brief introduction and answer questions.

- *Handouts* can provide additional information, lists of works cited, or copies of your slides.

What visual tools (if any) you decide to use are partly determined by how your presentation will be delivered: face to face? through a podcast? an online meeting? Make sure that any necessary equipment, programs, and electrical and internet connections are available—and that they work. Finally, remember that computers can fail; the internet may not work. Have a backup plan in case of problems.

Presentation software. *PowerPoint, Google Slides, Prezi*, or other presentation software enables you to include images, video, and sound in addition to written text. Here are some tips for writing and designing slides.

Thomas E. Dewey

- Appeared overconfident
- Ran a lackluster, "safe" campaign
- Was perceived as stuffy and aloof
- Made several blunders
- Would not address issues

This slide about the 1948 presidential election includes sans serif font and an image. Dark text on a white background provides a strong contrast.

- *Use lists or images, not paragraphs.* Use slides to emphasize your main points. A list of brief points, presented one by one, reinforces your words; charts and images can provide additional information that the audience can take in quickly.

- *Make your text easy for the audience to read.* FONTS should be at least 18 points. On slides, sans serif fonts like Arial and Helvetica are easier to read than serif fonts like Times New Roman. Avoid using all capital letters, which are hard to read.

- *Choose colors carefully.* Your text and illustrations need to contrast with the background. Dark content on a light background is easier to see and read than the reverse. And remember that not everyone sees all colors; be sure your audience doesn't need to see particular colors in order to get your meaning.

- *Use purely decorative elements sparingly, if at all.* Decorative backgrounds, animations, and sound effects can be more distracting than helpful; use them only if they help to make your point.

- *Mark your text.* Indicate in your notes each place where you need to advance to the next slide.

Handouts. Label handouts with your name and the date and title of the presentation. It's also good practice to provide printouts of your talk and slides in large-print (18 pt. or higher) for accessibility.

W-7c Delivering a Presentation

Practice. Practice, practice, and then practice some more. Practice builds confidence, and your audience will respond positively to that confidence. If you're reading a prepared text rather than using notes, practice by recording it as you read it; listen for spots that sound as if you're reading, and try to sound relaxed. Time your talk to be sure you don't go beyond your limit. If possible, practice with a small group of friends to get used to having an audience.

Speak clearly. If listeners miss important words or phrases because you don't pronounce them distinctly, that will limit your impact. Often you'll have to make yourself speak more slowly than usual.

Pause for emphasis. In writing, you have white space and punctuation to show readers where an idea or discussion ends. When speaking, a pause helps to signal the end of a thought, gives the audience a moment to consider what you've just said, or prepares them for a surprising or amusing statement.

Look directly at your audience. If you're in the same room as your audience, try to maintain eye contact. If that's uncomfortable, fake it: focus on the wall just above someone in the back of the room.

Use gestures for emphasis. To overcome any nervousness and stiffness, take some deep breaths, try to relax, and—if possible—move your arms and the rest of your body as you would if you were talking to a friend.

» **SEE W-1** for help analyzing your rhetorical context. See **W-4** for guidelines on drafting, revising, editing, and proofreading.
To read an example of a presentation, go to **digital.wwnorton.com /littleseagull4**.

W-8 Arguments

Everything we say or do presents some kind of argument, takes some kind of position. Often we take overt positions: "Everyone in the United States is entitled to affordable health care." "Photoshopped images should carry disclosure notices." In college course work, you are constantly called on to argue positions: in an English class, you may argue for a certain interpretation of a poem; in a business course, you may argue for the merits of a flat tax. All of those positions are arguable—people of goodwill can agree or disagree with them. This chapter provides a description of the key elements of an essay that argues a position and tips for writing one.

W-8a Key Elements of an Argument

A clear and arguable position. At the heart of every argument is a **CLAIM** with which people may reasonably disagree. Some claims are not arguable because they're matters of taste or opinion ("I love kale"), of fact ("The first *Star Wars* movie came out in 1977"), or belief or faith ("I believe in life after death"). To be arguable, a position must reflect one of at least two points of view, making reasoned argument necessary: ride-sharing companies such as Lyft and Uber should (or should not) be more tightly regulated; selling human organs should be legal (or illegal). In college writing, you will often argue not that a position is correct but that it is plausible—that it is reasonable, supportable, and worthy of being taken seriously.

Necessary background information. Sometimes, you need to provide some background on a topic so that readers can understand what is being argued. To argue that ride-sharing companies should be more regulated, for example, you might begin by explaining how they differ from traditional taxi companies.

Good reasons. By itself, a position does not make an argument; the argument comes when a writer offers reasons to support the position. There are many kinds of good **REASONS**. You might argue that ride-sharing services should be more tightly regulated by comparing their accident rates with those of traditional taxi services. You might base an argument in favor of legalizing the sale of human organs on the fact that transplants save lives and that regulation would protect impoverished people who currently sell their organs on the black market.

Convincing evidence. Once you've given reasons for your position, you then need to offer **EVIDENCE** for your reasons: facts, statistics, testimony, anecdotes, textual examples, and so on. For example, to support your position that soft drinks should be taxed, you might cite a nutrition expert who links frequent soda consumption to diabetes, offer facts that demonstrate the health-care costs of diabetes, and provide statistics that show how taxation affects behavior.

Appeals to readers' values. Effective arguments appeal to readers' values and emotions. For example, arguing that legalizing organ sales will save the lives of those in need of transplants appeals to compassion—a deeply held value. To appeal to readers' emotions, you might describe the plight of those who are dying in want of a transplant. Keep in mind, however, that emotional appeals can make readers feel manipulated—and then less likely to accept an argument.

A trustworthy TONE. Readers need to trust the person who's making the argument. There are many ways of establishing yourself (and your argument) as trustworthy: by providing facts that demonstrate your knowledge of the subject, by indicating that you have some experience with it, by demonstrating that you've considered perspectives other than your own, and by showing that you're fair and honest.

Careful consideration of other positions. No matter how reasonable you are in arguing your position, others may disagree or hold other positions. So you need to acknowledge any likely **COUNTERARGUMENTS** and, if possible, refute them. For example, you might acknowledge the argument that tighter regulation of ride-sharing apps might result in fewer work opportunities for part-time drivers, but you might counter that regulation could mean better pay and conditions for drivers.

W-8b **Tips for Writing an Argument**

Choosing a topic. A fully developed argument requires significant work and time, so choosing a topic in which you're interested is very important. Widely debated topics such as animal rights or gun control can be difficult to write on if you have no personal connection to them. Better topics include those that interest you right now, are focused, and have some personal connection to your life. Here's one good way to **GENERATE IDEAS** for a topic that meets those three criteria:

Start with your roles in life. Make four columns with the headings "Personal," "Family," "Public," and "School." Then list the roles you play in life that relate to each heading. Under "School," for example, your list might include "college student," "chemistry major," and "work-study employee."

Identify issues that interest you. Pick a few of the roles you list, and identify the issues that interest or concern you. Try wording each issue as a question starting with "should": Should college cost less than it does? Should student achievement be measured by standardized tests?

Try framing your topic as a problem: Why has college tuition risen so rapidly in recent decades? What would be better than standardized tests for measuring student achievement? This strategy will help you think about the issue and find a clear focus for your essay.

Choose one issue to write about. It is a preliminary choice; if you find later that you have trouble writing about it, you'll be able to go back to your list and choose another.

Generating ideas and text. Most essays that successfully argue a position share certain features that make them interesting and persuasive. Remember that your goal is to stake out a position and convince your readers that it's plausible.

Explore the issue. Write out whatever you know about the issue, perhaps by **FREEWRITING** or making an **OUTLINE**. Consider what interests you about the topic and what more you may need to learn in order to write about it. It may help to do some preliminary research;

start with one general source of information (a news magazine or *Wikipedia*, for example) to find out the main questions raised about your issue and to get some ideas about how you might argue it. Make sure your issue is arguable—and worth arguing about.

Draft a THESIS. Once you've explored the issue thoroughly, decide your position on it, and write it out as a sentence—for example, "Baseball players who have used steroids should not be eligible for the Hall of Fame." In most cases you'll then want to qualify your thesis—to acknowledge that yours is not the only plausible position, and to limit your topic and make it manageable. Use phrases like "in certain circumstances," "under certain conditions," or "with these limitations." For example, "Though baseball players who use steroids should not be eligible for the Hall of Fame, their records and achievements will still stand."

Come up with good REASONS. You need to convince your readers that your thesis is plausible. Start by stating your position and then answering the question "why?"

> **THESIS:**   Baseball players who have used steroids should not be eligible for the Hall of Fame.
>
> **REASON:**   (Because) Using steroids gives athletes unfair advantages.

Keep in mind that you will likely have a further reason, a principle that underlies the reason you give for your CLAIM.

> **UNDERLYING REASON:**   Gaining an unfair advantage is cheating.
> **UNDERLYING REASON:**   Cheating is wrong.

This analysis can continue indefinitely as the underlying reasons grow more and more general and abstract. When you've listed several reasons, consider which are the most persuasive ones given your PURPOSE and AUDIENCE.

Find EVIDENCE to support your reasons. Here are some kinds of evidence you can offer as support: facts; statistics; testimony by authorities and experts; ANECDOTES; case studies and observations; textual evidence; and visual evidence like photos, graphs, and videos.

Identify other positions. Think about positions that differ from yours and about the reasons that might be given for those positions. Even if you can't refute such doubts about and objections to your position, you need to acknowledge them to show that you've considered other perspectives. To refute other positions, state them as clearly and as fairly as you can, and then show why you believe they are wrong. Perhaps the reasoning is faulty or the supporting evidence is inadequate. Acknowledge their merits, if any, but emphasize their shortcomings.

Addressing a hostile audience. Sometimes your goal is to change your audience's minds, which is often more difficult than simply convincing them your position is plausible. In situations like these, **ROGERIAN ARGUMENT** techniques, based on the work of psychologist Carl Rogers, can help. Rogerian argument assumes that common ground exists between people who disagree and finding that common ground can lead to some agreement or compromise.

To write a Rogerian argument, begin by introducing the issue and acknowledging the sides of the controversy fairly. In the next section, summarize the opposing view accurately and neutrally, including circumstances when that view might be valid. Your goal is to show that you understand the opposing view and why some readers hold that view; you want those readers to agree that your summary is accurate, establishing your credibility and honest desire to understand those whose views differ from yours. Then go on to outline your position and defend it as you would in a traditional argument. In your conclusion, bring the two perspectives you've just outlined together to show how, while your opponent's views have merit, your position deals with the issue better—or how a compromise position, somewhere in the middle, allows both sides to benefit.

Ways of organizing an argument. Sometimes, you'll want to give all the reasons for your argument first, followed by discussion of all the counterarguments. Alternatively, you might discuss each reason and any counterargument to it together. And be sure to consider the order in which you discuss your reasons. Usually, what comes last makes the strongest impression on readers, and what comes in the middle makes the weakest impression.

[Reasons to support your argument, followed by counterarguments]

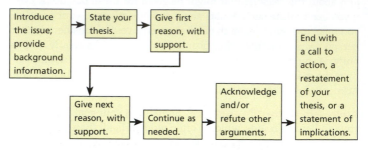

[Reason / counterargument, reason / counterargument]

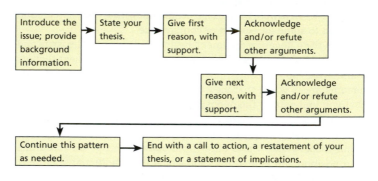

[Rogerian argument]

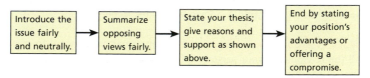

>> **SEE** **W-1** for help analyzing your writing context. See **W-4** for guidelines on drafting, revising, editing, and proofreading your argument. See **W-3c** for guidelines on analyzing an argument. To read additional examples of argument essays, go to **digital .wwnorton.com/littleseagull4**.

W-8c Sample Argument Essay

GAVIN REID

The Electoral College Embodies American Ideals

This essay written by chemical engineering student Gavin Reid using MLA style was published in Analog, *a collection of essays by first-year students at the University of Alabama.*

Imagine that you've just cast your vote for president, and you are now impatiently waiting for the election results to see who will be the next president of the United States of America. When the votes are counted, you are excited to see that the candidate you voted for won the majority of votes across the country . . . but then you realize that your candidate somehow lost in the Electoral College so will not become president. This was reality for many who voted in the US presidential elections of 1824, 1876, 1888, 2000, and 2016. It's strange that a candidate can win a majority of votes and yet still lose the presidential election. As a result, many people have argued that the Electoral College should be eliminated. However, the Electoral College should remain, because it was instated by the nation's founders for good reasons, it solidly embodies the ideals of the United States, and its benefits strongly outweigh possible shortcomings.

A clear and arguable position. The thesis previews the shape of the argument.

The Electoral College was created by our nation's founders to prevent one region from controlling the country. When the United States was founded, most of the population was concentrated within a few states, and those states would be able to dominate the country if the government were a pure democracy. Because of this population disparity, many small-population states feared that the larger ones would force them to conform to any laws and legislation that the larger states desired, creating a tyranny of the majority. So the founders put multiple measures in place to avoid this imbalance. One of those measures is the Electoral College, which gives each state a voice while also reflecting the opinion of the general population.

Necessary background information: reasoning behind creating the Electoral College.

The Electoral College consists of groups of electors from each state. The number of electors for each state is equal to the sum of the number of the state's representatives in the House of Representatives and its two senators, so there is a total of 538 electors (and

Additional background information: how the Electoral College works.

a candidate must earn 270 electoral votes to win the election). Each state legislature nominates the electors for the state, and all the electors in a state support a candidate based on how the general public in that state votes ("What"). This strategy grants each state two electors regardless of population and grants additional electors based on each state's population. Without the Electoral College, urban areas could potentially dominate politics. If the president were simply decided by the popular vote, then vast regions of America wouldn't be properly represented.

Reasons presented for keeping the Electoral College are supported with evidence from experts.

The founders also appreciated the quality of votes as opposed to the quantity. Michael Uhlmann, a political science professor at Claremont Graduate University, states that the Electoral College "teaches us that the character of a majority is more important than its size alone" (29). Richard Posner, a past judge on the United States Seventh Court of Appeals, a professor at the University of Chicago, and a Harvard Law School graduate, states that while a majority vote of the population could come solely from urban areas, "the Electoral College requires a presidential candidate to have trans-regional appeal." The president can't win the election by earning the support of simply one geographic area or demographic of the population. The Electoral College forces the future president to appeal to people of various demographics, regions, and subcultures.

The author acknowledges a counterargument, explains the reasoning underlying it, and responds.

Many Americans believe that since the Electoral College does not always reflect the will of the majority it is, in effect, undemocratic. The short response to that comment is "yes," but the longer response requires a more thorough understanding of the founding of our nation. The framers of the Constitution formed a government with characteristics of a democracy, a republic, and a federalist system. While a democracy focuses solely on the will and desires of the majority of its population, a republic allows the people to elect representatives who will represent the population in legal matters by doing what those representatives believe is best for the nation. A federalist system, in turn, separates the powers of a government into multiple tiers to ensure that local areas are governed in a way that accurately represents the local population. While the Electoral College may seem to contradict some ideals of a democracy, it accomplishes goals set forth by a republic and federalist system. Representatives chosen by the public ultimately are the ones responsible for electing the president, and the state legislatures assume responsibility for nominating the members of the Electoral College. Thomas Jefferson is said to have stated, "Democracy is nothing more than mob rule, where 51 percent of the people may take away the rights of the other 49 percent." The founders were wary of majority rule in a pure democracy and so ensured that the country was protected from itself by using principles of republic and federalist systems in the Electoral College. America is the great country that it is today because the founders promised American citizens certain unalienable rights through these systems, and we must be cautious of any political reform that could jeopardize those rights.

Some opponents of the Electoral College argue it should be removed because it has negative effects on campaigning strategy. Presidential campaigns tend to focus on certain key swing states and have "just taken a lot of states off of the presidential map" (Dotinga). Abolishing the Electoral College would supposedly "allow long-ignored states to get attention again in presidential campaigns" (Dotinga). While campaigns concentrating on certain states and not others is not ideal, it is unreasonable to assume that candidates would give equal attention to every region of the country if the Electoral College were abolished. In that case, it's more likely campaigns would instead focus on regions with concentrated population centers such as the Northeast and the West Coast. As a result, large sections of America, especially rural areas with low population density, would be ignored. So although it's fair to point out that presidential campaigns focus on certain geographic areas and leave out others, removing the Electoral College would not fix this problem.

Another counter-argument is presented and refuted with reasoning.

Another argument for abolishing the Electoral College is that every single vote would become more important and our political system would be more accommodating to third parties. Instead of ignoring the votes that do not align with the majority of voters in each state and the opinions of voters supporting third parties, every individual's vote would have an equal effect on the outcome of the election, allowing third parties the possibility to win. Uhlmann states, "What the people would get by choosing direct election is the disintegration of the state-based two-party system" (28). He notes that removing the Electoral College would allow "the rise of

A third counter-argument's validity is acknowledged and its shortcomings identified.

numerous factional parties based on region, class, ideology, or cult of personality" (28). Although this may be true and attractive, we must not lose sight of the initial purpose of the Electoral College and not let the appeal of the statement "Every vote counts" overshadow the purpose and intentions of the Electoral College. Just because a system has some flaws does not mean that extreme reform will lead us to a new system any more just and reasonable than what the founders designed. As long as government is organized by humans—and humans continue to be imperfect creatures—we must accept that our political system will include some flaws and carefully weigh whether reform would truly improve upon the founders' vision or leave us worse off. A single-vote system would leave us vulnerable to the "mob rule" that the founders worked to protect us against.

Appeals to our values, specifically our understanding of and perhaps pride in the ideas of the founders of our country.

For these reasons, the United States of America should keep the Electoral College. Although the complaints against it are understandable, we must consider the profound reasons it was initially created: to ensure a proper representation of each state, region, and person in the United States in the presidential election. The Electoral College prevents regional tyranny in our government, maintains our current government structure, and embodies the ideals that have helped our country survive and thrive. As appealing as a direct election may sound, we must remember what the founders had in mind for our country and that the institutions they put in place were created for the protection of our freedom.

Concludes by summarizing the reasons the Electoral College was invented and why it shouldn't be abolished— restating his thesis.

Works Cited

Dotinga, Randy. "A Backdoor Plan to Thwart the Electoral College." *Christian Science Monitor*, 16 June 2006, www .csmonitor.com/2006/0616/p01s02-uspo.html. Accessed 23 Jan. 2020.

Posner, Richard A. "In Defense of the Electoral College." *Slate*, 12 Nov. 2012, www.slate.com/news-and-politics/2012/11 /defending-the-electoral-college.html. Accessed 23 Jan. 2020.

Uhlmann, Michael M. "The Old (Electoral) College Cheer: Why We Have It; Why We Need It." *National Review*, 8 Nov. 2004, pp. 28–29.

"What Is the Electoral College?" *National Archives*, 23 Dec. 2019, www.archives.gov/federal-register/electoral-college/about .html. Accessed 23 Jan. 2020.

W-9   Rhetorical Analyses

Both *HuffPost* and the *National Review* cover the same events, but each interprets them differently. All toothpaste ads claim to make teeth "the whitest." Those are just a couple of examples that demonstrate why we need to be careful, analytical readers of magazines and newspapers, websites, ads, political documents, even textbooks—to understand not only what texts say but also how they say it. Assignments in many disciplines call for a rhetorical analysis: you may be asked to analyze the use of color and space in Edward Hopper's painting *Nighthawks* for an art history course, or to analyze a set of data to find the standard deviation in a statistics course. This chapter describes the key elements of an essay that analyzes a text and provides tips for writing one.

W-9a   Key Elements of a Rhetorical Analysis

A summary of the text. Your readers may not know the subject or text you are analyzing, so you need to include it or tell them about it before you can analyze it. A well-known text such as the Gettysburg Address may require only a brief description, but less well-known texts require a more detailed **SUMMARY**. For an analysis of several advertisements, for example, you'd probably show several ads and also describe them in some detail.

Attention to the context. All texts are part of ongoing conversations, controversies, or debates, so to understand a text, you need to understand its larger context. To analyze the lyrics of a new hip-hop song, you might need to introduce other artists that the lyrics refer to or explain how the lyrics relate to aspects of hip-hop culture.

A clear interpretation or judgment. Your goal is to lead readers through a careful examination of the text to some kind of interpretation or reasoned judgment, generally announced clearly in a **THESIS**

statement. When you interpret something, you explain what you think it means. If you're analyzing the TV show *Family Guy*, you might argue that a particular episode is a parody of the political controversy over health care. In an analysis of a cologne advertisement, you might explain how the ad encourages consumers to objectify themselves.

Reasonable support for your conclusions. You'll need to support your analysis with EVIDENCE from the text itself and sometimes from other sources. You might support your interpretation by quoting passages from a written text or referring to images in a visual text. To argue that Barack Obama's eulogy for the Reverend Clementa Pinckney aligns him with Martin Luther King Jr. and Abraham Lincoln, you might trace the ways his wording echoes that of "I Have a Dream" and Lincoln's second inaugural address, for example. Note that the support you offer need only be "reasonable"—there is never only one way to interpret something.

W-9b Tips for Writing a Rhetorical Analysis

Choosing a text to analyze. Most of the time, you will be assigned a text or a type of text to analyze: the work of a political philosopher in a political science class, a speech in a history or communications course, a painting or sculpture in an art class, and so on. If you must choose a text to analyze, look for one that suits the assignment—one that is neither too large or complex to analyze thoroughly nor too brief or limited to generate sufficient material. You might also analyze three or four texts by examining elements common to all.

Generating ideas and text. In analyzing a text, your goal is to understand what it says, how it works, and what it means. To do so, you may find it helpful to follow a certain sequence for your analysis: read, respond, summarize, analyze, and draw conclusions.

Read to see what the text says. Start by reading carefully, noting the main ideas, key words and phrases, and anything that seems noteworthy or questionable.

Once you have a sense of what the text says, consider your initial response. What's your reaction to the argument, the tone, the language, the images? Do you find the text difficult? puzzling? Do you agree with what the writer says? Whatever your reaction, think about how you react—and why.

Then consolidate your understanding of the text by **SUMMARIZING** or **DESCRIBING** it in your own words.

Decide what you want to analyze. Think about what you find most interesting about the text and why. Are you interested in the language? the imagery? the larger context? something else? You might begin your analysis by exploring what attracted your notice.

Think about the larger context. All texts are part of larger conversations, and academic texts include documentation partly to weave in voices from the conversation. Being aware of that larger context can help you better understand what you're reading; here are some things to consider:

- *What larger conversation does the text respond to?* What's motivated the writer? Are they responding to something others have said?

- *Who else cares about this topic?* Those cited could be assumed to care, but does the author indicate who else cares—and why the topic matters in the first place?

- *Where is the writer coming from?* Is there any terminology that suggests that they are allied with a particular intellectual school or academic discipline? Words like "intersectionality" or "mansplaining," for instance, might suggest that the text was written by a feminist scholar.

Consider what you know about the writer or artist. The credentials, other work, reputation, stance, and beliefs of the person who created the text are all useful windows into understanding it. Write a sentence or two summarizing what you know about the creator and how that information affects your understanding of the text.

Study how the text works. Written texts are made up of various components, including words, sentences, headings, punctuation—and sometimes images as well. Visual texts might be made up of images, lines, angles, color, light and shadow, and sometimes words. Look for patterns in the way these elements are used. Write a sentence or two describing the patterns you discover and how they contribute to what the text says.

Analyze the argument. An important part of understanding any text is to recognize its **ARGUMENT** —what the writer or artist wants the audience to believe, feel, or do.

- *What is the claim?* What is the main point the writer is trying to make? Is there a clearly stated **THESIS**, or is it merely implied?

- *What support does the writer offer for the claim?* What **REASONS** are given to support the claim, and what **EVIDENCE** backs up those reasons? Are the reasons plausible and sufficient?

- *How evenhandedly does the writer present the issues?* Are the arguments appropriately qualified? Is there any mention of **COUNTERARGUMENTS** —and if so, how does the writer deal with them?

- *What authorities or other sources of information are cited?* How credible and current are they?

- *Do you see any logical* **FALLACIES**? Arguments that rely on faulty reasoning can seem plausible, and they can be persuasive—but they're misleading.

After considering these questions, write a sentence or two summarizing the argument and your reactions to it.

Come up with a thesis. Once you've studied the text thoroughly, you need to identify your analytical goal. Do you want to show that the text has a certain meaning? uses certain techniques to achieve its purposes? tries to influence its audience in particular ways? relates to some larger context in some significant manner? something else? Come up with a tentative thesis to guide you—but be aware that your thesis may change as you work.

Ways of organizing a rhetorical analysis. Consider how to organize the information you've gathered to best support your thesis. Your analysis might be structured in at least two ways. You might discuss patterns or themes that run through the text. Alternatively, you might analyze each text or section of text separately.

[Thematically]

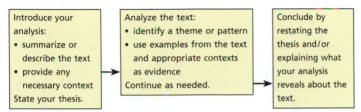

[Part by part, or text by text]

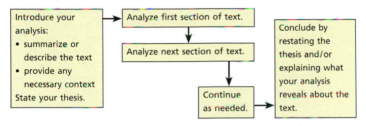

>> **SEE W-1** for help analyzing your writing context. See **W-4** for guidelines on drafting, revising, editing, and proofreading a textual analysis. To read additional examples of rhetorical analyses, go to **digital.wwnorton.com/littleseagull4**.

W-9c Sample Rhetorical Analysis Essay

PIERCE RENDALL

Hip-Hop's Potential Impact

Pierce Rendall wrote this analysis (using MLA style) of Logic's "1-800-273-8255" music video for a first-year writing course at Stephen F. Austin State University. It was a nominee for the Norton Writer's Prize.

Musical artists today have many tools at their disposal to influence the way an audience understands their message—from the tone of the music and the pronunciation of lyrics to the visual elements in music videos. In hip-hop artist Logic's music video "1-800-273-8255," he combines lyrics with a powerful visual story that results in raising real awareness and helping people. The video begins in a high school, where the lead character—an African American boy—flirts with a white male classmate. At home, the lead character's sexuality is questioned by his father, causing the lead to leave his house looking disappointed, frustrated, and lonely. The relationship between the two classmates develops until they're caught in bed by the white boy's father, who is not pleased. At school, the lead is bullied about his sexuality, and the following scenes show he's anguished and alone. He finds his father's gun and considers ending his life, but instead he makes a call—presumably to the suicide hotline whose phone number is the title of the song. One of the final scenes shows the lead, now grown up, at his wedding marrying a man, finally receiving acceptance from his father. By pairing his lyrics with an emotional visual story, Logic raises awareness of the struggles many LGBTQ people face and provides an ultimately uplifting message that has the power of positively impacting anyone facing a difficult time in their lives.

One of the main points of the video is to show the negative treatment LGBTQ people often face. Multiple scenes show the lead character enduring painful experiences both at home and school because of his sexuality. In one scene, the student finds his locker vandalized with spray paint and a sex toy (Logic 3:42–3:50). In another, the student sleeps at school and receives food from a teacher because he doesn't feel accepted at home. Both scenes show the kinds of inescapable discrimination many LGBTQ people

The video is briefly summarized.

The author makes a claim and supports it with evidence from the video and from a scholarly source.

face in their daily lives. In "'Like Walking through a Hailstorm': Discrimination against LGBT Youth in US Schools," a Human Rights Watch report, author Ryan Thoreson bluntly states:

> A lack of policies and practices that affirm and support LGBT youth—and a failure to implement protections that do exist—means that LGBT students nationwide continue to face bullying, exclusion, and discrimination in school, putting them at physical and psychological risk and limiting their education.

Logic's video provides a personal, powerful example of the struggles Thoreson describes: ignorance and a lack of acceptance leading to bullying, humiliation, and physical risk. The song's lyrics alone portray anguish: "I don't wanna be alive / I just wanna die today" (Logic 0:48–0:59). But it's the bullying scenes in the music video that represent the real, dangerous impacts that discrimination can have on LGBTQ individuals.

Throughout the music video, Logic uses emotional appeals by synchronizing lyrics with specific scenes—an effect that helps the audience empathize and relate. For example, when the lead character's father confronts him about finding a copy of a magazine published for gay men, the lyrics say:

> I know I'm hurting deep down but can't show it
> I never had a place to call my own
> I never had a home, ain't nobody calling my phone
> where you been? where you at? what's on your mind?
> they say every life precious but nobody care about mine.
> (Logic 1:13–1:28)

This synchronization helps the audience understand what the young man is feeling in the scene. Hearing these lyrics while watching someone experience an emotional and painful moment provokes empathy. This synchronization technique of combining powerful lyrics with emotional situations and images is used at several critical points in the video, and it effectively conveys what discrimination might feel like for the main character in the video. In "Exploring Hip-Hop Therapy with High-Risk Youth," human services consultant Nakeyshaey M. Tillie Allen examines the positive influence hip-hop lyrics can have on young people going through tough times. She

Another claim, supported by evidence from the video and from a scholarly source.

argues: "Analyzing Hip-Hop lyrics engages participants, stimulates discussion, and promotes the examination of life issues, struggles, and experiences in a way that participants experience as relevant to their own lives" (31). Allen's research suggests that hip-hop music has the power to help young people when it portrays challenges they can relate to. So by pairing hip-hop lyrics with a depiction of a young person's struggle, Logic does more than evoke empathy; he strives to have a positive impact on young people who need a lifeline.

An analysis of the response to the video as evidence for the author's interpretation.

Elements of the video and song suggest that Logic composed "1-800-273-8255" in an effort to speak to young people in crises, but it's the response to the video that proves Logic accomplished his goal. By using the National Suicide Prevention Lifeline's phone number as the song's title and ending the music video with the number, Logic spreads the word about this life-saving resource. In fact, the National Suicide Prevention Lifeline said in a press release about the song's impact that calls surged after the song's release and stated emphatically that "Logic addressed suicide thoughtfully and creatively to inspire fans to seek help and find hope" (@ Logic301). And Logic himself commented on the song's impact during his performance at the 2017 MTV Video Music Awards, where he was joined on stage by fifty suicide attempt survivors and people who had lost others to suicide. Concluding the performance, Logic announced:

> I just want to . . . thank you all so much for giving me a platform to talk about something that mainstream media doesn't want to talk about[:] . . . mental health, anxiety, suicide, depression and so much more that I talk about on this album . . . I'm gonna fight for your equality because I believe that we are all born equal, but we are not treated equal and that is why we must fight. (qtd. in Moniuszko)

The analysis leads to a clear interpretation of the video. The conclusion summarizes why the interpretation matters.

Logic's motivation is clear—he created the work to shine light on mental health issues and fight for the equality of those who are not treated equal. And the techniques he used worked to both raise awareness and connect many people to a life-saving resource.

Logic's "1-800-273-8255"—from the song to the music video to the VMA stage performance—was crafted to have an emotional and positive impact on audiences. This work achieves one of its main goals—to give struggling people hope and resources. But it also accomplishes a second goal: spreading awareness of common, painful experiences in the LGBTQ community in a sympathetic light so others who can't relate can at least empathize. For those naïve to the extent of discrimination against young LGBTQ people, the song and video provide a sympathetic viewpoint and way of understanding. As a result of seeing and hearing Logic's "1-800-273-8255," there's reason to hope people may change the way they treat others and consider other people's experiences and emotions more carefully.

Works Cited

@Logic301 (Logic). "The most important song I've ever wrote." *Twitter*, 15 Nov. 2017, 6:19 p.m., twitter.com/Logic301 /status/930938282539491328. Accessed 23 Jan. 2020.

Logic. "Logic - 1-800-273-8255 ft. Alessia Cara, Khalid." *YouTube*, 17 Aug. 2017, www.youtube.com/watch?v=Kb24RrHIbFk. Accessed 23 Jan. 2020.

Moniuszko, Sara M. "Logic's MTV VMAs Performance of '1-800' Was an Emotional Triumph with a Powerful Message." *USA Today*, 27 Aug. 2017, www.usatoday.com/story/life/entertainthis /2017/08/27/logics-mtv-vmas-performance-1-800-emotional -triumph-powerful-message/606928001/. Accessed 17 Jan. 2020.

Thoreson, Ryan. "'Like Walking through a Hailstorm': Discrimination against LGBT Youth in US Schools." *Human Rights Watch*, 7 Dec. 2016, www.hrw.org/sites/default/files /report_pdf/uslgbt1216web_2.pdf. Accessed 17 Jan. 2020.

Tillie Allen, Nakeyshaey M. "Exploring Hip-Hop Therapy with High-Risk Youth." *Praxis: Where Reflection & Practice Meet*, vol. 5, 2005, pp. 30–36, www.luc.edu/media/lucedu/socialwork /pdfs/praxis/Volume%205.pdf. Accessed 16 Jan. 2020.

W-10 Reports

Many kinds of writing report information. Newspapers report on local and world events; textbooks give information about biology, history, writing; websites provide information about products (uniqlo.com), people (avaduvernay.com), institutions (smithsonian.org). You've probably done a lot of writing that reports information, from a third-grade report on the water cycle to an essay for a history class reporting on migrants during the Great Depression. Very often this kind of writing calls for research: you need to know your subject in order to report on it. This chapter describes the key elements found in most reports and offers tips for writing one.

W-10a Key Elements of a Report

A tightly focused topic. The goal of this kind of writing is to inform readers about something without digressing—and without, in general, bringing in the writer's own opinions. If you're writing a report on the causes of air turbulence, for example, you probably shouldn't get into complaints about the delays on your last flight.

Accurate, well-researched information. Reports usually require some research. The kind of research depends on the topic. Library research may be necessary for some topics—for a report on migrant laborers during the Great Depression, for example. Most current topics, however, require internet research. Some topics may require FIELD RESEARCH —interviews, observations, and so on. For a report on local farming, for example, you might interview some local farmers.

Various writing strategies. You'll usually use a number of organizing STRATEGIES —to describe something, explain a process, and so on. For example, a report on the benefits of exercise might require that you classify types of exercise, analyze the effects of each type, and compare the benefits of each.

Clear definitions. Reports need to provide clear **DEFINITIONS** of any key terms that the audience may not know. For a report on the impeachment proceedings against President Donald Trump for a general audience, you might need to define terms such as "quid pro quo" and "high crimes and misdemeanors."

Appropriate design. Some information is best presented in paragraphs, but other information may be easier to present (and to read) in lists, tables, diagrams, and other **VISUALS**. Numerical data, for instance, can be easier to understand in a table than in a paragraph. A photograph can help readers see a subject, such as an image of someone texting while driving in a report on car accidents.

W-10b Tips for Writing a Report

Choosing a topic. If you get to choose your topic, consider what interests you and what you wish you knew more about. The possible topics for informational reports are limitless, but the topics that you're most likely to write well on are those that engage you. They may be academic in nature or reflect your personal interests, or both.

If your topic is assigned, be sure you understand what you're required to do. Some assignments are specific: "Explain the physics of roller coasters." If, however, your assignment is broad—"Explain some aspect of the US government"—try focusing on a more limited aspect of that topic, preferably one that interests you: federalism, the Electoral College, filibusters. Even if an assignment seems to offer little flexibility, you will need to decide how to research the topic and how to develop your report to appeal to your audience. And sometimes even narrow topics can be shaped to fit your own interests.

Generating ideas and text. Start by exploring whatever you know or want to know about your topic, perhaps by **FREEWRITING**, **LOOPING**, or **CLUSTERING**, all activities that will help you come up with ideas. Then you'll need to narrow your focus.

Narrow your topic. You may know which aspect of the topic you want to focus on, but often you'll need to do some research first—and that research may change your thinking and your focus. Start with sources that can give you a general sense of the subject, such as a *Wikipedia* entry or an interview with an expert. Your goal at this point is to find topics to report on and then to focus on one that you will be able to cover.

Come up with a tentative thesis. Once you narrow your topic, write out a statement saying what you plan to report on or explain. A good **THESIS** is potentially interesting (to you and your readers) and limits your topic enough to be manageable. For a report on the benefits of exercise, for instance, your thesis might be "While weight lifting can build strength and endurance, regular cardiovascular exercise offers greater overall health benefits."

Do any necessary research. Focus your efforts by **OUTLINING** what you expect to discuss. Identify any aspects you'll need to research. Think about what kinds of information will be most informative for your audience, and be sure to consult multiple sources and perspectives. Revisit and finalize your thesis in light of your research findings.

Ways of organizing a report

[Reports on topics that are unfamiliar to readers]

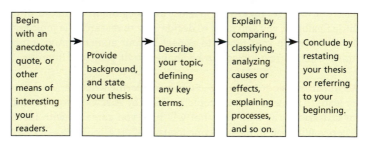

| Begin with an anecdote, quote, or other means of interesting your readers. | Provide background, and state your thesis. | Describe your topic, defining any key terms. | Explain by comparing, classifying, analyzing causes or effects, explaining processes, and so on. | Conclude by restating your thesis or referring to your beginning. |

[Reports on an event]

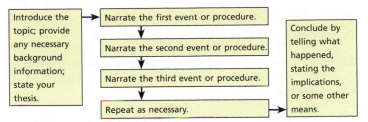

[Reports that compare by the block method]

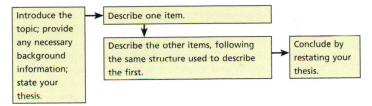

[Reports that compare by the point-by-point method]

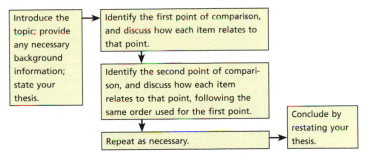

>> **SEE W-1** for help analyzing your writing context. See **W-4** for guidelines on drafting, revising, editing, and proofreading your report. To read additional examples of reports, go to **digital .wwnorton.com/littleseagull4**.

W-10c Sample Report Essay

ROCIO CELESTE MEJIA AVILA

Cyberloafing: Distraction or Motivation?

This report, a nominee for the Norton Writer's Prize, was written by Keiser University student and English tutor Rocio Celeste Mejia Avila. It follows APA style.

Increased technological advances and widespread internet access have revolutionized the workplace. But all this innovation has come with at least one questionable stowaway: cyberloafing—the act of browsing the internet for personal use while at work. It's becoming essential for organizations to understand cyberloafing: what it is, which factors lead employees to do it, and how it affects productivity. At its worst, cyberloafing can jeopardize an organization's information security, so awareness about cyberloafing is essential to both employees and employers in order to prevent its most negative consequences.

> *Narrow topic and a clear thesis.*

Cyberloafing refers to a behavior in which employees use their organization's internet access to spend work hours on nonwork-related tasks such as checking personal emails, playing games, social networking, or shopping online (Wagner et al., 2012, p. 1068). The work of organizational psychology researchers Henle and Blanchard (2008) showed two factors that lead to workplace cyberloafing behaviors: role ambiguity and role conflict. "Role ambiguity" refers to not being clear about a job's duties or roles; "role conflict" occurs when the job's actual demands do not match an individual's expectations. These stressors contribute to employee dissatisfaction, leading unhappy employees to escape their problems by using the internet for personal means.

> *Definitions of key terms. Several sources of information are synthesized.*

Mercado et al. (2017) conducted a meta-analysis of the current literature in order to examine the variables related to cyberloafing behaviors. Their database consisted of 54 independent samples contributing 609 effect sizes. The study concluded that boredom was highly correlated with cyberloafing, while self-control and engagement were qualities not associated with cyberloafing behaviors. Emotional stability, conscientiousness, and agreeableness showed a modest negative correlation with cyberloafing. Demographic

> *Comparison and contrast of effects on different populations.*

variables, such as age, showed little effect on an individual's cyber-loafing behavior. Tenure, organizational level, and income were also trivial (Mercado et al., 2017).

External factors play just as important a role as internal factors do when it comes to the causes of cyberloafing. Wagner et al. (2012) concluded that the Monday *after* a daylight savings time (DST) shift shows more employee *Google* searches related to entertainment websites than the Monday *prior* to the DST shift (p. 1071). This sud-den but slight interruption in sleeping habits has a demonstrated impact on workplace behavior. While employees who score high in conscientiousness on personality assessments are less likely to engage in cyberloafing after getting a bad night's sleep, they are the exception. For most people, sleep deprivation or low-quality sleep appears to decrease employees' optimum workplace perfor-mance (Wagner et al., 2012, pp. 1073–1074). Wagner et al. (2012) found that sleep deprivation may have considerable repercussions, such as the initiation of cyberloafing behaviors (p. 1071).

Analysis of causes and effects—with evidence from scholarly sources.

Although the consequences of cyberloafing are similar across different populations, Lim and Chen's 2012 study demonstrated there are some meaningful differences based on gender. Men were more likely to cyberloaf than women, but when it came to switch-ing back to work, women took around eight minutes, while men took only four (Lim & Chen, 2012, pp. 346–347). There were differ-ences, too, in how men and women thought cyberloafing affected their work: men were more likely to say cyberloafing activities have a positive impact while women tended to say they have a nega-tive impact (Lim & Chen, 2012, p. 347). However, the results of the study also showed overall that many workers—men and women—believe there are some positive effects: 75% of participants said that cyberloafing increases their engagement at work, and 49% said that cyberloafing helps them to solve problems at work (Lim & Chen, 2012, p. 348). And most respondents said they believe it's not breaking any rules to browse the internet for personal reasons while at work (Lim & Chen, 2012, p. 346).

One of the most pressing reasons for organizations to pay atten-tion to cyberloafing behavior is that it can make sensitive, secure information vulnerable. Indeed, organizations should be aware that sensitive information that is stored in their computers may be com-promised by malware that gets into the system through employees' internet browsing, especially on entertainment websites. Findings suggest that up to 60% of entertainment website traffic comes from people at the workplace (Wagner et al., 2012, p. 1071). So certain cyberloafing activities, such as visiting online gambling and adult websites, could expose an organization to a security breach (Hadlington & Parsons, 2017, pp. 570–571).

Proposals for reducing negative effects of cyberloafing.

Given the prevalence of cyberloafing and its potential to have serious negative effects, organizations might consider taking the following steps to combat workplace cyberloafing. First, employers can prevent role ambiguity and role conflict by providing accurate job descriptions and performing a thorough job analysis to assist potential employees, specifying exactly what is expected from them (Henle & Blanchard, 2008, pp. 393–394). Also, supervisors should avoid handing heavy workloads to employees, as doing so may increase stress levels while forcing them to lose sleep to complete their tasks (Wagner et al, 2012, p. 1074). Managers are encouraged to provide reasonable deadlines for their subordinates or at least ask if subordinates consider their deadlines reasonable. Cyberloafing levels should decrease when employees feel empowered and enabled to provide their input within a flexible work environment.

Further, organizational rules discouraging cyberloafing can be effective. By simply walking the halls of a department regularly, managers can notice disruptive levels of cyberloafing. It is important to note that the internet can be useful in solving work-related problems or even communicating family emergencies, so managers should take a holistic approach to determine if an employee's apparent cyberloafing is significantly disruptive. Training can help employees discern dangerous cyberloafing practices and consequences, and employees should also be encouraged to seek treatment for addictive internet behaviors (Henle & Blanchard, 2008, p. 394). Some cyberloafing can be healthy and positive, but enacting these suggestions will help ensure cyberloafing habits don't veer into a loss of productivity.

Acknowledging cyberloafing's presence and impact on an organization is the first step in figuring out a plan to address it—both at the upper levels of the organization and for each employee. And by training employees about cybersecurity, the organization's risk of breaches caused by personal internet use will be reduced.

Given the power and prevalence of the internet in our daily lives, cyberloafing in the workplace is almost certainly here to stay, but there is much that individuals and organizations can do to keep its negative consequences to a minimum.

References

Hadlington, L., & Parsons, K. (2017). Can cyberloafing and internet addiction affect organizational information security? *Cyberpsychology, Behavior & Social Networking*, *20*(9), 567–571. https://doi.org/10.1089/cyber.2017.0239

Henle, C. A., & Blanchard, A. L. (2008). The interaction of work stressors and organizational sanctions on cyberloafing. *Journal of Managerial Issues*, *20*(3), 383–400.

Lim, V. K. G., & Chen, D. J. Q. (2012). Cyberloafing at the workplace: Gain or drain on work? *Behaviour & Information Technology*, *31*(4), 343–353. https://doi.org/10.1080/01449290903353054

Mercado, B. K., Giordano, C., & Dilchert, S. (2017). A meta-analytic investigation of cyberloafing. *Career Development International*, *22*(5), 546–564. https://doi.org/10.1108/CDI-08-2017-0142

Wagner, D. T., Barnes, C. M., Lim, V. K. G., & Ferri, D. L. (2012). Lost sleep and cyberloafing: Evidence from the laboratory and a daylight saving time quasi-experiment. *Journal of Applied Psychology*, *97*(5), 1068–1076. https://doi.org/10.1037/a0027557

In-text citations and references list use APA style.

W-11   Personal Narratives

Narratives are stories, and we read and tell them for many different purposes. Parents read their children bedtime stories. Preachers base their sermons on religious stories to teach lessons about moral behavior. Grandparents tell how things used to be. College applicants write about significant moments in their lives. Writing students are often called on to compose narratives to explore their personal experiences. This chapter describes the key elements of personal narratives and provides tips for writing one.

W-11a Key Elements of a Personal Narrative

A well-told story. Most narratives set up a situation that needs to be resolved, which keeps your audience reading. You might write about a challenge you've overcome, for example, such as learning a new language or dealing with some kind of discrimination.

Vivid detail. Details can bring a narrative to life by giving readers vivid mental images of the sights, sounds, smells, tastes, and textures of the world in which your story takes place. The details you use when **DESCRIBING** something can help readers picture places, people, and events; **DIALOGUE** can help them hear what is being said. To give readers a picture of your childhood home in the city, you might describe the mouthwatering aromas from the street vendors on your block and the sounds of a nearby pick-up basketball game. Similarly, dialogue that lets readers hear your father's stern reminder after you forgot to lock your bike can help them understand how you felt at the time. Depending on your topic and your **MEDIUM**, you may want to provide some of the details in audio or visual form.

Some indication of the narrative's significance. Narratives usually have a point; you need to make clear why the incident matters to you or how it supports a larger argument. You may reveal its significance in various ways, but try not to state it outright, as if it were a kind of moral of the story.

W-11b Tips for Writing a Personal Narrative

Choosing a topic. In general, it's a good idea to focus on a single event that took place during a relatively brief period of time:

- an event that was interesting, humorous, or embarrassing
- something you found (or find) especially difficult or challenging
- the origins of an attitude or belief you hold
- a memory from your childhood that remains vivid

Make a list of possible topics, and choose one that will be interesting to you and to others—and that you're willing to share.

Generating ideas and text. Start by writing out what you remember about the setting and the people involved, perhaps **BRAIN-STORMING**, **LOOPING**, or **QUESTIONING** to help you generate ideas.

Describe the setting. List the places where your story unfolds. For each place, write informally for a few minutes, **DESCRIBING** what you remember seeing, hearing, smelling, tasting, and feeling.

Think about the key people. Narratives include people whose actions play an important role in the story. To develop your understanding of the people in your narrative, you might begin by describing them—their movements, their posture, their facial expressions. Try writing several lines of **DIALOGUE** between two people in your narrative, including distinctive words or phrases they used.

Write about what happened. At the heart of every good narrative is the answer to the question "What happened?" The action may be as dramatic as winning a championship or as subtle as a conversation between friends; both contain movement or change that the narrative dramatizes. Try narrating the action using active and specific **VERBS** (pondered, shouted) to capture what happened.

Consider the significance. You need to make clear why the event you are writing about matters. How did it change or otherwise affect you? What aspects of your life now can you trace to that event? How might your life have been different if this event had not happened?

Ways of organizing a personal narrative. Don't assume that the only way to tell your story is just as it happened. That's one way—starting at the beginning and continuing to the end. You might also start in the middle—or even at the end.

[Chronologically, from beginning to end]

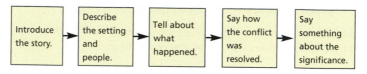

[Beginning in the middle]

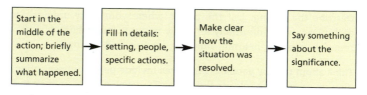

[Beginning at the end]

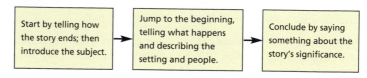

>> **SEE** W-1 for help analyzing your writing context. See W-4 for guidelines on drafting, revising, editing, and proofreading. To read additional examples of narratives, go to **digital.wwnorton.com /littleseagull4**.

W-11c Sample Personal Narrative Essay

MOHAMMED MASOOM SHAH

One Last Ride

A nominee for the Norton Writer's Prize, this personal narrative was written by Mohammed Masoom Shah while he was a student at St. John's University.

College Point, Queens. They called it "Garbage Point." I didn't agree with that for a while because it was home, but when I turned sixteen, I looked at College Point differently. Sure, it wasn't Compton or Chicago, but as in any city, it was easy to slip up if you hung out in the wrong places. I was still sixteen when a family member I'll call "T" shot up heroin right in front of me. He was driving, and I was unlucky enough to be in the passenger seat beside him; I was in for a rough ride.

It was ten o'clock on a summer night. We were double-parked on 14th Avenue, right by College Point Boulevard. T went across the street to grab some "snacks" from Walgreens, leaving me alone in the car. Just seconds after he left, I heard a blaring truck horn behind me, the driver growing increasingly impatient by the second. "Move the f---ing car!" he shouted. I still didn't have my permit at the time, so I just sat there listening to the cacophonous mix of deafening horns and explicit language, wondering what was taking T so long. Eventually, he came out holding a bag and exchanged a few colorful words with the truck driver. Then we were on our way home—or so I thought.

T pulled in to a quiet alleyway on 13th Avenue and pulled his keys from the ignition. The hum of the engine was the only noise within a mile radius, so when it stopped, all I could hear was the eerie whistling of the wind. There was a broken pause between the moment he shut off the car and the moment he reached for what was in the bag. At this point, I knew there weren't any snacks in there. His hands were trembling, and I tried reading his face, searching for what was troubling him. He avoided making eye contact, as if he was ashamed of what he was about to do, but it had to be done regardless. He reached into the plastic bag and pulled out a needle, a syringe, and a latex glove.

Sets up a situation to be resolved. What will happen next?

Vivid detail brings the story to life: the hum of the engine, the whistling of the wind, T's trembling hands.

My heart pounded uncontrollably in my chest, but I had to play it cool. I had looked up to T for as long as I could remember. When he lived in Pakistan, I'd stay over at his house and he'd take me out on his motorcycle. Its once-glossy red paint was chipping, worn-out and paper-thin, but the bike got the job done; it took us away, and that's all we asked from it. We went for long rides down the dirt roads around the village, and he'd pull over sometimes to light a cigarette. He'd stare blankly across the acres of wheat that swayed in the wind and tell me about how he wanted to be a doctor one day and make his dad proud. He said he didn't have the brains for that, though. Nonetheless, I aspired to be just like him. I admired his ability to remain composed about everything that life threw at him. I wanted to be as tough as he was, have as many friends as he did, and have the money he had. He knew just about everybody that walked down the boulevard at night, and he used to tell me stories about his fights back in high school—he never lost. He even had the blood-stained Timberlands to prove it. Yet here we were, sitting in an old gray Lincoln in silence, the moonlight beaming through the dark, and for the first time, I thought to myself: he was losing.

He must have sensed my uneasiness when he said, "My bad, I just need to do this really quickly. Then I'll drop you home." He reached over to the glove compartment, taking a vial of a dark, tar-like solution out of it. After a few more precision moves, the drugs were in him; he grunted and then went silent. His face looked relieved, but his eyes said otherwise. "I'ma drop you home now," he mumbled.

He yanked the steering wheel one way and then the other, speeding through narrow, two-way streets recklessly. Cars honked as he bolted past them and down College Point Boulevard, or what I now understood as "Garbage Point" Boulevard. I clenched my seat belt tightly, foolishly thinking that it'd protect me. We flew over bumps and past stop signs. I shot a quick glance at T; his grip was loosening on the wheel and his eyelids were almost completely draped over his eyes. I was glad I lived only a couple of blocks away. Somehow, I made it home, but when I looked back at T—droopy-eyed and dazed—I didn't know if he was going to make it back home.

I didn't tell anyone about that night—not even my parents—but eventually my whole family got word of T's new pastime. The news broke out when someone found him lying on the floor, unresponsive,

---

Details make the scene real.

The author's memories show the history of this important relationship.

Dialogue helps animate this key scene.

Active and specific verbs— "yanked," "bolted," "clenched"— narrate the action vividly.

in a gas station bathroom. He recovered, but my family never did. After that, there was a lot of finger-pointing. Some family members blamed T's parents, while our family in Pakistan blamed mine for advising others to come to America in the first place. "America this and America that, look what America did to him! He was just fine in Pakistan." Of course, no one was as angry as T's father. T was his eldest son and his mirror image, which is probably why he seemed to blame himself for every one of T's mistakes. I found myself doing the same—asking myself if there was something I could have done. I should've snatched that vial from his hands and shattered it on the ground when I had the chance. I could've said how I felt about him doing all this and he would've quit right there and then. I knew it wasn't that easy, but my family didn't. They insisted that he should make something out of nothing: get a degree and a job. All that pressure was bound to make him burst; he ended up in the hospital again due to another overdose.

Details about the family's reaction show their concern—and also their family history.

Years went by, but not much changed. T went in and out of rehab, unemployed and aging quickly. Recently I tried speaking to him about the direction that his life was going. I wish I could say he made a complete turnaround for the better. Instead, he told me that his days were over. Staring at the ground as he spoke, he said he'd "messed up, and there was no going back." Just as I was about to interject, he held up his hand to stop me.

"You can help me, though," he said, finally looking up.

"How?" I replied.

Dialogue puts the reader right in the action.

He paused, and then he said, "Do what I couldn't."

I went home and tried to decode what T meant. After some time, I realized the depth of the words that he uttered on that day. He wanted me to live out the life that he gave away. He had wanted to make his dad proud and to be a doctor, so I guessed it was up to me now to handle those responsibilities. But I believe there was more to it than pride and education. He knew what I had seen. I had seen him at his weakest; I had watched him surrender to a needle and syringe. He remembered, too. He remembered our motorcycle rides in Pakistan down the dusty roads and past the farmland. He didn't want pity either, nor did he pity himself—that wasn't how he operated. He wanted to be remembered for what he had been, not for what he turned into. I think that's where I come in: I'm what he was, and when I get to where I want to be—realize my full potential—so will he.

The significance of this story becomes clear: the author must do with his life what T proved unable to do.

W-12 Summary/Response Essays

Summarizing a text—boiling it down to its basic ideas—helps us to see and understand its main points, think about what it says, and incorporate it into our own writing. Responding to that text then prompts us to think about—*and say*—what we think. Together, summarizing and responding is one way that we engage with the ideas of others. In much of the writing that you do, you'll need to cite the ideas of others, both as context for your own thinking and as evidence to support your arguments. One way of introducing what you have to say is to frame it as a response to something others have said about your topic. A good way to do that is by summarizing what they've said, using the summary as a launching pad for what *you* say. This chapter provides advice for summarizing and responding, a description of the key elements of a summary/response essay, and tips for writing one.

W-12a Key Elements of a Summary/Response Essay

A clearly identified author and title.   Usually the author and title of the text being summarized are identified in a SIGNAL PHRASE in the first sentence. The author or title may then be abbreviated in the rest of the essay.

A concise summary of the text.   The summary presents only the main and supporting ideas in the text, usually in the order in which they appear. Leave out supporting EVIDENCE, ANECDOTES, and COUNTERARGUMENTS unless they are crucial to understanding the text.

An explicit response with support. Your essay should usually provide a concise statement (one sentence if possible) of your overall response to the text. Your response should be supported by reasons backed up with evidence from the text.

W-12b Tips for Writing a Summary/Response Essay

Writing a summary

Read the text carefully and annotate it. **SKIM** the text to get a general sense of what it's saying. Then reread the text slowly, **ANNOTATING** it paragraph by paragraph. If there's an explicit **THESIS** statement, highlight it. Try to restate the main idea of each paragraph in a single sentence.

State the main points concisely and accurately. Summaries of a complete text are generally between 100 and 250 words in length, so you need to choose your words carefully and to focus only on the text's main ideas. Leave out details like supporting evidence, anecdotes, and counterarguments unless they're crucial to understanding the text.

Describe the text accurately and fairly, using neutral language. Present the author's ideas evenhandedly; a summary isn't the place to share your opinion of what the text says. Use neutral verbs such as "states," "asserts," or "concludes," not verbs that imply praise or criticism like "proves" or "complains."

Use SIGNAL PHRASES to distinguish what the author says from what you say. At the start of your summary, you may begin with the author's credentials. For example:

> In "Always Living in Spanish," Spanish professor Marjorie Agosín describes her need to connect with her childhood by writing in Spanish.

> James Fallows, a contributing editor at the *Atlantic*, explains the mechanics of throwing baseballs in "Throwing Like a Girl."

Later in the text, you may need to refer to the author again as you summarize specific parts of the text. These signal phrases are typically briefer: "In Agosín's view . . . ," "Fallows then argues . . .".

Use quotations sparingly, if at all. You may need to **QUOTE** keywords or memorable phrases, but most or all of a summary should be written in your own words, using your own sentence structures. **DOCUMENT** any text you summarize in a works-cited or references list.

An example summary

This summary begins with a signal phrase stating the author's name, credentials, and the title of the text being summarized. It includes only the main ideas, in the summary writer's own words.

> In "The Reason College Costs More Than You Think," Jon Marcus, a higher-education editor at the *Hechinger Report*, states that a major reason that college educations are so expensive is the amount of time students stay in college. Although almost all first-year students and their families assume that earning a bachelor's degree will take four years, the reality is that more than half of all students take longer, with many taking six years or more. This delay happens for many reasons: students may change majors, have to take developmental courses, take fewer courses per term than they could have, and be unable to register for required courses. As a result, their expenses are much greater—financial aid seldom covers a fifth or sixth year, so students must borrow money to finish—and the additional time they spend in college is time they aren't working, leading to significant losses in wages.

Writing a response

Decide how to respond. You may be assigned to write a specific kind of response—an argument or analysis, for instance—but usually, the nature of your response is left up to you. You can respond to what the text says (its ideas), to how it says it (the way it's written), or to where it leads your own thinking (your own personal reaction). Or you might write a response that mixes those ways of responding.

Respond to what a text says. You might agree or disagree with the author's ARGUMENT, supporting your position with reasons and evidence. You might agree with parts of the argument and disagree with others. You might find that the author has ignored or downplayed some important aspect of the topic that should be discussed. The following questions can help you think about what a text says:

- What does the writer claim?
- What REASONS and EVIDENCE are provided to support that claim?
- What parts of the text do you agree with? disagree with? Why?
- Does the writer represent any views other than their own? If not, what other perspectives should be considered?
- Are there aspects of the topic that the writer overlooks or ignores?
- If you're responding to a visual text, how do the design and any images contribute to your understanding of what the text "says"?

As support for your response, you may offer facts, statistics, anecdotal evidence, and textual evidence. You'll also need to consider—and acknowledge—any possible COUNTERARGUMENTS.

Respond to how a text is written. Consider what elements the writer uses to convey the message—facts, stories, images, and so on. Pay attention to the writer's word choices and look for any patterns that lead you to understand the text in a particular way. The following questions can help you think about how a text is written:

- What is the writer's message or THESIS? Is it stated explicitly?
- How well has the writer communicated the message?
- How does the writer support the message: by citing facts or statistics? by quoting experts? by noting personal experiences? Are you persuaded?
- Are there any words, phrases, or sentences that you find notable and that contribute to the text's overall TONE?
- How does the text's DESIGN affect your response to it? In a visual text, how do the parts of the text contribute to its message?

To support your analysis, you'll need to cite specific patterns and evidence from the text itself.

Reflect on your own reaction to a text. You might focus on how your personal experiences or beliefs influenced the way you understood the text or on how it reinforced or prompted you to reassess some of those beliefs. You could also focus on how it led you to see the topic in new ways—or note questions that it's led you to wonder about. The following questions may help you reflect on your own reaction to a text:

- How did the text affect you personally?
- What, if anything, really grabbed your attention in the text?
- Did any parts of the text provoke an emotional reaction—make you laugh or cry, make you uneasy? What prompted that response?
- Did the text bring to mind any memories or past experiences? Can you see anything related to you and your life in the text?
- Did the text remind you of any other texts?
- Did the text support (or challenge) any of your beliefs? How?
- Has reading this text given you any new ideas or insight?

To support your reflection, you may connect the text's ideas with your own experiences or explore how it reinforced, challenged, or altered your beliefs.

Ways of organizing a summary/response essay. You can organize a summary and response essay in various ways. You may want to use a simple, straightforward structure that starts out by summarizing the text and then gives the **THESIS** of your response followed by details that develop the thesis. Or you may start out with your thesis and then, depending on whether your response focuses on the text's argument or its rhetorical choices, provide a paired summary of each main point or each aspect of the writing and a response to it.

[Summary, followed by response]

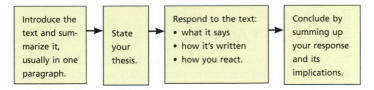

[Introduction and thesis, followed by point-by-point summary and response]

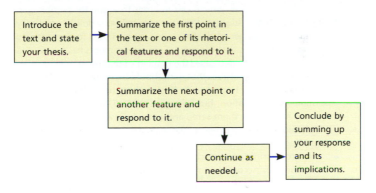

≫ **SEE W-3** for more strategies on reading, annotating, and summarizing texts. See **W-4** for guidelines on drafting, revising, editing, and proofreading your summary/response essay.

W-12c Sample Summary/Response Essay

JACOB MacLEOD

Guns and Cars Are Different

The following essay was written by Jacob MacLeod, a student at Wright State University, and responds to a New York Times column by Nicholas Kristof, "Our Blind Spot about Guns." You can read Kristof's piece at nytimes.com.

First paragraph summarizes main ideas of Kristof's essay. A signal phrase identifies Kristof. The final sentence outlines MacLeod's response.

In "Our Blind Spot about Guns," *The New York Times* columnist Nicholas Kristof compares guns to cars in order to argue for sensible gun regulation. Kristof suggests that gun regulations would dramatically decrease the number of deaths caused by gun use. To demonstrate this point, he shows that the regulations governments have instituted for cars have greatly decreased the number of deaths per million miles driven. Kristof then argues that guns should be regulated in the same way that cars are. I agree with Kristof that there should be more sensible gun regulation, but I disagree that all regulations imposed on cars have made them safer, and I also believe that not all of the safety regulations he proposes for guns would necessarily have positive effects.

MacLeod responds to Kristof's argument, agreeing and offering support for one claim.

Kristof is right that background checks for gun buyers should be expanded. According to Daniel Webster, director of the Johns Hopkins Center for Gun Policy and Research, state laws prohibiting firearm ownership by members of high-risk groups, such as perpetrators of domestic violence, have been shown to reduce violence. Therefore, Webster argues, universal background checks would significantly reduce the availability of guns to high-risk groups and reduce the number of guns diverted to the illegal market by making it easier to prosecute gun traffickers.

Kristof also argues that lowering the speed limit made cars safer. However, in 1987, forty states raised their top speed limit from 55 to 65 miles per hour. An analysis by the University of California Transportation Center shows that after the increase, traffic fatality rates on interstate highways in those forty states decreased between 3.4 percent and 5.1 percent. After the higher limits went into effect, the study suggested, some drivers may have switched to safer interstates, and highway patrols may have focused less on enforcing interstate speed limits and more on activities yielding greater benefits in terms of safety (Lave and Elias 58–61). Although common sense suggests that lowered speed limits would mean safer driving, research showed otherwise, and the same may be true for gun regulation.

MacLeod summarizes and disagrees with another of Kristof's claims.

Gun control advocates argue that more guns mean more deaths. However, an article by gun rights advocates Don B. Kates and Gary Mauser argues that murder rates in many developed nations bear no relation to the rate of gun ownership (652). The authors cite data on firearm ownership in the United States and England that suggest that crime rates are lowest where the density of gun ownership is highest and highest where gun density is lowest (653) and that increased gun ownership has often coincided with significant reductions in violence. For example, in the United States in the 1990s, criminal violence decreased, even though gun ownership increased (656). However, the authors acknowledge that "the notion that more guns reduce crime is highly controversial" (659).

MacLeod provides evidence for his stance.

All in all, then, Kristof is correct to suggest that sensible gun regulation is a good idea in general, but the available data suggest that some of the particular measures he proposes should not be instituted. While I agree that expanding background checks would be a good way to regulate guns, I disagree with reducing the rate of gun ownership. The problem with this solution is that although it is based on common-sense thinking, data show that it may not work.

MacLeod summarizes his response in his concluding paragraph.

Works Cited

Kates, Don B., and Gary Mauser. "Would Banning Firearms Reduce Murder and Suicide? A Review of International and Some Domestic Evidence." *Harvard Journal of Law and Public Policy*, vol. 30, no. 2, Jan. 2007, pp. 649–94.

Kristof, Nicholas. "Our Blind Spot about Guns." *The New York Times*, 31 July 2014, www.nytimes.com/2014/07/31/opinion/nicholas-kristof-our-blind-spot-about-guns.html. Accessed 23 Jan. 2020.

Lave, Charles, and Patrick Elias. "Did the 65 mph Speed Limit Save Lives?" *Accident Analysis & Prevention*, vol. 26, no. 1, Feb. 1994, pp. 49–62, www.sciencedirect.com/science/article/pii/000145759490068X. Accessed 23 Jan. 2020.

Webster, Daniel. "Why Expanding Background Checks Would, in Fact, Reduce Gun Crime." Interview conducted by Greg Sargent. *The Washington Post*, 3 Apr. 2013, www.washingtonpost.com/blogs/plum-line/wp/2013/04/03/why-expanding-background-checks-would-in-fact-reduce-gun-crime/. Accessed 23 Jan. 2020.

Sources cited in MacLeod's essay, including Kristof's essay, are acknowledged.

W-13   Literary Analyses

Literary analyses are essays in which we examine literary texts closely to understand their messages, interpret their meanings, and appreciate their writers' techniques. You might look for a pattern in the images of blood in Shakespeare's *Macbeth* or point out the differences between Stephen King's *The Shining* and Stanley Kubrick's screenplay based on that novel. You go below the surface to deepen your understanding of how texts work and what they mean. This chapter describes the key elements of most literary analyses and provides tips for writing one.

W-13a Key Elements of a Literary Analysis

An arguable THESIS. In a literary analysis, you are arguing that your **ANALYSIS** of a work is valid. Your thesis, then, should be arguable. You might argue, for example, that the dialogue between two female characters in a short story reflects stereotypes about gender. But a mere summary—"In this story, two women discuss their struggles to succeed"—would not be arguable and therefore is not a good thesis. (See **W-4b** for help developing an arguable thesis.)

Careful attention to the language of the text. Specific words, images, **METAPHORS**—these are the foundation of a text's meaning, and are where analysis begins. You might bring in contextual information or refer to similar texts, but the words and sentences that make up the text you're analyzing are your primary source. That's what's meant by "close reading": reading with the assumption that every word of a text is meaningful.

Attention to patterns or themes. Literary analyses are usually built on evidence of meaningful patterns or themes within a text or among several texts. For example, you might analyze how the images of snow and wind and the repetition of the word "nothing" contribute to a sense of desolation in a poem about a winter scene.

A clear INTERPRETATION. When you write a literary analysis, you show one way the text may be understood, using evidence from the text and relevant contextual evidence to support what you think the text means.

MLA style. Literary analyses usually follow MLA style.

W-13b Tips for Writing a Literary Analysis

Generating ideas and text. Start by considering whether your assignment specifies a particular kind of analysis or critical approach. Look for words that say what to do: "analyze," "compare," "interpret," and so on. Then you'll want to take a close look at the literary work.

Choose a method for analyzing the text. If your assignment doesn't specify a particular method, three common approaches are to focus on the text itself; on your own experience reading it; and on other cultural, historical, or literary contexts:

- *The text itself.* Trace the development and expression of themes, characters, and language through the work. How do they help to create particular meaning, tone, or effects?

- *Your own response as a reader.* Explore the way the text affects you. Read closely, noticing how the elements of the text shape your responses, both intellectual and emotional. How has the author evoked your response?

- *Context.* Analyze the text as part of some larger context—as part of a certain time or place in history or of a certain culture; or as one of many other texts like it, a representative of a genre.

Read the work more than once. When you first read a piece of literature, you usually focus on the plot and overall meaning. By rereading, you can see how its effects are achieved, what the pieces are and how they fit together, where different patterns emerge, and how the author crafted the work.

Compose a strong thesis. The **THESIS** of a literary analysis should be specific, limited, and open to potential disagreement. In addition, it should be **ANALYTICAL**, not **EVALUATIVE**. Your goal is not to pass judgment but to suggest one way of seeing the text.

Do a close reading. Find specific, brief passages that support your interpretation; then analyze those passages in terms of their language, their context, and your reaction to them as a reader. Do a close reading, questioning as you go:

- What does each word (phrase, passage) mean exactly? Why does the writer choose *this* language, *these* words?

- What images or metaphors are used? What is their effect?

- What patterns of language, imagery, or plot do you see? If something is repeated, what significance does the pattern have?

- What words, phrases, or passages connect to a larger context?

- How do elements of language, image, and pattern support your thesis?

Support your argument with evidence. The parts of the text you examine in your close reading become the evidence you use to support your interpretation. Treat your analysis like any other **ARGUMENT**: discuss how the text creates an effect or expresses a theme, and then show **EVIDENCE** from the text—significant plot or structural elements; important characters; patterns of language, imagery, or action—to back up your argument.

Paying attention to matters of style. Literary analyses have certain conventions for using pronouns and verbs. In informal papers, it's OK to use the first person: "I believe Frost's narrator provides little basis for claiming that one road is 'less traveled.'" In more formal essays, make assertions directly: "Frost's narrator provides no basis for claiming that one road is 'less traveled.'" Discuss textual features in the present tense even if quotations from the text are in another tense. Describe the historical context of the setting in the past tense.

One way of organizing a literary analysis

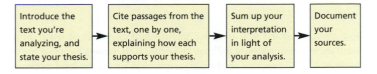

Introduce the text you're analyzing, and state your thesis. → Cite passages from the text, one by one, explaining how each supports your thesis. → Sum up your interpretation in light of your analysis. → Document your sources.

>> **SEE** W-1 for help analyzing your writing context. See W-3 for more help reading with a critical eye. For guidelines on drafting, revising, editing, and proofreading, see W-4. To read an example of literary analysis, go to **digital.wwnorton.com/littleseagull4**.

W-14 Proposals

You need a car, so you propose paying half the cost of a car and insurance if your parents will pay the other half. Lovers propose marriage; students propose that colleges provide healthier food options on campus. These are all examples of proposals, ideas that offer solutions to some problem. All proposals are arguments: you propose something in order to persuade others to consider—and hopefully to accept—your solution to the problem. This chapter describes the key elements of a proposal and provides tips for writing one.

W-14a Key Elements of Proposals

A well-defined problem. Some problems are self-evident and relatively simple and don't require much to make people act. While some might not care about colleges wasting paper, for example, most are likely to agree that recycling is good. Other issues are more controversial: some people see them as problems while others do not. For example, some believe that motorcycle riders who do not wear helmets risk serious injury and raise the cost of health care for all of us, but others think that wearing a helmet—or not—should be a personal choice; you would have to present arguments to convince your readers that not wearing a helmet is a problem needing a solution. Any written proposal must establish that there is a problem—and that it's serious enough to require a solution.

A solution to the problem. Once you've defined the problem, you need to describe the solution you are suggesting and to explain it in enough detail for readers to understand what you are proposing. You might suggest several possible solutions, analyze their merits, and choose one you think is most likely to solve the problem.

A convincing argument for your proposed solution. You need to provide evidence to convince readers that your solution is feasible—and that it will, in fact, solve the problem. If, for example, you're proposing that motorcycle riders be required to wear helmets, you might provide data about the serious injuries suffered by those not wearing helmets—and note that insurance rates are tied to the costs of dealing with such injuries. Sometimes you'll want to explain in detail how your proposed solution would work.

A response to questions readers may have. You need to consider any questions readers may have about your proposal—and to show how its advantages outweigh any disadvantages. A proposal for recycling paper, for example, would need to address questions about the costs of recycling bins and separate trash pickups.

A call to action. The goal of a proposal is to persuade readers to accept your proposed solution—and perhaps to take action. You may want to conclude by noting the outcomes likely to result from following your suggestions.

An appropriate tone. Since you're trying to persuade readers to act, your tone is important. Readers will always react better to a reasonable, respectful presentation than to anger or self-righteousness.

W-14b Tips for Writing a Proposal

Choosing a topic. Choose a problem that can be solved. Large, complex problems such as poverty or terrorism usually require large, complex solutions. Focusing on a smaller problem or a limited aspect of a large problem will usually yield a more manageable proposal. Rather than tackling the problem of world poverty, for example, think about the problem faced by people in your community who are dealing with food or housing insecurity.

Generating ideas and text. Most successful proposals share certain features that make them persuasive. Remember that your goal is to identify a problem that matters, come up with a feasible solution, and convince readers that it will solve the problem.

Explore several possible solutions to the problem. Many problems can be solved in more than one way, and you need to show that you've examined several potential solutions. You may develop solutions on your own; more often, though, you'll need to **RESEARCH** how others have solved—or tried to solve—similar problems. Don't settle on a solution too quickly; compare the advantages and disadvantages of several solutions in order to argue convincingly for one.

Decide on the most desirable solution(s). One solution may be clearly the best, but be open to rejecting all the possible solutions on your list and starting over if you need to, or to combining a few potential solutions in order to come up with an acceptable fix.

Think about why your solution is the best one. What has to be done to enact it? What will it cost? What makes you think it can be done? Why will it work better than others?

Ways of organizing a proposal. You can organize a proposal in various ways, but you should always begin by establishing that there is a problem. You may then identify several possible solutions before recommending one of them or a combination of several.

[Several possible solutions]

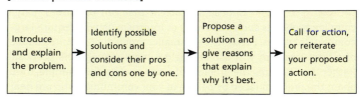

| Introduce and explain the problem. | Identify possible solutions and consider their pros and cons one by one. | Propose a solution and give reasons that explain why it's best. | Call for action, or reiterate your proposed action. |

[A single solution]

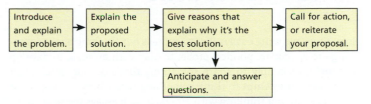

Introduce and explain the problem. → Explain the proposed solution. → Give reasons that explain why it's the best solution. → Call for action, or reiterate your proposal.

Anticipate and answer questions.

≫ **SEE W-1** for help analyzing your writing context. See **W-4** for guidelines on drafting, revising, editing, and proofreading. To read an example of a proposal, go to **digital.wwnorton.com /littleseagull4**.

W-15 Reflections

Sometimes we write essays just to express our thinking about something—to speculate, ponder, probe; to play with an idea; to develop a thought; or simply to share something that's on our mind. Such essays are our attempt to think something through by writing about it and to share our thinking with others. If such essays make an argument, it is about things we're thinking about more than about what we believe to be "true." This chapter describes the key elements of a reflective essay and tips for writing one.

W-15a Key Elements of a Reflection

A topic that intrigues you. A reflective essay has a dual purpose: to ponder something you find interesting or puzzling and to share your thoughts with an audience. Your topic may be anything that interests you—someone you're curious about, something that happened that's got you thinking, some idea you want to contemplate, something you've done or experienced that you're reflective about. Whatever your subject, your goal is to explore it in a way that will interest others. One way to do that is to start by considering your own experience and then moving on to think about more universal experiences that your readers may share. For example, you might write about your dog, and in doing so you could raise questions and offer insights about the ways that people and animals interact.

Some kind of structure. A reflective essay can be organized in many ways, but it needs to have a clear structure. Whether you move from detail to detail or focus your reflection on one central question or insight about your subject, all your ideas need to relate, one way or another. The challenge is to keep your readers interested as you explore your topic and to leave them satisfied that the journey was interesting and thought-provoking.

Specific details. You'll need to provide concrete details to help readers understand and connect with your subject. In an essay about his dog, Jonathan Safran Foer offers a wealth of **DESCRIPTIVE** details ("She mounts guests, eats my son's toys . . . lunges at skateboarders and Hasids. . . ."). **ANECDOTES** can bring your subject to life, as Foer shows when he tells us that sometimes his dog will "tear into a full sprint" and that "other dog owners can't help but watch her. Every now and then someone will cheer her on." You might explore **CAUSES** (why are Labrador retrievers so popular?) or make **COMPARISONS** (how's your dog better than all the others?). Details such as these will help your readers understand and care about your subject.

A questioning, speculative tone. In a reflective essay, you're usually looking for answers, not providing them neatly organized and ready for consumption. So your tone will often be tentative and open, demonstrating a willingness to entertain, try out, accept, and reject various ideas as your essay progresses from beginning to end, maybe even asking questions for which you can provide no direct answers.

W-15b Tips for Writing a Reflection

Choosing a topic. Choose a subject you want to explore. Make a list of things that you think about, wonder about, find puzzling or annoying. They may be big things (work, relationships) or little things (a friend's quirky behavior, an everyday event). Begin by **FREEWRITING** to see what comes to mind as you write, and then try **CLUSTERING** to see how your ideas relate to one another.

Generating ideas and text. Start by exploring your topic, perhaps by **BRAINSTORMING**, **LOOPING**, **QUESTIONING**, even doodling—all activities that will help you come up with ideas.

Explore your subject in detail. Reflections often include descriptive details that provide a base for the speculations to come. Foer, for example, **DESCRIBES** the many ways he encounters dogs in New York: "Retrievers in elevators, Pomeranians on No. 6 trains, bull mastiffs crossing the Brooklyn Bridge." You may also use other **STRATEGIES** to explore your subject: **DEFINING**, **COMPARING**, **CLASSIFYING**, and so on.

Back away. Ask yourself why your subject matters: why is it important or intriguing or otherwise significant? You may try **LISTING** or **OUTLINING** possible answers, or you may want to start **DRAFTING** to see where it takes your thinking. Your goal is to think on screen or paper about your subject, to see where it leads you.

Think about how to keep readers with you. Reflections must be carefully crafted so that readers can follow your train of thought. It's a good idea to sketch out a rough **THESIS** to help focus your thoughts. Even if you don't include the thesis in the essay itself, every part of the essay should in some way relate to it.

Ways of organizing a reflective essay. Reflections may be organized in many ways because they mimic the way we think, sometimes associating one idea with another in ways that make sense but do not necessarily follow the kinds of logical progression found in academic arguments or reports. Here are two ways you might organize a reflection.

[Exploring a subject using various strategies]

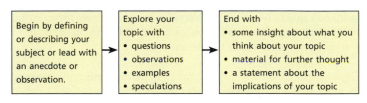

| Begin by defining or describing your subject or lead with an anecdote or observation. | Explore your topic with • questions • observations • examples • speculations | End with • some insight about what you think about your topic • material for further thought • a statement about the implications of your topic |

[Presenting a series of reflections on your subject]

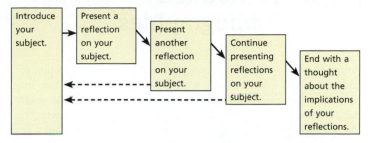

Introduce your subject. → Present a reflection on your subject. → Present another reflection on your subject. → Continue presenting reflections on your subject. → End with a thought about the implications of your reflections.

>> **SEE W-1** for help analyzing your writing context. See **W-4** for guidelines on drafting, revising, editing, and proofreading your reflection. To read an example of a reflective essay, go to **digital .wwnorton.com/littleseagull4**.

W-16 Annotated Bibliographies

Annotated bibliographies describe, give publication information for, and sometimes evaluate each work on a list of sources. You may be assigned to create annotated bibliographies to weigh the potential usefulness of sources and to document your search efforts. This chapter describes the key elements of an annotated bibliography and provides tips for writing two kinds of annotations: descriptive and evaluative.

Descriptive annotations simply SUMMARIZE the contents of each work, without comment or evaluation. They may be very short, just long enough to capture the flavor of the work, like this excerpt from a bibliography of books and articles on teen films, documented with MLA style and published in the *Journal of Popular Film and Television*.

> Doherty, Thomas. *Teenagers and Teenpics: The Juvenilization of American Movies in the 1950s.* Unwin Hyman, 1988.
>
> A historical discussion of the identification of teenagers as a targeted film market.
>
> Foster, Harold M. "Film in the Classroom: Coping with Teen Pics." *English Journal*, vol. 76, no. 3, Mar. 1987, pp. 86-88.
>
> An evaluation of the potential of using teen films such as *Sixteen Candles* and *The Karate Kid* to instruct adolescents on the difference between film as communication and film as exploitation.
>
> —Michael Benton, Mark Dolan, and Rebecca Zisch, "Teen Film$"

Evaluative annotations offer opinions on each source as well as describe it. They are often helpful in assessing how useful a source will be for your own writing. The following evaluative annotation is from an APA-style bibliography written by a student. Following her instructor's directions, the writer labeled each part of her annotation: summary, degree of advocacy, credibility, and reliability.

United States Census Bureau. (2015, November 2). *Facts for features: American Indian and Alaska Native heritage month* (Report No. CB15-FF.22). US Department of Commerce. http://www.census.gov/newsroom/facts-for-features/2015/cb15-ff22.html

The site contains statistical data on American Indian and Alaska Native populations in the United States during 2014 and 2015. Data include percentages regarding population size, housing and education, and income and poverty [Summary]. The site is objective in the presentation of data. Only raw data are presented without any degree of bias [Degree of Advocacy]. The data are current and relevant to the topic. The site is managed by a government agency, rendering it credible [Credibility]. The data posted on this site are updated regularly and retrieved from a number of sources. Concerns can be directed to the Census Bureau's Public Information Office in order to maintain accuracy of information [Reliability].

Fording, R. C., & Berry, W. D. (2007). The historical impact of welfare programs on poverty: Evidence from the American states. *Policy Studies Journal, 35*(1), 37–60. https://doi.org/10.1111/j.1541-0072.2007.00206.x

The authors present the history of welfare programs and assess their efficiency in decreasing poverty rates in the United States [Summary]. The authors maintain an objective view of the material. They explore different viewpoints with no apparent bias toward any stance [Degree of Advocacy]. Both authors have backgrounds in political science and the article contains a vast list of cited sources used, which lead to additional useful sources [Credibility]. The article was published in *Policy Studies Journal*, an academic journal that aims to provide articles focused on many aspects of policy studies and political science [Reliability].

—Kelly Green, "Researching Hunger and Poverty"

W-16a Key Elements of Annotated Bibliographies

A statement of scope. You may need a brief introductory statement to explain what you're covering. This might be one paragraph or several—but it should establish a context for the bibliography and announce your purpose for compiling it.

Complete bibliographic information. Provide all the information about each source using one documentation system (MLA, APA, Chicago, CSE, or another one) so that your readers or other researchers will be able to find the source easily.

A concise description of the work. A good annotation describes each item as carefully and objectively as possible, giving accurate, specific information and showing that you understand the source—and how it relates to your topic.

Relevant commentary. If you write an evaluative bibliography, your comments should be relevant to your purpose and audience. To achieve relevance, consider what questions a potential reader might have about the sources. Your evaluation might also focus on the text's suitability as a source for your writing.

Consistent presentation. All annotations should be consistent in content, sentence structure, and format. If you're evaluating, don't evaluate some sources and just describe others. If one annotation is written in complete sentences, they should all be. Also be sure to use one documentation style—and to treat all book titles consistently, all italicized and following a consistent capitalization style.

W-16b Tips for Annotating a Bibliography

Generating ideas and text. You'll need to do some research to locate potential sources for your bibliography. As you consider which to include, keep your AUDIENCE and PURPOSE in mind.

Decide what sources to include. Though you may be tempted to include every source you find, a better strategy is to include only those sources that you or your readers may find useful in researching your topic. Consider these qualities:

- *Appropriateness.* Is this source relevant to your topic? Is it a PRIMARY or SECONDARY source? Is it general or specialized?

- *Credibility.* Are the author and the publisher or sponsor reputable? Do their ideas agree with those in other sources you've read?

- *Balance.* Does the source present enough evidence? Does it show any particular bias? Does it present COUNTERARGUMENTS?

- *Timeliness.* Does the source reflect current thinking or research?

See R-2 for more information on determining the best sources for your purposes.

Decide whether the bibliography should be descriptive or evaluative. If you're writing a descriptive bibliography, your reading goal will be just to understand and capture each writer's message clearly. If you're writing an evaluative bibliography, you'll also need to assess the source as you read in order to include your own opinions of it.

Read carefully. To write an annotation, you must understand the source's argument, but for some assignments, you may have neither the time nor the need to read the whole text. To quickly determine whether a source is likely to serve your needs, first check the publisher or sponsor; then read the preface, abstract, or introduction; skim the table of contents or the headings; scan the index, if there is one, for relevant words and phrases; and read the parts that relate specifically to your topic.

Research the writer, if necessary. You may need to find information about the writer's credentials; try looking them up online or in *Contemporary Authors*. In any case, information about the writer should take up no more than one sentence in your annotation.

Summarize the work. Summarize it as objectively as possible: even if you are writing an evaluative annotation, you can evaluate the central point of a work better by stating it clearly first. Your SUMMARY should be concise, but try to be specific and detailed enough to give readers a clear understanding not only of the scope and content of the source, but also of the author's perspective on the topic. *If you're writing a descriptive annotation, you're done after completing this step.*

If you're writing an evaluative bibliography, EVALUATE your sources in terms of their usefulness for your project, their STANCE, and their overall CREDIBILITY. If you can generalize about the worth of the entire work, fine. You may find, however, that some parts are useful while others are not, and your evaluation should reflect that mix.

Ways of organizing an annotated bibliography. Depending on their purpose, annotated bibliographies may or may not include an introduction. Consult the documentation system you're using for details about alphabetizing works appropriately.

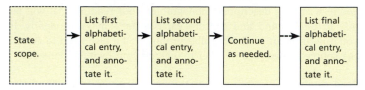

Sometimes an annotated bibliography needs to be organized into several subject areas (or genres, periods, or some other category); if so, the entries are listed alphabetically within each category.

[Multicategory bibliography]

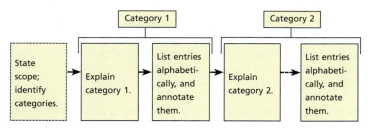

>> SEE W-1 for help analyzing your writing context. See W-4 for guidelines on drafting, revising, editing, and proofreading your bibliography. For help finding and evaluating sources, see R-1 and R-2. To read an example of an annotated bibliography, go to **digital.wwnorton.com/littleseagull4**.

W-17 Abstracts

Abstracts are brief summaries written to give readers the gist of a report or presentation. You may be required to include an abstract in a **REPORT** or as a preview of a presentation for an academic or professional conference. This chapter provides tips for writing three common kinds: informative, descriptive, and proposal.

Informative abstracts state in one paragraph the essence of a whole study or research project. The abstract should include all the main points of the paper: a description of the study or project, its methods, the results, and the conclusions. Here, for example, is the abstract accompanying a seven-page essay that appeared in the *Journal of Clinical Psychology*:

> The relationship between boredom proneness and health-symptom reporting was examined. Undergraduate students (N = 200) completed the Boredom Proneness Scale and the Hopkins Symptom Checklist. A multiple analysis of covariance indicated that individuals with high boredom-proneness total scores reported significantly higher ratings on all five subscales of the Hopkins Symptom Checklist (Obsessive-Compulsive, Somatization, Anxiety, Interpersonal Sensitivity, and Depression). The results suggest that boredom proneness may be an important element to consider when assessing symptom reporting. Implications for determining the effects of boredom proneness on psychological- and physical-health symptoms, as well as the application in clinical settings, are discussed.   —Jennifer Sommers and Stephen J. Vodanovich, "Boredom Proneness"

Descriptive abstracts are usually much briefer than informative abstracts; they provide a quick overview that invites the reader to read the whole paper. They usually do not summarize the entire paper, give results, or set out conclusions. A descriptive abstract of the boredom-proneness essay might be:

The relationship between boredom proneness and health-symptom reporting was examined. The findings and their application in clinical settings were discussed.

Proposal abstracts contain the same basic information as informative abstracts. You prepare them to persuade someone to let you write on a topic, pursue a project, conduct an experiment, or present at a scholarly conference; usually the abstract is written before the paper itself. You may use the future tense to describe work not yet completed. Here is a possible proposal for doing research on boredom and health problems:

Undergraduate students will complete the Boredom Proneness Scale and the Hopkins Symptom Checklist. A multiple analysis of covariance will be performed to determine the relationship between boredom-proneness total scores and ratings on the five subscales of the Hopkins Symptom Checklist (Obsessive-Compulsive, Somatization, Anxiety, Interpersonal Sensitivity, and Depression).

W-17a Key Elements of an Abstract

A summary of basic information. An informative abstract includes enough information to substitute for the report itself; a descriptive abstract offers only enough information to let the audience decide whether to read further; and a proposal abstract gives an overview of the planned work.

Objective description. Abstracts present information on the contents of a report or a proposed study; they do not present arguments about or personal perspectives on those contents.

Brevity. Although the length of abstracts may vary, journals and organizations often restrict them to 120–200 words.

W-17b Tips for Writing an Abstract

Generating ideas and text. Unless you are writing a proposal abstract, write the paper first. You can then use the finished work to guide the abstract, which should follow the same structure.

Copy and paste key statements. If you've already written the work, highlight your **THESIS**, objective, or purpose; basic information on your methods; your results; and your conclusion. Copy and paste those sentences into a new document to create a rough draft.

Pare down the rough draft. **SUMMARIZE** the key ideas, editing out any nonessential words and details. Introduce the overall scope of your study, and include any other information that seems crucial to understanding your work. In general, avoid using "I"; an abstract should cover ideas, not say what you personally think or will do.

Conform to any length requirements. In general, an informative abstract should be at most 10 percent as long as the original. Descriptive abstracts should be shorter still, and proposal abstracts should conform to the requirements of the organization calling for the proposal.

Ways of organizing an abstract

[An informative abstract]

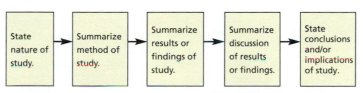

[A descriptive abstract]   **[A proposal abstract]**

   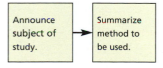

>> **SEE** **W-1** for help analyzing your writing context. See **W-4** for guidelines on drafting, revising, editing, and proofreading your abstract. To read an example of an abstract, go to **digital .wwnorton.com/littleseagull4**.

Research

Research is formalized curiosity.
It is poking and prying with a purpose.

— ZORA NEALE HURSTON

R-1　Doing Research

We do research all the time, for many different reasons. We search the internet for information about a new cell phone, ask friends about the best place to get coffee, try on several pairs of jeans before deciding which ones to buy. When you write something that uses facts, statistics, theories, or other information from sources, you're doing research. This chapter will help you get started with the kind of research you'll need to do for academic work.

R-1a Thinking about What You Already Know and Believe

Research is a process of inquiry—you approach a topic ready to learn, rather than committed to finding sources that support what you think. When you begin, outline what you already know and believe about your subject. Then, look for sources that expand, question, and contradict your preconceptions—not just ones that confirm your beliefs. Doing so will reduce CONFIRMATION BIAS, the tendency to look for information that supports what you already believe and to ignore information that doesn't. Make it a habit to seek out different perspectives, read sources with an open mind, and check your own biases.

R-1b Considering the Context for Your Research, Choosing a Topic

When you begin a research project, consider your purpose and overall context. If your topic is assigned, make sure you understand what the assignment asks you to do. If the assignment offers only broad guidelines, identify the requirements and range of possibilities, and define what topic you're most interested in exploring within those constraints. If you get to choose a topic to research, consider your interests. What do you want to learn more about?

- What is your **PURPOSE** for the project? Does the assignment specify a **GENRE** of writing—to argue for a position? report on a topic? analyze something? do something else?
- Who is your **AUDIENCE**, and what do they know about your topic? Will you need to provide background information? What kinds of evidence will your audience find persuasive? What attitudes do they hold, and how can you best appeal to them?
- What is your **STANCE** toward your topic? What accounts for that stance or attitude? Are you objective? skeptical? passionate? confused? indifferent?
- Do you get to choose your **MEDIUM**? If so, which media will best reach your audience, and how will your medium affect the kind of information you search for?
- How much time do you have to complete the project? Is there a due date? How much time will your project take, and how can you best schedule your time in order to complete it?

R-1c Narrowing Your Topic's Focus

As you consider topics, look to narrow your focus to be specific enough to cover in a research paper. For example, "fracking and the environment" is probably too broad; a better topic might be "the potential environmental risks from fracking." Narrowing your topic will make it easier to find and manage specific information that you can address in your project.

Doing some preliminary research can help you explore your topic and start to articulate a research question that will drive your research. You may choose to begin by using a general search engine or the library website. Starting with the library saves you time in the long run since reference librarians can direct you to the most appropriate resources, ones that have been selected and verified by experts. General encyclopedias and other reference works can provide an overview of your topic, while more specialized encyclopedias cover subjects in greater depth and provide other scholarly references for further research.

Be sure to keep a **WORKING BIBLIOGRAPHY** that lists all the sources you consult. Include all the information you'll need later to follow the documentation style you'll use when you write. You'll find more on documentation in the chapters on **MLA**, **APA**, **Chicago**, and **CSE** styles.

R-1d Posing a Research Question, Drafting a Tentative Thesis

Posing a research question. Once you have narrowed your topic, you need to come up with a research question—a specific question that you will then work to answer through your research. Generate a list of questions beginning with "what," "when," "where," "who," "how," "why," "would," "could," and "should." For example, here are some questions about the tentative topic "the potential environmental risks from fracking":

> <u>What</u> are the environmental effects of fracking?
> <u>Who</u> should determine when and where fracking can be done?
> <u>Should</u> fracking be expanded?

Select one question and use it to help guide your research.

Drafting a tentative thesis. When your research has led you to a possible answer to your question, try to formulate your answer as a tentative **THESIS**. Here are three tentative thesis statements, each one based on a previous research question about fracking:

> By injecting sand, water, and chemicals into rock, fracking may pollute drinking water and air.
> The federal government should strictly regulate the production of natural gas by fracking.
> Fracking can greatly increase our supplies of natural gas, but other methods of producing energy should still be pursued.

A tentative thesis will guide your research, but you should be ready to revise it as you learn more about your subject. If you hold too tightly to a tentative thesis, you risk focusing only on evidence that supports your own views through **CONFIRMATION BIAS**. Instead, stay open to the possibility that your ideas—and your thesis—will change as you uncover new information.

R-1e Finding Appropriate Sources

You'll need to choose from many sources for your research—from reference works, books, periodicals, and websites to surveys, interviews, and other kinds of field research that you yourself conduct. Which sources you turn to will depend on your topic. If you're researching a literary topic, you might consult biographical reference works and scholarly works of criticism. If you're researching a current issue, you'd likely consult news articles, books, and social media posts on your topic. For a report on career opportunities in psychology, you might interview someone working in the field.

Primary and secondary sources. Check your assignment to see if you are required to use primary or secondary sources—or both. Primary sources are original works, such as historical documents, literary works, eyewitness accounts, diaries, letters, and lab studies, as well as your own original field research. Secondary sources include scholarly books and articles, reviews, biographies, and other works that interpret or discuss primary sources.

Whether a source is considered primary or secondary sometimes depends on your topic and purpose. If you're analyzing a poem, a critic's article analyzing the poem is a secondary source—but if you're investigating the critic's work, the article would be a primary source.

Scholarly and popular sources. In many of your college courses, you'll be expected to rely primarily on scholarly sources that are written by experts for readers knowledgeable on the topic and that treat their subjects in depth. Popular sources, on the other hand, are written for a general audience, and while they may discuss scholarly research, they are more likely to summarize that research than to report on it in detail. That said, the distinction can be blurry: many scholars write books for a general readership that are informed by those authors' own scholarship, and many writers of popular sources

Scholarly Source

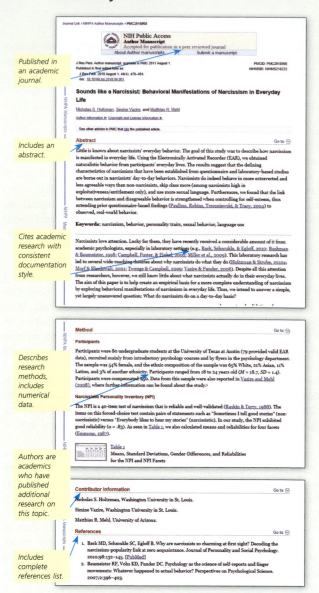

Published in an academic journal.

Includes an abstract.

Cites academic research with consistent documentation style.

Describes research methods, includes numerical data.

Authors are academics who have published additional research on this topic.

Includes complete references list.

Popular Sources

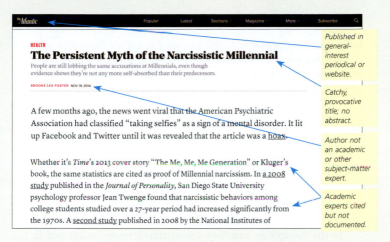

The Atlantic | Popular | Latest | Sections ⌄ | Magazine ⌄ | More ⌄ | Subscribe

HEALTH

The Persistent Myth of the Narcissistic Millennial

People are still lobbing the same accusations at Millennials, even though evidence shows they're not any more self-absorbed than their predecessors.

BROOKE LEA FOSTER NOV 19, 2014

A few months ago, the news went viral that the American Psychiatric Association had classified "taking selfies" as a sign of a mental disorder. It lit up Facebook and Twitter until it was revealed that the article was a hoax.

Whether it's *Time*'s 2013 cover story "The Me, Me, Me Generation" or Kluger's book, the same statistics are cited as proof of Millennial narcissism. In a 2008 study published in the *Journal of Personality*, San Diego State University psychology professor Jean Twenge found that narcissistic behaviors among college students studied over a 27-year period had increased significantly from the 1970s. A second study published in 2008 by the National Institutes of

Published in general-interest periodical or website.

Catchy, provocative title; no abstract.

Author not an academic or other subject-matter expert.

Academic experts cited but not documented.

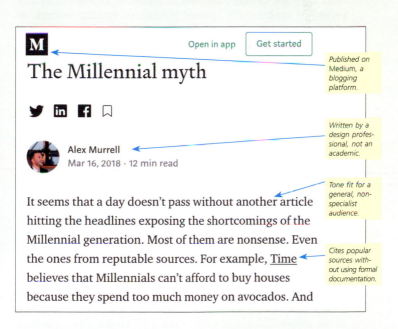

M | Open in app | Get started

The Millennial myth

Alex Murrell
Mar 16, 2018 · 12 min read

It seems that a day doesn't pass without another article hitting the headlines exposing the shortcomings of the Millennial generation. Most of them are nonsense. Even the ones from reputable sources. For example, Time believes that Millennials can't afford to buy houses because they spend too much money on avocados. And

Published on Medium, a blogging platform.

Written by a design professional, not an academic.

Tone fit for a general, non-specialist audience.

Cites popular sources without using formal documentation.

121

have extensive expertise in the subject. Even if it's not a requirement, citing scholarly sources often contributes to your own authority as a writer, demonstrating that you are familiar with important research and scholarship and that your own writing is informed by it.

HOW TO DETERMINE IF A SOURCE IS SCHOLARLY

There are several criteria to consider when determining whether or not a source is scholarly or reflects appropriate expertise. Ask these questions of each of your sources:

- *What kind of source is it?* A book from a scholarly press? A journal article? Scholarly sources present original academic research; they are peer-reviewed, meaning they are evaluated by experts in the discipline; and they are written largely for experts in the field. They are usually published in academic journals or by university or academically focused publishers. Popular sources, on the other hand—such as online magazine articles, blog posts, and news articles—usually report on the scholarship of others and tend to simplify concepts and facts to make them understandable to nonspecialists.

- *Who's the author?* Scholarly sources are written by authors with academic credentials (an advanced degree in the field in which they are writing and a position at a university, for example); popular sources are most often written by journalists or staff writers. What's most important, though, is that the author has some expertise on the topic being discussed.

- *Who's the intended audience?* Consider how much prior knowledge readers are assumed to have. Are specialized terms defined? If not, you can assume it's a scholarly work. Look as well at the detail: scholarly sources describe methods and give considerable detail, such as extensive analyses or numerical data; popular sources give less detail, often in the form of anecdotes or simple examples.

- *Who's the publisher?* Scholarly sources are published by academic journals, university presses, and professional organizations such as the Modern Language Association; popular sources come from general interest publications such as *Time* or the *Atlantic*, trade publishers such as Random House or HarperCollins, or online platforms such as *Medium*.

- *Does the source cite other academic studies and include formal documentation?* Scholarly sources do; popular sources may link to academic work in the text but generally do not list references. Or they might provide references at the end but omit in-text documentation.

- *Is there an abstract?* Scholarly journal articles often begin with an abstract or summary of the article; popular magazine articles may include a tag line giving some sense of what the article covers, but less than a formal summary.

R-1f Using Popular Sites and Search Engines

When we need to find something out, many of us begin with *Google* or *Wikipedia*. If you aren't familiar with your research topic, these sites provide general information and a variety of perspectives. However, using general search engines can present challenges: paywalls limit access, it's easy to be overwhelmed by the number of sources, and determining what's trustworthy can be difficult. So you'll want to rely primarily on your library's resources to find accurate, up-to-date, scholarly sources. However, the following sites can still serve as helpful starting points.

Wikipedia. An open, online reference, *Wikipedia* often serves as a starting point for preliminary research. Reading a *Wikipedia* entry can help you understand background information, come up with **KEYWORDS** to search, and discover related topics. A list of references—often hyperlinked—at the bottom of each entry can lead to potential sources. Check information you find on *Wikipedia* for accuracy, since entries can be written or edited by anyone.

Google, Google Scholar, **and other free search tools.** To search *Google*, use simple but specific **KEYWORDS** . Googling "fracking environmental effects" will turn up more focused results than googling "what is fracking." Scan the list of results and open sources that look promising in a new tab instead of stopping to read the first result that catches your eye. Be sure to look beyond the first page of results; higher placement doesn't always mean most relevant to your topic.

Google Scholar limits your search results to scholarly literature such as researched articles, theses, books, abstracts, and court opinions. A keyword search in *Google Scholar* will often give you an initial idea of the scholarly authors, publications, and databases publishing on your topic. Sort results by publication date to check if there's recent research. Some articles and books in *Google Scholar* are full-text, but many are behind paywalls and so must be accessed through your campus library.

Here are several more tools for searching online, outside of the library, to get started:

- *Keyword search engines.* Search engines use algorithms to tailor results to you, so search engines—and the results they show you—are not all the same. Compare results from *Google*, *Bing*, *Yahoo!*, and other search sites to get more varied results.

- *Metasearch engines. Yippy*, *Dogpile*, *Creafy*, and *Metacrawler* let you use several search sites simultaneously.

- *Nonlibrary, academic searches.* In addition to *Google Scholar*, search *Microsoft Academic* or *Base* for peer-reviewed academic writing in many disciplines. *Science.gov* offers results from more than fifteen US federal agencies, and *Core* collects open-access research papers.

- *Social media searches. Google Social Search*, *Social Searcher*, and *Talkwalker* let you search various social media platforms. Use **HASHTAGS** (#) or *Tagboard*, a hashtag-based search engine, to search the contents of social media posts.

Image, video, and audio platforms. *Google Images* and *TinEye* allow you to search for images by keyword or by uploading an image. *Google Video Search* lets you search for videos by keyword, and *You-Tube*'s search function allows you to find videos by relevance, upload date, view count, or rating. *Audioburst Search* provides results from podcast and radio segments.

News sites. Sites for newspapers, magazines, and radio and TV stations provide both up-to-the-minute information and also archives of older stories online. News-aggregating sites like *Google News* and *Apple News* collect worldwide news from a wide range of sources. *Google News Archive* has news archives extending back to the 1700s. Beware that MISINFORMATION is spread most often as news, so evaluating sources that appear to be news is essential.

Government sites. Many government agencies and departments maintain websites where you can find government reports, statistics, legislative information, and other resources. *USA.gov* offers resources from the US government.

Digital archives. You can find primary sources from the past, including drawings, maps, recordings, speeches, and historic documents at sites maintained by the National Archives, the Library of Congress, the New York Public Library, and others.

Although many websites provide authoritative information, content found online varies greatly in stability and reliability: what you see on a site today may be different (or gone) tomorrow, so save copies of pages you use. In addition, many reference and news sites are behind paywalls, their content unavailable unless you pay a fee or subscribe. If a source you need is behind a paywall, check if it is available through your library or through interlibrary loan.

R-1g Using Library Resources

Your school's library is your main source for finding reliable books, articles, media (images, audio, video), and many other potential sources of information. In addition to consulting librarians, you can search for information in four main ways.

Your library's homepage. Many academic libraries' homepages feature a search box that lets you search the library's full holdings, including physical books, media collections, and online databases of academic journals and articles. Searching by **KEYWORD**, subject, title, or author is a good way to get started if you don't know what kinds of sources you need. The homepage may also provide links to research guides that the library has created which recommend resources for specific disciplines. Look for librarian contact information on the homepage.

The library catalog. To find books, journals, and media physically available in your library, narrow your search by using the library catalog. The library catalog is a list of all the resources physically housed there (though many items will be available digitally, too). Access the catalog on the library's homepage (often you can limit search results to show only items in the library's catalog), and search by **KEYWORD**, author, title, or subject.

Databases. To find journal, magazine, and newspaper articles as well as video, audio, and images, narrow your search by using a database. You can search using multidisciplinary databases such as *Academic Search Premier* or *JSTOR*, but there are also many databases dedicated to single subjects. Browse the databases available to you by visiting your library's website; librarians can also recommend databases based on your topic.

To search for sources within a database, start with a **KEYWORD** search. Try narrowing your search using the strategies in R-1h. When you access a source through a database, the URL may not be permanent, so look for a **PERMALINK** or **DOI** to copy and paste into your working list of sources.

Reference works. Every library has a reference section, where you'll find encyclopedias, dictionaries, atlases, almanacs, bibliographies, and other reference works that can provide an overview as you begin your search. Reference works are helpful starting points for gathering background information and leading you to other sources and ideas. Many reference sources, such as *CREDO Reference* and *Gale Virtual Reference*, are online and collect specialized reference works across disciplines.

R-1h Narrowing Search Results

When you use digital search engines to find sources, in or outside of the library, you'll need to come up with **KEYWORDS** to focus search results on the information you need. Specific commands vary among sites and databases, but many offer advanced-search options that allow you to narrow (or expand) your search by typing keywords into search boxes using these tips:

- All of these words (insert commas between the words)
- The exact phrase (place quotation marks around it)
- Any of these words (insert "or" between each term)

In addition, look for features that allow you to filter results to include a specific date range; only full-text articles (articles that are available in full online); and only scholarly, peer-reviewed resources.

Some databases may require that you use symbols or Boolean operators (AND, OR, NOT) to combine search functions. See the databases' advanced-search instructions for help with such symbols, which may be called "field tags."

If a search turns up too many sources, be more specific ("homeopathy" instead of "medicine"). If your original keywords don't generate good results, try synonyms ("home remedy" instead of "folk medicine"). Keep in mind that searching requires flexibility, both in the words you use and in the methods you try.

And remember that the first items in a results list are not necessarily the most useful; scan what appears beyond page 1 of your results. Exercise "click restraint" by scanning through many items in the results and choosing only the ones that look most promising to open, each in its own separate tab for evaluation.

R-1i Doing Field Research

Sometimes you'll need to go beyond the information you find in published sources and gather your own data by doing field research. Three kinds of field research that you might consider are interviews, observations, and surveys.

Interviews. Some kinds of writing—a **PROFILE** of a living person, for instance—almost require that you conduct an interview, whether it's face-to-face or by telephone, email, or videoconference.

1. *Before the interview,* email or call to contact the person, stating your purpose for the request. If you wish to record the interview, ask for permission. Write out questions in advance—and bear in mind that open-ended questions are likely to elicit a more extended response than those that can be answered with a simple "yes" or "no."

2. *At the interview,* note the full name of the person and the date, time, and place. Take notes, even if you are recording the interview, and don't take more time than you agreed to beforehand.

3. *After the interview,* flesh out your notes with details right away, and send a thank-you note or email.

Observations. Some writing projects are based on information you get by observing something.

1. *Before observing,* think about your research purpose. How does this observation relate to your research goals, and what do you expect to find? If necessary, set up an appointment, and ask your subjects' permission to observe them. You may also need to get your school's permission.

2. *While observing,* divide your document into two columns, and make notes only in the left column. Describe who is there, what they are doing, what they look like, what they say, and any other relevant details. Also note details about the setting.

3. *After observing,* use the right column of your notes to fill in additional details. Then analyze your notes, looking for patterns. What did you learn? Did anything surprise or puzzle you?

Surveys. One way of gathering information from a large number of people is to use a questionnaire.

1. *Start by thinking* about your research question and what you can learn with a survey.

2. *Decide whom you'll send it to* and how you'll reach them: face-to-face? on the phone? on a website such as *Google Forms* or *SurveyMonkey*? via email?

3. *Write questions* that require specific answers and can be answered easily. Multiple-choice questions will be easier to tally than open-ended questions.

4. *Write an introduction* that explains the survey's purpose. Be sure to give a due date and to say thank you.

5. *Test your questions* on several people, making sure that the questions and any instructions are clear.

R-2 Evaluating Sources

Searching the *Health Source* database for information on the incidence of meningitis among college students, you find twenty-eight articles. A *Google* search on the same topic produces almost 12 million hits. How do you decide which ones to read? This chapter presents advice on evaluating potential sources and reading your chosen sources critically.

R-2a Considering Whether a Source Might Be Useful

As you consider potential sources, keep your **PURPOSE** in mind. If you're trying to persuade readers to believe something, look for sources representing various stances; if you're reporting on a topic, you may need sources that are more factual or informative. Consider your **AUDIENCE**. What kinds of sources will they find persuasive? If you're writing for readers in a particular field, what counts as **EVIDENCE** in that field? The following questions can help you select useful sources—consider most or all of the questions, don't rely on a single criterion:

- *Is the source relevant?* How well does it relate to your purpose? What would it add to your work? To see what it covers, look at the title and at any introductory material (such as a preface or an abstract).

- *What are the author's credentials?* Has the author written other works on this subject? Is the author known for a particular position on it? Is the author an expert? a scholar? a journalist? Will your audience find this person credible? If their credentials are not stated, search to see what reliable sources say about the author.

- *What is the* STANCE*?* Does the source explain various points of view or advocate only one perspective? Does its title suggest a certain slant? If it's online, check to see whether it includes links to other sites and, if so, what their perspectives are. You'll want to consult sources with various viewpoints and understand the biases of each source you use.

- *Who is the publisher?* If the source is a book, what kind of company published it? If an article, what kind of periodical did it appear in? Books published by university presses and articles in scholarly journals are reviewed by experts before they are published. Many books and articles written for the general public also undergo careful fact-checking, but some do not.

- *At what level is it written?* How hard is it to understand? Texts written for a general audience might be easier to understand but not authoritative enough for academic work. Scholarly texts will be more authoritative but may be hard to comprehend.

- *How current is it?* Check to see when books and articles were published and when websites were last updated. (If a site lists no date, see if links to other sites still work; if not, the site is probably too dated to use.) A recent publication date or update, however, does not necessarily mean that a potential source is good—some topics require current information; others call for older sources.

- *Is it cited in other works?* If so, you can probably assume that some other writers regard it as trustworthy.

- *Is it available?* If it's a book and your school's library doesn't have it, can you get it through interlibrary loan? If it's online and there's a paywall, can your library get you access?

- *Does it include other useful information?* Is there a bibliography that might lead you to other sources? How current or authoritative are the sources it cites?

R-2b Fact-Checking Popular Sources Online

Scholarly books are edited; scholarly articles are reviewed by experts; established news sources employ professionals to **FACT-CHECK** information. But many websites and social media sites aren't vetted by anyone. As a result, when you're using *Google* and other nonlibrary resources, you may find misleading information, data, images, and videos. To conduct sound research—and to use reliable information to form your own ideas—you need to determine what is true, what is false, and what is trying to manipulate you. Professional fact-checkers use the following methods to evaluate accuracy.

Fact-checkers begin not by jumping into something they find online that looks relevant, but by first moving *outside* the source—opening new tabs in the same browser—to search and see what other reliable sites say about it. Only after they've done some research to confirm a source's accuracy do they read the source itself.

When you find something online that looks relevant, first stop and ask yourself if you know the website publishing the source and have reason to trust it. If not, take the following steps to assess the source before reading any further:

- *Look up the main* **CLAIMS**. Copy and paste the title or a few key words of the article, essay, or post into *Google* to see if a reliable fact-checking site—*Snopes*, *FactCheck*, or *Politifact*—has already evaluated it. If several reputable sources report the same information, it's probably true. If the information appears in only one source—even if many other people are quoting it—it's worth taking more steps to check whether it's reliable enough for your academic writing.

- *Investigate the author's expertise and* **STANCE**. Use *Wikipedia*, *Google News*, or *Google Scholar* to verify if the author is an expert on the topic they're weighing in on. Signs that the author has expertise include an academic position in a relevant field, pieces on the same topic published in reputable sources, and considerable experience in the area being written about. If you can't find any evidence of the author's expertise on the topic, don't depend on the information as authoritative. Also, the author's affiliations—the groups they're members of or the places they've published—can help you determine their stance.

Fact-Checking Popular Sources

Once you've got a source to fact-check, begin by looking outside the site itself following the steps below.

LOOK UP THE CLAIM

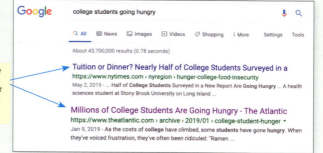

Other reliable news organizations report similar claims from various sources.

CHECK OUT THE WEBSITE

Wikipedia says the site began in 2008 and closed in 2019. Be skeptical of a new site or one that no longer exists.

A New York Times *article confirms the site was funded by a well-established academic publisher and won two awards for quality, so it appears trustworthy.*

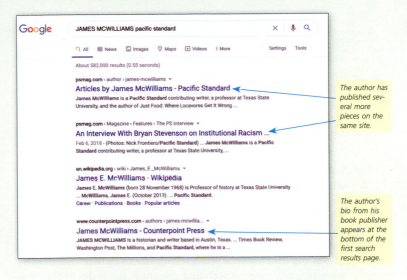

Google   JAMES MCWILLIAMS pacific standard   ✕   🎤   🔍

🔍 All   📰 News   🖼 Images   📍 Maps   ▶ Videos   ⋮ More   Settings   Tools

About 582,000 results (0.55 seconds)

psmag.com › author › james-mcwilliams ▾

Articles by James McWilliams - Pacific Standard ◀

James McWilliams is a **Pacific Standard** contributing writer, a professor at Texas State University, and the author of Just Food: Where Locavores Get It Wrong ...

The author has published several more pieces on the same site.

psmag.com › Magazine › Features › The PS Interview ▾

An Interview With Bryan Stevenson on Institutional Racism ... ◀

Feb 6, 2018 - (Photos: Nick Frontiero/**Pacific Standard**) ... **James McWilliams** is a **Pacific Standard** contributing writer, a professor at Texas State University, ...

en.wikipedia.org › wiki › James_E._McWilliams ▾

James E. McWilliams - Wikipedia

James E. McWilliams (born 28 November 1968) is Professor of history at Texas State University ... **McWilliams**, James E. (October 2013). ... **Pacific Standard**.
Career · Publications · Books · Popular articles

www.counterpointpress.com › authors › james-mcwillia... ▾

James McWilliams - Counterpoint Press ◀

JAMES MCWILLIAMS is a historian and writer based in Austin, Texas. ... Times Book Review, Washington Post, The Millions, and **Pacific Standard**, where he is a ...

The author's bio from his book publisher appears at the bottom of the first search results page.

gato-docs.its.txstate.edu › McWilliams_CV_2019 ▾ PDF

James McWilliams - Texas State University ◀

James McWilliams. Curriculum Vita. Degree Year. Ph.D. 2001 The ... Columnist, Freakonomics.com (2009-2011). Columnist, **Pacific Standard** (2013-present).

james-mcwilliams.com › wp-content › uploads › 2014/06 ▾ DOC

Slow-Food-version-2.doc - James McWilliams

... Salatin / Polyface farm here: http://james-mcwilliams.com/?p=598. On local slaughterhouses, a reply in "The **Pacific Standard**" to Nicolette Niman's NYT Op-Ed: ...

www.ourhenhouse.org › 2017/09 › episode-402-james-... ▾

Episode 402: James McWilliams & Julia Feliz Brueck | Our ...

Sep 23, 2017 - He writes a column at **Pacific Standard**, where he is a contributing writer. His literary non-fiction has appeared in The Millions, Quarterly ...

Opening the author's academic webpage shows he's a professor at Texas State University, teaching courses in American history and writing about the history of eating habits.

www.amazon.com › Eating-Promiscuously-Adventures... ▾

Eating Promiscuously: Adventures in the Future of Food ... ◀

Eating Promiscuously: Adventures in the Future of Food [McWilliams, James] ... Review, The Washington Post, The Millions, and **Pacific Standard**, where he is a ...

An Amazon page shows the author's published a book on food and eating. So he appears credible on this topic.

133

- *Check out who runs the site.* Don't rely on the site's "about" page alone. Instead, google the organization's name in quotation marks and add keywords like "who sponsors" or "funding." What do other reputable sites say about the publisher or sponsoring organization? Take note of controversies or a specific agenda attached to the organization. Do reliable sources say the organization has a good reputation? a lot of members? a long history? Those are all good signs the publication is trustworthy.

- *Take stock and use your judgment.* Consider your **PURPOSE** and what you've found about the source's main claims, author, and publisher. Does the source seem accurate and trustworthy, given what you know about the world and how it works? Do the claims seem designed to generate a strong emotional response rather than appealing to logic or sound evidence? If taking these steps shows you that a source has a strong stance or bias, that doesn't automatically mean you should discard it, but it does mean you should keep that stance in mind as you work with the source.

If even just one of these steps reveals troubling information, move on to find a different, more solidly reliable source. As you use these fact-checking moves, don't just click on the first item in a list of search results. Instead, scan the results to get a broad sense of what others are saying, and choose the most trustworthy ones to read.

Photos and Videos. Visual media—especially images and videos spread online—can also be manipulated to present misleading information. Hoax photos are images taken out of context or doctored in order to deceive using photo-editing tools. To identify the source of most photos, you can do a reverse image search using these tools:

- *Google Images.* Click on the small camera icon to the right of the search box and paste in the image's web address. The results will show other uses of the image as well as similar images.

- *TinEye.* Upload the image or enter its URL in the search box to get a list of other places where the image has appeared online.

Hoax videos are ones altered or presented in misleading ways. The *Washington Post* identifies three ways hoax videos are made:

- *Missing context.* The video itself is not altered, but it is misrepresented in order to mislead the viewer—using an incorrect date, location, or summary. Or it's a brief clip from a longer video taking an event out of context.

- *Deceptive editing.* Portions of the video have been edited out and the remaining parts spliced together to create a misleading narrative. Or videos shot on two different occasions have been spliced together to create a single false narrative.

- *Malicious transformation.* The video is altered to deceive the viewer, or artificial intelligence is used to create fake images and audio.

To evaluate the accuracy of videos, type a brief summary of the video into *Google* to see if fact-checking sites like *Snopes* have reported on it. Also, do your own analysis: does anything in the video seem doctored? Are the events depicted believable or unlikely? If the video appears on several websites, do its details change from site to site? Use *YouTube DataViewer*, available at citizenevidence.amnestyusa.org, to see where else a *YouTube* video has been posted and to do a reverse image search on stills from any video.

R-2c Reading Sources with a Critical Eye

Approach your sources with an open mind, but consider their arguments with a critical eye. Pay attention to what they say, to the reasons and evidence they offer to support what they say, and to whether they address viewpoints other than their own. Assume that each author is responding to some other argument.

- *What* **ARGUMENTS** *does the author make?* Does the author present several different positions or argue for a particular position? What arguments is the author responding to?

- *How persuasive do you find the argument to be?* What REASONS and EVIDENCE does the author provide? Are there references or links—and if so, are they CREDIBLE? Are any of the author's assumptions questionable? How thoroughly does the author consider alternative arguments?

- *What is the author's STANCE?* Does it seem objective, or does the content or language reveal a particular bias? Are opposing views considered and treated fairly? Do the headlines and text try to elicit an emotional reaction?

- *Do you recognize ideas you've run across in other sources?* Does the source leave out any information or perspective that other sources include—or does it include any that they leave out?

- *Does this source support or challenge your own position—or does it do both?* Does it support a different argument altogether? Does it represent a position you need to address? Don't reject a source just because it challenges your views—instead, to avoid CONFIRMATION BIAS, work to understand various perspectives on your topic.

- *What can you tell about the intended AUDIENCE and PURPOSE?* Are you a member of the audience addressed—and if not, does that affect the way you interpret what you read? Is the main purpose to inform readers about a topic or to argue a certain point?

R-3   Synthesizing Ideas

Whatever topic you are researching, you need to constantly synthesize the information you find—that is, to sift through your sources in order to identify patterns, themes, and main points—and then use these data to help generate your own ideas. This chapter focuses on going beyond what your sources say, using them to inspire and support what *you* want to say.

R-3a Reading for Patterns and Connections

Your task as a writer is to find as much information as you can on your topic and then to study the data you find to determine what you think and to support what you yourself then write. Read with an open mind, taking careful notes to help you see patterns, themes, and connections among your sources. Pay attention to your first reactions: you'll probably have many ideas to work with, but your first thoughts can often lead somewhere interesting. Here are some questions that can help you discover patterns and connections:

- Which sources make the strongest arguments? What makes them so strong?
- Which arguments do you agree with? disagree with?
- Are there any arguments, distinctive terms, themes, or data that you see in more than one source?
- Are there any disagreements among sources? Are there any that you need to address in what you write?
- How have your sources affected your thinking on your topic? Have you discovered new questions you need to investigate?
- Have you found the information you need that will achieve your **PURPOSE**, appeal to your **AUDIENCE**, and suit your **MEDIUM**?

The ideas and insights that emerge from this questioning can become the basis for your own ideas—and for what *you* have to say about the topic.

R-3b Moving from What Your Sources Say to What You Say

As you work to make sense of what your sources say, you'll be figuring out what you yourself think—where you stand on your topic and what you want to say. You'll have some understanding of what others believe, which will affect what you think. But when you formulate your own argument, you'll need to be careful to draw from your sources to support what *you* want to say to weave their ideas in with your ideas.

Entering the conversation. As you read and think about your topic, you'll come to understand the concepts, interpretations, and controversies relating to it—and you'll become aware that there's a larger conversation going on. When you formulate and write out your own ideas on the topic, you'll begin to find your way into that conversation. This is the exciting part of a research project. Remember that your **STANCE** as an author needs to be clear: simply stringing together the words and ideas of others isn't enough. You need to show readers how your source materials relate to one another and to your **THESIS** .

R-4   Integrating Sources, Avoiding Plagiarism

When you include the ideas and words of others in your writing, you need to clearly distinguish those ideas and words from your own and give credit to their authors. This chapter will help you with the specifics of integrating source materials into your writing and acknowledging your sources appropriately.

R-4a Incorporating the Words and Ideas of Others into Your Text

When you incorporate source materials into your own writing, you'll need to decide how to do so—whether to quote, paraphrase, or summarize. This is a judgment call, but you might follow this rule of thumb: **QUOTE** texts when the wording is worth repeating, when you want to cite the exact words of a known authority on your topic, or when the author's opinions challenge or disagree with those of others. **PARAPHRASE** texts that are not worth quoting but that contain information you need to include. **SUMMARIZE** passages whose main points are important but whose details are not.

In addition, you'll need to introduce any words or ideas that are not your own with a SIGNAL PHRASE in order to clearly distinguish what your sources say from what you have to say.

R-4b Quoting

Quoting is a way of weaving someone's exact words into your text. When you quote, you reproduce the source exactly, though you can omit unnecessary details (adding ELLIPSES to show that you've done so) or modify the quotation to make it fit smoothly into your text (enclosing any changes in BRACKETS).

Incorporate short quotations into your text, enclosed in quotation marks. What counts as a short quotation varies, however; consult the chapters on MLA, APA, Chicago, or CSE for guidelines in each of those styles. The following examples are shown in MLA style.

> Gerald Graff argues that colleges leave many students with "the misconception that the life of the mind is a secret society for which only an elite few qualify" (1).

To quote three lines or less of poetry in MLA style, run them in with your text, enclosed in quotation marks. Separate lines with slashes, leaving one space on each side of the slash. Include the line numbers in parentheses at the end of the quotation.

> Emma Lazarus almost speaks for the Statue of Liberty with the words inscribed on its pedestal: "Give me your tired, your poor, / Your huddled masses yearning to breathe free, / The wretched refuse of your teeming shore" (10-12).

Set off long quotations block style. Longer quotations should not be run in with quotation marks but instead are set off from your text and indented from the left margin. Block quotations are usually introduced by a full sentence. Again, what counts as long varies across disciplines; consult the chapters on MLA, APA, Chicago, or CSE for specific guidelines on when to format a quotation as a block and how much to indent. Whatever style you're following, do not add quotation marks; the indent signals that you are quoting someone's exact words. Remember to document the source, using the format required by the style you're following. Here is an example shown in MLA style, indented one-half inch from the left margin:

> Organizations such as Oxfam rely on visual representations of the poor. What better way to get our attention? asks Diana George:
>> In a culture saturated by the image, how else do we convince Americans that—despite the prosperity they see all around them—there is real need out there? The solution for most nonprofits has been to show the despair. To do that they must represent poverty as something that can be seen and easily recognized: fallen down shacks and trashed out public housing, broken windows, dilapidated porches, barefoot kids with stringy hair, emaciated old women and men staring out at the camera with empty eyes. (210)

If you quote four lines or more of poetry in MLA style, they need to be set off block style in the same way.

Indicate any omissions with ellipses, inserting three ellipsis dots with space around each one to indicate deleted words. Be careful not to distort your source's meaning.

> In her essay, Antonia Peacocke argues that *Family Guy* provides an astute satire of American society, though she concedes that it does sometimes "seem to cross . . . the line of indecency" (266).

If you omit a sentence or more in the middle of a quotation, put a period before the three ellipsis dots.

> According to Kathleen Welch, "Television is more acoustic than visual. . . . One can turn one's gaze away from the television, but one cannot turn one's ears from it without leaving the area where the monitor leaks its aural signals into every corner" (102).

Indicate any additions or changes with brackets. Sometimes, you'll need to change or add words to make a quotation fit grammatically within your sentence, or you'll want to add a comment. Here the writer changes the word "our" to "their" so that the quotation fits grammatically into her own text:

> Writing about the dwindling attention of some composition scholars to the actual teaching of writing, Susan Miller notes that "few discussions of writing pedagogy take it for granted that one of [their] goals is to teach how to write" (480).

In this example, brackets are used to add an explanatory word:

> As Barbosa notes, Chico Buarque's lyrics include "many a metaphor of *saudades* [yearning] so characteristic of fado music" (207).

Keep in mind that too many ellipses and brackets can make a text choppy and hard to read, so it's best to keep such editing to a minimum.

>> **SEE P-4** for guidance in using other punctuation inside or outside quotation marks.

R-4c Paraphrasing

When you paraphrase, you restate material from a source in your own words, using your own sentence structure. Paraphrase when the source material is important but the original wording is not. Because it includes all the main points and details of the source material, a paraphrase is usually about the same length as the original.

Here is an excerpt from a source, followed by a paraphrase:

ORIGINAL SOURCE

In 1938, in a series of now-classic experiments, exposure to synthetic dyes derived from coal and belonging to a class of chemicals called aromatic amines was shown to cause bladder cancer in dogs. These results helped explain why bladder cancers had become so prevalent among dyestuffs workers. With the invention of mauve in 1854, synthetic dyes began replacing natural plant-based dyes in the coloring of cloth and leather. By the beginning of the twentieth century, bladder cancer rates among this group of workers had skyrocketed, and the dog experiments helped unravel this mystery.
—Sandra Steingraber, "Pesticides, Animals, and Humans," p. 976

PARAPHRASE

Biologist Sandra Steingraber explains that pathbreaking experiments in 1938 demonstrated that dogs exposed to aromatic amines (chemicals used in coal-derived synthetic dyes) developed cancers of the bladder that were similar to cancers common among dyers in the textile industry. After mauve, the first synthetic dye, was invented in 1854, leather and cloth manufacturers replaced most natural dyes made from plants with synthetic dyes, and by the early 1900s textile workers had very high rates of bladder cancer, according to Steingraber. The experiments with dogs revealed the connection (976).

Now see two examples that demonstrate some of the challenges of paraphrasing. The paraphrase below borrows too much of the original language or changes it only slightly, as the words and phrases highlighted in yellow show.

Now-classic experiments in 1938 showed that when dogs were exposed to aromatic amines, chemicals used in synthetic dyes derived from coal, they developed bladder cancer. Similar cancers were prevalent among dyestuffs workers, and these experiments helped to explain why. Mauve, a synthetic dye, was invented in 1854, after which cloth and leather manufacturers replaced most of the natural plant-based dyes with synthetic dyes. By the early twentieth century, this group of workers had skyrocketing rates of bladder cancer, a mystery the dog experiments helped to unravel (Steingraber 976).

This next paraphrase uses different language but follows the sentence structure of Steingraber's text too closely.

In 1938, several pathbreaking experiments showed that being exposed to synthetic dyes that are made from coal and belong to a type of chemicals called aromatic amines caused dogs to get bladder cancer. These results helped researchers identify why cancers of the bladder had become so common among textile workers who worked with dyes. With the development of mauve in 1854, synthetic dyes began to be used instead of dyes based on plants in the dyeing of leather and cloth. By the end of the nineteenth century, rates of bladder cancer among these workers had increased dramatically, and the experiments using dogs helped clear up this oddity (Steingraber 976).

It can be a challenge to write a paraphrase without inadvertently copying some of the original text's wording or sentence structures, especially when you're paraphrasing complex or unfamiliar ideas. One common mistake many writers make is to start by copying a passage directly from a source and then changing it: adding some words or deleting some words, replacing others with synonyms, altering sentence structures. The result is **PATCHWRITING**, patching together passages from another source; even if the source is documented, patchwriting is considered plagiarism.

To avoid problems of this kind, read over the original passages you're paraphrasing carefully, but do not look at them while you're writing. Use your own words and sentence structure. If you use any words from the original, put them in quotation marks. And be sure to indicate the source: the wording may be yours, but the ideas and information come from another source; name the author and include **DOCUMENTATION**.

R-4d Summarizing

A summary states the main ideas in a source concisely and in your own words. Unlike a paraphrase, a summary does *not* present the details, and it is generally as brief as possible. Summaries may boil down an entire book or essay into a single sentence, or they may take a paragraph or more to present the main ideas. Here, for example, is a summary of the original excerpt from Steingraber (see p. 141):

> Steingraber explains that experiments with dogs demonstrated that aromatic amines, chemicals used in synthetic dyes, can cause bladder cancer (976).

As with a paraphrase, if you include any language from the original, put it in quotation marks—and indicate the source, naming the author and including **DOCUMENTATION**.

R-4e Using Signal Phrases to Introduce Source Materials

You need to introduce quotations, paraphrases, and summaries with a signal phrase, usually letting readers know who the author is and, if need be, something about the writer's credentials. Consider this sentence:

> Professor and textbook author Elaine Tyler May argues that many high school history books are far too bland to interest young readers (531).

The signal phrase ("Professor and textbook author Elaine Tyler May") tells readers who is making the assertion and why she has the authority to speak on the topic.

Signal verbs. The language you use in a signal phrase can be neutral, like "X says" or "according to Y." Or it can suggest something about the STANCE—the source's or your own. The example above referring to the textbook author uses the verb "argues," suggesting that what she says is disputable (or that the writer believes it is).

SOME COMMON SIGNAL VERBS

acknowledge	claim	disagree	observe
admit	comment	dispute	point out
advise	conclude	emphasize	reason
agree	concur	grant	reject
argue	confirm	illustrate	report
assert	contend	imply	respond
believe	declare	insist	suggest
charge	deny	note	think

Sometimes "X says" or "according to Y" will be the most appropriate phrasing, but you can usually make your writing more precise and lively by choosing verbs that better signal the stance of the source you're citing—and by varying the placement of your signal phrases. In addition, it's a good idea to include information about authors' institutional affiliations and academic or professional specialties as well as other context that lets your readers judge the CREDIBILITY of your sources. For example:

> Suzanne Clark, professor of English at the University of Oregon, argues that . . .
>
> Science writer Isaac McDougal questions whether . . .
>
> Writing in *Psychology Today*, Amanda Chao-Fitz speculates that . . .

If your primary language isn't English, some uses of these verbs may seem odd to you. For example:

> In other words, the data suggest that . . .
>
> Our theory challenges common assumptions about . . .
>
> Their hypothesis supposes . . .

In many languages, it's unheard of for data to "suggest" anything or for a theory to "challenge" assumptions or anything else; only people can do those things. But in English, abstract nouns—a paper, new data, these conclusions—can perform "human" actions as well, and are often paired with the signal verbs above.

Verb tenses. Each documentation style has its own conventions regarding the verbs that are used in signal phrases.

MLA generally requires present tense verbs (notes, contends) in signal phrases that introduce source material. If, however, you mention the date when the source was written, the verb should be in the past tense.

> As Benjamin Franklin <u>notes</u> in *Poor Richard's Almanack*, "He that cannot obey, cannot command" (739).
>
> In a 2012 interview, Susan Miller <u>said</u> that "if you want to know how power works, you must understand how language works—and that's what the study of rhetoric is all about" (36).

APA uses the past tense or PRESENT PERFECT to introduce quotations or to present research results.

> Dowdall et al. (2020) <u>observed</u> that women at women's colleges are less likely to engage in binge drinking than are women at coeducational colleges (p. 713).
>
> Dowdall et al. (2020) <u>have observed</u> that . . . .

But to discuss the implications of an experiment or conclusions that are generally agreed on, APA requires the use of the present tense: the findings of the study <u>suggest</u>, most researchers <u>concur</u>.

Chicago uses the present tense (As Eric Foner <u>notes</u>) or **PRESENT PERFECT** (As Eric Foner <u>has noted</u>) to introduce most quotations. Use the past tense, however, when you are focusing on the fact that the action took place in the past: Just before signing the Declaration of Independence, John Adams <u>wrote</u> to his wife.

CSE uses the past tense or **PRESENT PERFECT** to refer to research from the past (Gillen's 2005 paper <u>argued</u>, his early studies <u>have demonstrated</u>) or to discuss methods (our subjects <u>received</u>) or findings: his earlier studies (1999, 2003) <u>showed</u>. Use the present tense, however, when citing research reports: Gillen (2010) <u>provides</u> the most detailed evidence.

Statistics and facts. You may introduce a statistic or a specific fact with a signal phrase—but you don't need to. Most of the time, it will be clear that you are documenting only the statistic or fact. The following examples introduce statistics with and without a signal phrase in **MLA** style.

> Puzzanchera notes that almost half of the people arrested for arson in 2008—47 percent—were juveniles (2).
>
> Almost half of the people arrested for arson in 2008—47 percent—were juveniles (Puzzanchera 2).

R-4f Acknowledging Sources

When you insert into your text any information that you've obtained from others, your reader needs to know where your source's words or ideas begin and end. Usually, you should introduce a source by naming the author in a **SIGNAL PHRASE** and follow it with brief

DOCUMENTATION; then provide full publication information in your WORKS CITED, REFERENCES, or BIBLIOGRAPHY. Conventions for acknowledging sources vary across disciplines, however; see the chapters on MLA, APA, Chicago, and CSE for specific advice.

Citing images or video requires that you provide a citation in your list of works cited or references—and if you're writing online, through a link. When deciding whether or not to use a video from *YouTube* or elsewhere, see if the content is original or comes from another source; if possible, use the original source.

Material that needs acknowledgment

- Direct quotations (unless they're well known), paraphrases, and summaries
- Controversial statements
- Information that may not be common knowledge
- The opinions and ideas of others
- Any information that you didn't generate or create yourself—charts, graphs, interviews, statistics
- Videos, photographs, audio, images
- Help from others

Material that doesn't need acknowledgment. Widely available information and common knowledge do not require acknowledgment—but what constitutes common knowledge isn't always clear. When in doubt, provide documentation or ask your instructor for advice. You generally do not need to document the following material:

- Facts that most readers are likely to know or that are found in reference sources (such as the date when Martin Luther King Jr. died)
- Information that you see mentioned in several sources
- Well-known quotations (name the person who said it; for example, "As Socrates said, 'The unexamined life is not worth living.'")
- Material that you created or gathered yourself, such as photos you took or data from your own field research (make sure, however, that readers know the work is yours)

A good rule of thumb: when in doubt, acknowledge your source. Assuming that the majority of an essay is your own writing, you won't be criticized for documenting too much—but you may invite charges of plagiarism by documenting too little.

R-4g Avoiding Plagiarism

In North America, authors' words and ideas are considered to belong to them, so using others' words or ideas without acknowledging the source is considered to be a serious offense called plagiarism. Plagiarism is often unintentional, as when a writer paraphrases someone else's ideas in language that is close to the original. It is essential, therefore, to know what constitutes plagiarism: (1) using another writer's words, ideas, videos, or other media without acknowledging and documenting the source; (2) using another writer's exact words without quotation marks; and (3) paraphrasing or summarizing another writer's text by using language or sentence structures that are too close to the originals. The following practices will help you avoid plagiarizing.

- *Take careful notes*, clearly labeling quotations and using your own phrasing and sentence structure in paraphrases and summaries.

- *Know what sources you must document*, and give credit to them both in the text and in a works-cited list (MLA), a references list (APA or CSE), or a bibliography (Chicago).

- *Be especially careful with online material*—it is all too easy to copy source material directly into a document you are writing and then forget to put quotation marks around it or document it. Like other sources, information from the internet must be acknowledged.

- *Check all paraphrases and summaries* to be sure they are in *your* words and sentence structures—and that you put quotation marks around any of the source's original phrasing.

- *Check to see that all quotations are both documented and enclosed in quotation marks* (or indented as a block); it's not enough to do just one or the other.

Whether it's deliberate or accidental, plagiarism has consequences. Students who plagiarize fail courses or might even be expelled from school. If you're having trouble figuring out when or how to cite your sources, seek assistance from your instructor or your school's writing center.

R-4h Understanding Documentation Styles

When we write up the results of a research project, we cite the sources we use and acknowledge those sources through **DOCUMENTATION**. Documenting our sources not only helps establish our credibility as researchers and writers, but also enables our readers to find our sources themselves (if they wish to).

The Little Seagull Handbook provides guidelines on four documentation styles, each of which is commonly used in specific disciplines.

- **MLA** (Modern Language Association): mainly used in English, foreign languages, and other humanities
- **APA** (American Psychological Association): mainly used in psychology and other social sciences
- **Chicago** (University of Chicago Press): mainly used in history, philosophy, and other humanities
- **CSE** (Council of Science Editors): mainly used in physical and biological sciences and mathematics

Each system has two parts: (1) an acknowledgment of each quotation, paraphrase, or summary in the text and (2) a detailed list of sources at the end of the text. Although the specific guidelines for the styles differ, they all require that you provide basic information about the authors, titles, and publication of your sources. To help you see the crucial parts of each source documentation in this book, the examples throughout the following chapters are color-coded: tan for author and editor, yellow for title, and gray for publication information: place of publication, name of publisher, date of publication, page number(s), medium of publication, and so on.

MLA Style

MLA style calls for (1) brief in-text documentation and (2) complete bibliographic information in a list of works cited at the end of your text. The models and examples in this chapter draw on the eighth edition of the *MLA Handbook*, published by the Modern Language Association in 2016. For additional information, visit **style.mla.org**.

A DIRECTORY TO MLA STYLE

Notes   160

List of Works Cited   160

Formatting a Research Paper   189
Sample Research Paper   191

Throughout this chapter, you'll find color-coded templates and examples to help you see how writers include source information in their texts and in their lists of works cited: tan for author, editor, translator, and other contributors; yellow for titles; gray for publication information—date of publication, page number(s) or other location information, and so on.

MLA-a In-Text Documentation

Brief documentation in your text tells your readers what you took from a source and where in the source you found the information.

You have three options for citing a source in your text: quoting, paraphrasing, and summarizing. As you cite each source, you will need to decide whether or not to name the author in a signal phrase—"as Toni Morrison writes"—or in parentheses—(Morrison 24).

The first examples below show basic in-text documentation of a work by one author. Variations on those examples follow. The examples illustrate the MLA style of using quotation marks around titles of short works and italicizing titles of long works.

1. AUTHOR NAMED IN A SIGNAL PHRASE

If you mention the author in a signal phrase, put only the page number(s) in parentheses. Do not write "page" or "p."

> McCullough describes John Adams's hands as those of someone used to manual labor (18).

2. AUTHOR NAMED IN PARENTHESES

If you do not mention the author in a signal phrase, put the author's last name in parentheses along with the page number(s). Do not use punctuation between the name and the page number(s).

> Adams is said to have had "the hands of a man accustomed to pruning his own trees, cutting his own hay, and splitting his own firewood" (McCullough 18).

Whether you use a signal phrase and parentheses or parentheses only, try to put the parenthetical documentation at the end of the sentence or as close as possible to the material you've cited—without awkwardly interrupting the sentence. Notice that in the example above, the parenthetical reference comes after the closing quotation marks but before the period at the end of the sentence.

3. TWO OR MORE WORKS BY THE SAME AUTHOR

If you cite multiple works by one author, include the title of the work you are citing either in the signal phrase or in parentheses. Give the full title if it's brief; otherwise, give a short version.

> Kaplan insists that understanding power in the Near East requires "Western leaders who know when to intervene, and do so without illusions" (*Eastward* 330).

author   title   publication

Put a comma between author and title if both are in the parentheses.

> Understanding power in the Near East requires "Western leaders
> who know when to intervene, and do so without illusions"
> (Kaplan, *Eastward* 330).

4. AUTHORS WITH THE SAME LAST NAME

Give the author's first and last names in any signal phrase, or add
the author's first initial in the parenthetical reference.

> "Imaginative" applies not only to modern literature but also to
> writing of all periods, whereas "magical" is often used in
> writing about Arthurian romances (A. Wilson 25).

5. TWO OR MORE AUTHORS

For a work with two authors, name both, either in a signal phrase
or in parentheses.

> Carlson and Ventura's stated goal is to introduce Julio Cortázar,
> Marjorie Agosín, and other Latin American writers to an
> audience of English-speaking adolescents (v).

For a work by three or more authors, name the first author followed
by "et al."

> One popular survey of American literature breaks the contents
> into sixteen thematic groupings (Anderson et al. A19-24).

6. ORGANIZATION OR GOVERNMENT AS AUTHOR

Acknowledge the organization either in a signal phrase or in parentheses. It's acceptable to shorten long names.

> The US government can be direct when it wants to be. For
> example, it sternly warns, "If you are overpaid, we will recover
> any payments not due you" (Social Security Administration 12).

7. AUTHOR UNKNOWN

If you don't know the author, use the work's title or a shortened version of the title in the parenthetical reference.

> A powerful editorial in last week's paper asserts that healthy liver donor Mike Hurewitz died because of "frightening" faulty postoperative care ("Every Patient's Nightmare").

8. LITERARY WORKS

When referring to literary works that are available in many different editions, give the page numbers from the edition you are using, followed by information that will let readers of any edition locate the text you are citing.

NOVELS. Give the page and chapter number, separated by a semicolon.

> In *Pride and Prejudice,* Mrs. Bennet shows no warmth toward Jane when she returns from Netherfield (105; ch. 12).

VERSE PLAYS. Give act, scene, and line numbers, separated with periods.

> Macbeth continues the vision theme when he says, "Thou hast no speculation in those eyes / Which thou dost glare with" (3.3.96-97).

POEMS. Give the part and the line numbers (separated by periods). If a poem has only line numbers, use the word "line(s)" only in the first reference.

> Whitman sets up not only opposing adjectives but also opposing nouns in "Song of Myself" when he says, "I am of old and young, of the foolish as much as the wise, / . . . a child as well as a man" (16.330-32).

author   title   publication

One description of the mere in *Beowulf* is "not a pleasant place" (line 1372). Later, it is labeled "the awful place" (1378).

9. WORK IN AN ANTHOLOGY

Name the author(s) of the work, not the editor of the anthology—either in a signal phrase or in parentheses.

"It is the teapots that truly shock," according to Cynthia Ozick in her essay on teapots as metaphor (70).

In *In Short: A Collection of Creative Nonfiction*, readers will find both an essay on Scottish tea (Hiestand) and a piece on teapots as metaphors (Ozick).

10. ENCYCLOPEDIA OR DICTIONARY

Acknowledge an entry in an encyclopedia or dictionary by giving the author's name, if available. For an entry without an author, give the entry's title in parentheses. If entries are arranged alphabetically, no page number is needed.

According to *Funk & Wagnall's New World Encyclopedia*, early in his career Kubrick's main source of income came from "hustling chess games in Washington Square Park" ("Kubrick, Stanley").

11. LEGAL AND HISTORICAL DOCUMENTS

For legal cases and acts of law, name the case or act in a signal phrase or in parentheses. Italicize the name of a legal case.

In 2005, the Supreme Court confirmed in *MGM Studios, Inc. v. Grokster, Ltd.* that peer-to-peer file sharing is copyright infringement.

Do not italicize the titles of laws, acts, or well-known historical documents such as the Declaration of Independence. Give the title and any relevant articles and sections in parentheses. It's fine to use common abbreviations such as "art." or "sec." and to abbreviate well-known titles.

The president is also granted the right to make recess appointments (US Const., art. 2, sec. 2).

12. SACRED TEXT

When citing a sacred text such as the Bible or the Qur'an for the first time, give the title of the edition, and in parentheses give the book, chapter, and verse (or their equivalent), separated by periods. MLA recommends abbreviating the names of the books of the Bible in parenthetical references. Later citations from the same edition do not have to repeat its title.

> The wording from *The New English Bible* follows: "In the beginning of creation, when God made heaven and earth, the earth was without form and void, with darkness over the face of the abyss, and a mighty wind that swept over the surface of the waters" (Gen. 1.1-2).

13. MULTIVOLUME WORK

If you cite more than one volume of a multivolume work, each time you cite one of the volumes, give the volume *and* the page number(s) in parentheses, separated by a colon and a space.

> Sandburg concludes with the following sentence about those paying last respects to Lincoln: "All day long and through the night the unbroken line moved, the home town having its farewell" (4: 413).

If your works-cited list includes only a single volume of a multivolume work, give just the page number in parentheses.

14. TWO OR MORE WORKS CITED TOGETHER

If you're citing two or more works closely together, you will sometimes need to provide a parenthetical reference for each one.

> Tanner (7) and Smith (viii) have looked at works from a cultural perspective.

author   title   publication

If you include both in the same parentheses, separate the references with a semicolon.

> Critics have looked at both *Pride and Prejudice* and *Frankenstein* from a cultural perspective (Tanner 7; Smith viii).

15. SOURCE QUOTED IN ANOTHER SOURCE

When you are quoting text that you found quoted in another source, use the abbreviation "qtd. in" in the parenthetical reference.

> Charlotte Brontë wrote to G. H. Lewes: "Why do you like Miss Austen so very much? I am puzzled on that point" (qtd. in Tanner 7).

16. WORK WITHOUT PAGE NUMBERS

For works without page numbers, including many online sources, identify the source using the author or other information either in a signal phrase or in parentheses.

> Studies show that music training helps children to be better at multitasking later in life ("Hearing the Music").

If the source has chapter, paragraph, or section numbers, use them with the abbreviations "ch.," "par.," or "sec.": ("Hearing the Music," par. 2). Alternatively, you can refer to a heading on a screen to help readers locate text.

> Under the heading "The Impact of the Railroad," Rawls notes that the transcontinental railroad was called an iron horse and a greedy octopus.

For an audio or a video recording, give the hours, minutes, and seconds (separated by colons) as shown on the player: (00:05-08:30).

17. AN ENTIRE WORK OR A ONE-PAGE ARTICLE

If you cite an entire work rather than a part of it, or if you cite a single-page article, there's no need to include page numbers.

> Throughout life, John Adams strove to succeed (McCullough).

MLA-b Notes

Sometimes you may need to give information that doesn't fit into the text itself—to thank people who helped you, to provide additional details, to refer readers to other sources, or to add comments about sources. Such information can be given in a footnote (at the bottom of the page) or an endnote (on a separate page with the heading "Notes" just before your works-cited list). Put a superscript number at the appropriate point in your text, signaling to readers to look for the note with the corresponding number. If you have multiple notes, number them consecutively throughout your paper.

TEXT

This essay will argue that small liberal arts colleges should not recruit athletes and, more specifically, that giving student athletes preferential treatment undermines the larger educational goals.[1]

NOTE

1. I want to thank all those who have contributed to my thinking on this topic, especially my classmates and my teacher Marian Johnson.

MLA-c List of Works Cited

A works-cited list provides full bibliographic information for every source cited in your text. See page 191 for guidelines on formatting this list and page 199 for a sample works-cited list.

Core Elements

MLA style provides a list of "core" elements for documenting sources in a works-cited list. Not all sources will include each of these elements; include as much information as is available for any title you cite. For guidance about specific sources you need to document, see

author   title   publication

the templates and examples on pages 165–89, but here are some general guidelines for how to treat each of the core elements.

CORE ELEMENTS FOR ENTRIES IN A WORKS-CITED LIST

- Author
- Title of the source
- Title of any "container," MLA's term for a larger work in which the source is found—an anthology, a website, a journal or magazine, a database, even a streaming service like *Netflix*
- Editor, translator, director, or other contributors
- Version
- Volume and issue numbers
- Publisher (or sponsor)
- Date of publication
- Location of the source: page numbers, URL, **PERMALINK, DOI**, etc.

The above order is the general order MLA recommends, but there will be exceptions. To document a translated essay that you found in an anthology, for instance, you'd identify the translator after the title of the essay rather than after that of the anthology. Remember that your goal is to tell readers what sources you've consulted and where they can find them. Providing this information is one way you can engage with readers—and enable them to join in the conversation with you and your sources.

AUTHORS AND OTHER CONTRIBUTORS

- If there is one author, put the last name first, followed by a comma and the first name: Morrison, Toni.
- If there are two authors, list the first author last name first and the second one first name first: Lunsford, Andrea, and Lisa Ede. Put their names in the order given in the work. For three or more authors, give the first author's name followed by "et al.": Greenblatt, Stephen, et al.
- Include any middle names or initials: Toklas, Alice B.

- If there's no known author, start the entry with the title.
- If you're citing an editor, translator, or other contributors, specify their role. If there are multiple contributors, put the one whose work you wish to highlight before the title, and list any others you want to mention after the title. For contributors named before the title, specify their role after the name: Fincher, David, director. For those named after the title, specify their role first: directed by David Fincher.

TITLES

- Include any subtitles and capitalize all the words except for articles ("a," "an," "the"), prepositions ("to," "at," "from," and so on), and coordinating conjunctions ("and," "but," "for," "or," "nor," "yet")—unless they are the first or last word of a title or subtitle.
- Italicize the titles of books, periodicals, and other long works: *Pride and Prejudice*, *Wired*.
- Put quotation marks around the titles of articles and other short works: "Letter from Birmingham Jail."
- To document a source that has no title, describe it without italics or quotation marks: Letter to the author, Review of rap concert.

VERSIONS

- If you cite a source that's available in more than one version, specify the one you consulted in your works-cited entry. Write ordinal numbers with numerals, and abbreviate "edition": 2nd ed. Write out names of specific versions, and capitalize if the name is a **PROPER NOUN**: King James Version, unabridged version, director's cut.

NUMBERS

- If you cite a book that's published in multiple volumes, indicate the volume number. Abbreviate "volume," and write the number as a numeral: vol. 2.
- Indicate any volume and issue numbers of journals, abbreviating both "volume" and "number": vol. 123, no. 4.

PUBLISHERS

- Write publishers' names in full, but omit business words like "Inc." or "Company."

- For university presses, use "U" for "University" and "P" for "Press": Princeton UP, U of California P.

DATES

- Whether to give just the year or to include the month and day depends on the source. Give the full date that you find there. If the date is unknown, simply omit it.

- Abbreviate the months except for May, June, and July: Jan., Feb., Mar., Apr., Aug., Sept., Oct., Nov., Dec.—9 Sept. 2020.

- For books, give the year of publication: 1948. If a book lists more than one date, use the most recent one.

- Periodicals may be published annually, monthly, seasonally, weekly, or daily. Give the full date that you find in the periodical: 2019, Apr. 2019, Spring 2019, 16 Apr. 2019.

- For online sources, use the copyright date or the most recent update, giving the full date that you find in the source. If the source does not give a date, use the date of access: Accessed 6 June 2020. And if the source includes the time when it was posted or updated, give the time along with the date: 18 Oct. 2020, 9:20 a.m.

- Because online sources may change or even disappear, the date of access can be important for indicating the exact version you've cited. Some instructors may require this information, so we've included access dates in this chapter's guidelines for specific kinds of sources, but check with your instructor to see if you're required to include this information.

LOCATION

- For most print articles and other short works, give a page number or range of pages: p. 24, pp. 24-35. For articles that are not on consecutive pages, give the first page number with a plus sign: pp. 24+.

- Indicate the location of most online sources by giving their URL, omitting "http://" or "https://." If a source has a **PERMALINK** (a stable version of its URL), give that instead. Some of the scholarly journal articles you'll find in a database provide a **DOI** (a stable digital object identifier) instead; if so, give that.

- For physical objects that you find in a museum, archive, or some other place, give the name of the place and its city: Menil Collection, Houston. Omit the city if it's part of the place's name: Boston Public Library.

- For performances or other live presentations, name the venue and its city: Mark Taper Forum, Los Angeles. Omit the city if it's part of the place's name: Berkeley Repertory Theatre.

PUNCTUATION

- Use a period after the author name(s) that start an entry (Morrison, Toni.) and the title of the source you're documenting (*Beloved.*)

- Use a comma between the author's last and first names: Ede, Lisa.

- Some URLs will not fit on one line. MLA does not specify where to break a URL, but we recommend breaking it before a punctuation mark. Do *not* add a hyphen.

- Sometimes you'll need to provide information about more than one work for a single source—for instance, when you cite an article from a periodical that you access through a database. MLA refers to the periodical and database (or any other entity that holds a source) as "containers" and specifies certain punctuation. Use commas between elements within each container, and put a period at the end of each container. For example:

  Semuels, Alana. "The Future Will Be Quiet." *The Atlantic*, Apr. 2016,
  pp. 19-20. *ProQuest*, search.proquest.com/docview
  /1777443553?accountid+42654. Accessed 5 Apr. 2016.

The guidelines that follow will help you document kinds of sources you're likely to use. The first section shows how to acknowledge

author   title   publication

authors and other contributors and applies to all kinds of sources—print, online, or others. Later sections show how to treat titles, publication information, location, and access information for many specific kinds of sources. In general, provide as much information as possible for each source—enough to tell readers how to find a source if they wish to access it themselves.

Authors and Other Contributors

When you name authors and other contributors in your citations, you are crediting them for their work and letting readers know who's in on the conversation. The following guidelines for citing authors and other contributors apply to all sources you cite: in print, online, or in some other media.

1. ONE AUTHOR

Author's Last Name, First Name. *Title*. Publisher, Date.

Anderson, Curtis. *The Long Tail: Why the Future of Business Is Selling Less of More.* Hyperion, 2006.

2. TWO AUTHORS

1st Author's Last Name, First Name, and 2nd Author's First and Last Names. *Title*. Publisher, Date.

Lunsford, Andrea, and Lisa Ede. *Singular Texts/Plural Authors: Perspectives on Collaborative Writing*. Southern Illinois UP, 1990.

3. THREE OR MORE AUTHORS

1st Author's Last Name, First Name, et al. *Title*. Publisher, Date.

Sebranek, Patrick, et al. *Writers INC: A Guide to Writing, Thinking, and Learning.* Write Source, 1990.

4. TWO OR MORE WORKS BY THE SAME AUTHOR

Give the author's name in the first entry, and then use three hyphens in the author slot for each of the subsequent works, listing them alphabetically by the first important word of each title.

> Author's Last Name, First Name. *Title That Comes First Alphabetically.* Publisher, Date.
> ---. *Title That Comes Next Alphabetically.* Publisher, Date.
> Kaplan, Robert D. *The Coming Anarchy: Shattering the Dreams of the Post Cold War.* Random House, 2000.
> ---. *Eastward to Tartary: Travels in the Balkans, the Middle East, and the Caucasus.* Random House, 2000.

5. AUTHOR AND EDITOR OR TRANSLATOR

> Author's Last Name, First Name. *Title.* Role by First and Last Names, Publisher, Date.
> Austen, Jane. *Emma.* Edited by Stephen M. Parrish, W. W. Norton, 2000.
> Dostoevsky, Fyodor. *Crime and Punishment.* Translated by Richard Pevear and Larissa Volokhonsky, Vintage Books, 1993.

Start with the editor or translator if you are focusing on that contribution rather than the author's.

> Pevear, Richard, and Larissa Volokhonsky, translators. *Crime and Punishment.* By Fyodor Dostoevsky, Vintage Books, 1993.

6. NO AUTHOR OR EDITOR

When there's no known author or editor, start with the title.

> *The Turner Collection in the Clore Gallery.* Tate Publications, 1987.
> "Being Invisible Closer to Reality." *The Atlanta Journal-Constitution,* 11 Aug. 2008, p. A3.

author   title   publication

7. ORGANIZATION OR GOVERNMENT AS AUTHOR

Organization Name. *Title.* Publisher, Date.

Diagram Group. *The Macmillan Visual Desk Reference.* Macmillan, 1993.

For a government publication, give the name of the government first, followed by the names of any department and agency.

United States, Department of Health and Human Services, National

Institute of Mental Health. *Autism Spectrum Disorders.*
Government Printing Office, 2004.

When the organization is both author and publisher, start with the title and list the organization only as the publisher.

Stylebook on Religion 2000: A Reference Guide and Usage Manual.
Catholic News Service, 2002.

Articles and Other Short Works

Articles, essays, reviews, and other shorts works are found in journals, magazines, newspapers, other periodicals, and books—all of which you may find in print, online, or in a database. For most short works, you'll need to provide information about the author, the titles of both the short work and the longer work, any page numbers, and various kinds of publication information, all explained below.

8. ARTICLE IN A JOURNAL

PRINT

Author's Last Name, First Name. "Title of Article." *Name of Journal*, Volume, Issue, Date, Pages.

Cooney, Brian C. "Considering *Robinson Crusoe*'s 'Liberty of Conscience' in an Age of Terror." *College English*, vol. 69, no. 3, Jan. 2007, pp. 197-215.

Documentation Map (MLA)

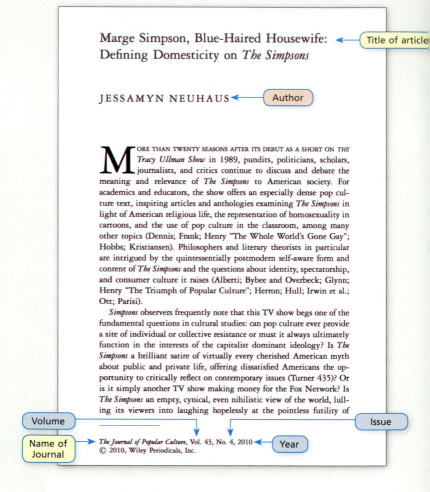

Marge Simpson, Blue-Haired Housewife: Defining Domesticity on *The Simpsons* — Title of article

JESSAMYN NEUHAUS — Author

MORE THAN TWENTY SEASONS AFTER ITS DEBUT AS A SHORT ON *THE Tracy Ullman Show* in 1989, pundits, politicians, scholars, journalists, and critics continue to discuss and debate the meaning and relevance of *The Simpsons* to American society. For academics and educators, the show offers an especially dense pop culture text, inspiring articles and anthologies examining *The Simpsons* in light of American religious life, the representation of homosexuality in cartoons, and the use of pop culture in the classroom, among many other topics (Dennis; Frank; Henry "The Whole World's Gone Gay"; Hobbs; Kristiansen). Philosophers and literary theorists in particular are intrigued by the quintessentially postmodern self-aware form and content of *The Simpsons* and the questions about identity, spectatorship, and consumer culture it raises (Alberti; Bybee and Overbeck; Glynn; Henry "The Triumph of Popular Culture"; Herron; Hull; Irwin et al.; Ott; Parisi).

Simpsons observers frequently note that this TV show begs one of the fundamental questions in cultural studies: can pop culture ever provide a site of individual or collective resistance or must it always ultimately function in the interests of the capitalist dominant ideology? Is *The Simpsons* a brilliant satire of virtually every cherished American myth about public and private life, offering dissatisfied Americans the opportunity to critically reflect on contemporary issues (Turner 435)? Or is it simply another TV show making money for the Fox Network? Is *The Simpsons* an empty, cynical, even nihilistic view of the world, lulling its viewers into laughing hopelessly at the pointless futility of

Volume — Issue

Name of Journal — *The Journal of Popular Culture*, Vol. 43, No. 4, 2010 — Year
© 2010, Wiley Periodicals, Inc.

Neuhaus, Jessamyn. "Marge Simpson, Blue-Haired Housewife: Defining Domesticity on *The Simpsons." The Journal of Popular Culture*, vol. 43, no. 4, 2010, pp. 761-81.

Documentation Map (MLA)

ARTICLE IN AN ONLINE MAGAZINE

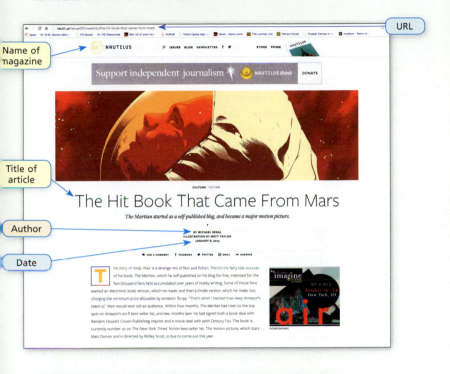

URL

Name of magazine

Title of article

Author

Date

Segal, Michael. "The Hit Book That Came from Mars." *Nautilus*,
8 Jan. 2015, nautil.us/issue/20/creativity/the-hit-book-that
-came-from-mars. Accessed 10 Oct. 2016.

ONLINE

Author's Last Name, First Name. "Title of Article." *Name of Journal,*
Volume, Issue, Date, Pages (if any), URL. Accessed Day Month
Year.

Gleckman, Jason. "Shakespeare as Poet or Playwright? The Player's
Speech in *Hamlet.*" *Early Modern Literary Studies,* vol. 11, no.
3, Jan. 2006, purl.oclc.org/emls/11-3/glechaml.htm. Accessed 31
Mar. 2020.

9. ARTICLE IN A MAGAZINE

PRINT

Author's Last Name, First Name. "Title of Article." *Name of*
Magazine, Date, Pages.

Neyfakh, Leon. "The Future of Getting Arrested." *The Atlantic,*
Jan.-Feb. 2015, pp. 26+.

ONLINE

Author's Last Name, First Name. "Title of Article." *Name of*
Magazine, Date on web, Pages (if any), URL. Accessed Day
Month Year.

Khazan, Olga. "Forgetting and Remembering Your First Language."
The Atlantic, 24 July 2014, www.theatlantic.com/international
/archive/2014/07/learning-forgetting-and-remembering-your
-first-language/374906/. Accessed 2 Apr. 2020.

10. ARTICLE IN A NEWSPAPER

PRINT

Author's Last Name, First Name. "Title of Article." *Name of*
Newspaper, Date, Pages.

Saulny, Susan, and Jacques Steinberg. "On College Forms, a Question
of Race Can Perplex." *The New York Times,* 14 June 2011, p. A1.

author   title   publication

Documentation Map (MLA)

JOURNAL ARTICLE ACCESSED THROUGH A DATABASE

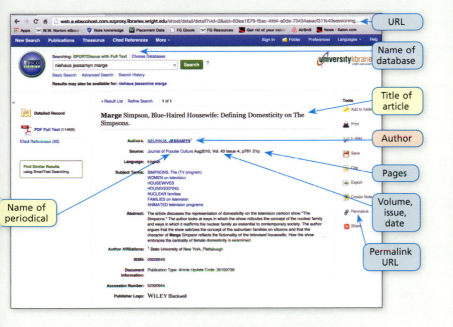

Neuhaus, Jessamyn. "Marge Simpson, Blue-Haired Housewife:
Defining Domesticity on The Simpsons." *Journal of Popular
Culture*, vol. 43, no. 4, Aug. 2010, pp. 761-81. *SPORT
Discus with Full Text*, http://eds.a.ebscohost.com.ezproxy
.libraries.wright.edu/eds/detail/detail?vid=3&sid=1115d897
-ef7a-478f-83ad80b949f71078%40sessionmgr4009&hid=4110
&bdata=JnNpdGU9ZWRzLWxpdmU%3d#. Accessed 24 Mar.
2020.

To document a particular edition of a newspaper, list the edition ("late ed.," "natl. ed.," and so on) after the date. If a section of the newspaper is numbered, put that detail after the edition information.

> Burns, John F., and Miguel Helft. "Under Pressure, YouTube Withdraws Muslim Cleric's Videos." *The New York Times,* 4 Nov. 2010, late ed., sec. 1, p. 13.

ONLINE

> Author's Last Name, First Name. "Title of Article." *Name of Newspaper*, Date on web, URL. Accessed Day Month Year.
>
> Banerjee, Neela. "Proposed Religion-Based Program for Federal Inmates Is Canceled." *The New York Times,* 28 Oct. 2006, www.nytimes.com/2006/10/28/us/28prison.html?_r=0. Accessed 4 Apr. 2020.

11. ARTICLE ACCESSED THROUGH A DATABASE

> Author's Last Name, First Name. "Title of Article." *Name of Periodical*, Volume, Issue, Date, Pages. Name of Database, DOI or URL. Accessed Day Month Year.
>
> Stalter, Sunny. "Subway Ride and Subway System in Hart Crane's 'The Tunnel.'" *Journal of Modern Literature,* vol. 33, no. 2, Jan. 2010, pp. 70-91. *JSTOR*, doi: 10.2979/jml.2010.33.2.70. Accessed 30 Mar. 2020.

12. ENTRY IN A REFERENCE WORK

PRINT

> Author's Last Name, First Name (if any). "Title of Entry." *Title of Reference Book*, edited by Editor's First and Last Names (if any), Edition number, Publisher, Date, Pages.
>
> "California." *The New Columbia Encyclopedia*, edited by William H. Harris and Judith S. Levey, 4th ed., Columbia UP, 1975, pp. 423-24.

author   title   publication

"Feminism." *Longman Dictionary of American English*, Longman,
1983, p. 252.

If there's no author given, start with the title of the entry.

ONLINE

Document online reference works the same as print ones, adding the
URL and access date after the date of publication.

"Baseball." *The Columbia Electronic Encyclopedia*, edited by
Paul Lagassé, 6th ed., Columbia UP, 2012. www.infoplease
.com/encyclopedia. Accessed 25 May 2020.

13. EDITORIAL

PRINT

"Title of Editorial." *Name of Periodical*, Date, Page. Editorial.

"Gas, Cigarettes Are Safe to Tax." *The Lakeville Journal*, 17 Feb.
2005, p. A10. Editorial.

ONLINE

"Title of Editorial." *Name of Periodical*, Date on web, URL.
Accessed Day Month Year. Editorial.

"Keep the Drinking Age at 21." *Chicago Tribune*, 28 Aug. 2008,
articles.chicagotribune.com/2008-08-26/news/0808250487_1
_binge-drinking-drinking-age-alcohol-related-crashes. Accessed
26 Apr. 2020. Editorial.

14. LETTER TO THE EDITOR

Author's Last Name, First Name. "Title of Letter (if any)." Letter.
Name of Periodical, Date on web, URL. Accessed Day Month
Year.

Pinker, Steven. "Language Arts." Letter. *The New Yorker*, 4 June
2012, www.newyorker.com/magazine/2012/06/04/language
-arts-2. Accessed 6 Apr. 2020.

15. REVIEW

PRINT

Reviewer's Last Name, First Name. "Title of Review." Review of
    Title, by Author's First and Last Names. *Name of
    Periodical*, Date, Pages.

Frank, Jeffrey. "Body Count." Review of *The Exception*, by Christian
    Jungersen. *The New Yorker*, 30 July 2007, pp. 86-87.

If a review has no author or title, start with what's being reviewed:

Review of *Ways to Disappear*, by Idra Novey. *The New Yorker*, 28
    Mar. 2016, p. 79.

ONLINE

Reviewer's Last Name, First Name. "Title of Review." Review of
    Title, by Author's First and Last Names. *Name of Periodical*,
    Date, URL. Accessed Day Month Year.

Donadio, Rachel. "Italy's Great, Mysterious Storyteller." Review
    of *My Brilliant Friend*, by Elena Ferrante. *The New York
    Review of Books*, 18 Dec. 2014, www.nybooks.com
    /articles/2014/12/18/italys-great-mysterious-storyteller.
    Accessed 28 Sept. 2020.

16. COMMENT ON AN ONLINE ARTICLE

Commenter. Comment on "Title of Article." *Name of Periodical*,
    Date posted, Time posted, URL. Accessed Day Month Year.

Simone de Rochefort. Comment on "The Post-Disaster Artist."
    Polygon, 5 May 2020, 4:33 p.m., www.polygon.com/2020
    /5/5/21246679/josh-trank-capone-interview-fantastic-four
    -chronicle#comments. Accessed 17 June 2020.

Books and Parts of Books

For most books, you'll need to provide information about the author, the title, the publisher, and the year of publication. If you found the book inside a larger volume, a database, or some other work, be sure to specify that as well.

17. BASIC ENTRIES FOR A BOOK

PRINT

Author's Last Name, First Name. *Title*. Publisher, Year of
    publication.

Watson, Brad. *Miss Jane*. W. W. Norton, 2016.

EBOOK

Document an ebook as you would a print book, but add information about the ebook—or the type of ebook if you know it.

Watson, Brad. *Miss Jane*. Ebook, W. W. Norton, 2016.

Watson, Brad. *Miss Jane*. Kindle ed., W. W. Norton, 2016.

IN A DATABASE

Author's Last Name, First Name. *Title*. Publisher, Year of
    publication. *Name of Database*, DOI or URL. Accessed Day
    Month Year.

Anderson, Sherwood. *Winesburg, Ohio*. B. W. Huebsch, 1919.
    Bartleby.com, www.bartleby.com/156/. Accessed 8 Apr. 2020.

18. ANTHOLOGY

Last Name, First Name, editor. *Title*. Publisher, Year of publication.

Kitchen, Judith, and Mary Paumier Jones, editors. *In Short: A
    Collection of Brief Nonfiction*. W. W. Norton, 1996.

19. WORK IN AN ANTHOLOGY

Author's Last Name, First Name. "Title of Work." *Title of
    Anthology*, edited by First and Last Names, Publisher, Year of
    publication, Pages.

Documentation Map (MLA)

PRINT BOOK

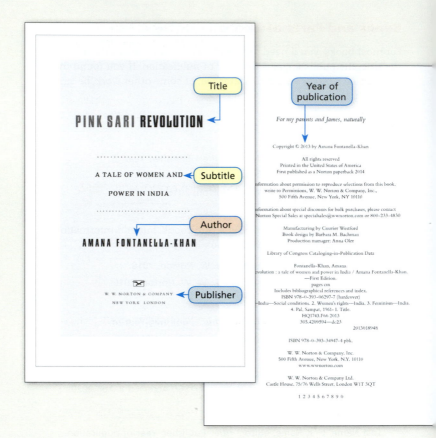

Fontanella-Khan, Amana. *Pink Sari Revolution: A Tale of Women and Power in India.* W. W. Norton, 2013.

Achebe, Chinua. "Uncle Ben's Choice." *The Seagull Reader:*
Literature, edited by Joseph Kelly, W. W. Norton, 2005, pp.
23-27.

TWO OR MORE WORKS FROM ONE ANTHOLOGY

Prepare an entry for each selection by author and title, followed by
the anthology editors' last names and the pages of the selection. Then
include an entry for the anthology itself (see no. 18).

Author's Last Name, First Name. "Title of Work." Anthology
Editors' Last Names, Pages.

Hiestand, Emily. "Afternoon Tea." Kitchen and Jones, pp. 65-67.

Ozick, Cynthia. "The Shock of Teapots." Kitchen and Jones, pp.
68-71.

20. MULTIVOLUME WORK

ALL VOLUMES

Author's Last Name, First Name. *Title of Work.* Publisher, Year(s) of
publication. Number of vols.

Churchill, Winston. *The Second World War.* Houghton Mifflin, 1948-
53. 6 vols.

SINGLE VOLUME

Author's Last Name, First Name. *Title of Work.* Vol. number,
Publisher, Year of publication. Number of vols.

Sandburg, Carl. *Abraham Lincoln: The War Years.* Vol. 2, Harcourt,
Brace & World, 1939. 4 vols.

21. BOOK IN A SERIES

Author's Last Name, First Name. *Title of Book.* Edited by First and
Last Names, Publisher, Year of publication. Series Title.

Walker, Alice. *Everyday Use.* Edited by Barbara T. Christian, Rutgers
UP, 1994. Women Writers: Texts and Contexts.

22. GRAPHIC NARRATIVE

> Author's Last Name, First Name. *Title.* Publisher, Year of publication.
> Bechdel, Alison. *Fun Home: A Family Tragicomedy.* Houghton Mifflin, 2006.

If the work has both an author and an illustrator, start with the one whose work is more relevant to your research, and label the role of anyone who's not an author.

> Pekar, Harvey. *Bob & Harv's Comics.* Illustrated by R. Crumb, Running Press, 1996.
> Crumb, R., illustrator. *Bob & Harv's Comics.* By Harvey Pekar, Running Press, 1996.

23. SACRED TEXT

If you cite a specific edition of a religious text, you need to include it in your works-cited list.

> *The New English Bible with the Apocrypha.* Oxford UP, 1971.
> *The Torah: A Modern Commentary.* Edited by W. Gunther Plaut, Union of American Hebrew Congregations, 1981.

24. EDITION OTHER THAN THE FIRST

> Author's Last Name, First Name. *Title.* Name *or* number of edition, Publisher, Year of publication.
> Fowler, H. W. *A Dictionary of Modern English.* 2nd ed., Oxford UP, 1965.

25. REPUBLISHED WORK

> Author's Last Name, First Name. *Title.* Year of original publication. Current publisher, Year of republication.
> Bierce, Ambrose. *Civil War Stories.* 1909. Dover, 1994.

author   title   publication

26. FOREWORD, INTRODUCTION, PREFACE, OR AFTERWORD

Part Author's Last Name, First Name. Name of Part. *Title of Book*, by Author's First and Last Names, Publisher, Year of publication, Pages.

Tanner, Tony. Introduction. *Pride and Prejudice*, by Jane Austen, Penguin, 1972, pp. 7-46.

27. PUBLISHED LETTER

Letter Writer's Last Name, First Name. Letter to First and Last Names. Day Month Year. *Title of Book*, edited by First and Last Names, Publisher, Year of publication, Pages.

White, E. B. Letter to Carol Angell. 28 May 1970. *Letters of E. B. White*, edited by Dorothy Lobarno Guth, Harper & Row, 1976, p. 600.

28. PAPER AT A CONFERENCE

PAPER PUBLISHED IN CONFERENCE PROCEEDINGS

Author's Last Name, First Name. "Title of Paper." *Title of Published Conference Proceedings*, edited by First and Last Names, Publisher, Year of publication, Pages.

Flower, Linda. "Literate Action." *Composition in the Twenty-first Century: Crisis and Change*, edited by Lynn Z. Bloom et al., Southern Illinois UP, 1996, pp. 249-60.

PAPER HEARD AT A CONFERENCE

Author's Last Name, First Name. "Title of Paper." Title of Conference, Day Month Year, Location, City.

Hern, Katie. "Inside an Accelerated Reading and Writing Classroom." Conference on Acceleration in Developmental Education, 15 June 2016, Sheraton Inner Harbor Hotel, Baltimore.

29. DISSERTATION

> Author's Last Name, First Name. *Title.* Year. Institution, PhD
> dissertation. *Name of Database,* URL. Accessed Day Month
> Year.

> Simington, Maire Orav. *Chasing the American Dream Post World
> War II: Perspectives from Literature and Advertising.* 2003.
> Arizona State University, PhD dissertation. *ProQuest,* search
> .proquest.com/docview/305340098?accountid=42654. Accessed
> 5 Oct. 2020.

For an unpublished dissertation, end with the institution and a description of the work.

> Kim, Loel. *Students Respond to Teacher Comments: A Comparison
> of Online Written and Voice Modalities.* 1998. Carnegie
> Mellon U, PhD dissertation.

Websites

Many sources are available in multiple media—for example, a print periodical that is also on the web and contained in digital databases—but some are published only on websites. This section covers the latter.

30. ENTIRE WEBSITE

> Last Name, First Name, role. *Title of Site.* Publisher, Date, URL.
> Accessed Day Month Year.

> Zalta, Edward N., principal editor. *Stanford Encyclopedia of Philosophy.*
> Metaphysics Research Lab, Center for the Study of Language,
> Stanford U, 1995-2015, plato.stanford.edu/index.html. Accessed
> 21 Apr. 2020.

PERSONAL WEBSITE

> Author's Last Name, First Name. *Title of Site.* Date, URL. Accessed
> Day Month Year.

> Heath, Shirley Brice. *Shirley Brice Heath.* 2015, shirleybriceheath.net.
> Accessed 6 June 2020.

author   title   publication

Documentation Map (MLA)

WORK ON A WEBSITE

URL

Title of site

Publisher

Title of work

Authors

Date posted

McIlwain, John, et al. "Housing in America: Integrating Housing,
Health, and Resilience in a Changing Environment." *Urban
Land Institute*, Urban Land Institute, 28 Aug. 2014, uli.org
/report/housing-in-america-housing-health-resilience.
Accessed 17 May 2020.

31. WORK ON A WEBSITE

Author's Last Name, First Name (if any). "Title of Work." *Title of Site*, Publisher, Date, URL. Accessed Day Month Year.

"Global Minnesota: Immigrants Past and Present." *Immigration History Research Center*, U of Minnesota, 2015, cla.umn.edu /ihrc. Accessed 25 May 2020.

32. BLOG ENTRY

Author's Last Name, First Name. "Title of Blog Entry." *Title of Blog*, Date, URL. Accessed Day Month Year.

Hollmichel, Stefanie. "Bringing Up the Bodies." *So Many Books*, 10 Feb. 2014, somanybooksblog.com/2014/02/10/bring-up -the-bodies/. Accessed 12 Feb. 2020.

Document a whole blog as you would an entire website (no. 30) and a comment on a blog as you would a comment on an online article (no. 16).

33. WIKI

"Title of Entry." *Title of Wiki*, Publisher, Date, URL. Accessed Day Month Year.

"Pi." *Wikipedia*, Wikimedia Foundation, 28 Aug. 2013, en.wikipedia .org/wiki/Pi. Accessed 25 Oct. 2020.

Personal Communication and Social Media

34. PERSONAL LETTER

Sender's Last Name, First Name. Letter to the author. Day Month Year.

Quindlen, Anna. Letter to the author. 11 Apr. 2013.

35. EMAIL

Sender's Last Name, First Name. "Subject Line." Received by First and Last Names, Day Month Year.

author   title   publication

Smith, William. "Teaching Grammar—Some Thoughts." Received by
Richard Bullock, 19 Nov. 2013.

36. TEXT MESSAGE

Sender's Last Name, First Name. Text message. Received by First and
Last Names, Day Month Year.

Douglass, Joanne. Text message. Received by Kim Yi, 4 June 2015.

37. POST TO AN ONLINE FORUM

Author. "Subject line" or "Full text of short untitled post." *Name of
Forum*, Day Month Year, URL.

@somekiryu. "What's the hardest part about writing for you?"
Reddit, 22 Apr. 2016, redd.it/4fyni0.

38. POST TO *TWITTER*, *FACEBOOK*, OR OTHER SOCIAL MEDIA

Author. "Full text of short untitled post" or "Title" or Descriptive
label. *Name of Site*, Day Month Year, Time, URL. Accessed Day
Month Year.

@POTUS44 (Barack Obama). "I'm proud of the @NBA for taking a
stand against gun violence. Sympathy for victims isn't
enough—change requires all of us speaking up." *Twitter*,
23 Dec. 2015, 1:21 p.m., twitter.com/POTUS44/status
/679773729749078016. Accessed 20 Apr. 2020.

Black Lives Matter. "Rise and Grind! Did you sign this petition yet?
We now have a sign on for ORGANIZATIONS to lend their
support." *Facebook*, 23 Oct. 2015, 11:30 a.m., www.facebook
.com/BlackLivesMatter/photos/a.294807204023865.1073741829
.180212755483311/504711973033386/?type=3&theater.
Accessed 20 Apr. 2020.

@quarterlifepoetry. Illustrated poem about girl at Target. *Instagram*,
22 Jan. 2015, www.instagram.com/p/yLO6fSurRH/. Accessed 20
Apr. 2020.

Audio, Visual, and Other Sources

39. ADVERTISEMENT

PRINT

Name of Product or Company. Advertisement *or* Description of ad. *Title of Periodical*, Date, Page.

Cal Alumni Association. Sports Merchandise ad. *California*, Spring 2016, p. 3.

AUDIO OR VIDEO

Name of Product or Company. Advertisement *or* Description of ad. Date. *Name of Host Site*, URL. Accessed Day Month Year.

Microsoft. Super Bowl commercial. 28 Jan. 2020. *YouTube*, www .youtube.com/watch?v=_xPn4DXIj5w. Accessed 17 June 2020.

40. ART

ORIGINAL

Artist's Last Name, First Name. *Title of Art.* Year created, Site, City.

Van Gogh, Vincent. *The Potato Eaters.* 1885, Van Gogh Museum, Amsterdam.

REPRODUCTION

Artist's Last Name, First Name. *Title of Art.* Year created. *Title of Book*, by First and Last Names, Publisher, Year of publication, Page.

Van Gogh, Vincent. *The Potato Eaters.* 1885. *History of Art: A Survey of the Major Visual Arts from the Dawn of History to the Present Day*, by H. W. Janson, Prentice-Hall/Harry N. Abrams, 1969, p. 508.

ONLINE

Artist's Last Name, First Name. *Title of Art.* Year created. *Name of Site*, URL. Accessed Day Month Year.

Warhol, Andy. *Self-portrait.* 1979. *J. Paul Getty Museum*, www.getty
.edu/art/collection/objects/106971/andy-warhol-self-portrait
-american-1979/. Accessed 20 Jan. 2020.

41. CARTOON

PRINT

Author's Last Name, First Name. "Title of Cartoon." *Title of
Periodical*, Date, Page. Cartoon.

Chast, Roz. "The Three Wise Men of Thanksgiving." *The New Yorker*,
1 Dec. 2003, p. 174. Cartoon.

ONLINE

Author's Last Name, First Name. "Title of Cartoon." *Title of Site*,
Date, URL. Accessed Day Month Year. Cartoon.

Munroe, Randall. "Up Goer Five." *xkcd*, 12 Nov. 2012, xkcd
.com/1133/. Accessed 22 Apr. 2020. Cartoon.

42. SUPREME COURT CASE

United States, Supreme Court. *First Defendant v. Second
Defendant.* Date of decision. *Name of Source Site*, Publisher,
URL. Accessed Day Month Year.

United States, Supreme Court. *District of Columbia v. Heller.* 26 June
2008. *Legal Information Institute*, Cornell U Law School, www
.law.cornell.edu/supct/html/07-290.ZS.html. Accessed 25 Feb.
2020.

43. FILM

Name individuals based on the focus of your project—the director,
the screenwriter, the cinematographer, or someone else. If your essay
focuses on one or more contributors, you may put their names before
the title.

Title of Film. Role by First and Last Names, Production Studio, Date.
Breakfast at Tiffany's. Directed by Blake Edwards, Paramount, 1961.

STREAMING

Title of Film. Role by First and Last Names, Production Studio,
Date. *Streaming Service,* URL. Accessed Day Month Year.

Interstellar. Directed by Christopher Nolan, Paramount, 2014.
Amazon Prime Video, www.amazon.com/Interstellar-Matthew
-McConaughey/dp/B00TU9UFTS. Accessed 2 May 2020.

44. INTERVIEW

If the interviewer's name is known and relevant to your argument,
include it after the word "Interview" or the title: Interview by Stephen
Colbert.

BROADCAST

Subject's Last Name, First Name. Interview *or* "Title of Interview."
Title of Program, Network, Day Month Year.

Gates, Henry Louis, Jr. Interview. *Fresh Air,* NPR, 9 Apr. 2002.

PUBLISHED

Subject's Last Name, First Name. Interview *or* "Title of Interview."
Title of Publication, Date, Pages.

Stone, Oliver. Interview. *Esquire,* Nov. 2004, pp. 170-71.

PERSONAL

Subject's Last Name, First Name. Personal interview. Day Month Year.

Roddick, Andy. Personal interview. 17 Aug. 2013.

45. MAP

If the title doesn't make clear it's a map, add a label at the end.

"Title of Map." Publisher, URL. Accessed Day Month Year.

"National Highway System." US Department of Transportation
Federal Highway Administration, www.fhwa.dot.gov/planning
/images/nhs.pdf. Accessed 10 May 2020. Map.

author   title   publication

46. MUSICAL SCORE

Composer's Last Name, First Name. *Title of Composition.* Year of
        composition. Publisher, Year of publication.

Stravinsky, Igor. *Petrushka*. 1911. W. W. Norton, 1967.

47. ONLINE VIDEO

Author's Last Name, First Name. *Title. Name of Host Site*, Date,
        URL. Accessed Day Month Year.

Westbrook, Adam. *Cause/Effect: The Unexpected Origins of Terrible
        Things. Vimeo*, 9 Sept. 2014, vimeo.com/105681474. Accessed
        20 Dec. 2020.

48. ORAL PRESENTATION

Presenter's Last Name, First Name. "Title of Presentation."
        Sponsoring Institution, Date, Location.

Cassin, Michael. "Nature in the Raw—The Art of Landscape
        Painting." Berkshire Institute for Lifelong Learning, 24 Mar.
        2005, Clark Art Institute, Williamstown, MA.

49. PODCAST

If you accessed a podcast online, give the URL and date of access; if
you accessed it through a service such as Stitcher or Spotify, indicate
that instead.

Last Name, First Name, role. "Title of Episode." *Title of Program*,
        season, episode, Sponsor, Date, URL. Accessed Day Month Year.

Koenig, Sarah, host. "DUSTWUN." *Serial*, season 2, episode 1, WBEZ,
        10 Dec. 2015, serialpodcast.org/season-two/1/dustwun.
        Accessed 23 Apr. 2020.

Foss, Gilad, author and performer. "Aquaman's Brother-in-Law."
        Superhero Temp Agency, season 1, episode 1, 16 Apr. 2015.
        Stitcher.

50. RADIO PROGRAM

Last Name, First Name, role. "Title of Episode." *Title of Program*, Station, Day Month Year of broadcast, URL. Accessed Day Month Year.

Glass, Ira, host. "In Defense of Ignorance." *This American Life*, WBEZ, 22 Apr. 2016, thisamericanlife.org/radio-archives /episode/585/in-defense-of-ignorance. Accessed 2 May 2020.

51. SOUND RECORDING

ONLINE

Last Name, First Name. "Title of Work." *Title of Album*, Distributor, Date. *Name of Audio Service.*

Simone, Nina. "To Be Young, Gifted and Black." *Black Gold*, RCA Records, 1969. *Spotify*.

CD

Last Name, First Name. "Title of Work." *Title of Album*, Distributor, Date.

Brown, Greg. "Canned Goods." *The Live One*, Red House, 1995.

52. TV SHOW

Name contributors based on the focus of your project—director, writers, actors, or others. If there's a key contributor, you might include that contributor's name and role before the episode title.

"Title of Episode." *Title of Program*, role by First and Last Names, season, episode, Network, Day Month Year.

"The Silencer." *Criminal Minds*, written by Erica Messer, season 8, episode 1, NBC, 26 Sept. 2012.

DVD

"Title of Episode." Broadcast Year. *Title of DVD*, role by First and Last Names, season, episode, Production Studio, Release Year, disc number.

author   title   publication

"The Pants Tent." 2003. *Curb Your Enthusiasm: Season One*,
        performance by Larry David, season 1, episode 1, HBO Video,
        2006, disc 1.

ONLINE

"Title of Episode." *Title of Program*, role by First and Last Names (if
        any), season, episode, Production Studio, Day Month Year.
        Name of Host Site, URL. Accessed Day Month Year.

"Shadows in the Glass." *Marvel's Daredevil*, season 1, episode 8,
        Netflix, 10 Apr. 2015. *Netflix*, www.netflix.com/watch
        /80018198. Accessed 3 Nov. 2020.

53. VIDEO GAME

Last Name, First Name, role. *Title of Game*. Distributor, Date of
        release. Gaming System or Platform.

Metzen, Chris, and James Waugh, writers. *StarCraft II: Legacy of the
        Void*. Blizzard Entertainment, 2015. OS X.

MLA-d Formatting a Research Paper

Name, course, title. MLA does not require a separate title page. In
the upper left-hand corner of your first page, include your name,
your professor's name, the name of the course, and the date. Center
the title of your paper on the line after the date; capitalize it as you
would a book title.

Page numbers. In the upper right-hand corner of each page, one-
half inch below the top of the page, include your last name and the
page number. Number pages consecutively throughout your paper.

Font, spacing, margins, and indents. Choose a font that is easy to
read (such as Times New Roman) and that provides a clear contrast
between regular and italic text. Double-space the entire paper, includ-

ing your works-cited list. Set one-inch margins at the top, bottom, and sides of your text; do not justify your text. The first line of each paragraph should be indented one-half inch from the left margin.

Long quotations. When quoting more than three lines of poetry, more than four lines of prose, or dialogue between characters in a drama, set off the quotation from the rest of your text, indenting it one-half inch (or five spaces) from the left margin. Do not use quotation marks, and put any parenthetical documentation *after* the final punctuation.

> In *Eastward to Tartary*, Kaplan captures ancient and
> contemporary Antioch for us:
>> At the height of its glory in the Roman-Byzantine age,
>> when it had an amphitheater, public baths, aqueducts,
>> and sewage pipes, half a million people lived in Antioch.
>> Today the population is only 125,000. With sour relations
>> between Turkey and Syria, and unstable politics
>> throughout the Middle East, Antioch is now a backwater—
>> seedy and tumbledown, with relatively few tourists. I
>> found it altogether charming. (123)

> In the first stanza of Arnold's "Dover Beach," the exclamations
> make clear that the speaker is addressing someone who is also
> present in the scene:
>> Come to the window, sweet is the night air!
>> Only, from the long line of spray
>> Where the sea meets the moon-blanched land,
>> Listen! You hear the grating roar
>> Of pebbles which the waves draw back, and fling. (6-10)

Be careful to maintain the poet's line breaks. If a line does not fit on one line of your paper, put the extra words on the next line. Indent that line an additional quarter inch (or two spaces).

Illustrations. Insert illustrations close to the text that discusses them. For tables, provide a number (Table 1) and a title on separate lines above the table. Below the table, provide a caption and information about the source. For graphs, photos, and other figures, provide a figure number (Fig. 1), caption, and source information below the figure. If you give only brief source information (such as a parenthetical note), or if the source is cited elsewhere in your text, include it in your list of works cited. Be sure to make clear how any illustrations relate to your point.

List of Works Cited. Start your list on a new page, following any notes. Center the title and double-space the entire list. Begin each entry at the left margin, and indent subsequent lines one-half inch (or five spaces). Alphabetize the list by authors' last names (or by editors' or translators' names, if appropriate). Alphabetize works with no author or editor by title, disregarding "A," "An," and "The." To cite more than one work by a single author, list them as in no. 4 on page 166.

MLA-e Sample Research Paper

The following report was written by Dylan Borchers for a first-year writing course. It's formatted according to the guidelines of the MLA (**style.mla.org**).

Sample Research Paper, MLA Style

Dylan Borchers

Professor Bullock

English 102, Section 4

4 May 2019

Against the Odds:

Harry S. Truman and the Election of 1948

Just over a week before Election Day in 1948, a *New York
Times* article noted "[t]he popular view that Gov. Thomas E. Dewey's
election as President is a foregone conclusion" (Egan). This
assessment of the race between incumbent Democrat Harry S.
Truman and Dewey, his Republican challenger, was echoed a week
later when *Life* magazine published a photograph whose caption
labeled Dewey "The Next President" (Photo of Truman 37). In a
Newsweek survey of fifty prominent political writers, each one
predicted Truman's defeat, and *Time* correspondents declared that
Dewey would carry 39 of the 48 states (Donaldson 210). Nearly
every major media outlet across the United States endorsed Dewey
and lambasted Truman. As historian Robert H. Ferrell observes,
even Truman's wife, Bess, thought he would be beaten (270).

The results of an election are not so easily predicted, as the
famous photograph in fig. 1 shows. Not only did Truman win the
election, but he won by a significant margin, with 303 electoral
votes and 24,179,259 popular votes, compared to Dewey's 189
electoral votes and 21,991,291 popular votes (Donaldson 204-07). In
fact, many historians and political analysts argue that Truman
would have won by an even greater margin had third-party
Progressive candidate Henry A. Wallace not split the Democratic

Borchers   2

Fig. 1. President Harry S. Truman holds up an edition of the *Chicago Daily Tribune* that mistakenly announced "Dewey Defeats Truman." (Rollins).

Illustration is positioned close to the text to which it relates, with figure number, caption, and parenthetical documentation.

vote in New York State and Dixiecrat Strom Thurmond not won four states in the South (McCullough 711). Although Truman's defeat was heavily predicted, those predictions themselves, Dewey's passiveness as a campaigner, and Truman's zeal turned the tide for a Truman victory.

In the months preceding the election, public opinion polls predicted that Dewey would win by a large margin. Pollster Elmo Roper stopped polling in September, believing there was no reason to continue, given a seemingly inevitable Dewey landslide. Although the margin narrowed as the election drew near, the other pollsters predicted a Dewey win by at least 5 percent (Donaldson 209). Many

No signal phrase; author and page number in parentheses.

1" margin

historians believe that these predictions aided the president in the long run. First, surveys showing Dewey in the lead may have prompted some of Dewey's supporters to feel overconfident about their candidate's chances and therefore to stay home from the polls on Election Day. Second, these same surveys may have energized Democrats to mount late get-out-the-vote efforts ("1948 Truman-Dewey Election"). Other analysts believe that the overwhelming predictions of a Truman loss also kept at home some Democrats who approved of Truman's policies but saw a Truman loss as inevitable. According to political analyst Samuel Lubell, those Democrats may have saved Dewey from an even greater defeat (Hamby, *Man* 465). Whatever the impact on the voters, the polling numbers had a decided effect on Dewey.

Historians and political analysts alike cite Dewey's overly cautious campaign as one of the main reasons Truman was able to achieve victory. Dewey firmly believed in public opinion polls. With all indications pointing to an easy victory, Dewey and his staff believed that all he had to do was bide his time and make no foolish mistakes. Dewey himself said, "When you're leading, don't talk" (Smith 30). Each of Dewey's speeches was well crafted and well rehearsed. As the leader in the race, he kept his remarks faultlessly positive, with the result that he failed to deliver a solid message or even mention Truman or any of Truman's policies. Eventually, Dewey began to be perceived as aloof and stuffy. One observer compared him to the plastic groom on top of a wedding cake (Hamby, "Harry S. Truman"), and others noted his stiff, cold demeanor (McCullough 671-74).

Short title given for author with multiple works cited.

Paragraphs indent 1/2 inch or 5 spaces.

Two works cited within the same sentence.

Borchers   4

As his campaign continued, observers noted that Dewey seemed uncomfortable in crowds, unable to connect with ordinary people. And he made a number of blunders. One took place at a train stop when the candidate, commenting on the number of children in the crowd, said he was glad they had been let out of school for his arrival. Unfortunately for Dewey, it was a Saturday ("1948: The Great Truman Surprise"). Such gaffes gave voters the feeling that Dewey was out of touch with the public.

Title used when there's no known author.

Again and again through the autumn of 1948, Dewey's campaign speeches failed to address the issues, with the candidate declaring that he did not want to "get down in the gutter" (Smith 515). When told by fellow Republicans that he was losing ground, Dewey insisted that his campaign not alter its course. Even *Time* magazine, though it endorsed and praised him, conceded that his speeches were dull (McCullough 696). According to historian Zachary Karabell, they were "notable only for taking place, not for any specific message" (244). Dewey's numbers in the polls slipped in the weeks before the election, but he still held a comfortable lead over Truman. It would take Truman's famous whistle-stop campaign to make the difference.

Few candidates in US history have campaigned for the presidency with more passion and faith than Harry Truman. In the autumn of 1948, he wrote to his sister, "It will be the greatest campaign any President ever made. Win, lose, or draw, people will know where I stand" (91). For thirty-three days, Truman traveled the nation, giving hundreds of speeches from the back of the *Ferdinand Magellan* railroad car. In the same letter, he described the

Borchers   5

pace: "We made about 140 stops and I spoke over 147 times, shook hands with at least 30,000 and am in good condition to start out again tomorrow for Wilmington, Philadelphia, Jersey City, Newark, Albany and Buffalo" (91). McCullough writes of Truman's campaign:

> No President in history had ever gone so far in quest of
> support from the people, or with less cause for the effort, to
> judge by informed opinion. . . . As a test of his skills and
> judgment as a professional politician, not to say his stamina
> and disposition at age sixty-four, it would be like no other
> experience in his long, often difficult career, as he himself
> understood perfectly. More than any other event in his public
> life, or in his presidency thus far, it would reveal the kind of
> man he was. (655)

He spoke in large cities and small towns, defending his policies and attacking Republicans. As a former farmer and relatively late bloomer, Truman was able to connect with the public. He developed an energetic style, usually speaking from notes rather than from a prepared speech, and often mingled with the crowds that met his train. These crowds grew larger as the campaign progressed. In Chicago, over half a million people lined the streets as he passed, and in St. Paul the crowd numbered over 25,000. When Dewey entered St. Paul two days later, he was greeted by only 7,000 supporters ("1948 Truman-Dewey Election"). Reporters brushed off the large crowds as mere curiosity seekers wanting to see a president (McCullough 682). Yet Truman persisted, even if he often seemed to be the only one who thought he could win. By

Quotations of more than 4 lines indented 1/2 inch (5 spaces) and double-spaced.

Parenthetical reference after final punctuation.

going directly to the American people and connecting with them, Truman built the momentum needed to surpass Dewey and win the election.

The legacy and lessons of Truman's whistle-stop campaign continue to be studied by political analysts, and politicians today often mimic his campaign methods by scheduling multiple visits to key states, as Truman did. He visited California, Illinois, and Ohio 48 times, compared with 6 visits to those states by Dewey. Political scientist Thomas M. Holbrook concludes that his strategic campaigning in those states and others gave Truman the electoral votes he needed to win (61, 65).

The 1948 election also had an effect on pollsters, who, as Elmo Roper admitted, "couldn't have been more wrong." *Life* magazine's editors concluded that pollsters as well as reporters and commentators were too convinced of a Dewey victory to analyze the polls seriously, especially the opinions of undecided voters (Karabell 256). Pollsters assumed that undecided voters would vote in the same proportion as decided voters—and that turned out to be a false assumption (Karabell 257). In fact, the lopsidedness of the polls might have led voters who supported Truman to call themselves undecided out of an unwillingness to associate themselves with the losing side, further skewing the polls' results (McDonald et al. 152). Such errors led pollsters to change their methods significantly after the 1948 election.

Work by 3 or more authors is shortened using "et al."

After the election, many political analysts, journalists, and historians concluded that the Truman upset was in fact a victory for the American people, who, the *New Republic* noted, "couldn't be ticketed by the polls, knew its own mind and had picked the rather unlikely but courageous figure of Truman to carry its banner" (T.R.B. 3). How "unlikely" is unclear, however; Truman biographer Alonzo Hamby notes that "polls of scholars consistently rank Truman among the top eight presidents in American history" (*Man* 641). But despite Truman's high standing, and despite the fact that the whistle-stop campaign is now part of our political landscape, politicians have increasingly imitated the style of the Dewey campaign, with its "packaged candidate who ran so as not to lose, who steered clear of controversy, and who made a good show of appearing presidential" (Karabell 266). The election of 1948 shows that voters are not necessarily swayed by polls, but it may have presaged the packaging of candidates by public relations experts, to the detriment of public debate on the issues in future presidential elections.

1" margin

Borchers   8

Works Cited

Donaldson, Gary A. *Truman Defeats Dewey*. UP of Kentucky, 1999.

Egan, Leo. "Talk Is Now Turning to the Dewey Cabinet." *The New York Times*, 20 Oct. 1948, p. 8E, www.nytimes.com /timesmachine/1948/10/26/issue.html. Accessed 18 Apr. 2019.

Ferrell, Robert H. *Harry S. Truman: A Life*. U of Missouri P, 1994.

Hamby, Alonzo L., editor. "Harry S. Truman: Campaigns and Elections." *American President*, Miller Center, U of Virginia, 11 Jan. 2012, millercenter.org/president/biography/truman -campaigns-and-elections. Accessed 17 Mar. 2019.

---. *Man of the People: A Life of Harry S. Truman*. Oxford UP, 1995.

Holbrook, Thomas M. "Did the Whistle-Stop Campaign Matter?" *PS: Political Science and Politics,* vol. 35, no. 1, Mar. 2002, pp. 59-66.

Karabell, Zachary. *The Last Campaign: How Harry Truman Won the 1948 Election*. Alfred A. Knopf, 2000.

McCullough, David. *Truman*. Simon and Schuster, 1992.

McDonald, Daniel G., et al. "The Spiral of Silence in the 1948 Presidential Election." *Communication Research,* vol. 28, no. 2, Apr. 2001, pp. 139-55.

"1948: The Great Truman Surprise." *The Press and the Presidency*, Dept. of Political Science and International Affairs, Kennesaw State U, 29 Oct. 2003, kennesaw.edu/pols.3380/pres/1984.html. Accessed 10 Apr. 2019.

"1948 Truman-Dewey Election." *American Political History*, Eagleton Institute of Politics, Rutgers, State U of New Jersey, 1995-2012, www.eagleton.rutgers.edu/research/americanhistory /ap_trumandewey.php. Accessed 18 Apr. 2019.

Heading centered.

Double-spaced.

Alphabetized by authors' last names.

Each entry begins at the left margin; subsequent lines are indented.

Multiple works by a single author listed alphabetically by title. For subsequent works, replace author's name with three hyphens.

Sources beginning with numerals are alphabetized as if the number were spelled out.

A range of dates is given for web projects developed over a period of time.

Photo of Truman in San Francisco. "The Next President Travels by
 Ferry Boat over the Broad Waters of San Francisco Bay." *Life*, 1 Nov.
 1948, p. 37. *Google Books*, books.google.com/books?id
 =ekoEAAAAMBAJ&printsec=frontcover#v=onepage&q&f=false.
 Accessed 20 Apr. 2019.

Rollins, Byron. "President Truman with *Chicago Daily Tribune*
 Headline of 'Dewey Defeats Truman.'" Associated Press,
 4 Nov. 1948. Harry S. Truman Library & Museum, www
 .trumanlibrary.org/photographs/view.php?id=25248. Accessed
 20 Apr. 2019.

Roper, Elmo. "Roper Eats Crow; Seeks Reason for Vote Upset."
 Evening Independent, 6 Nov. 1948, p. 10. *Google News*, news
 .google.com/newspapers?nid=PZE8UkGerEcC&dat=19481106
 &printsec=frontpage&hl=en. Accessed 13 Apr. 2019.

Smith, Richard Norton. *Thomas E. Dewey and His Times*. Simon and
 Schuster, 1982.

T.R.B. "Washington Wire." *The New Republic*, 15 Nov. 1948, pp. 3-4.
 EBSCOhost, search.ebscohost.com/login.aspx?direct=true&db
 =tsh&AN=14779640&site=ehost-live. Accessed 20 Apr. 2019.

Truman, Harry S. "Campaigning, Letter, October 5, 1948." *Harry S.
 Truman*, edited by Robert H. Ferrell, CQ P, 2003, p. 91.

Every source used is in the list of works cited.

APA Style

American Psychological Association (APA) style calls for (1) brief documentation in parentheses near each in-text citation and (2) complete documentation in a list of references at the end of your text. The models in this chapter draw on the *Publication Manual of the American Psychological Association*, 7th edition (2020). Additional information is available at **www.apastyle.org**.

A DIRECTORY TO APA STYLE

In-Text Documentation 204

Notes 208
Reference List 209

201

author   title   publication

Throughout this chapter, you'll find models and examples that are color-coded to help you see how writers include source information in their texts and reference lists: <mark>tan</mark> for author or editor, <mark>yellow</mark> for title, <mark>gray</mark> for publication information—publisher, date of publication, page number(s), DOI or URL, and so on.

APA-a In-Text Documentation

Brief documentation in your text makes clear to your readers precisely what you took from a source. If you are quoting, provide the page number(s) or other information that will help readers find the quotation in the source. You're not required to give the page number(s) with a paraphrase or summary, but you may want to do so if you are citing a long or complex work.

<mark>PARAPHRASES</mark> and <mark>SUMMARIES</mark> are more common than <mark>QUOTATIONS</mark> in APA-style projects. See <mark>R-4</mark> for more on all three kinds of citation. As you cite each source, you will need to decide whether to name the author in a signal phrase—"as McCullough (2020) wrote"—or in parentheses—"(McCullough, 2020)." Note that APA requires you to use the past tense or present perfect tense for verbs in <mark>SIGNAL PHRASES</mark>: "Moss (2019) argued," "Moss (2019) has argued."

1. AUTHOR NAMED IN A SIGNAL PHRASE

Put the date in parentheses after the author's last name, unless the year is mentioned in the sentence. Put any page number(s) you're including in parentheses after the quotation, paraphrase, or summary.

Parenthetical documentation should come *before* the period at the end of the sentence and *after* any quotation marks.

> McCullough (2001) described John Adams as having "the hands of a man accustomed to pruning his own trees, cutting his own hay, and splitting his own firewood" (p. 18).

> In 2001, McCullough noted that John Adams's hands were those of a laborer (p. 18).

> John Adams had "the hands of a man accustomed to pruning his own trees," according to McCullough (2001, p. 18).

If the author is named after a quotation, as in this last example, put the page number(s) after the date within the parentheses.

2. AUTHOR NAMED IN PARENTHESES

If you do not mention an author in a signal phrase, put the name, the year of publication, and any page number(s) in parentheses at the end of the sentence or right after the quotation, paraphrase, or summary.

> John Adams had "the hands of a man accustomed to pruning his own trees, cutting his own hay, and splitting his own firewood" (McCullough, 2001, p. 18).

3. AUTHORS WITH THE SAME LAST NAME

If your reference list includes more than one first author with the same last name, include initials in all documentation to distinguish the authors from one another.

> Eclecticism is common in modern criticism (J. M. Smith, 1992, p. vii).

4. TWO AUTHORS

Always mention both authors. Use "and" in a signal phrase, but use an ampersand (&) in parentheses.

> Carlson and Ventura (1990) wanted to introduce Julio Cortázar, Marjorie Agosín, and other Latin American writers to an audience of English-speaking adolescents (p. v).

According to the Peter Principle, "In a hierarchy, every employee tends to rise to his level of incompetence" (Peter & Hull, 1969, p. 26).

5. THREE OR MORE AUTHORS

When you refer to a work by three or more contributors, name only the first author followed by "et al.," Latin for "and others."

Peilen et al. (1990) supported their claims about corporate corruption with startling anecdotal evidence (p. 75).

6. ORGANIZATION OR GOVERNMENT AS AUTHOR

If an organization name has a familiar abbreviation, give the full name and the abbreviation the first time you cite the source. In subsequent references, use only the abbreviation. If the organization does not have a familiar abbreviation, always use its full name.

FIRST REFERENCE

The American Psychological Association (APA, 2020)

(American Psychological Association [APA], 2020)

SUBSEQUENT REFERENCES

The APA (2020)

(APA, 2020)

7. AUTHOR UNKNOWN

Use the complete title if it's short; if it's long, use the first few words of the title under which the work appears in the reference list. Italicize the title if it's italicized in the reference list; if it isn't italicized there, enclose the title in quotation marks.

According to *Feeding Habits of Rams* (2000), a ram's diet often changes from one season to the next (p. 29).

The article noted that one donor died because of "frightening" postoperative care ("Every Patient's Nightmare," 2007).

author   title   publication

8. TWO OR MORE WORKS TOGETHER

If you document multiple works in the same parentheses, place the source information in alphabetical order, separated by semicolons.

> Many researchers have argued that what counts as "literacy" is
> not necessarily learned at school (Heath, 1983; Moss, 2003).

Multiple authors in a signal phrase can be named in any order.

9. TWO OR MORE WORKS BY ONE AUTHOR IN THE SAME YEAR

If your list of references includes more than one work by the same author published in the same year, order them alphabetically by title, adding lowercase letters ("a," "b," and so on) to the year.

> Kaplan (2000a) described orderly shantytowns in Turkey that
> did not resemble the other slums he visited.

10. SOURCE QUOTED IN ANOTHER SOURCE

When you cite a source that was quoted in another source, add the words "as cited in." If possible, cite the original source instead.

> Thus, Modern Standard Arabic was expected to serve as the
> "moral glue" holding the Arab world together (Choueri, 2000,
> as cited in Walters, 2019, p. 475).

11. WORK WITHOUT PAGE NUMBERS

Instead of page numbers, some works have paragraph numbers, which you should include (preceded by the abbreviation "para.") if you are referring to a specific part of such a source.

> Russell's dismissals from Trinity College at Cambridge and from
> City College in New York City have been seen as examples of
> the controversy that marked his life (Irvine, 2006, para. 2).

In sources with neither page nor paragraph numbers, point to a particular part of the source if possible: (Brody, 2020, Introduction, para. 2).

12. AN ENTIRE WORK

You do not need to give a page number if you are directing readers' attention to an entire work.

> Kaplan (2000) considered Turkey and Central Asia explosive.

When you're citing an entire website, give the URL in the text. You do not need to include the website in your reference list. To document a webpage, see no. 18 on page 218.

> Beyond providing diagnostic information, the website for the
> Alzheimer's Association (http://www.alz.org) includes a variety
> of resources for the families of patients.

13. PERSONAL COMMUNICATIONS

Document emails, telephone conversations, personal interviews, personal letters, messages from nonarchived online discussion sources, and other personal texts as "personal communication," along with the person's initial(s), last name, and the date. You do not need to include such personal communications in your reference list.

> L. Strauss (personal communication, December 6, 2013) told
> about visiting Yogi Berra when they both lived in Montclair,
> New Jersey.

APA-b Notes

You may need to use footnotes to give an explanation or information that doesn't fit into your text. To signal a content footnote, place a superscript numeral at the appropriate point in your text. Include this information in a footnote, either at the bottom of that page or on a separate page with the heading "Footnotes" centered and in bold, after your reference list. If you have multiple notes, number them consecutively throughout your text. Here is an example from *In Search of Solutions: A New Direction in Psychotherapy* (2003).

author   title   publication

TEXT WITH SUPERSCRIPT

An important part of working with teams and one-way mirrors is taking the consultation break, as at Milan, BFTC, and MRI.[1]

FOOTNOTE

[1]It is crucial to note here that while working within a team is fun, stimulating, and revitalizing, it is not necessary for successful outcomes. Solution-oriented therapy works equally well when working solo.

APA-c Reference List

A reference list provides full bibliographic information for every source cited in your text with the exception of entire websites, common computer software and mobile apps, and personal communications. See page 231 for guidelines on preparing such a list; for a sample reference list, see page 238.

Key Elements for Documenting Sources

To document a source in APA style, you need to provide information about the author, the date, the title of the work you're citing, and the source itself (who published it; volume, issue, and page numbers; any DOI or URL). The following guidelines explain how to handle each of these elements generally, but there will be exceptions. For that reason, you'll want to consult the entries for the specific kinds of sources you're documenting; these entries provide templates showing which details you need to include. Be aware, though, that sometimes the templates will show elements that your source doesn't have; if that's the case, just omit those elements.

AUTHORS

Most entries begin with the author's last name, followed by the first and any middle initials: Smith, Z. for Zadie Smith; Kinder, D. R. for Donald R. Kinder.

- If the author is a group or organization, use its full name: Black Lives Matter, American Historical Association.

- If there is no author, put the title of the work first, followed by the date.

- If the author uses a screen name, first give their real name, followed by the screenname in brackets: Scott, B. [@BostonScott2]. If only the screen name is known, leave off the brackets: Avalon-Girl1990.

DATES

Include the date of publication, in parentheses right after the author. Some sources require only the year; others require the year, month, and day; and still others require something else. Consult the entry in this chapter for the specific source you're documenting.

- For a book, use the copyright year, which you'll find on the copyright page. If more than one year is given, use the most recent one.

- For most magazine or newspaper articles, use the full date that appears on the work, usually the year followed by the month and day.

- For a journal article, use the year of the volume.

- For a work on a website, use the date when the work was last updated. If that information is not available, use the date when the work was published.

- If a work has no date, use "n.d." for "no date."

- For online content that is likely to change, include the month, day, and year when you retrieved it. No need to include a retrieval date for materials that are unlikely to change.

TITLES

Capitalize only the first word and any proper nouns and adjectives in the title and subtitle of a work. But sometimes you'll also need to provide the title of a periodical or website where a source was found,

author   title   publication

and those are treated differently: capitalize all the principal words (excluding articles and prepositions).

- For books, reports, webpages, podcasts, and any other works that stand on their own, italicize the title: *White fragility*, *Radiolab*, *The 9/11 report*. Do not italicize the titles of the sources where you found them, however: NPR, ProQuest.

- For journal articles, book chapters, TV series episodes, and other works that are part of a larger work, do not italicize the title: The snowball effect, Not your average Joe. But do italicize the title of the larger work: *The Atlantic*, *Game of Thrones*.

- If a work has no title, include a description in square brackets after the date: [Painting of sheep on a hill].

- If the title of a work you're documenting includes another title, italicize it: *Frog and Toad and the self*. If the title you're documenting is itself in italics, do not italicize the title within it: *Stay, Illusion!: The* Hamlet *Doctrine*.

- For untitled social media posts or comments, include the first twenty words as the title, in italics, followed by a bracketed description: *TIL pigeons can fly up to 700 miles in one day* [Tweet].

SOURCE INFORMATION

This indicates where the work can be found (in a database or on a website, for example, or in a magazine or on a podcast) and includes information about the publisher; any volume, issue, and page numbers; and, for some sources, a DOI or URL. DOIs and URLs are included in all the templates; if the work you are documenting doesn't have one, just leave it off.

- For a work that stands on its own (a book, a report, a webpage), the source might be the publisher, a database, or a website.

- For a work that's part of a larger work (an article, an episode in a TV series, an essay in a collection), the source might be a magazine, a TV series, or an anthology.

- Give the volume and issue for journals and magazines that include that information. No need to give them for newspapers.

- Include a **DOI** for any work that has one, whether you accessed the source in print or online. For an online work with no DOI, include a working URL unless the work is from an academic database. You can use a shortDOI (**https://shortdoi.org/**) or a URL shortened using an online URL shortener, as long as the shorter DOI or URL leads to the correct work. No need to include a URL for a print work with no DOI.

Authors and Other Contributors

Most entries begin with authors—one author, two authors, or twenty-five. And some include editors, translators, or others who've contributed. The following templates show you how to document the various kinds of authors and other contributors.

1. ONE AUTHOR

Author's Last Name, Initials. (Year of publication). *Title.*
Publisher. DOI *or* URL

Lewis, M. (2003). *Moneyball: The art of winning an unfair game.*
W. W. Norton.

2. TWO AUTHORS

First Author's Last Name, Initials, & Second Author's Last Name,
Initials. (Year of publication). *Title.* Publisher. DOI *or* URL

Montefiore, S., & Montefiore, S. S. (2016). *The royal rabbits of London.* Aladdin.

3. THREE OR MORE AUTHORS

For three to 20 authors, include all names.

First Author's Last Name, Initials, Next Author's Last Name, Initials, &
Final Author's Last Name, Initials. (Year of publication).
Title. Publisher. DOI *or* URL

Greig, A., Taylor, J., & MacKay, T. (2013). *Doing research with children: A practical guide* (3rd ed.). Sage.

For a work by 21 or more authors, name the first 19 authors, followed by three ellipsis points, and end with the final author.

Gao, R., Asano, S. M., Upadhyayula, S., Pisarev, I., Milkie, D. E., Liu, T.-L., Singh, V., Graves, A., Huynh, G. H., Zhao, Y., Bogovic, J., Colonell, J., Ott, C. M., Zugates, C., Tappan, S., Rodriguez, A., Mosaliganti, K. R., Sheu, S.-H., Pasolli, H. A., . . . Betzig, E. (2019, January 18). Cortical column and whole-brain imaging with molecular contrast and nanoscale resolution. *Science, 363*(6424). https://doi.org/10.1126/science.aau8302

4. TWO OR MORE WORKS BY THE SAME AUTHOR

If the works were published in different years, list them chronologically.

Lewis, B. (1995). *The Middle East: A brief history of the last 2,000 years.* Scribner.

Lewis, B. (2003). *The crisis of Islam: Holy war and unholy terror.* Modern Library.

If the works were published in the same year, list them alphabetically by title (ignoring "A," "An," and "The"), adding "a," "b," and so on to the year.

Kaplan, R. D. (2000a). *The coming anarchy: Shattering the dreams of the post cold war.* Random House.

Kaplan, R. D. (2000b). *Eastward to Tartary: Travels in the Balkans, the Middle East, and the Caucasus.* Random House.

5. AUTHOR AND EDITOR

If a book has an author and an editor who is credited on the cover, include the editor in parentheses after the title.

Author's Last Name, Initials. (Year of publication). *Title* (Editor's Initials Last Name, Ed.). Publisher. DOI *or* URL (Original work published Year)

Dick, P. F. (2008). *Five novels of the 1960s and 70s* (J. Lethem, Ed.). Library of America. (Original works published 1964–1977)

6. AUTHOR AND TRANSLATOR

Author's Last Name, Initials. (Year of publication). *Title*
(Translator's Initials Last Name, Trans.). Publisher. DOI *or*
URL (Original work published Year)

Hugo, V. (2008). *Les misérables* (J. Rose, Trans.). Modern Library.
(Original work published 1862)

7. EDITOR

Editor's Last Name, Initials (Ed.). (Year of publication). *Title.*
Publisher. DOI *or* URL

Jones, D. (Ed.). (2007). *Modern love: 50 true and extraordinary tales
of desire, deceit, and devotion.* Three Rivers Press.

8. UNKNOWN OR NO AUTHOR OR EDITOR

Title. (Year of Publication). Publisher. DOI *or* URL

Feeding habits of rams. (2000). Land's Point Press.

Clues in salmonella outbreak. (2008, June 21). *The New York Times*, A13.

If the author is listed as "Anonymous," use that as the author's name
in the reference list.

9. ORGANIZATION OR GOVERNMENT AS AUTHOR

Sometimes an organization or a government agency is both author
and publisher. If so, omit the publisher.

Organization Name *or* Government Agency. (Year of publication).
Title. DOI *or* URL

Catholic News Service. (2002). *Stylebook on religion 2000: A
reference guide.*

Articles and Other Short Works

Articles, essays, reviews, and other short works are found in periodicals
and books—in print, online, or in a database. For most short works,
provide information about the author, the date, the titles of both the

author   title   publication

short work and the longer work, plus any volume and issue numbers, page numbers, and a DOI or URL if there is one.

10. ARTICLE IN A JOURNAL

Author's Last Name, Initials. (Year). Title of article. *Title of Journal, volume*(issue), page(s). DOI *or* URL

Gremer, J. R., Sala, A., & Crone, E. E. (2010). Disappearing plants: Why they hide and how they return. *Ecology, 91*(11), 3407–3413. https://doi.org/10.1890/09-1864.1

11. ARTICLE IN A MAGAZINE

If a magazine is published weekly, include the year, month, and day. Put any volume number and issue number after the title.

Author's Last Name, Initials. (Year, Month Day). Title of article. *Title of Magazine, volume*(issue), page(s). DOI *or* URL

Klump, B. (2019, November 22). Of crows and tools. *Science, 366*(6468), 965. https://doi.org/10.1126/science.aaz7775

12. ARTICLE IN A NEWSPAPER

If page numbers are consecutive, separate them with an en dash. If not, separate them with a comma.

Author's Last Name, Initials. (Year, Month Day). Title of article. *Title of Newspaper,* page(s). URL

Schneider, G. (2005, March 13). Fashion sense on wheels. *The Washington Post,* F1, F6.

13. ARTICLE ON A NEWS WEBSITE

Italicize the titles of articles on CNN, HuffPost, Salon, Vox, and other news websites. Do not italicize the name of the website.

Author's Last Name, Initials. (Year, Month Day). *Title of article.* Name of Site. URL

Travers, C. (2019, December 3). *Here's why you keep waking up at the same time every night.* HuffPost. https://bit.ly/3drSwAR

14. JOURNAL ARTICLE FROM A DATABASE

Author's Last Name, Initials. (Year). Title of article. *Title of
Journal*, *volume*(issue), pages. DOI

Simpson, M. (1972). Authoritarianism and education: A comparative
approach. *Sociometry, 35*(2), 223–234. https://doi
.org/10.2307/2786619

15. EDITORIAL

Editorials can appear in journals, magazines, and newspapers. If the
editorial is unsigned, put the title in the author position.

Author's Last Name, Initials. (Year, Month Day). Title of editorial
[Editorial]. *Title of Periodical*. DOI *or* URL

The Guardian view on local theatres: The shows must go on [Editorial].
(2019, December 6). *The Guardian*. https://bit.ly/2VZHIUg

16. REVIEW

Use this general format to document a review that appears in a periodical or on a blog.

Reviewer's Last Name, Initials. (Year, Month Day). Title of review
[Review of the work *Title*, by Author's Initials Last
Name]. *Title of Periodical* or *Name of Blog*. DOI *or* URL

Joinson, S. (2017, December 15). Mysteries unfold in a land of
minarets and magic carpets [Review of the book *The city of
brass,* by S. A. Chakraborty]. *The New York Times*. https://nyti
.ms/2kvwHFP

For a review published on a website that is not associated with a
periodical or a blog, italicize the title of the review and do not italicize
the website name.

Documentation Map (APA)

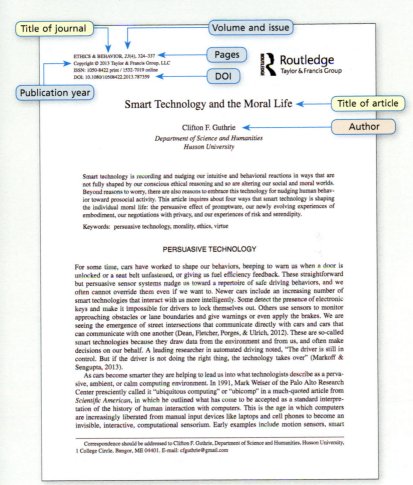

Title of journal

Volume and issue

Pages

DOI

Publication year

Title of article

Author

ETHICS & BEHAVIOR, *23*(4), 324–337
Copyright © 2013 Taylor & Francis Group, LLC
ISSN: 1050-8422 print / 1532-7019 online
DOI: 10.1080/10508422.2013.787359

Routledge
Taylor & Francis Group

Smart Technology and the Moral Life

Clifton F. Guthrie

*Department of Science and Humanities
Husson University*

Smart technology is recording and nudging our intuitive and behavioral reactions in ways that are not fully shaped by our conscious ethical reasoning and so are altering our social and moral worlds. Beyond reasons to worry, there are also reasons to embrace this technology for nudging human behavior toward prosocial activity. This article inquires about four ways that smart technology is shaping the individual moral life: the persuasive effect of promptware, our newly evolving experiences of embodiment, our negotiations with privacy, and our experiences of risk and serendipity.

Keywords: persuasive technology, morality, ethics, virtue

PERSUASIVE TECHNOLOGY

For some time, cars have worked to shape our behaviors, beeping to warn us when a door is unlocked or a seat belt unfastened, or giving us fuel efficiency feedback. These straightforward but persuasive sensor systems nudge us toward a repertoire of safe driving behaviors, and we often cannot override them even if we want to. Newer cars include an increasing number of smart technologies that interact with us more intelligently. Some detect the presence of electronic keys and make it impossible for drivers to lock themselves out. Others use sensors to monitor approaching obstacles or lane boundaries and give warnings or even apply the brakes. We are seeing the emergence of street intersections that communicate directly with cars and cars that can communicate with one another (Dean, Fletcher, Porges, & Ulrich, 2012). These are so-called smart technologies because they draw data from the environment and from us, and often make decisions on our behalf. A leading researcher in automated driving noted, "The driver is still in control. But if the driver is not doing the right thing, the technology takes over" (Markoff & Sengupta, 2013).

As cars become smarter they are helping to lead us into what technologists describe as a pervasive, ambient, or calm computing environment. In 1991, Mark Weiser of the Palo Alto Research Center presciently called it "ubiquitous computing" or "ubicomp" in a much-quoted article from *Scientific American*, in which he outlined what has come to be accepted as a standard interpretation of the history of human interaction with computers. This is the age in which computers are increasingly liberated from manual input devices like laptops and cell phones to become an invisible, interactive, computational sensorium. Early examples include motion sensors, smart

Correspondence should be addressed to Clifton F. Guthrie, Department of Science and Humanities, Husson University, 1 College Circle, Bangor, ME 04401. E-mail: cfguthrie@gmail.com

Guthrie, C. F. (2013). Smart technology and the moral life. *Ethics & Behavior*, *23*(4), 324–337. https://doi.org/10.1080/10508422.2013.787359

17. COMMENT ON AN ONLINE PERIODICAL ARTICLE OR BLOG POST

Writer's Last Name, Initials [username]. (Year, Month Day). Text of comment up to 20 words [Comment on the article "Title of work"]. *Title of Publication.* DOI *or* URL

PhyllisSurprise. (2020, May 10). How about we go all the way again? It's about time . . . [Comment on the article "2020 Eagles schedule: Picking wins and losses for all 16 games"]. *The Philadelphia Inquirer.* https://rb.gy/iduabz

Link to the comment if possible; if not, include the URL of the article.

18. WEBPAGE

Author's Last Name, Initials. (Year, Month Day). *Title of work.* Title of Site. URL

Pleasant, B. (n.d.). *Annual bluegrass.* The National Gardening Association. https://garden.org/learn/articles/view/2936/

If the author and the website name are the same, use the website name as the author. If the content of the webpage is likely to change and no archived version exists, use "n.d." as the date and include a retrieval date.

Centers for Disease Control and Prevention. (2019, December 2). *When and how to wash your hands.* https://www.cdc.gov /handwashing/when-how-handwashing.html

Worldometer. (n.d.). *World population.* Retrieved February 2, 2020, from https://www.worldometers.info/world-population/

Books, Parts of Books, and Reports

19. BASIC ENTRY FOR A BOOK

Author's Last Name, Initials. (Year of publication). *Title.* Publisher. DOI *or* URL

PRINT BOOK

Schwab, V. E. (2018). *Vengeful.* Tor.

author   title   publication

Documentation Map (APA)

WEBPAGE

URL

Title of site

Title of work

Date of publication

Author

Lazette, M. P. (2015, February 24). *A hurricane's hit to households.* Federal Reserve Bank of Cleveland. https:// www.clevelandfed.org/en/newsroom-and-events /publications/forefront/ff-v6n01/ff-20150224-v6n0107-a -hurricanes-hit-to-households.aspx

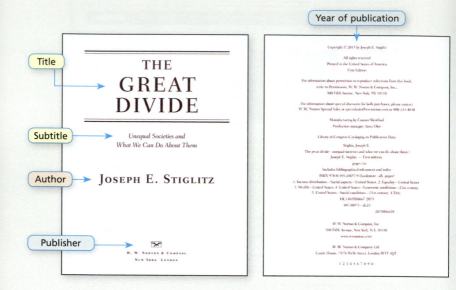

Year of publication

Title

Subtitle

Author

Publisher

THE
GREAT
DIVIDE

*Unequal Societies and
What We Can Do About Them*

JOSEPH E. STIGLITZ

W. W. NORTON & COMPANY
NEW YORK LONDON

Stiglitz, J. E. (2015). *The great divide: Unequal societies and what we can do about them.* W. W. Norton.

EBOOK

Jemisin, N. K. (2017). *The stone sky*. Orbit. https://amzn.com
/B01N7EQOFA

AUDIOBOOK

Obama, M. (2018). *Becoming* (M. Obama, Narr.) [Audiobook].
Random House Audio. http://amzn.com/B07B3JQZCL

Include the word "Audiobook" in brackets and the name of the narrator
only if the format and the narrator are something you've mentioned in
what you've written.

20. EDITION OTHER THAN THE FIRST

Author's Last Name, Initials. (Year). *Title* (Name *or* number
ed.). Publisher. DOI *or* URL

Burch, D. (2008). *Emergency navigation: Find your position and
shape your course at sea even if your instruments fail* (2nd
ed.). International Marine/McGraw-Hill.

21. EDITED COLLECTION OR ANTHOLOGY

Editor's Last Name, Initials (Ed.). (Year). *Title* (Name *or* number ed.,
Vol. number). Publisher. DOI *or* URL

Gilbert, S. M., & Gubar, S. (Eds.). (2003). *The Norton anthology of
literature by women: The traditions in English* (3rd ed., Vol. 2).
W. W. Norton.

22. WORK IN AN EDITED COLLECTION OR ANTHOLOGY

Author's Last Name, Initials. (Year of edited edition). Title of
work. In Editor's Initials Last Name (Ed.), *Title of
collection* (Name *or* number ed., Vol. number, pp. pages).
Publisher. DOI *or* URL (Original work published Year)

Baldwin, J. (2018). Notes of a native son. In M. Puchner, S. Akbari,
W. Denecke, B. Fuchs, C. Levine, P. Lewis, & E. Wilson (Eds.),
The Norton anthology of world literature (4th ed., Vol. F, pp.
728–743). W. W. Norton. (Original work published 1955)

23. CHAPTER IN AN EDITED BOOK

Author's Last Name, Initials. (Year). Title of chapter. In Editor's Initials Last Name (Ed.), *Title of book* (pp. pages). Publisher. DOI *or* URL

Amarnick, S. (2009). Trollope at fuller length: Lord Silverbridge and the manuscript of *The duke's children*. In M. Markwick, D. Denenholz Morse, & R. Gagnier (Eds.), *The politics of gender in Anthony Trollope's novels: New readings for the twenty-first century* (pp. 193–206). Routledge.

24. ENTRY IN A REFERENCE WORK (DICTIONARY, THESAURUS, OR ENCYCLOPEDIA)

If the entry has no author, use the name of the publisher as the author. If the reference work has an editor, include their name after the title of the entry. If the entry is archived or is not likely to change, use the publication date and do not include a retrieval date.

Author's Last Name, Initials. (Year). Title of entry. In Editor's Initials Last Name (Ed.), *Title of reference work* (Name *or* number ed., Vol. number, pp. pages). Publisher. URL

Merriam-Webster. (n.d.). Epoxy. In *Merriam-Webster.com dictionary*. Retrieved January 29, 2020, from https://www.merriam-webster.com/dictionary/epoxy

25. BOOK IN A LANGUAGE OTHER THAN ENGLISH

Author's Last Name, Initials. (Year). *Title of book* [English translation of title]. Publisher. DOI *or* URL

Ferrante, E. (2011). *L'amica geniale* [My brilliant friend]. Edizione E/O.

26. ONE VOLUME OF A MULTIVOLUME WORK

Author's Last Name, Initials. (Year). *Title of entire work* (Vol. number). Publisher. DOI *or* URL

Spiegelman, A. (1986). *Maus* (Vol. 1). Random House.

If the volume has a separate title, include the volume number and title in italics after the main title.

author   title   publication

Ramazani, J., Ellmann, R., & O'Clair, R. (Eds.). (2003). *The Norton
anthology of modern and contemporary poetry: Vol. 1.
Modern poetry* (3rd ed.). W. W. Norton.

27. RELIGIOUS WORK

Do not include an author for most religious works. If the date of
original publication is known, include it at the end.

Title. (Year of publication). Publisher. URL (Original work published
Year)

The New American Bible. (2002). United States Conference of
Catholic Bishops. http://www.vatican.va/archive/ENG0839/_
INDEX.HTM (Original work published 1970)

28. REPORT BY A GOVERNMENT AGENCY OR OTHER ORGANIZATION

Author's Last Name, Initials. (Year). *Title* (Report No.
number). Publisher. DOI *or* URL

Centers for Disease Control and Prevention. (2009). *Fourth national
report on human exposure to environmental chemicals.* US
Department of Health and Human Services. https://www.cdc
.gov/exposurereport/pdf/fourthreport.pdf

Include the year, month, and day if the report you're documenting
includes that information. Omit the report number if one is not given.
If more than one government department is listed as the publisher,
list the most specific department as the author and the larger department as the publisher.

29. DISSERTATION

Author's Last Name, Initials. (Year). *Title* (Publication No. number)
[Doctoral dissertation, Name of School]. Database *or* Archive
Name. URL

Solomon, M. (2016). *Social media and self-examination: The
examination of social media use on identity, social comparison,
and self-esteem in young female adults* (Publication No.
10188962) [Doctoral dissertation, William James College].
ProQuest Dissertations and Theses Global.

If the dissertation is in a database, do not include a URL. Include a URL if it is published elsewhere online. If it is unpublished, write "Unpublished doctoral dissertation" in brackets, and use the name of the school in place of the database.

30. PAPER OR POSTER PRESENTED AT A CONFERENCE

Presenter's Last Name, Initials. (Year, Month First Day–Last Day).
   Title [Paper *or* Poster presentation]. Name of Conference, City,
   State, Country. URL

Dolatian, H., & Heinz, J. (2018, May 25–27). *Reduplication and
   finite-state technology* [Paper presentation]. The 53rd
   Annual Meeting of the Chicago Linguistic Society, Chicago, IL,
   United States. http://shorturl.at/msuB2

Audio, Visual, and Other Sources

If you are referring to an entire website, do not include it in your reference list; simply mention the website's name in the body of your paper and include the URL in parentheses. Do not include email, personal communication, or other unarchived discussions in your list of references.

31. *WIKIPEDIA* ENTRY

Wikipedia has archived versions of its pages, so give the date when you accessed the page and the permanent URL of the archived page, which is found by clicking "View history."

Title of entry. (Year, Month Day). In *Wikipedia*. URL

List of sheep breeds. (2019, September 9). In *Wikipedia*.
   https://en.wikipedia.org/w/index.php?title=List_of_sheep
   _breeds&oldid=914884262

32. ONLINE FORUM POST

Author's Last Name, Initials [username]. (Year, Month Day). *Content of
   the post up to 20 words* [Online forum post]. Name of Site. URL

author   title   publication

Hanzus, D. [DanHanzus]. (2019, October 23). *GETCHA DAN HANZUS. ASK ME ANYTHING!* [Online forum post]. Reddit. https://bit.ly/38WgmSF

33. BLOG POST

Author's Last Name, Initials [username]. (Year, Month Day). Title of post. *Name of Blog.* URL

gcrepps. (2017, March 28). Shania Sanders. *Women@NASA.* https://blogs.nasa.gov/womenatnasa/2017/03/28/shania-sanders/

If only the username is known, use it without brackets.

34. ONLINE STREAMING VIDEO

Uploader's Last Name, Initials [username]. (Year, Month Day). *Title* [Video]. Name of Video Platform. URL

CinemaSins. (2014, August 21). *Everything wrong with* National treasure *in 13 minutes or less* [Video]. YouTube. https://www.youtube.com/watch?v=1ul-_ZWvXTs

Whoever uploaded the video is considered the author, even if someone else created the content. If only the username is known, use it without brackets.

35. PODCAST

Host's Last Name, Initials (Host). (First Year–Last Year). *Podcast name* [Audio podcast]. Production Company. URL

Poor, N., Woods, E., & Thomas, R. (Hosts). (2017–present). *Ear hustle* [Audio podcast]. PRX. https://www.earhustlesq.com/

36. PODCAST EPISODE

Host's Last Name, Initials (Host). (Year, Month Day). Episode title (No. number) [Audio podcast episode]. In *Podcast name.* Production Company. URL

Tamposi, E., & Samocki, E. (Hosts). (2020, January 8). The year of the broads [Audio podcast episode]. In *The broadcast podcast.* Podcast One. https://podcastone.com/episode/the-year-of-the-broads

Omit the episode number if one is not given.

37. FILM

> Director's Last Name, Initials (Director). (Year). *Title* [Film].
> Production Company. URL

Jenkins, B. (Director). (2016). *Moonlight* [Film]. A24; Plan B; PASTEL.

Cuarón, A. (Director). (2016). *Harry Potter and the prisoner of
Azkaban* [Film; two-disc special ed. on DVD]. Warner Brothers.

List the director as the author of the film. Indicate how you watched
the film only if the format is relevant to what you've written.

38. TELEVISION SERIES

> Executive Producer's Last Name, Initials (Executive Producer). (First
> Year–Last Year). *Title of series* [TV series]. Production
> Company. URL

Iungerich, L., Gonzalez, E., & Haft, J. (Executive Producers). (2018–
present). *On my block* [TV series]. Crazy Cat Lady Productions.

Indicate how you watched the TV series (two-disc DVD set, for example) only if the format is relevant to your essay.

39. TELEVISION SERIES EPISODE

> Writer's Last Name, Initials (Writer), & Director's Last Name, Initials
> (Director). (Year, Month Day). Title of episode (Season
> number, Episode number) [TV series episode]. In Executive
> Producer's Initials Last Name (Executive Producer), *Title of
> series.* Production Company. URL

Siegal, J. (Writer), Morgan, D. (Writer), & Sackett, M. (Director).
(2018, December 6). Janet(s) (Season 3, Episode 10) [TV series
episode]. In M. Schur, D. Miner, M. Sackett, & D. Goddard
(Executive Producers), *The good place*. Fremulon; 3 Arts
Entertainment; Universal Television.

40. MUSIC ALBUM

> Artist's Last Name, Initials. (Year). *Title of album* [Album]. Label. URL

Jonas Brothers. (2019). *Happiness begins* [Album]. Republic.

author   title   publication

41. SONG

Artist's Last Name, Initials. (Year). Name of song [Song]. On *Title of album*. Label. URL

Giddens, R. (2015). Shake sugaree [Song]. On *Tomorrow is my turn*. Nonesuch.

42. *POWERPOINT* SLIDES

Author's Last Name, Initials. (Year, Month Day). *Title of presentation* [PowerPoint slides]. Publisher. URL

Pavliscak, P. (2016, February 21). *Finding our happy place in the internet of things* [PowerPoint slides]. Slideshare. https://bit.ly/3aOcfs7

43. RECORDING OF A SPEECH OR WEBINAR

Author's Last Name, Initials. (Year, Month Day). *Title of speech* [Speech audio recording]. Publisher. URL

Kennedy, J. F. (1961, January 20). *Inaugural address* [Speech audio recording]. American Rhetoric. https://bit.ly/339Gc3e

44. PHOTOGRAPH

Photographer's Last Name, Initials. (Year). *Title of photograph* [Photograph]. Name of Site. URL

Kudacki, P. (2013). [Photograph of Benedict Cumberbatch]. Time. http://content.time.com/time/covers/asia/0,16641,20131028,00.html

Use this format to document a photograph that is not in a museum or on a museum website. For a photograph with no title, include a description of the photograph in brackets after the date.

45. MAP

Mapmaker's Last Name, Initials. (Year). *Title of map* [Map]. Publisher. URL

Daniels, M. (2018). *Human terrain: Visualizing the world's population, in 3D* [Map]. The Pudding. https://pudding .cool/2018/10/city_3d/

46. SOCIAL MEDIA POSTS

If only the username is known, provide it without brackets. List any audiovisual content (e.g., videos, images, or links) in brackets. Replicate emoji or include a bracketed description.

Author's Last Name, Initials [@username]. (Year, Month Day). *Content of post up to 20 words* [Description of any audiovisual content] [Type of post]. Platform. URL

TWEET

Baron, D. [@DrGrammar]. (2019, November 11). *Gender conceal: Did you know that pronouns can also hide someone's gender?* [Thumbnail with link attached] [Tweet]. Twitter. https://bit .ly/2vaCcDc

INSTAGRAM PHOTOGRAPH OR VIDEO

Jamil, J. [@jameelajamilofficial]. (2018, July 18). *Happy Birthday to our leader. I steal all my acting faces from you. @kristenanniebell* [Face with smile and sunglasses emoji] [Photograph]. Instagram. https://www.instagram.com/p/BlYX5F9FuGL/

FACEBOOK POST

Raptor Resource Project. (2020, May 8). *Happy Fri-yay, everyone! We'll keep the news short and sweet: today Decorah eaglets D34 and D35 turn 33 days* [Images attached]. Facebook. https://bit.ly/3icwFzN

47. DATA SET

Author's Last Name, Initials. (Year). *Title of data set* (Version number) [Data set]. Publisher. DOI *or* URL

Pew Research Center. (2019). *Core trends survey* [Data set]. https://www.pewresearch.org/internet/dataset/core-trends -survey/

Omit the version number if one is not given. If the publisher is the author, no need to list it twice; omit the publisher.

author   title   publication

48. SUPREME COURT CASE

Name of Case, volume US pages (year). URL

Plessy v. Ferguson, 163 US 537 (1896). https://www.oyez.org
/cases/1850-1900/163us537

Obergefell v. Hodges, 576 US ___ (2015). https://www.oyez.org
/cases/2014/14-556

The source for most Supreme Court cases is United States Reports, which is abbreviated "US" in the reference list entry. If the case does not yet have a page number, use three underscores instead.

Sources Not Covered by APA

To document a source for which APA does not provide guidelines, look at models similar to the source you have cited. Give any information readers will need in order to find the source themselves—author; date of publication; title; and information about the source itself (including who published it; volume, issue, and page numbers; and a DOI or URL). You might want to check your reference note to be sure it will lead others to your source.

APA-d Formatting a Research Essay

Title page. APA generally requires a title page. The page number should go in the upper right-hand corner. Center the full title of the paper in bold in the top half of the page. Center your name, the name of your department and school, the course number and name, the instructor's name, and the due date on separate lines below the title. Leave one line between the title and your name.

Page numbers. Place the page number in the upper right-hand corner. Number pages consecutively throughout.

Fonts, spacing, margins, and indents. Use a legible font that will be accessible to everyone, either a serif font (such as Times New Roman or Bookman) or a sans serif font (such as Calibri or Verdana). Use a sans serif font within figure images. Double-space the entire paper, including any notes and your list of references; the only exception is footnotes at the bottom of a page, which should be single-spaced, and text within tables and images, the spacing of which will vary. Leave one-inch margins at the top, bottom, and sides of your text; do not justify the text. The first line of each paragraph should be indented one-half inch (or five to seven spaces) from the left margin. APA recommends using one space after end-of-sentence punctuation.

Headings. Though they are not required in APA style, headings can help readers follow your text. The first level of heading should be bold and centered; the second level of heading should be bold and flush with the left margin; the third level should be bold, italicized, and flush left. Capitalize all headings as you would any other title within the text.

First Level Heading

Second Level Heading

Third Level Heading

Abstract. An abstract is a concise summary of your paper that introduces readers to your topic and main points. Most scholarly journals require an abstract; an abstract is not typically required for student papers, so check your instructor's preference. Put your abstract on the second page, with the word "Abstract" centered and in bold at the top. Unless your instructor specifies a length, limit your abstract to 250 words or fewer.

Long quotations. Indent quotations of forty or more words one-half inch (or five to seven spaces) from the left margin. Do not use quotation marks, and place the page number(s) or documentation information in parentheses *after* the end punctuation. If there are paragraphs in the quotation, indent the first line of each paragraph another one-half inch.

> Kaplan (2000) captured ancient and contemporary Antioch:
>> At the height of its glory in the Roman-Byzantine age, when it had an amphitheater, public baths, aqueducts, and sewage pipes, half a million people lived in Antioch. Today the population is only 125,000. With sour relations between Turkey and Syria, and unstable politics throughout

the Middle East, Antioch is now a backwater—seedy and
tumbledown, with relatively few tourists. (p. 123)

Antioch's decline serves as a reminder that the fortunes of cities
can change drastically over time.

List of references. Start your list on a new page after the text but before any endnotes. Title the page "References," centered and in bold, and double-space the entire list. Each entry should begin at the left margin, and subsequent lines should be indented one-half inch (or five to seven spaces). Alphabetize the list by authors' last names (or by editors' names, if appropriate). Alphabetize works that have no author or editor by title, disregarding "A," "An," and "The." Be sure every source listed is cited in the text; do not include sources that you consulted but did not cite.

Tables and figures. Above each table or figure (charts, diagrams, graphs, photos, and so on), provide the word "Table" or "Figure" and a number, flush left and in bold (e.g., **Table 1**). On the following line, give a descriptive title, flush left and italicized. Below the table or figure, include a note with any necessary explanation and source information. Number tables and figures separately, and be sure to discuss them in your text so that readers know how they relate.

Table 1

Hours of Instruction Delivered per Week

	American classrooms	Japanese classrooms	Chinese classrooms
First grade			
Language arts	10.5	8.7	10.4
Mathematics	2.7	5.8	4.0
Fifth grade			
Language arts	7.9	8.0	11.1
Mathematics	3.4	7.8	11.7

Note. Adapted from *Peeking Out from Under the Blinders: Some Factors We Shouldn't Forget in Studying Writing* (Occasional Paper No. 25), by J. R. Hayes, 1991, National Center for the Study of Writing and Literacy (https://archive.nwp.org/cs/public/print/resource/720). Copyright 1991 by the Office of Educational Research and Improvement.

APA-e Sample Pages

The following sample pages are from "Early Word Production: A Study of One Child's Word Productions," a paper written by Katryn Sheppard for a linguistics course. They are formatted according to the guidelines of the *Publication Manual of the American Psychological Association*, 7th edition (2020). To see the complete paper, go to **digital.wwnorton .com/littleseagull4**. See pages 76–79 for another model essay written by a student following APA style.

Sample Title Page, APA Style

1

Page numbers appear in the upper right corner.

The title is bold, centered, and placed in the upper half of the page.

Early Word Production: A Study of One Child's Word Productions

Your name is centered below the title, with one double-spaced line in between.

Katryn Sheppard

The school name and department, course number and name, professor's name, and due date of the paper are centered below your name.

Department of Applied Linguistics, Portland State University

LING 437: First Language Acquisition

Dr. Lynn Santelmann

October 31, 2019

Sample Abstract, APA Style

2

Abstract

Early word production, one of the initial stages of language development in children, plays an important role in the development of later language skills. This study identifies the word classes and number of words spoken in a recorded interaction (Bloom, 1973) by one normally developing child of sixteen months and analyzes aspects of the child's speech, with the goal of noting if the characteristics observed were supported by the existing research on early word production or if they deviated from those findings. The words that I analyzed fell into six categories: nouns, spatial terms, adjectives, negatives, social phrases, and verbs. Although the frequency with which the child used words from some of these categories reflected the expectations established by previous research, her use of words in other categories was less predictable. Noting word usage in the six categories led to an analysis of the functions that those categories served in the child's semantic communication at this early stage of language development.

Abstract begins on a new page. Heading is centered and bold. An abstract is not generally required for a student paper, so check with your professor.

Abstract text does not need a paragraph indent.

Use one space after each sentence.

250 words or fewer.

Sample Pages of Research Paper, APA Style

3

Text starts on a new page. Title is centered and bold.

Early Word Production: A Study of One Child's Word Productions

Each step in the course of language development and acquisition in children provides a foundation for later skills and eventual mastery of the language. Early word production, a stage of language development in which children have only a few words in their vocabularies, provides the foundation for later vocabulary building and language production and has been shown to be closely linked to later language performance skills (Walker et al., 1994). The early word production stage is therefore worthy of examination, as it "signals that children have a new tool that will enable them to learn about and participate more fully in their society" (Uccelli & Pan, 2013, p. 95).

Because so few words are produced by children in this early stage, the analysis of their word production focuses on the frequency of particular word classes in speech. When examining typically developing English-speaking children who have few words in their productive vocabulary, Bates et al. (1994) found that the words produced were most often nouns, while other categories more seldom appeared. These less frequent categories included verbs and closed-class words. *Closed-class* words are function words, categories to which new members cannot easily be added: articles, conjunctions, numbers, pronouns, and prepositions.

Reporting on the most common kinds of the nouns uttered in early vocabularies, Nelson (1973) found that children "began by naming objects exhibiting salient properties of change whether as the result of the child's own action . . . or independent of it" (p. 1).

Essay is double-spaced.

Because this source has more than two authors, the in-text documentation begins with the first author's name followed by "et al." The year of publication is included in the reference.

The signal phrase uses past tense, and the year of publication is given in parentheses.

Indent each paragraph ½" (5–7 spaces).

Sample Pages of Research Paper, APA Style

1" margins

4

The author, year, and page number are given in parentheses right after a quotation.

In other words, nouns that point to consistent, concrete objects are most prevalent in early speech because "children learn to name and understand categories that are functionally relevant to them" (Anglin, 1995, p. 165)—they learn to name the objects they see and interact with day to day.

1" margin

Because the authors are not named in a signal phrase, their names are given in parentheses, with an ampersand rather than "and" between them. A page number is provided for a direct quotation.

Although nouns make up the largest percentage of the words produced by children in the earlier stages of language acquisition, other word classes also appear. While occurring in children's first fifty words, "verbs, adjectives, and function words each account for less than 10 percent" of total utterances (Uccelli & Pan, 2013, p. 96). Infrequent use of these categories supports the idea that, while all word classes are represented, nouns are expected to occur most often.

Other lexical items found in the speech of children with limited vocabulary are words indicating spatial relationships, how things relate to one another in physical space. According to Bowerman (2007), "among children's earliest spatial words are

The page number is provided in parentheses for a direct quotation when the author and year of the work are given earlier in the signal phrase.

topological forms like 'in' and 'on'" (p. 177). This observation supports the hypothesis that those prepositions are among the first lexical items acquired (Brown, 1973; Zukowski, 2013).

Multiple sources documented in the same parentheses are ordered alphabetically and separated by semicolon.

Overall, the research on early word production in children just beginning to acquire their first language has found that the majority of words produced will be nouns that refer to concrete objects. According to Pine (1992), children frequently use their early words to describe or label or to do both. Pine concluded that "children are making referential statements about the world with the kind of

1" margins

vocabulary items which they . . . have available to them" (p. 53). That is, children try to comment on referents.

Sample Pages of Research Paper, APA Style

7

The category of nouns contained the largest number of distinct types as well as the largest number of tokens, as shown in Figure 1. Allison used a total of 12 nouns, and all reflected concrete concepts. These included household objects, nouns that referenced people, and the names of animals referring to toys in the recording room. The most frequently used noun was "baby" (n=25); "chair" was second (n=24). The total number of nouns represented 122 occurrences, or 34% of the total words uttered.

Figure 1 is referred to in the text.

Figure 1

Figure number is bold and flush left

Categories of Words Uttered by the Subject

Descriptive figure title is italicized and appears below the figure number.

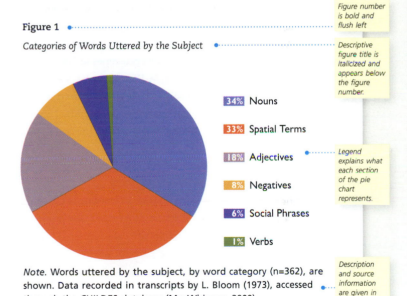

34% Nouns

33% Spatial Terms

18% Adjectives

8% Negatives

6% Social Phrases

1% Verbs

Legend explains what each section of the pie chart represents.

Note. Words uttered by the subject, by word category (n=362), are shown. Data recorded in transcripts by L. Bloom (1973), accessed through the CHILDES database (MacWhinney, 2000).

Description and source information are given in the figure note.

Sample Page of Reference List, APA Style

List of references begins on a new page. Heading is centered and bold.

Entries are arranged alphabetically.

All entries are double-spaced, and all lines except the first are indented ½" (5–7 spaces).

DOI given when one is available. Do not add a period at the end of a DOI or a URL.

Entry for a work found in an edited collection includes the editors' names, first initial followed by last name.

14

References

Anglin, J. M. (1995). Classifying the world through language: Functional relevance, cultural significance, and category name learning. *International Journal of Intercultural Relations,* 19(2), 161–181. http://doi.org/bg4cz3

Bates, E., Marchman, V., Thal, D., Fenson, L., Dale, P., Reznick, J. S., & Hartung, J. (1994). Developmental and stylistic variation in the composition of early vocabulary. *Journal of Child Language,* 21(1), 85–123. http://doi.org/fbjfz6

Bloom, L. (1973). *One word at a time: The use of single-word utterances before syntax.* Mouton.

Bowerman, M. (2007). Containment, support, and beyond: Constructing topological spatial categories in first language acquisition. In M. Aurnague, M. Hickmann, & L. Vieu (Eds.), *The categorization of spatial entities in language and cognition* (pp. 177–203). John Benjamins. http://doi.org/dffs

Brown, R. (1973). *A first language: The early stages.* Harvard University Press.

MacWhinney, B. (2000). *The CHILDES Project: Tools for analyzing talk* (3rd ed.). Lawrence Erlbaum Associates.

Nelson, K. (1973). Structure and strategy in learning to talk. *Monographs of the Society for Research in Child Development,* 38(1), 1–135. http://doi.org/fpfm6f

Chicago Style

The University of Chicago Press presents two systems of documentation. This chapter shows the notes-and-bibliography system, which calls for (1) a superscript number for each in-text citation, (2) a correspondingly numbered footnote or endnote, and (3) an end-of-paper bibliography. The models in this chapter draw on *The Chicago Manual of Style*, 17th edition (2017), and Kate L. Turabian's *A Manual for Writers of Research Papers, Theses, and Dissertations*, 8th edition (2013). Additional information about CMS style is available at **www.chicago manualofstyle.org** and within that site at "Chicago Style Q&A."

A DIRECTORY TO CHICAGO STYLE

author   title   publication

Throughout this chapter, you'll find models that are color-coded to help you see how writers include source information in their notes and bibliographies: tan for author or editor, yellow for title, gray for publication information—place of publication, publisher, date of publication, page number(s), and so on.

CMS-a Documenting with Notes and Bibliography

Put a superscript number in your text to indicate to your reader that you are citing material from a source. The superscript should follow the **QUOTATION**, **PARAPHRASE**, or **SUMMARY** of the source you are cit-ing, as in the example below. Note that CMS requires you to use the present tense for verbs in **SIGNAL PHRASES**.

IN-TEXT CITATION

Kaplan insists that understanding power in the Near East requires "Western leaders who know when to intervene, and do so without illusions."[1]

The superscript number directs your reader to a footnote or an end-note that gives more information about the source; these in-text references are numbered sequentially throughout your text. The number that introduces the footnote or endnote should not be set superscript and should be followed by a period. Here is the full ver-sion of the note that documents the quote from Kaplan's book.

FULL NOTE

1. Robert D. Kaplan, *Eastward to Tartary: Travels in the Balkans, the Middle East, and the Caucasus* (New York: Random House, 2000), 330.

If your bibliography does not include all the works you reference in your notes, you should use the full version of the note the first time you cite a source. If you cite the same source later in your paper, give a shorter form of the note that lists just the author's last name, an abbreviated title, and the page(s) cited. If your bibliography does include all the works you reference in your notes, CMS allows for the use of the shorter form of the note the first time you cite a source as well. The models that follow indicate which kinds of sources do not require bibliography entries. It's a good idea to check your instructor's preference, however.

SHORTER NOTE

> 4. Kaplan, *Eastward*, 332.

If you cite the same source in two consecutive notes, omit the shortened title but include the page number in the second note. When your next citation is to the same page of that source, repeat the author and page number. (The use of "Ibid." is discouraged.)

> 5. Kaplan, 334.
> 6. Kaplan, 334.

BIBLIOGRAPHY

The bibliography at the end of your paper is an alphabetical list of the sources you've cited or consulted. Here is how Kaplan's book would appear in a bibliography.

> Kaplan, Robert D. *Eastward to Tartary: Travels in the Balkans, the Middle East, and the Caucasus.* New York: Random House, 2000.

CMS-b Note and Bibliography Models

Because Chicago style requires notes and a bibliography for documentation, this chapter provides examples of both. See page 272 for guidelines on preparing notes and a bibliography; for samples, see pages 275–76.

Print Books

For most books, you'll need to provide information about the author; the title and any subtitle; and the place of publication, publisher, and year of publication. Treat pamphlets and brochures like books, giving whatever information is available.

KEY DETAILS FOR DOCUMENTING PRINT BOOKS

- **AUTHORS:** Include the author's middle name or initial, if any.

author   title   publication

- **TITLES:** Capitalize the first and last words and all principal words of titles and subtitles. Italicize book titles. Use quotation marks around titles of chapters or other short works within books.

- **PUBLICATION PLACE:** If there's more than one city, use only the first. If a city may be unfamiliar or could be confused with another of the same name, give the state, province, or country. For the US capital, use "Washington, DC." Do not list the state or country if that information is part of the publisher's name.

- **PUBLISHER:** Omit "The" at the start of a publisher's name, along with abbreviations such as "Inc." If you shorten a publisher's name (e.g., "Wiley" for "John Wiley"), be consistent.

1. ONE AUTHOR

NOTE

1. Author's First Name Last Name, *Title* (Publication City: Publisher, Year of publication), Page(s).

1. Erik Larson, *The Devil in the White City: Murder, Mayhem, and Madness at the Fair That Changed America* (New York: Crown, 2003), 113.

BIBLIOGRAPHY

Author's Last Name, First Name. *Title.* Publication City: Publisher, Year of publication.

Larson, Erik. *The Devil in the White City: Murder, Mayhem, and Madness at the Fair That Changed America*. New York: Crown, 2003.

TWO OR MORE WORKS BY THE SAME AUTHOR

If you include more than one work by the same author, give the author's name in the first entry, and then use a long dash (three-em dash or six hyphens) in the author slot for each of the subsequent works, listing them alphabetically by the first important word of each title. Some people prefer to repeat the author's name instead, so check with your professor.

Caro, Robert A. *Master of the Senate*. New York: Knopf, 2002.
———. *The Passage of Power.* New York: Knopf, 2012.

Documentation Map (Chicago)

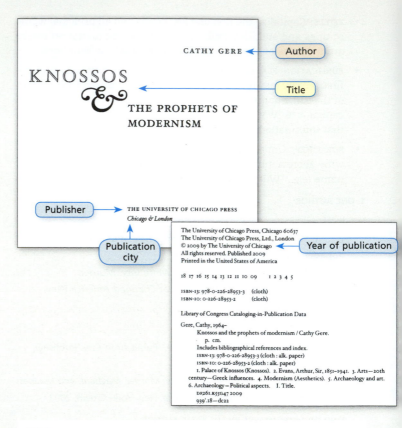

NOTE

1. Cathy Gere, *Knossos & the Prophets of Modernism* (Chicago: University of Chicago Press, 2009), 18.

BIBLIOGRAPHY

Gere, Cathy. *Knossos & the Prophets of Modernism.* Chicago: University of Chicago Press, 2009.

2. MULTIPLE AUTHORS

NOTE

2. First Author's First Name Last Name, Next Author's First Name Last Name, and Third Author's First Name Last Name, *Title* (Publication City: Publisher, Year of publication), Page(s).

2. Ronald W. Walker, Richard E. Turley Jr., and Glen M. Leonard, *Massacre at Mountain Meadows* (New York: Oxford University Press, 2008), 225.

For more than three authors, give the first author's name followed by "et al.," Latin for "and others."

2. David Goldfield et al., *Twentieth-Century America: A Social and Political History* (Upper Saddle River, NJ: Pearson Prentice Hall, 2005), 376.

BIBLIOGRAPHY

Give all authors' names for works with ten or fewer authors.

First Author's Last Name, First Name, Next Author's First Name Last Name, . . . and Final Author's First Name Last Name. *Title.* Publication City: Publisher, Year of publication.

Goldfield, David, Carl E. Abbott, Jo Ann E. Argersinger, and Peter H. Argersinger. *Twentieth-Century America: A Social and Political History.* Upper Saddle River, NJ: Pearson Prentice Hall, 2005.

For more than ten authors, give the first seven names, followed by "et al."

3. ORGANIZATION OR CORPORATION AS AUTHOR

NOTE

3. Organization Name, *Title* (Publication City: Publisher, Year of publication), Page(s).

3. Johnson County Historical and Genealogical Society, *Historic Sites of Paintsville and Johnson County, Kentucky* (Paintsville: East Kentucky Press, 2012), 27.

BIBLIOGRAPHY

Organization Name. *Title.* Publication City: Publisher, Year of publication.

Johnson County Historical and Genealogical Society. *Historic Sites of Paintsville and Johnson County, Kentucky.* Paintsville: East Kentucky Press, 2012.

4. AUTHOR AND EDITOR

NOTE

4. Author's First Name Last Name, *Title,* ed. Editor's First Name Last Name (Publication City: Publisher, Year of publication), Page(s).

4. Raphael Lemkin, *Totally Unofficial: The Autobiography of Raphael Lemkin,* ed. Donna-Lee Frieze (New Haven, CT: Yale University Press, 2013), 288.

BIBLIOGRAPHY

Author's Last Name, First Name. *Title.* Edited by Editor's First Name Last Name. Publication City: Publisher, Year of publication.

Lemkin, Raphael. *Totally Unofficial: The Autobiography of Raphael Lemkin.* Edited by Donna-Lee Frieze. New Haven, CT: Yale University Press, 2013.

5. EDITOR ONLY

NOTE

5. Editor's First Name Last Name, ed., *Title* (Publication City: Publisher, Year of publication), Page(s).

5. Eric Foner and John A. Garraty, eds., *The Reader's Companion to American History* (Boston: Houghton Mifflin, 1991), xix.

author   title   publication

BIBLIOGRAPHY

Editor's Last Name, First Name, ed. *Title.* Publication City: Publisher,
    Year of publication.
Foner, Eric, and John A. Garraty, eds. *The Reader's Companion to
    American History.* Boston: Houghton Mifflin, 1991.

6. PART OF A BOOK

WORK IN AN EDITED COLLECTION OR ANTHOLOGY
NOTE

6. Author's First Name Last Name, "Title of Work," in *Title
of Book*, ed. Editor's First Name Last Name (Publication City:
Publisher, Year of publication), Page(s).

6. Lee Sandlin, "Losing the War," in *The New Kings of
Nonfiction*, ed. Ira Glass (New York: Riverhead Books, 2007), 355.

BIBLIOGRAPHY

Author's Last Name, First Name. "Title of Work." In *Title of Book*,
    edited by Editor's First Name Last Name, Page range.
    Publication City: Publisher, Year of publication.
Sandlin, Lee. "Losing the War." In *The New Kings of Nonfiction*,
    edited by Ira Glass, 315–61. New York: Riverhead Books, 2007.

CHAPTER IN A BOOK
NOTE

6. Author's First Name Last Name, "Title of Chapter," in *Title
of Book* (Publication City: Publisher, Year of publication), Page(s).

6. Nate Silver, "Less and Less and Less Wrong," in *The Signal
and the Noise* (New York: Penguin Press, 2012), 236–37.

BIBLIOGRAPHY

Author's Last Name, First Name. "Title of Chapter." In *Title of Book*,
    Page range. Publication City: Publisher, Year of publication.
Silver, Nate. "Less and Less and Less Wrong." In *The Signal and the
    Noise*, 232–61. New York: Penguin Press, 2012.

FOREWORD, INTRODUCTION, PREFACE, OR AFTERWORD

NOTE

6. Part Author's First Name Last Name, part to *Title of Book*, by *or* ed. First Name Last Name (Publication City: Publisher, Year of publication), Page(s).

6. Tony Tanner, introduction to *Pride and Prejudice*, by Jane Austen (New York: Penguin, 1972), 8.

BIBLIOGRAPHY

Part Author's Last Name, First Name. Part to *Title of Book*, by *or* ed. First Name Last Name, Page range. Publication City: Publisher, Year of publication.

Tanner, Tony. Introduction to *Pride and Prejudice*, by Jane Austen, 7–46. New York: Penguin, 1972.

7. UNKNOWN AUTHOR

NOTE

7. *Title* (Publication City: Publisher, Year of publication), Page(s).

7. *All States Tax Handbook* (New York: Thomson Reuters, 2009), 5.

BIBLIOGRAPHY

Title. Publication City: Publisher, Year of publication.

All States Tax Handbook. New York: Thomson Reuters, 2009.

8. TRANSLATION

NOTE

8. Author's First Name Last Name, *Title*, trans. Translator's First Name Last Name (Publication City: Publisher, Year of publication), Page(s).

8. Norberto Fuentes, *The Autobiography of Fidel Castro*, trans. Anna Kushner (New York: Norton, 2009), 49.

author   title   publication

BIBLIOGRAPHY

Author's Last Name, First Name. *Title.* Translated by Translator's
First Name Last Name. Publication City: Publisher, Year of
publication.

Fuentes, Norberto. *The Autobiography of Fidel Castro.* Translated by
Anna Kushner. New York: Norton, 2009.

9. EDITION OTHER THAN THE FIRST

NOTE

9. Author's First Name Last Name, *Title,* name *or* number of
ed. (Publication City: Publisher, Year of publication), Page(s).

9. Michael D. Coe and Rex Koontz, *Mexico: From the Olmecs to
the Aztecs,* 6th ed. (London: Thames & Hudson, 2008), 186–87.

BIBLIOGRAPHY

Author's Last Name, First Name. *Title.* Name *or* number of ed.
Publication City: Publisher, Year of publication.

Coe, Michael D., and Rex Koontz. *Mexico: From the Olmecs to the
Aztecs.* 6th ed. London: Thames & Hudson, 2008.

10. VOLUME OF A MULTIVOLUME WORK

NOTE

10. Author's First Name Last Name, *Title of Multivolume Work,*
vol. number of individual volume, *Title of Individual Volume*
(Publication City: Publisher, Year of publication), Page(s).

10. Bruce Catton, *The Army of the Potomac,* vol. 2, *Glory Road*
(Garden City, NY: Doubleday, 1952), 169–70.

BIBLIOGRAPHY

Author's Last Name, First Name. *Title of Multivolume Work.* Vol.
number, *Title of Individual Volume.* Publication City: Publisher,
Year of publication.

Catton, Bruce. *The Army of the Potomac.* Vol. 2, *Glory Road.* Garden
City, NY: Doubleday, 1952.

11. DICTIONARY OR ENCYCLOPEDIA ENTRY

Well-known reference works can be documented in a note without any publication information and do not need to be included in your bibliography. Use the abbreviation "s.v.," meaning "under the word," before the name of the entry.

NOTE

11. *Title,* name or number of ed. (year), s.v. "name of entry."

11. *The Random House Dictionary of the English Language*, 2nd ed. (1987), s.v. "ethos."

11. *The New Encyclopaedia Britannica*, 15th ed. (1992), s.v. "Klee, Paul."

12. LETTER IN A PUBLISHED COLLECTION

NOTE

12. Sender's First Name Last Name to Recipient's First Name Last Name, Month Day, Year, in *Title of Collection*, ed. Editor's First Name Last Name (Publication City: Publisher, Year of publication), Page(s).

12. Abigail Adams to John Adams, August 14, 1776, in *My Dearest Friend: Letters of Abigail and John Adams,* ed. Margaret A. Hogan and C. James Taylor (Cambridge, MA: Harvard University Press, 2007), 139–41.

BIBLIOGRAPHY

Sender's Last Name, First Name. Sender's First Name Last Name to Recipient's First Name Last Name, Month Day, Year. In *Title of Collection of Letters*, edited by Editor's First Name Last Name, Pages. Publication City: Publisher, Year.

Adams, Abigail. Abigail Adams to John Adams, August 14, 1776. In *My Dearest Friend: Letters of Abigail and John Adams*, edited by Margaret A. Hogan and C. James Taylor, 139–41. Cambridge, MA: Harvard University Press, 2007.

author   title   publication

13. BOOK IN A SERIES

NOTE

13. Author's First Name Last Name, *Title of Book*, Title of Series (Publication City: Publisher, Year of publication), Page(s).

13. Karen Armstrong, *Buddha*, Penguin Lives (New York: Viking, 2004), 135.

BIBLIOGRAPHY

Author's Last Name, First Name. *Title of Book*. Title of Series. Publication City: Publisher, Year of publication.

Armstrong, Karen. *Buddha*. Penguin Lives. New York: Viking, 2004.

14. SACRED TEXT

Document a sacred work in a note but not in your bibliography. Provide section information, such as book, chapter, and verse—but never a page number. If you are documenting the Bible, identify the version. Translated texts should give the name of the version or translator.

NOTE

14. Exod. 6:26–27 (New Revised Standard Version).

14. Qur'an 19:17–21.

15. SOURCE QUOTED IN ANOTHER SOURCE

Give the author, title, publication, and page information for the source quoted, followed by information on the source where you found it.

NOTE

15. John Gunther, *Inside USA* (New York: Harper and Brothers, 1947), 259, quoted in Thomas Frank, *What's the Matter with Kansas?* (New York: Henry Holt, 2004), 29.

BIBLIOGRAPHY

Gunther, John. *Inside USA*. New York: Harper and Brothers, 1947. Quoted in Thomas Frank, *What's the Matter with Kansas?* New York: Henry Holt, 2004.

Print Periodicals

For most articles, you'll need to list the author, the article title and any subtitle, the periodical title, volume and issue numbers (for journals), and date information. Include page references only for journals and magazines.

KEY DETAILS FOR DOCUMENTING PRINT PERIODICALS

- **AUTHORS:** If there is more than one author, follow the models for a book with multiple authors (see no. 2).

- **TITLES:** Capitalize article titles and subtitles as you would a work in an edited collection (see no. 6). Use quotation marks around article titles. Italicize periodical titles.

- **VOLUME, ISSUE, AND DATE:** Use Arabic numbers (1, 2, 3, etc.) for the volume even if a journal uses roman numerals. Include the month or season in your documentation whenever that information is given. Magazines and newspapers are documented by date only.

- **PAGES:** Notes for journal and magazine articles need a specific page number; notes for newspapers do not. For the bibliography, give the full page range for journal articles; omit this information for newspapers and for magazine articles.

16. ARTICLE IN A JOURNAL

> **NOTE**
>
> 16. Author's First Name Last Name, "Title of Article," *Title of Journal* volume, no. issue (Month Year): Page(s).
>
> 16. Jeremy Adelman, "An Age of Imperial Revolutions," *American Historical Review* 113, no. 2 (April 2008): 336.

> **BIBLIOGRAPHY**
>
> Author's Last Name, First Name. "Title of Article." *Title of Journal* volume, no. issue (Month Year): Page range.

author   title   publication

Adelman, Jeremy. "An Age of Imperial Revolutions." *American Historical Review* 113, no. 2 (April 2008): 319–40.

17. ARTICLE IN A MAGAZINE

Include the day for a weekly magazine. For a monthly magazine, give only the month and year with no comma in between.

NOTE

17. Author's First Name Last Name, "Title of Article," *Title of Magazine*, Month Day, Year, Page(s).

17. Tony Horwitz, "One Man's Epic Quest to Visit Every Former Slave Dwelling in the United States," *Smithsonian*, October 2013, 42.

BIBLIOGRAPHY

Author's Last Name, First Name. "Title of Article." *Title of Magazine*, Month Day, Year.

Horwitz, Tony. "One Man's Epic Quest to Visit Every Former Slave Dwelling in the United States." *Smithsonian*, October 2013.

18. ARTICLE IN A NEWSPAPER

NOTE

18. Author's First Name Last Name, "Title of Article," *Title of Newspaper*, Month Day, Year, edition (if any), sec. (if any).

18. Nicholas J. C. Pistor, "Arch Is Endangered Monument, Group Says," *St. Louis Post-Dispatch*, October 10, 2013, early edition, sec. A.

BIBLIOGRAPHY

Author's Last Name, First Name. "Title of Article." *Title of Newspaper*, Month Day, Year, edition (if any), sec. (if any).

Pistor, Nicholas J. C. "Arch Is Endangered Monument, Group Says." *St. Louis Post-Dispatch*, October 10, 2013, early edition, sec. A.

19. UNSIGNED ARTICLE

When the author is unknown, put the article title first in notes. In the bibliography entry, put the name of the periodical first.

NOTE

19. "Title of Article," *Title of Newspaper*, Month Day, Year, edition (if any), sec. (if any).

19. "The Next Campaign," *New York Times*, November 8, 2010, New York edition, sec. A.

BIBLIOGRAPHY

Title of Newspaper. "Title of Article." Month Day, Year, edition (if any), sec. (if any).

New York Times. "The Next Campaign." November 8, 2010, New York edition, sec. A.

20. BOOK REVIEW

NOTE

20. Reviewer's First Name Last Name, review of *Title of Book*, by Author's First Name Last Name, *Title of Periodical* volume, no. issue (Month Year): Page(s).

20. Gary K. Waite, review of *The Path of the Devil: Early Modern Witch Hunts*, by Gary Jensen, *American Historical Review* 113, no. 2 (April 2008): 453.

BIBLIOGRAPHY

Reviewer's Last Name, First Name. Review of *Title of Book*, by Author's First Name Last Name. *Title of Periodical* volume, no. issue (Month Year): Page range.

Waite, Gary K. Review of *The Path of the Devil: Early Modern Witch Hunts*, by Gary Jensen. *American Historical Review* 113, no. 2 (April 2008): 453–54.

For a review in a magazine or newspaper, replace the volume and issue numbers with the publication date, as in nos. 17 and 18.

Documentation Map (Chicago)

ARTICLE IN A PRINT JOURNAL

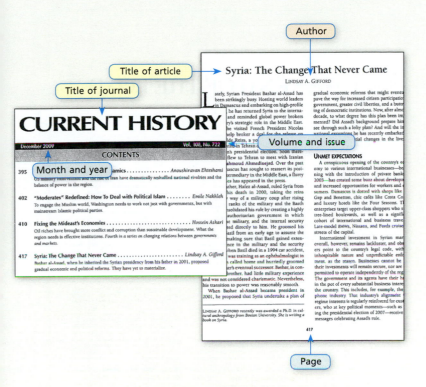

Author

Title of article → Syria: The Change That Never Came

Title of journal

CURRENT HISTORY

December 2009 | Vol. 108, No. 722

CONTENTS

Volume and issue

395 Month and year amics . . . . Anoushiravan Ehteshami
US military intervention and the rise of Iran have dramatically reshuffled national rivalries and the
balance of power in the region.

402 "Moderates" Redefined: How To Deal with Political Islam . . . . Emile Nakhleh
To engage the Muslim world, Washington needs to work not just with governments, but with
mainstream Islamic political parties.

410 Fixing the Mideast's Economies . . . . Hossein Askari
Oil riches have brought more conflict and corruption than sustainable development. What the
region needs is effective institutions. Fourth in a series on changing relations between governments
and markets.

417 Syria: The Change That Never Came . . . . Lindsay A. Gifford
Bashar al-Assad, when he inherited the Syrian presidency from his father in 2001, proposed
gradual economic and political reforms. They have yet to materialize.

Page

NOTE

16. Lindsay A. Gifford, "Syria: The Change That Never Came,"
Current History 108, no. 722 (December 2009): 417.

BIBLIOGRAPHY

Gifford, Lindsay A. "Syria: The Change That Never Came." *Current
History* 108, no. 722 (December 2009): 417–23.

Documentation Map (Chicago)

ARTICLE IN A PRINT MAGAZINE

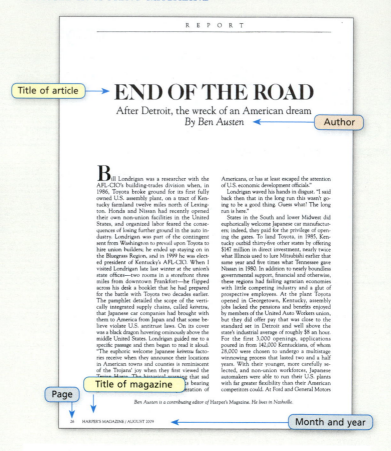

REPORT

Title of article →

END OF THE ROAD

After Detroit, the wreck of an American dream

By Ben Austen ← Author

Bill Londrigan was a researcher with the AFL-CIO's building-trades division, in 1986, Toyota broke ground for its first fully owned U.S. assembly plant, on a tract of Kentucky farmland twelve miles north of Lexington. Honda and Nissan had recently opened their own non-union facilities in the United States, and organized labor feared the consequences of losing further ground in the auto industry. Londrigan was part of the contingent sent from Washington to prevail upon Toyota to hire union builders; he ended up staying on in the Bluegrass Region, and in 1999 he was elected president of Kentucky's AFL-CIO. When I visited Londrigan late last winter at the union's state offices—two rooms in a storefront three miles from downtown Frankfort—he flipped across his desk a booklet that he had prepared for the battle with Toyota two decades earlier. The pamphlet detailed the scope of the vertically integrated supply chains, called *keiretsu*, that Japanese car companies had brought with them to America from Japan and that some believe violate U.S. antitrust laws. On its cover was a black dragon hovering ominously above the middle United States. Londrigan guided me to a specific passage and then began to read it aloud. "The euphoric welcome Japanese *keiretsu* factories receive when they announce their locations in American towns and counties is reminiscent of the Trojans' joy when they first viewed the Trojan Horse. The historical warning that sad ... bearing ... eration of

Americans, or has at least escaped the attention of U.S. economic development officials."

Londrigan waved his hands in disgust. "I said back then that in the long run this wasn't going to be a good thing. Guess what? The long run is here."

States in the South and lower Midwest did euphorically welcome Japanese car manufacturers; indeed, they paid for the privilege of opening the gates. To land Toyota, in 1985, Kentucky outbid thirty-five other states by offering $147 million in direct investment, nearly twice what Illinois used to lure Mitsubishi earlier that same year and five times what Tennessee gave Nissan in 1980. In addition to nearly boundless governmental support, financial and otherwise, these regions had failing agrarian economies with little competing industry and a glut of prospective employees. At the plant Toyota opened in Georgetown, Kentucky, assembly jobs lacked the pensions and benefits enjoyed by members of the United Auto Workers union, but they did offer pay that was close to the standard set in Detroit and well above the state's industrial average of roughly $8 an hour. For the first 3,000 openings, applications poured in from 142,000 Kentuckians, of whom 28,000 were chosen to undergo a multistage winnowing process that lasted two and a half years. With their younger, more carefully selected, and non-union workforces, Japanese automakers were able to run their U.S. plants with far greater flexibility than their American competitors could. At Ford and General Motors

Ben Austen is a contributing editor of Harper's Magazine. He lives in Nashville.

Page → 26 HARPER'S MAGAZINE / AUGUST 2009 ← Month and year

Title of magazine

NOTE

17. Ben Austen, "End of the Road: After Detroit, the Wreck of an American Dream," *Harper's*, August 2009, 26.

BIBLIOGRAPHY

Austen, Ben. "End of the Road: After Detroit, the Wreck of an American Dream." *Harper's*, August 2009.

256

Online Sources

Documentation for many online sources begins with the same elements you'd provide for a print source: author or editor; title of the work; publisher, place of publication, periodical title, publication date, and so on. Provide a **DOI** (Digital Object Identifier, a string of numbers that identifies an online document) or URL whenever possible. For websites you'll also need to include the site's title, sponsor, and a URL.

KEY DETAILS FOR DOCUMENTING ONLINE SOURCES

- **AUTHORS:** If there is more than one author, list subsequent authors as you would for a book with multiple authors (see no. 2).

- **PAGES OR OTHER LOCATORS:** When an online book or journal article has no page numbers, you may give another locator such as a paragraph number, chapter number, or section heading. Be sure to make it clear (with an abbreviation such as "par.," for example) that the locator you cite is not a page number. See no. 25 (pp. 260, 262) for examples that use part and chapter headings as locators.

- **ACCESS DATES:** Chicago requires access dates only when a publication or revision date cannot be determined, or when a source is likely to be updated or removed without notice. However, some instructors require access dates for all online sources, so most of the following models include them.

- **DOI OR URL:** Use a **DOI** if available, starting with "https://doi.org/" and then adding the string of numbers. If a DOI is not available, use a **PERMALINK** if one is provided, or, if not, use the URL that appears in your browser's address bar. Break a DOI or URL that won't fit on one line after a colon or a double slash, before a slash or other punctuation mark, or to either side of an equals sign or an ampersand. Do not add a hyphen or break the URL at one. Put a period at the end. A long DOI can be shortened using the shortDOI service provided by the International DOI Foundation. Do not use online services to shorten URLs.

21. ARTICLE IN AN ONLINE JOURNAL

NOTE

21. Author's First Name Last Name, "Title of Article," *Title of Journal* volume, no. issue (Month Year): Page(s) *or* other locator, accessed Month Day, Year, DOI *or* URL.

21. Gary Gerstle, "A State Both Strong and Weak," *American Historical Review* 115, no. 3 (June 2010): 780, accessed October 7, 2019, https://doi.org/10.1086/ahr.115.3.779.

BIBLIOGRAPHY

Author's Last Name, First Name. "Title of Article." *Title of Journal* volume, no. issue (Month Year): Page(s) *or* other locator. Accessed Month Day, Year. DOI *or* URL.

Gerstle, Gary. "A State Both Strong and Weak." *American Historical Review* 115, no. 3 (June 2010): 778–85. Accessed October 7, 2019. https://doi.org/10.1086/ahr.115.3.779.

22. ARTICLE IN AN ONLINE MAGAZINE

NOTE

22. Author's First Name Last Name, "Title of Article," *Title of Magazine*, Month Day, Year, accessed Month Day, Year, DOI *or* URL.

22. Rozina Kanchwala, "Dating with Climate Anxiety during the Apocalypse," *Teen Vogue*, April 2, 2020, accessed April 8, 2020, https://www.teenvogue.com/story/climate-anxiety-and-dating.

BIBLIOGRAPHY

Author's Last Name, First Name. "Title of Article." *Title of Magazine*, Month Day, Year. Accessed Month Day, Year. DOI *or* URL.

Kanchwala, Rozina. "Dating with Climate Anxiety during the Apocalypse." *Teen Vogue*, April 2, 2020. Accessed April 8, 2020. https://www.teenvogue.com/story /climate-anxiety-and-dating.

author   title   publication

23. ARTICLE IN AN ONLINE NEWSPAPER

Very lengthy URLs can usually be shortened to end after the first single forward slash.

NOTE

23. Author's First Name Last Name, "Title of Article," *Title of Newspaper*, Month Day, Year, accessed Month Day, Year, DOI *or* URL.

23. Quan Truong, "Fundraising Begins for Wheaton Grand Renovation," *Chicago Tribune*, February 27, 2013, accessed March 4, 2020, http://www.chicagotribune.com/.

BIBLIOGRAPHY

Author's Last Name, First Name. "Title of Article." *Title of Newspaper*, Month Day, Year. Accessed Month Day, Year. DOI *or* URL.

Truong, Quan. "Fundraising Begins for Wheaton Grand Renovation." *Chicago Tribune*, February 27, 2013. Accessed March 4, 2020. http://www.chicagotribune.com/.

24. ARTICLE ACCESSED THROUGH A DATABASE

Give the DOI of the article if one is available; if not, include the URL supplied with the article. If no URL is supplied, or if the URL will work only for subscribers, include the database name.

NOTE

24. Author's First Name Last Name, "Title of Article," *Title of Journal* volume, no. issue (Month Year): Page(s) *or* other locator, accessed Month Day, Year, DOI *or* URL *or* Database Name.

24. David W. Galenson, "Analyzing Artistic Innovation," *Historical Methods* 41, no. 3 (2008): 114, accessed August 23, 2013, Academic Search Premier.

BIBLIOGRAPHY

Author's Last Name, First Name. "Title of Article." *Title of Journal*
　　　volume, no. issue (Month Year): Page range. Accessed Month
　　　Day, Year. DOI *or* URL *or* Database Name.

Galenson, David W. "Analyzing Artistic Innovation." *Historical
　　　Methods* 41, no. 3 (2008): 111–20. Accessed August 23, 2013.
　　　Academic Search Premier.

For magazines and newspapers, add the appropriate information
about the month, day, and year as shown in nos. 22 and 23. See
page 259 for a journal article accessed through a database.

25. EBOOK

To document a downloaded ebook of a print work, follow the setup
for a print book but indicate the format of the ebook (PDF ebook,
Kindle). Be aware that the publisher and year may be different from
the print edition's. Because pagination can vary depending on factors
such as text size, notes should include the chapter or section instead
of a page reference.

NOTE

　　25. Author's First Name Last Name, *Title* (Publication City:
Publisher, Year of publication), locator, Format.

　　25. Erik Larson, *In the Garden of Beasts: Love, Terror, and an
American Family in Hitler's Berlin* (New York: Crown, 2011), pt. 1,
under "Dread," Kindle.

BIBLIOGRAPHY

Author's Last Name, First Name. *Title.* Publication City: Publisher,
　　　Year of publication. Format.

Larson, Erik. *In the Garden of Beasts: Love, Terror, and an
　　　American Family in Hitler's Berlin*. New York: Crown, 2011.
　　　Kindle.

Documentation Map (Chicago)

ARTICLE ACCESSED THROUGH A DATABASE

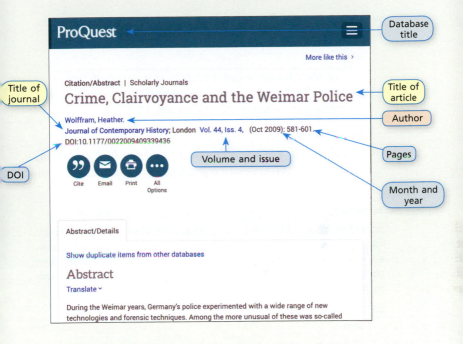

NOTE

24. Heather Wolffram, "Crime, Clairvoyance and the Weimar Police," *Journal of Contemporary History* 44, no. 4 (October 2009): 581, accessed June 25, 2020. https://doi.org/10.1177 /0022009409339436.

BIBLIOGRAPHY

Wolffram, Heather. "Crime, Clairvoyance and the Weimar Police." *Journal of Contemporary History* 44, no. 4 (October 2009): 581– 601. Accessed June 25, 2020. https://doi.org/10.1177 /0022009409339436.

For a book consulted online, include a DOI or URL at the end of the reference.

NOTE

   25. Mark Rowlands, *Can Animals Be Moral?* (Oxford: Oxford Scholarship Online, 2013), under "The Problem," https://doi.org /10.1093/acprof:oso/9780199842001.003.0002.

BIBLIOGRAPHY

Rowlands, Mark. *Can Animals Be Moral?* Oxford: Oxford Scholarship
   Online, 2013. https://doi.org/10.1093/acprof:oso/9780199842001
   .003.0002.

26. WEBSITE

According to the *Chicago Manual of Style*, titles of sites don't generally call for italics. For many sites, the author, the title, and the sponsor of the site are one and the same. If that is the case, simply give the name once. If no publication or revision date can be determined, include an access date.

WHOLE WEBSITE

NOTE

   26. Title of Site, Sponsor, Date of publication *or* last modification, accessed Month Day, Year, URL.

   26. National Weather Service, US Department of Commerce, accessed June 25, 2020, www.weather.gov.

BIBLIOGRAPHY

Title of Site. Sponsor. Date of publication *or* last modification.
   Accessed Month Day, Year. URL.
National Weather Service. US Department of Commerce. Accessed
   June 25, 2020. www.weather.gov.

author   title   publication

WORK FROM A WEBSITE

NOTE

26. "Title of Work," Title of Site, Sponsor, Month Day, Year of publication *or* modification, accessed Month Day, Year, URL.

26. "Copyright Statement," The Field Museum, last modified May 21, 2018, accessed April 8, 2020, https://www.fieldmuseum.org /about/copyright-statement.

BIBLIOGRAPHY

Sponsor. "Title of Work." Title of Site. Month Day, Year of publication *or* modification. Accessed Month Day, Year. URL.

The Field Museum. "Copyright Statement." Last modified May 21, 2018. Accessed April 8, 2020. https://www.fieldmuseum.org /about/copyright-statement.

27. BLOG ENTRY

Unlike a website, the title of a blog is usually set in italics. Omit "(blog)" if that word is included in the title.

NOTE

27. Author's First Name Last Name, "Title of Entry," *Title of Blog* (blog), Month Day, Year, accessed Month Day, Year, URL.

27. Randall Blomquist, "The Artwork of Wo-Haw," *History Happens Here* (blog), April 7, 2020, accessed April 8, 2020, https:// mohistory.org/blog/wo-haw.

BIBLIOGRAPHY

Author's Last Name, First Name. "Title of Entry." *Title of Blog* (blog). Month Day, Year. Accessed Month Day, Year. URL.

Blomquist, Randall. "The Artwork of Wo-Haw." *History Happens Here* (blog). April 7, 2020. Accessed April 8, 2020. https://mohistory.org/blog/wo-haw.

Documentation Map (Chicago)

WORK FROM A WEBSITE

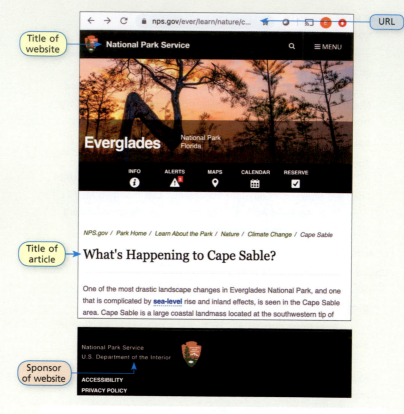

Title of website

URL

National Park Service

Everglades — National Park, Florida

INFO · ALERTS · MAPS · CALENDAR · RESERVE

NPS.gov / Park Home / Learn About the Park / Nature / Climate Change / Cape Sable

Title of article

What's Happening to Cape Sable?

One of the most drastic landscape changes in Everglades National Park, and one that is complicated by sea-level rise and inland effects, is seen in the Cape Sable area. Cape Sable is a large coastal landmass located at the southwestern tip of

National Park Service
U.S. Department of the Interior

Sponsor of website

ACCESSIBILITY
PRIVACY POLICY

NOTE

26. "What's Happening to Cape Sable?," National Park Service, U.S. Department of the Interior, accessed August 5, 2020, https://www.nps.gov/ever/learn/nature/cceffectscapesable.htm.

BIBLIOGRAPHY

U.S. Department of the Interior. "What's Happening to Cape Sable?" National Park Service. Accessed August 5, 2020, https://www.nps.gov/ever/learn/nature/cceffectscapesable.htm.

28. ONLINE VIDEO

The information you provide will vary depending on what you're citing and what information is available. For instance, you may not always find complete author information for online videos. If the video has an author, give that person's name first. If it was posted under a pseudonym or by someone else, indicate that as well.

NOTE

28. Author's First Name Last Name (if any), "Title of Video," produced by *or* streamed by Publisher on Date of online publication, Medium, duration, URL.

28. "Michael Lewis: Wall Street Can't Control Itself," produced by CBS on April 19, 2010, YouTube video, 9:57, http://www.youtube.com/watch?v=M93YUdbAVDA.

BIBLIOGRAPHY

Author's Last Name, First Name (if any). "Title of Video." Produced by *or* Streamed by Publisher on Date of online publication. Medium, duration, URL.

"Michael Lewis: Wall Street Can't Control Itself." Produced by CBS on April 19, 2010. YouTube video, 9:57, http://www.youtube.com/watch?v=M93YUdbAVDA.

29. EMAIL OR POSTING TO AN ONLINE FORUM

Include these sources in notes but not in a bibliography.

EMAIL

NOTE

29. Writer's First Name Last Name, email message to recipient, Month Day, Year.

29. Ana Cooke, email message to Richard Bullock, February 22, 2020.

POSTING TO AN ELECTRONIC FORUM

NOTE

29. Writer's First Name Last Name to Name of Forum, Month Day, Year, accessed Month Day, Year, URL.

29. David Elbert to New American Folk Music Listserv, July 3, 1998, accessed March 3, 2020, http://www.folkmusic.org/archives /fm/0492.html.

Other Kinds of Sources

30. BROADCAST INTERVIEW

NOTE

30. Subject's First Name Last Name, interview by First Name Last Name, *Title of Program*, Network, Month Day, Year.

30. Clive Davis, interview by Don Gonyea, *Weekend Edition Saturday*, NPR, February 22, 2013.

BIBLIOGRAPHY

Subject's Last Name, First Name. Interview by Interviewer's First Name Last Name. *Title of Program.* Network, Month Day, Year.

Davis, Clive. Interview by Don Gonyea. *Weekend Edition Saturday.* NPR, February 22, 2013.

31. SOUND RECORDING

NOTE

31. Composer's *or* Author's First Name Last Name, *Title of Work*, other appropriate information about the performer, conductor, recording, etc., Recording Company identifying number of recording, year of release, medium.

31. Giuseppe Verdi, *Rigoletto*, London Symphony Orchestra, conducted by Richard Bonynge, with Joan Sutherland, Luciano Pavarotti, Sherrill Milnes, et al., recorded at Kingsway Hall, June 1971, London 414269, 1990, MP3 file.

BIBLIOGRAPHY

Composer's *or* Author's Last Name, First Name. *Title of Work.* Other appropriate information about the performer, conductor, recording, etc. Recording Company identifying number of recording, year of release, medium.

Verdi, Giuseppe. *Rigoletto*. London Symphony Orchestra. Richard Bonynge. With Joan Sutherland, Luciano Pavarotti, Sherrill Milnes, et al. Recorded at Kingsway Hall, June 1971. London 414269, 1990, MP3 file.

To document a particular person's work, start with their name.

31. Bruce Springsteen, vocal performance of "Shenandoah," by Pete Seeger, on *We Shall Overcome: The Seeger Sessions*, Columbia 82867, 2006, compact disc.

To document a speech or lecture, begin with the speaker's name.

31. Lt. Ernest H. Shackleton, "My South Polar Expedition" (speech), March 30, 1910, Edison Amberol cylinder, 4M-473, July 1910, Thomas Edison National Historical Park, "Documentary Recordings and Political Speeches," MP3 file, http://www.nps.gov/edis /photosmultimedia/documentary-recordings-and-political-speeches.htm.

32. VIDEO OR DVD

To document a particular person's work, start with their name.

NOTE

32. Writer's First Name Last Name, *Title,* directed by First Name Last Name (Original release year; City: Studio, Year of recording release), Medium.

32. Chris Terrio, *Argo,* directed by Ben Affleck (2012; Burbank, CA: Warner Home Video, 2013), DVD.

BIBLIOGRAPHY

Writer's Last Name, First Name. *Title.* Directed by First Name Last Name. Original release year; City: Studio, Year of recording release. Medium.

> Terrio, Chris. *Argo*. Directed by Ben Affleck. 2012; Burbank, CA: Warner Home Video, 2013. DVD.

33. PODCAST

NOTE

33. Author's *or* Host's First Name Last Name, "Title of Podcast Episode," Month Day, Year, in *Title of Podcast*, produced by Producer's First Name Last Name *or* Production Company, podcast, format, duration, accessed Month Day, Year, URL.

33. Jen Yamato and Frank Shyong, "John Cho," March 17, 2020, in *Asian Enough*, produced by Liyna Anwar, Rina Palta, and Abbie Fentress Swanson, podcast, MP3 audio, 45:36, accessed June 18, 2020, https://www.latimes.com/california /story/2020-03-10/asian-enough-podcast.

BIBLIOGRAPHY

Author's *or* Host's Last Name, First Name. "Title of Podcast Episode." Month Day, Year. In *Title of Podcast*. Produced by Producer's First Name Last Name or Production Company. Podcast. Format. Duration. Accessed Month Day, Year. URL.

Yamato, Jen, and Frank Shyong. "John Cho." March 17, 2020. In *Asian Enough*. Produced by Liyna Anwar, Rina Palta, and Abbie Fentress Swanson. Podcast. MP3 audio. 45:36. Accessed June 18, 2020. https://www.latimes.com/california/story /2020-03-10/asian-enough-podcast.

34. SOCIAL MEDIA POST

Use this format to document any kind of social media post. A bibliography entry is needed only if the account or post is referred to frequently or is particularly important. If the author's real name isn't known, include the username in place of the author's name. Include the text of the post up to the first 160 characters. Include a time stamp only if needed to distinguish the post from others.

author   title   publication

NOTE

34. Writer's First Name Last Name (@username), "Text of post," Title of Site, Month Day, Year, Time, URL.

34. Barack Obama (@POTUS44), "Dr. King and those who marched with him proved that people who love their country can change it. As Americans, we all owe them a great deal," Twitter, January 16, 2017, https://twitter.com/POTUS44/status /821081947728412672.

BIBLIOGRAPHY

Writer's Last Name, First Name (@username). "Text of post." Title of
    Site, Month Day, Year, Time. URL.

Obama, Barack (@POTUS44). "Dr. King and those who marched with
    him proved that people who love their country can change it.
    As Americans, we all owe them a great deal." Twitter,
    January 16, 2017. https://twitter.com/POTUS44/status
    /821081947728412672.

35. GOVERNMENT PUBLICATION

Most government publications can be documented like a work by an organization or corporation (no. 3) or a work by an unknown author (no. 7).

NOTE

35. *The 9/11 Commission Report: Final Report of the National Commission on Terrorist Attacks upon the United States*, official government ed. (Washington, DC: US Government Printing Office, 2004), 33.

BIBLIOGRAPHY

*The 9/11 Commission Report: Final Report of the National
    Commission on Terrorist Attacks upon the United States*,
    official government ed. Washington, DC: US Government
    Printing Office, 2004.

Sources Not Covered by Chicago

To document a source for which Chicago does not provide guidelines, look for models similar to the source you have cited. Give any information readers will need in order to find your source themselves—author, title, publisher, date of publication, information about electronic retrieval (such as the URL or DOI and date of access), and any other pertinent information. You might want to try out your reference note yourself, to be sure it will lead others to your source.

CMS-c Formatting a Paper

Name, course, title. Type the title of your paper about one-third of the way down the page; capitalize it as you would the title of a book. Place your name several lines below the title, along with information such as the title of your course, your instructor's name, and the date. Center each element on the title page on a separate line.

Page numbers. Number all pages consecutively, but do not put a page number on the title page. If your instructor asks you to include your name, the date, or draft number alongside the page number, place the page number and this information in either the upper-right-hand or bottom-right-hand corner of the page; if all you need is a page number, you may also follow this setup or simply center it at the top or bottom of the page.

Spacing and margins. Double-space the main text of the paper as well as block quotations, table titles, captions, footnotes, endnotes, and the bibliography. Set one-inch margins on all sides.

Long quotations. When quoting a hundred or more words or two or more paragraphs, set off the quotation as a block, indenting it one-half inch (or five spaces) from the left margin. Double-space the quotation and do not add extra line space above or below it. Block quotations should not be enclosed in quotation marks.

author   title   publication

N. K. Jemisin describes how writing short stories helped improve her novels:

> And along the way, I learned that short stories *were* good for my longer-form fiction. Writing short stories taught me about the quick hook and the deep character. Shorts gave me space to experiment with unusual plots and story forms—future tense, epistolic format, black characters—which otherwise I would've considered too risky for the length investment of a novel.
>
> I started to *enjoy* writing short fiction, for itself and not just as novel practice. And of course, after all those rejections, my emotional skin grew as thick as an elephant's.[1]

Poetry should be set off when you're quoting two or more lines.

> By referring to him as both "Captain" and "father," Walt Whitman makes clear the strong sense of identification he has felt with the now-fallen Lincoln:
>
> > My Captain does not answer, his lips are pale and still,
> > My father does not feel my arm, he has no pulse nor will.[2]

Illustrations. You may wish to include figures and tables. Figures include charts, diagrams, graphs, maps, photographs, and other illustrations. Figures and tables should be numbered and given a title (Figure 1. A Map of Columbus, Ohio, 2010; Table 1. Telephone Ownership, 1900–1920). Any illustration that comes from another source should include documentation—*Source:* David Siegel, *Creating Killer Web Sites* (Indianapolis, IN: Hayden Books, 1996), 72. If you've created the illustration yourself with data from another source, add "Data from" before the author's name. Put the title above the illustration and any source note below. Position illustrations as soon as possible after they are discussed in your text—and be sure to explain how they relate to your point.

Notes. You may choose to give notes as footnotes at the bottom of the page on which you cite the source or as endnotes that are grouped at the end of your text under the heading "Notes." For both footnotes and endnotes, indent the first line one-half inch (five spaces); do not indent subsequent lines. Footnotes and endnotes should be double-spaced.

Bibliography. Start your list on a new page at the end of your paper, following any notes. Center the heading. Double-space each entry. Each entry should begin at the left margin, and subsequent lines should be indented one-half inch (or five spaces). Alphabetize the list by authors' or editors' last names; for works with no author or editor, or for multiple works by the same author, use the first important words of titles. If you include multiple works by the same author, use a three-em dash (or six hyphens) in place of the author's name in every entry after the first.

CMS-d Sample Pages

The following sample pages are from "History at Home: Leighton House, Sambourne House, and the Heritage Debate," written by Erika Graham for a museum studies course and internship during a study-abroad program in London. They are formatted according to the guidelines of the *Chicago Manual of Style*, 17th edition, and *A Manual for Writers of Research Papers, Theses, and Dissertations*, 8th edition. The sample notes are written in the style you would use if you weren't including a full bibliography; however, a sample bibliography is provided here as well. To read Graham's complete research paper, go to **digital.wwnorton.com /littleseagull4**.

author   title   publication

Sample Title Page, Chicago Style

History at Home:

Leighton House, Sambourne House, and the Heritage Debate •·········· *Title.*

Erika Graham

Grinnell-in-London Internship

December 3, 2019

•···················· *Name, course information, and date.*

Sample Page of Research Paper, Chicago Style

1" margin

Double-spaced throughout.

The Royal Borough of Kensington and Chelsea, a residential district in London, was home to a number of prominent Victorian artists, many of whose houses are still standing today. Two of these buildings have since become museums: Leighton House, home to Frederic Lord Leighton, P.R.A., and Linley Sambourne House, residence of the premier cartoonist for *Punch* magazine and his family. Though managed by the same team of curators and staff, the houses have distinct characters, which stem from the finery of their interiors: Sambourne House sports almost entirely original furnishings and decor, while Leighton House has been painstakingly restored to its intended grandeur as a "palace of art."

But although it might not be apparent to an average visitor overwhelmed by these displays, both museums are unavoidably involved in the fierce debate that surrounds all sites that present "the past." This debate is multifaceted, but all strands return eventually to the issue of whether or not such presentations can educate the visitor—the key role of the museum. As museum-studies scholar Eilean Hooper-Greenhill observes, "Knowledge is now well understood as the commodity that museums offer."[1] The details of this knowledge vary by museum; we will here be focusing on the transmission of historical knowledge. The history museum, however, has an interesting place in the discourse on museum education, for not everyone accepts that these institutions fulfill their didactic role. The accusation runs that some history museums have abandoned their educational duties by moving beyond the glass case format to display history in context through reconstruction, preservation, and, most feared of all, living history

1" margin

1" margin

Author in signal phrase; superscript number to cite source.

1" margin

Sample Endnotes, Chicago Style

21

Notes •·····················

Heading centered.

1. Eilean Hooper-Greenhill, *Museums and the Shaping of Knowledge,* Heritage: Care-Preservation-Management (London: Routledge, 1992), 2.

First line indented; subsequent lines flush left.

2. Emma Barker, "Heritage and the Country House," in *Contemporary Cultures of Display,* ed. Emma Barker (New Haven, CT: Yale University Press, 1999), 206.

Double-spaced.

3. G. Ellis Burcaw, *Introduction to Museum Work,* 3rd ed. (London: AltaMira Press, 1997), 177; Beth Goodacre and Gavin Baldwin, *Living the Past: Reconstruction, Recreation, Re-Enactment and Education at Museums and Historical Sites* (London: Middlesex University Press, 2002), 44.

Multiple sources in a note separated by semicolons.

4. Kevin Walsh, *The Representation of the Past: Museums and Heritage in the Post-Modern World,* Heritage: Care-Preservation-Management (London: Routledge, 1992), 102; Paul Greenhalgh, "Education, Entertainment and Politics: Lessons from the Great International Exhibitions," in *The New Museology,* ed. Peter Vergo (London: Reaktion Books, 1989). •····················

Page number omitted in a reference to the source as a whole.

5. Though a criticism here, not everyone believes this modification is a bad thing. For example, see Kevin Moore, *Museums and Popular Culture,* Contemporary Issues in Museum Culture (London: Cassell, 1997).

6. Goodacre and Baldwin, *Living,* 9 (italics added). •··················

Shorter note form.

7. Walsh, *Representation,* 94; Peter J. Fowler, *The Past in Contemporary Society: Then, Now,* Heritage: Care-Preservation-Management (London: Routledge, 1992), 5.

8. Walsh, *Representation,* 102.

Sample Bibliography, Chicago Style

Bibliography

Heading centered.

Alphabetized by author's last name.

Barker, Emma. "Heritage and the Country House." In *Contemporary Cultures of Display*, edited by Emma Barker, 200–228. New Haven, CT: Yale University Press, 1999.

First line flush left; subsequent lines indented.

Burcaw, G. Ellis. *Introduction to Museum Work.* 3rd ed. London: AltaMira Press, 1997.

Fowler, Peter J. *The Past in Contemporary Society: Then, Now.* Heritage: Care-Preservation-Management. London: Routledge, 1992.

Double-spaced.

Goodacre, Beth, and Gavin Baldwin. *Living the Past: Reconstruction, Recreation, Re-Enactment and Education at Museums and Historical Sites.* London: Middlesex University Press, 2002.

Greenhalgh, Paul. "Education, Entertainment and Politics: Lessons from the Great International Exhibitions." In *The New Museology*, edited by Peter Vergo, 74–98. London: Reaktion Books, 1989.

Handler, Richard. "Authenticity." *Anthropology Today* 2, no. 1 (1986): 2–4. Accessed September 30, 2013. https://doi.org/10.2307/3032899.

DOI.

3-em dash or 6 hyphens replace author's name for subsequent works by the same author.

———. "Heritage and Hegemony: Recent Works on Historic Preservation and Interpretation." *Anthropological Quarterly* 60, no. 3 (1987): 137–41. Accessed October 22, 2013. http://www.jstor.org/stable/i274779.

A stable URL is given for an article accessed from a database.

Hooper-Greenhill, Eilean. *Museums and the Shaping of Knowledge.* Heritage: Care-Preservation-Management. London: Routledge, 1992.

James, Simon. "Imag(in)ing the Past: The Politics and Practicalities of Reconstructions in the Museum Gallery." In *Making Early Histories in Museums*, edited by Nick Merriman, 117–35. London: Leicester University Press, 1999.

CSE Style

Many courses in the sciences will require you to follow the documentation style recommended by the Council of Science Editors (CSE) in *Scientific Style and Format: The CSE Manual for Authors, Editors, and Publishers*. This chapter provides models for documenting sources using the style recommended in the eighth edition of the *CSE Manual*, published in 2014. For more guidance on following CSE style, go to **www.scientificstyleandformat.org/Tools.html**.

A DIRECTORY TO CSE STYLE

Throughout this chapter, models are color-coded to help you see how writers present source information in their texts and in reference lists: tan for author or editor; yellow for title; gray for publication information, which may include place of publication, publisher, date of publication, volume and issue numbers, section and page numbers, and so on.

CSE-a In-Text Documentation

The CSE *Manual* offers three ways of indicating in your text that you are citing material from a source. You can use any of these styles, but CSE recommends citation–sequence style.

author   title   publication

Citation–Sequence Style calls for you to put a number (either a superscript or a number in parentheses) after any reference to a source. Number sources in the order you mention them—the first source you mention is numbered 1, the second one is numbered 2, and so on. Once you number a source, use that same number each time you mention that source: if your first reference to a source is numbered 3, every citation of that source thereafter should be numbered 3 regardless of where it appears in your paper.

Citation–Name Style calls for you first to alphabetize your list of references and then number the sources consecutively in the order they appear on the list: the first source on the list—say, Ackerman—is number 1, the second—perhaps, Bond—is number 2, and so on. Then put the appropriate number (either a superscript or a number in parentheses) after each mention of that source. So if Zuefle is the tenth source on your alphabetical list of references, every citation of the same work by this author will get Zuefle[10], even if Zuefle is the first source you cite in your paper.

Name–Year Style calls for you to give the author's last name and the year of publication in parentheses after any mention of a source. If you mention the author's name in a **SIGNAL PHRASE**, you need to put only the year in parentheses. For instance:

> Atherosclerosis seems to predate our modern lifestyles (Singer 2009).

> Singer (2009) questions whether atherosclerosis is inevitable.

If a work has two authors, give both names: (Davidson and Lyon 1987). For three or more authors, give only the first author, followed by "et al.," a Latin abbreviation meaning "and others": (Rathus et al. 2010). If you include more than one work in parentheses, separate them with a semicolon: (Gilder 2008; Singer 2009).

CSE-b List of References

The in-text documentation corresponds to the sources you give at the end of your paper in a list of references. How you arrange sources in your References, whether you number them, and where you put publication dates depend on which style you use.

- *In citation–sequence style,* arrange and number the sources in the order in which you first cite them in your text. Put the date for a book at the end of the publication information; put the date for a periodical article after the periodical's title.
- *In citation–name style,* arrange and number the sources in alphabetical order. Put the date for a book at the end of the publication information and the date for a periodical article after its title.
- *In name–year style,* arrange the sources alphabetically, and do not number them. Put the date after the name(s) of the author(s).

The models and examples that follow demonstrate citation–sequence style. See page 294 for guidelines on organizing and formatting a list of references and pages 296–97 for samples from a paper using citation–sequence style.

Print Books

For most books, you'll need to provide information about the author; the title and any subtitle; and the place of publication, publisher, and year of publication.

KEY DETAILS FOR DOCUMENTING PRINT BOOKS

- **AUTHORS:** Put each author's last name first, and give initials for first and middle names. Do not add space between initials, and omit punctuation except a period after the final initial.
- **TITLES:** For book and chapter titles, capitalize only the first word, any acronyms, and proper nouns or adjectives. Do not italicize, underline, or put quotation marks around any title.

author   title   publication

- **PUBLICATION PLACE:** Place the two-letter abbreviation for state, province, or country within parentheses after the city.
- **PUBLISHER:** Shorten a publisher's name by omitting "the" and abbreviations such as "Inc."

1. ONE AUTHOR

1. Author's Last Name Initials. Title. Publication City (State): Publisher; Year of publication.

1. Singh S. Big bang: the origin of the universe. New York (NY): Fourth Estate; 2004.

2. MULTIPLE AUTHORS

List up to ten authors, separating them with commas and putting a period after the last author's initials.

2. First Author's Last Name Initials, Next Author's Last Name Initials, Final Author's Last Name Initials. Title. Publication City (State): Publisher; Year of publication.

2. Gaines SM, Eglinton G, Rullkotter J. Echoes of life: what fossil molecules reveal about Earth history. New York (NY): Oxford University Press; 2009.

For a work by eleven or more authors, list the first ten, followed by a comma and "et al."

3. ORGANIZATION OR CORPORATION AS AUTHOR

3. Organization Name. Title. Publication City (State): Publisher; Year of publication.

3. National Research Council. Black and smokeless powders: technologies for finding bombs and the bomb makers. Washington (DC): National Academy Press; 1998.

Documentation Map (CSE)

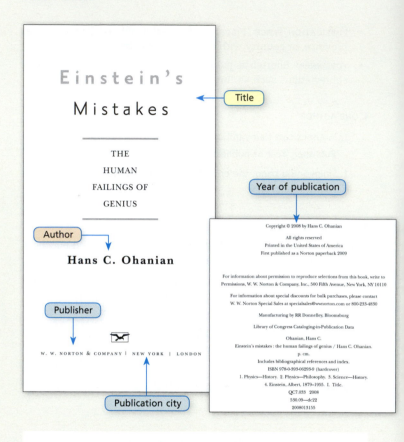

1. Ohanian HC. Einstein's mistakes: the human failings of genius. New York (NY): W. W. Norton; 2008.

4. EDITOR

4. Editor's Last Name Initials, editor. Title. Publication City (State): Publisher; Year of publication.

4. Dawkins R, editor. The Oxford book of modern science writing. New York (NY): Oxford University Press; 2009.

5. WORK IN AN EDITED COLLECTION

5. Author's Last Name Initials. Title of work. Year of publication if earlier than year of collection. In: Editor's Last Name Initials, editor. Title of book. Publication City (State): Publisher; Year of publication of collection. p. Pages.

5. Carson R. The sea around us. 1951. In: Dawkins R, editor. The Oxford book of modern science writing. New York (NY): Oxford University Press; 2009. p. 130–137.

6. CHAPTER OF A BOOK

6. Author's Last Name Initials. Title of book. Publication City (State): Publisher; Year of publication. Chapter number, Title of chapter; p. Pages.

6. Gilder L. The age of entanglement: when quantum physics was reborn. New York (NY): Knopf; 2008. Chapter 13, Solvay 1927; p. 110–127.

7. PAPER OR ABSTRACT FROM CONFERENCE PROCEEDINGS

If you cite an abstract of a paper rather than the paper itself, place [abstract] after the paper's title but before the period.

7. Author's Last Name Initials. Title of paper. In: Editor's Last Name Initials, editor. Title of book. Number and Name of Conference; Year Month Day of Conference; Place of Conference. Publication City (State): Publisher; Year of publication. p. Pages.

7. Polivy J. Physical activity, fitness, and compulsive behaviors. In: Bouchard C, Shephard RJ, Stephens T, editors. Physical activity, fitness, and health: international proceedings and consensus statement. 2nd International Consensus Symposium on Physical Activity, Fitness, and Health; 1992 May 5–9; Toronto, Canada. Champaign (IL): Human Kinetics Publishers; 1994. p. 883–897.

8. EDITION OTHER THAN THE FIRST

8. Author's Last Name Initials. Title of book. Name *or* number of ed. Publication City (State): Publisher; Year of publication.

8. Marshak S. Geology. 4th ed. New York (NY): W. W. Norton; 2012.

Print Periodicals

For most journal articles, you'll need to list the author, title, and any subtitle of the article; the title of the periodical; the volume and issue numbers; the year; and the inclusive page numbers of the article. Newspaper and some magazine articles have different requirements.

KEY DETAILS FOR DOCUMENTING PRINT PERIODICALS

- **AUTHORS:** List authors as you would for a book (nos. 1 and 2).
- **TITLES:** Capitalize only the first word, any acronyms, and proper nouns or adjectives in article titles. Abbreviate titles of journals and capitalize all major words, even if abbreviated. Do not italicize, underline, or put quotation marks around any titles.
- **DATE:** For periodicals with no volume or issue numbers, provide the year, month, and day. Abbreviate months to the first three letters: Jan, Feb, Mar, and so on.

9. ARTICLE IN A JOURNAL

9. Author's Last Name Initials. Title of article. Title of Journal. Year;Volume(issue):Pages.

9. Reutemann A, Lucero L, Guarise N, Vigetti AC. Structure of the Cyperaceae inflorescence. Bot Rev. 2012;78(2):184–204.

author   title   publication

Documentation Map (CSE)

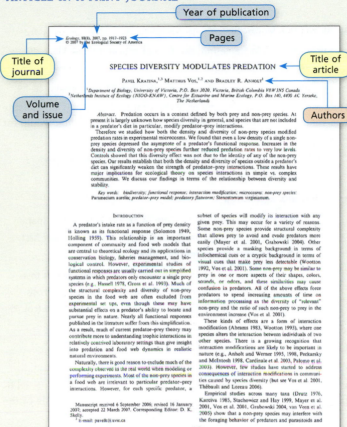

Year of publication

Pages

Title of journal

Title of article

Volume and issue

Authors

Ecology, 88(8), 2007, pp. 1917–1923
© 2007 by the Ecological Society of America

SPECIES DIVERSITY MODULATES PREDATION

PAVEL KRATINA,[1,3] MATTHIJS VOS,[1,2] AND BRADLEY R. ANHOLT[1]

[1]*Department of Biology, University of Victoria, P.O. Box 3020, Victoria, British Columbia V8W 3N5 Canada*
[2]*Netherlands Institute of Ecology (NIOO-KNAW), Centre for Estuarine and Marine Ecology, P.O. Box 140, 4400 AC Yerseke, The Netherlands*

Abstract. Predation occurs in a context defined by both prey and non-prey species. At present it is largely unknown how species diversity in general, and species that are not included in a predator's diet in particular, modify predator–prey interactions.

Therefore we studied how both the density and diversity of non-prey species modified predation rates in experimental microcosms. We found that even a low density of a single non-prey species depressed the asymptote of a predator's functional response. Increases in the density and diversity of non-prey species further reduced predation rates to very low levels. Controls showed that this diversity effect was not due to the identity of any of the non-prey species. Our results establish that both the density and diversity of species outside a predator's diet can significantly weaken the strength of predator–prey interactions. These results have major implications for ecological theory on species interactions in simple vs. complex communities. We discuss our findings in terms of the relationship between diversity and stability.

Key words: biodiversity; functional response; interaction modification; microcosms; non-prey species; Paramecium aurelia; predator–prey model; predatory flatworm; Stenostomum virginianum.

INTRODUCTION

A predator's intake rate as a function of prey density is known as its functional response (Solomon 1949, Holling 1959). This relationship is an important component of community and food web models that are central to theoretical ecology and its applications in conservation biology, fisheries management, and biological control. However, experimental studies of functional responses are usually carried out in simplified systems in which predators only encounter a single prey species (e.g., Hassell 1978, Gross et al. 1993). Much of the structural complexity and diversity of non-prey species in the food web are often excluded from experimental set ups, even though these may have substantial effects on a predator's ability to locate and pursue prey in nature. Nearly all functional responses published in the literature suffer from this simplification. As a result, much of current predator–prey theory may contribute more to understanding trophic interactions in relatively contrived laboratory settings than give insight into predation and food web dynamics in realistic natural environments.

Naturally, there is good reason to exclude much of the complexity observed in the real world when modeling or performing experiments. Most of the non-prey species in a food web are irrelevant to particular predator–prey interactions. However, for each specific predator, a subset of species will modify its interaction with any given prey. This may occur for a variety of reasons. Some non-prey species provide structural complexity that allows prey to avoid and evade predators more easily (Mayer et al. 2001, Grabowski 2004). Other species provide a masking background in terms of infochemical cues or a cryptic background in terms of visual cues that make prey less detectable (Wootton 1992, Vos et al. 2001). Some non-prey may be similar to prey in one or more aspects of their shapes, colors, sounds, or odors, and these similarities may cause confusion in predators. All of the above effects force predators to spend increasing amounts of time on information processing as the diversity of "relevant" non-prey and the ratio of such non-prey to prey in the environment increase (Vos et al. 2001).

These kinds of effects are a form of interaction modification (Abrams 1983, Wootton 1993), where one species alters the interaction between individuals of two other species. There is a growing recognition that interaction modifications are likely to be important in nature (e.g., Anholt and Werner 1995, 1998, Peckarsky and McIntosh 1998, Cardinale et al. 2003, Palomo et al. 2003). However, few studies have started to address consequences of interaction modifications in communities caused by species diversity (but see Vos et al. 2001, Thébault and Loreau 2006).

Empirical studies across many taxa (Drutz 1976, Kareiva 1985, Stachowicz and Hay 1999, Mayer et al. 2001, Vos et al. 2001, Grabowski 2004, van Veen et al. 2005) show that a non-prey species may interfere with the foraging behavior of predators and parasitoids and

Manuscript received 6 September 2006; revised 16 January 2007; accepted 22 March 2007. Corresponding Editor: D. K. Skelly.
[3] E-mail: pavelk@uvic.ca

1917

9. Kratina P, Vos M, Anholt BR. Species diversity modulates predation. Ecology. 2007;88(8):1917–1923.

285

10. ARTICLE IN A MAGAZINE

> 10. Author's Last Name Initials. Title of article. Title of Magazine.
> Year Month Day:Pages.

> 10. Wood, G. Scrubbed. New York. 2013 Jun 24–Jul 1:44–46, 48–49.

For a monthly magazine, give only the year and month. If a magazine
has volume and issue numbers, you can give them as you would for
a journal.

> 10. Millius S. Virus makes liars of squash plants. Science News.
> 2010;177(2):8.

11. ARTICLE IN A NEWSPAPER

> 11. Author's Last Name Initials. Title of article. Title of Newspaper
> (Edition). Year Month Day;Sect. section letter *or* number:first
> page of article (col. column number).

> 11. Singer N. Artery disease in some very old patients: doctors test
> mummies at a Cairo museum and find signs of atherosclerosis.
> New York Times (New England Ed.). 2009 Nov 24;Sect. D:6 (col. 3).

Online Sources

Documentation for online sources begins with basic elements—
author and title of the work and publication information. In addition, you usually need to include several other items: the title of the
website, access date, URL, DOI, and so on.

KEY DETAILS FOR DOCUMENTING ONLINE SOURCES

- **AUTHORS:** List authors as you would for a book (nos. 1 and 2).
- **TITLES:** Format the titles of books, journals, and articles on the
  web as you would print sources (see pp. 280 and 284). For titles of
  other web materials, including homepages, reproduce the wording, capitalization, and punctuation as they appear on the site.

author   title   publication

- **PUBLICATION CITY:** If you cannot identify the city of publication of an online book, write [place unknown].

- **PUBLISHER:** List as the publisher the person or organization that sponsors the website. If you cannot identify the publisher of an online book, write [publisher unknown].

- **DATES:** Whenever possible, give three dates: the date a work was first published online or the copyright date; the date of its latest update; and the date you accessed it.

- **PAGES, LENGTH:** If there are no page numbers, indicate the length in brackets: [2 screens], [8 paragraphs].

- **URL, DOI, DOCUMENT NUMBER:** Give whatever URLs, DOIs, and database document numbers are available, in that order. Break URLs that don't fit on one line after a slash or other punctuation, but do not add a hyphen. Put a period at the end.

12. ONLINE BOOK

12. Author's Last Name Initials. Title. Publication City (State): Publisher; Year of publication [updated Year Month Day; accessed Year Month Day]. URL.

12. Dean L. Blood groups and red cell antigens. Bethesda (MD): National Library of Medicine; 2005 [accessed 2020 Jun 23]. http://www.ncbi.nlm.nih.gov/bookshelf/br.fcgi?book=rbcantigen.

To document a part of an online book, include the title of the part after the publication information (as in no. 6).

13. ARTICLE ACCESSED THROUGH A DATABASE

Include the DOI and document number if the database assigns them.

13. Author's Last Name Initials. Title of article. Title of Periodical. Date of publication [updated Year Month Day; accessed Year Month Day];Volume(issue):Pages *or* [length]. Name of Database. URL. doi: DOI. Database Doc No number.

13. Kemker BE, Stierwalt JAG, LaPointe LL, Heald GR. Effects of a cell phone conversation on cognitive processing performances. J Am Acad Audiol. 2009 [accessed 2015 Nov 29];20(9):582–588. Academic Search Premier. https://web.ebscohost.com/academic/academic-search-premier. Database Doc No 45108388.

14. ARTICLE IN AN ONLINE JOURNAL

14. Author's Last Name Initials. Title of article. Title of Journal. Year of publication [updated Year Month Day; accessed Year Month Day];Volume(issue):Pages *or* [length]. URL.

14. Voelker R. Medical simulation gets real. JAMA. 2009 [accessed 2020 Jun 21];302(20):2190–2192. http://jama.ama-assn.org/cgi/content/full/302/20/2190.

15. ARTICLE IN AN ONLINE NEWSPAPER

15. Author's Last Name Initials. Title of article. Title of Newspaper. Year Month Day of publication [updated Year Month Day; accessed Year Month Day];Pages *or* [length]. URL.

15. Levey NN. Doctors list overused medical treatments. Los Angeles Times. 2013 Feb 20 [accessed 2020 Jun 21];[about 4 screens]. http://www.latimes.com/health/la-na-medical-procedures-20130221,0,6234009.story.

16. WEBSITE

If there is a known author, begin with the author's name before the title of the site. If the author is an organization, begin with the title of the site, and give the organization's name as the publisher.

16. Author's Last Name Initials (if any). Title of Site. Publication City (State): Publisher; Year of publication [updated Year Month Day; accessed Year Month Day]. URL.

author   title   publication

Documentation Map (CSE)

ARTICLE ACCESSED THROUGH A DATABASE

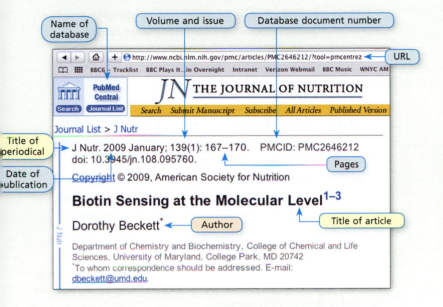

13. Beckett D. Biotin sensing at the molecular level. J Nutr. 2009
    [accessed 2015 Mar 2];139(1):167-170. PubMed Central. http://
    www.ncbi.nlm.nih.gov/pmc. Database Doc No PMC2646212.

16. American Wind Energy Association. Washington (DC): American Wind Energy Association; 1996–2013 [accessed 2020 May 15]. http://www.awea.org.

17. PART OF A WEBSITE

17. Title of Site. Publication City (State): Publisher; Year of site publication. Title of part; Date of part publication [updated Year Month Day; accessed Year Month Day]; [length of part]. URL of part.

17. US Environmental Protection Agency. Research Triangle Park (NC): US Environmental Protection Agency, Air Quality Analysis Group; 2011. Nitrogen dioxide; 2011 [updated 2012 Nov 28; accessed 2020 Apr 5];[about 3 screens]. http://www.epa.gov/airtrends/nitrogen.html.

If the author of the part you are citing is different from the author of the site, begin with the author and title of the part and do not give the title of the complete website.

17. Author's Last Name Initials. Title of part. Publication City (State): Publisher; Date of part publication [updated Year Month Day; accessed Year Month Day];[length of part]. URL of part.

17. Macklin SA. PICES Metadata Federation. Sidney (BC): PICES North Pacific Marine Science Organization; 2008 Nov [accessed 2020 Jun 2];[15 paragraphs]. http://www.pices.int/projects/npem/default.aspx.

18. IMAGE OR INFOGRAPHIC

18. Author's Last Name Initials. Title [image *or* infographic]. Publication City (State): Publisher *or* Producer; Date of publication: [updated Year Month Day; accessed Year Month Day]. URL.

author   title   publication

18. Watson JD, Crick FHC. Molecular structure of nucleic acids [image]. London (UK): Nature Publishing Group; 1953 [accessed 2020 Jun 14]. https://www.nature.com/articles/171737a0.

19. PODCAST OR WEBCAST

19. Host's Last Name Initials. Title of episode [podcast *or* webcast, episode number if any]. Name of series. Producer. Year Month Day of broadcast *or* posting, length. [accessed Year Month Day]. URL.

19. Benson M. Astrogeology—meteorites and spacecraft missions [webcast]. Smithsonian Science How. Smithsonian National Museum of Natural History. 2015 Jun 25, 36:38 minutes. [accessed 2020 Jun 14]. https://naturalhistory.si.edu/education /teaching-resources/earth-science/astrogeology-meteorites-and -spacecraft-missions.

19. Britt M. Why replications sometimes don't agree with the original study [podcast, episode 246]. The Psych Files. Boot & Eddy Productions. 2015 Sep 4, 12:36 minutes. [accessed 2020 Jun 23]. https://thepsychfiles.com/2015/09/ep-246-why-replications -sometimes-dont-agree-with-the-original-study/.

20. VIDEO

20. Title of video [video, episode number if any]. Name of series. Producer. Year Month Day of broadcast *or* posting, length. [accessed Year Month Day]. URL.

20. Making North America: origins [video]. NOVA ScienceNOW. WGBH. 2016 Jun 29, 53:04 minutes. [accessed 2020 Jun 23]. https://www.pbs.org/video/nova-making-north-america-origins/.

21. BLOG ENTRY

21. Author's Last Name Initials. Title of post [blog entry]. Title of blog. Year Month Day of posting. [accessed Year Month Day]. URL.

21. Blair ME. Calls of the forest [blog entry]. Scientist at Work: Notes from the Field. 2013 May 29. [accessed 2020 May 15]. http://scientistatwork.blogs.nytimes.com/2013/05/29/calls-of-the-forest.

22. SOCIAL MEDIA POST

22. Author's First Name Last Name *or* Organization's page name. Name of social media site [page type, post type]. Year Month Day, Time posted. [accessed Year Month Date]. URL.

22. Barack Obama. Facebook [profile page, shared link]. 2016 Apr 26, 12:09 p.m. [accessed 2020 Jan 20]. https://www.facebook.com/barackobama.

Sources Not Covered by CSE

To document a source for which CSE does not provide guidelines, look for models similar to the source you have cited. Give any information readers will need in order to find your source themselves—author, title, publisher, date of publication, information about electronic retrieval (such as the database, URL, and date of access), and any other pertinent information. You might want to try your reference note yourself, to be sure it will lead others to your source.

CSE-c Formatting a Paper

Title page. CSE does not provide guidelines for college papers. Check to see whether your instructor prefers a separate title page; if so, include the title of your paper, your name, the name of the course, your instructor's name, and the date. Otherwise, place that information at the top of the first page of your text.

Page numbers and running head. Put the page number and a short version of your title in the top right-hand corner of each page except for the title page.

author   title   publication

Margins and line spacing. Leave one-inch margins all around the page. Double-space your text but single-space your list of references, leaving one line space between entries. Some instructors prefer the list of references instead to be double-spaced with no extra spaces between entries; check which style your instructor prefers.

Headings. Especially when your paper is long or when it has clear parts, headings can help readers to follow your argument. Center headings but without adding any extra space above or below.

Abstract. If you include an **ABSTRACT**, put it on its own page after the title page, with the word "Abstract" centered at the top of the page.

Long quotations. When you are quoting forty or more words, reduce the text size slightly and set them off from your text, indented a little from the left margin. Do not enclose such quotations in quotation marks. Indicate the source in a sentence that introduces the quotation. Include a superscript or a number in parentheses pointing to the full documentation.

> The simulations identify observable criteria for sympatric speciation and resolve the question of whether Darwin correctly identified the trends he observed in nature.[1]
>
> > How many of those birds and insects in North America and Europe, which differ very slightly from each other, have been ranked by one eminent naturalist as undoubted species, and by another as varieties, or, as they are often called, as geographical races!

FROM LIST OF REFERENCES

1. Darwin C. The origin of species: Darwin's four great books. In: Wilson EO, editor. From so simple a beginning. New York (NY): W. W. Norton; 2006. p. 441–760.

Illustrations. Insert each illustration close to where you mention it in your text. Number and label each one (Table 1, Figure 3), and provide a descriptive title (Figure 5 Bonding in ethylene). Titles use sentence–style capitalization. Figures include charts, graphs, maps, photographs, and other types of illustrations. Number tables and figures consecutively, using separate numbering for tables and for figures.

References. Start your list of sources on a new page at the end of your paper; center the heading "References" at the top of the page. CSE single-spaces entries and separates them with a line space. For citation–sequence style, number entries according to the order in which you first cite them in your text. Align subsequent lines of each entry below the first word of the first line.

CSE-d Sample Pages

The following sample pages are from "Guppies and Goldilocks: Models and Evidence of Two Types of Speciation," a paper written by Pieter Spealman for an undergraduate biology course. They are formatted in the citation–sequence format according to the guidelines of *Scientific Style and Format: The CSE Manual for Authors, Editors, and Publishers*, 8th edition (2014). To read the complete paper, go to **digital.wwnorton.com/littleseagull4**.

author   title   publication

Sample Title Page, CSE Style

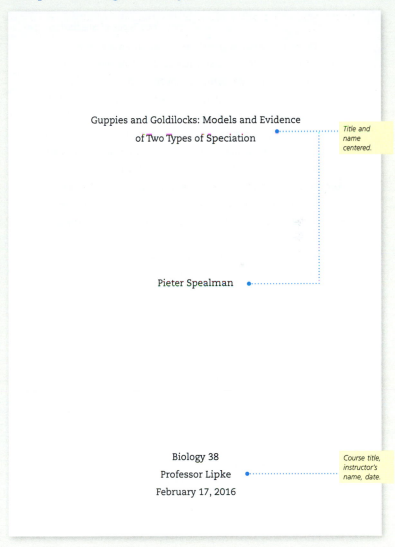

Guppies and Goldilocks: Models and Evidence
of Two Types of Speciation

Title and name centered.

Pieter Spealman

Biology 38
Professor Lipke
February 17, 2016

Course title, instructor's name, date.

Sample Page of Research Paper, CSE Style

1" margin Two Types of Speciation 1 *Brief title and page number.*

Determining how a given species has arisen is a central question for any field biologist. There are two competing models of speciation: allopatric and sympatric. In 1859, Charles Darwin[1] *Superscript number to mark citation* asserted that speciation could be sympatric, saying, "I believe that *Double-spaced text.* many perfectly defined species have been formed on strictly continuous areas." One hundred years later, Ernst Mayr[2] contested Darwin's assertion, saying, "All the evidence that has accumulated since Darwin indicates that this assumption [that species have been *Words added to a quotation are enclosed in brackets.* formed on strictly continuous areas] is unwarranted as far as higher animals are concerned." Was Mayr right to condemn Darwin for failing to assess correctly the lessons of nature that he observed in the Galapagos archipelago? The difficulty of determining the provenance of a species—whether it arose through sympatric or allopatric speciation—lies in knowing what to look for. And while recent research employing computer simulations[3] suggests a solution to the problem by providing a set of criteria necessary for sympatric speciation, the results predicted by those simulations did not actually arise in the field study that provides the most comprehensive data available to test the model. Rather than

1" margin invalidating the model, however, this research points to the *1" margin* challenges that complex natural environments pose to the isolation of observable criteria for distinguishing the two types of speciation.

Headings help organize the paper. Allopatric and Sympatric: Conditions and Examples

The two types of speciation differ in their view of what conditions are crucial in determining whether speciation can *In citation-sequence style, source previously cited uses same number as first citation.* occur. Allopatric speciation, which Mayr[2] championed, explains the divergence of species by physical isolation, as when a population

1" margin

Sample Page of Reference List, CSE Style

Two Types of Speciation   9

References ●··· *Heading centered.*

1. Darwin C. The origin of species: Darwin's four great books. In:
   Wilson EO, editor. From so simple a beginning. New York (NY):
   W. W. Norton; 2006. p. 441–760.

2. Mayr E. Isolation as an evolutionary factor. Proc Am Philos Soc.
   1959;103(2):221–230.

3. van Doorn GS, Edelaar P, Weissing FJ. On the origin of species by
   natural and sexual selection. Science. 2009;326(5960):1704–1707.

4. Schilthuizen M. Frogs, flies, and dandelions: speciation—the
   evolution of new species. New York (NY): Oxford University Press;
   2001.

5. Grant BR, Grant PR. Darwin's finches: population variation and
   sympatric speciation. Proc Nat Acad Sci USA. 1979;76(4):2359–
   2363.

6. Endler JA. Natural selection on color patterns in *Poecilia reticulata*.
   Evolution. 1980 [accessed 2016 Feb 7];34(1):76–91. JSTOR. http://
   jstor.org/stable/2408316.

7. Weiner J. The beak of the finch. New York (NY): Vintage; 1994.

8. Smith JM. Sympatric speciation. Am Nat. 1966 [accessed 2016
   Feb 7];100(916):637–650. JSTOR. http://jstor.org/stable/2459301.

9. Stewart P. Galapagos: islands that changed the world. New Haven ●···
   (CT): Yale University Press; 2006.

Entries are single-spaced with a line space between each. Subsequent lines of an entry align below the first word of the first line.

Citation-sequence style: Sources numbered according to the sequence in which they appear in the text.

Edit

We edit to let the fire show through
the smoke.

—ARTHUR PLOTNIK

Editing the Errors That Matter

In writing, as in life, no one's perfect. We make mistakes. Some of our errors are no big deal, barely noticeable, not worth mentioning. Others, however, are more serious—deal breakers, maybe—and we try hard to avoid them. One of the great things about writing is that we have time to edit our work and fix our errors. Our team asked seventy-five writing instructors which errors really matter to them—which ones are most bothersome and do the most damage to a writer's credibility and ideas. Their responses covered a wide gamut, from sentence structure to punctuation. This section focuses on those errors that matter in **EDITED ACADEMIC ENGLISH**, showing how to spot them in a draft, explaining why they're so troublesome, and suggesting strategies for editing them out.

Throughout this chapter, you'll find opportunities to practice editing in adaptive InQuizitive activities. For more information on InQuizitive, see the access card at the front of your book or visit **digital.wwnorton.com/littleseagull4**.

E-1 Editing Sentences

Fragments, comma splices, fused sentences, and mixed constructions are all types of sentence-structure errors. Such sentences are usually comprehensible in context, so as long as readers understand the message, what makes them errors? Here's what. Solid sentence structure matters for two reasons:

- The perception of your competence hangs on it: readers don't trust writers who write sloppy sentences.

- Even if a poorly structured sentence can be understood, your readers have to work a little harder to do so, and they may not want to put forth the effort. Your job is to make it easy for readers, to keep them reading smoothly all the way to the end.

Every sentence is composed of one or more **CLAUSES**, and every clause needs to have a **SUBJECT**, a **VERB**, and appropriate punctuation. Don't underestimate those little dots and squiggles; they often make all the difference in how a sentence is read and understood. Consider these two examples:

▶ Let's eat Grandma.

▶ Let's eat, Grandma.

Are you inviting your grandmother to eat a meal right now, or are you inviting someone else to eat *her*? That one little comma in the right place can save grandma's life (or at least make it clear to your readers that you aren't proposing to make a meal of her). This chapter will help you examine your writing with an eye to four common sentence-structure errors: fragments, comma splices, fused sentences, and mixed constructions.

E-1a Fragments

At first glance, a fragment looks like a complete sentence—it begins with a capital letter and concludes with end punctuation—but on closer examination, a key element, usually a **SUBJECT** or a **VERB**, is missing. For example: "Forgot to vote." Who forgot to vote? We don't know; the subject is missing. "Two bottles of rancid milk." Wow. That sounds interesting, but what about them? There's no verb, so we don't know. A fragment also occurs when a sentence begins with a **SUBORDINATING WORD** such as "if" or "because," but the **SUBORDINATE CLAUSE** is not followed by an **INDEPENDENT CLAUSE**. "If the ball game is rained out." Well, what happens if the ball game is rained out? Again, we don't know.

Checking for fragments

Sometimes writers use fragments for stylistic reasons, but it's best to avoid them in academic writing. To check your text for fragments, examine each sentence one by one, making sure there's both a subject and a verb. (It might take you a while to do this at first, but the process will go much faster with practice, and it's worth the time.) Check also for subordinating words (see **S-2a** for a list of common ones), and if there's a subordinate clause, make sure there's also an independent clause.

Editing fragments

Let's look at some fragments and see what we can do about them.

NEEDS A SUBJECT

▶ The Centipedes were terrible last night. *Started late, played three songs, and left.*

Context makes it clear that it was the Centipedes who started late. Still, the italicized part is a fragment because there is no explicit subject. We have two good options here. One is to add a subject to the fragment in order to make the sentence complete; the other is to attach the fragment to a nearby sentence. Both strategies will work, and you can choose whichever sounds better to you.

▶ The Centipedes were terrible last night. ~~Started~~ *They started* late, played three songs, and left.

▶ The Centipedes were terrible last night. ~~Started~~ *because they started* late, played three songs, and left.

In the first example, we've added a subject, "they," which refers to "Centipedes." In the second, we've attached the fragment to the preceding sentence using a subordinating word, "because," followed by an explicit subject, "they."

NEEDS A VERB

▶ Malik heard a knock on the door. *Then a loud thud.*

The example makes sense: we know that Malik heard a loud thud after the knock. But the italicized part is a fragment because between the capital "T" at the beginning and the period at the end, there is no verb. Again, there are two strategies for editing: to add a verb to the fragment in order to make the sentence complete, or to incorporate the fragment into the previous sentence so that its verb can do double duty.

▶ Malik heard a knock on the door. Then *came* a loud thud.

▶ Malik heard a knock on the door, ~~Then~~ *followed by* a loud thud.

NEEDS MORE INFORMATION

▶ Olga nearly missed her plane. *Because the line at security was so long.* She got flustered and dropped her change purse.

The italicized part of the example above does have a subject and a verb, but it can't stand alone as a sentence because it starts with "because," a subordinating word that leads readers to expect more information. Did the long security line cause Olga to nearly miss her plane? Or did the long line fluster her? We can't be sure. How you edit this fragment depends on what you're trying to say—and how the ideas relate to one another. For example:

▶ Olga nearly missed her plane. ~~Because~~ *because* the line at security was so long.

▶ Because the line at security was so long, ~~She~~ *she* got flustered and dropped her change purse.

The first option explains why Olga nearly missed her plane, and the second explains why she got flustered and dropped her change purse.

> Edit

The word "if" leads readers to expect a clause explaining what will happen. Consider the following example:

> If you activate the alarm.

This example is a fragment. We need the sentence to show the "what-if": what happens if you activate the alarm? Otherwise, we have an incomplete thought—and readers will be confused.

> The whole lab will be destroyed. If you activate the alarm.
> Spider-Man, you can avert the tragedy.

Will the lab be destroyed if Spider-Man activates the alarm? Or will activating the alarm avert the tragedy? There is no way for readers to know. This example needs to be edited! You try. Edit the example above for both possible interpretations.

≫ SEE **S-2** for more on how to edit fragments. Go to **digital.wwnorton .com/littleseagull4** for additional practice.

E-1b Comma Splices

A comma splice looks like a complete sentence in that it starts with a capital letter, concludes with end punctuation, and contains two INDEPENDENT CLAUSES. The problem is that there is only a comma between the two clauses. Here's an example:

▶ It was the coldest day in fifty years, the marching band performed brilliantly.

Both clauses are perfectly clear, and we expect that they are connected in some way—but we don't know how. Did the band play well because of the cold or in spite of it? Or is there no connection at all? In short, comma splices can leave your readers confused.

Checking for comma splices

Writers sometimes use comma splices to create a certain stylistic effect, but it's best to avoid them in academic writing. To check your work for comma splices, look at each sentence one by one and identify the **VERBS**. Next, look for their **SUBJECTS**. If you find two or more sets of subjects and verbs that form **INDEPENDENT CLAUSES**, make sure they are connected appropriately.

Editing comma splices

What are the appropriate ways to connect two independent clauses? Let's look at some of the possibilities.

CHANGE THE COMMA TO A PERIOD

One of your options is to create two separate sentences by inserting a period (.) after the first clause and capitalizing the first letter of the following word.

▶ It was the coldest day in fifty years. The marching band performed brilliantly.

This might be your preferred choice if you want to write tersely, with short sentences, perhaps to open an essay in a dramatic way. Maybe there is a connection between the two sentences; maybe there's not. Readers will want to keep going in order to find out.

CHANGE THE COMMA TO A SEMICOLON

Another simple way to edit a comma splice is to insert a semicolon (;) between the two clauses.

▶ It was the coldest day in fifty years; the marching band performed brilliantly.

The semicolon lets readers know that there is a definite connection between the weather and the band's brilliant performance, but they can't be certain what it is. The sentence is now correct, if not terribly interesting. You can make the connection clearer and even make the sentence more interesting by adding a **TRANSITION** (nevertheless, still, in any event; see **W-5c** for a complete list).

► It was the coldest day in fifty years/; *nevertheless,* the marching band performed brilliantly.

ADD A COORDINATING CONJUNCTION

You can also insert a **COORDINATING CONJUNCTION** (and, but, or, nor, so, for, yet) after the comma between the two clauses. A coordinating conjunction typically gives both clauses equal weight.

► It was the coldest day in fifty years, *but* the marching band performed brilliantly.

With this option, the two clauses are separated clearly, both clauses have equal weight, and the word "but" indicates that the band played brilliantly in spite of the cold weather.

ADD A SUBORDINATING WORD

Another way to show a relationship between the two clauses is with a **SUBORDINATING WORD** (while, however, thus; see **S-2a** for a full list). A subordinating word usually gives the clause it introduces less importance.

► *Although it* It was the coldest day in fifty years, the marching band performed brilliantly.

Here, the logical relationship between the two clauses is clear and explicit: the clause about cold weather is subordinated, and the band's performance becomes the important part of the sentence. But what if you wanted to suggest that the cold weather was responsible for the band playing so well? You could use the same clauses, but with a different subordinating word, as in the example below.

► *Possibly because it* It was the coldest day in fifty years, the marching band performed brilliantly.

You may also want to experiment with changing the order of the clauses; in many cases, that will cause the emphasis to change. Sometimes, too, changing the order will help you transition to the next sentence.

▶ *The marching band performed brilliantly, even though it*
It was the coldest day in fifty years/. ~~the marching band performed brilliantly.~~ Fans huddled together under blankets in the stands.

> Edit

Consider the following example:

> Transit officials estimate that the new light-rail line will be 20 percent faster than the express bus, the train will cost $1.85 per ride regardless of distance traveled.

Try editing this comma splice in two ways: one that emphasizes the speed of the train and another that emphasizes the cost.

≫ SEE S-3 for more advice and examples on how to edit comma splices. Go to **digital.wwnorton.com/littleseagull4** for additional practice.

E-1c Fused Sentences

A fused sentence looks like a complete sentence at first glance because it begins with a capital letter, concludes with end punctuation, and contains two **INDEPENDENT CLAUSES**. The reason it is problematic is that there is no explicit connection between the two clauses. A fused sentence will make sense to readers most of the time, but most of the time isn't quite often enough, and you don't want your readers to struggle to understand what you're saying. A sentence can contain more than one independent clause, no problem, but if it does, there needs to be some signal indicating how the clauses relate to one another. That signal could be a punctuation mark, a word that shows how the clauses are related, or both.

Checking for fused sentences

To check your text for fused sentences, look at each sentence one by one and identify any that have more than one **INDEPENDENT CLAUSE**. Then see how the clauses are connected: is there a word or punctuation mark that indicates how they relate? If not, you've got a fused sentence.

Editing fused sentences

Let's look at a typical fused sentence and some ways it can be edited.

▶   The fire alarm went off the senator spilled her latte all over her desk.

Perfectly clear, right? Or did you have to read it twice to make sure? This example is a fused sentence because it contains two independent clauses but offers no way of knowing where one stops and the next begins, and no indication of how the clauses relate to one another. Here are some options for editing this fused sentence.

ADD A PERIOD

One option is to make the fused sentence into two separate sentences by inserting a period after the first independent clause and capitalizing the first letter of the following clause.

▶   The fire alarm went off. ~~the~~ *The* senator spilled her latte all over her desk.

Now you have two complete sentences, but they are a little dry and lifeless. Readers may think the two events have nothing to do with each other, or they may think some explanation is missing. In some cases, you may want to choose this solution—if you are merely reporting what happened, for example—but it might not be the best one for this example.

ADD A SEMICOLON

Another option is to insert a semicolon (;) between the two clauses.

▶   The fire alarm went off; the senator spilled her latte all over her desk.

This is another simple way to deal with a fused sentence, although it still doesn't help readers know *how* the two clauses relate. The relationship between the clauses is fairly clear here, but that won't always be the case, so make sure the logical connection between the two clauses is very obvious before you use a semicolon. You can also add a TRANSITION (nevertheless, still, in any event; see W-5c for a complete list) after the semicolon to make the relationship between the two clauses more explicit.

▶ The fire alarm went off; *as a result,* the senator spilled her latte all over her desk.

ADD A COMMA AND A COORDINATING CONJUNCTION

In order to clarify the relationship between the clauses a little more, you could insert a comma and a COORDINATING CONJUNCTION (and, but, or, nor, so, for, yet) between the two clauses.

▶ The fire alarm went off, *and* the senator spilled her latte all over her desk.

Here the division between the two clauses is clearly marked, and readers will generally understand that the latte spilled right after (and the spill was possibly caused by) the fire alarm. With this solution, both clauses have equal importance.

ADD A SUBORDINATING WORD

One of the clearest ways to show the relationship between two clauses is by using a SUBORDINATING WORD (see S-2a for a full list).

▶ *When the* ~~The~~ fire alarm went off, the senator spilled her latte all over her desk.

Adding the subordinating word "when" to the first clause makes it clear that the fire alarm caused the senator to spill her latte and also puts emphasis on the spilled coffee. Note that you need to add a comma after the introductory clause. You can also change the order of the two clauses; see how the emphasis changes slightly. Note, too, that in this case, you should not add a comma.

▶ The senator spilled her latte all over her desk *when* the fire alarm went off.

> Edit

Using the editing options explained above, edit the following fused sentence in two different ways. Make one of your solutions short and snappy. In the other solution, show that the banging and the shouting were happening at the same time.

> The moderator banged his gavel the candidates continued to shout at each other.

>> **SEE S-3** for more on how to edit fused sentences. Go to **digital .wwnorton.com/littleseagull4** for additional practice.

E-1d Mixed Constructions

A MIXED CONSTRUCTION is a sentence that starts out with one structure and ends up with another one. Such a sentence may be understandable, but more often it leaves readers scratching their heads in confusion. There are many different ways to end up with a mixed construction, and this fact alone makes it difficult to identify one. Here are two examples of a common type of mixed construction:

▶ Décollage is when you take away pieces of an image to create a new image.

▶ Mosaic is where you assemble small bits of colored glass, stone, or other materials to create an image.

The two sentences are clear enough, but look again at the words "when" and "where." "When" locates an event in time (I'll call <u>when</u> I get there. The baby woke up <u>when</u> the phone rang. <u>When</u> the armistice was signed, everyone cheered.). In the first example above, there is no time associated with décollage; the sentence is simply describing the process. Similarly, "where" locates something in space (I don't remember <u>where</u> I put my keys. The man fell <u>where</u> the floor is uneven. <u>Where</u> does it hurt?). In the second example above, mosaic is not associated with any particular place; the sentence is describing a process. To edit these sentences, replace "when" and "where" with more appropriate words or phrases, and make adjustments as needed.

▶ Décollage is ~~when you take~~ *the technique of taking* away pieces of an image to create a new image.

> Mosaic is ~~where you assemble~~ small bits of colored glass, stone, or
>   ^ *the process of making a picture from*
> other materials.

Checking for mixed constructions

Let's consider another example:

> Nutritionists disagree about the riskiness of eating raw eggs and also
> more healthful compared with cooked ones.

What? It's hard to even know where to start. Let's begin by identifying the **VERB(S)**. Take a good look—there's only one verb here, "disagree." Next, let's identify the **SUBJECT**. Who disagrees? Nutritionists. OK, now we have a subject and a verb. What do nutritionists disagree about? It's clear enough that they disagree about the riskiness of eating raw eggs, but after that, it gets confusing. Consider the next words: "and also." Also what? Do nutritionists also disagree that raw eggs are more nutritious than cooked eggs? Or is the writer claiming that raw eggs *are* more healthful? It's impossible to tell, which suggests that we have a mixed construction.

Editing mixed constructions

Let's look at a couple of ways we might edit the sentence about raw eggs. Here's one way:

> Nutritionists disagree about the riskiness of eating raw eggs and also
> *about their healthfulness*
> ~~more healthful~~ compared with cooked ones.
> ^

Notice that we added another "about," which makes it clear that what follows is also something nutritionists disagree about. Notice, too, that we added the suffix "-ness" to "healthful" so that the word would be **PARALLEL** to "riskiness." Now the verb "disagree" applies to both "riskiness" and "healthfulness": nutritionists disagree about the riskiness of eating raw eggs, and they also disagree about the healthfulness of raw eggs compared with cooked ones.

What if the writer's original intention was to claim that raw eggs are more healthful than cooked ones? Since the two parts of the sentence express two different ideas, an editor might choose to simply make the mixed construction into two separate sentences.

▶ Nutritionists disagree about the riskiness of eating raw eggs. ~~and also~~ [Raw eggs are]
  more healthful ~~compared with~~ [than] cooked ones.

Just considering sentence structure, now we have two good sentences, but even though they both focus on raw eggs, the two sentences are not clearly connected. And besides, who is saying that eating raw eggs is more healthful? The author or the nutritionists? Adding just a couple of words links the sentences together and helps readers follow the ideas.

▶ Nutritionists disagree about the riskiness of eating raw eggs. ~~Raw~~ eggs [Some claim raw] are more healthful than cooked ones.

Here we've added a new subject, "some" (which refers to "nutritionists"), and we've also given the second sentence a verb, "claim." Now the two sentences have a logical sequence and are easier to read.

  Next, let's look at one other mixed construction:

▶ Because air accumulates under the eggshell is why an egg stands up underwater.

This sentence is more or less clear, but its parts don't fit together properly. What can we do about that? Same procedure as before—first, look for the verbs. This time, it's more complicated because there are three: "accumulates," "is," and "stands up." Next, we look for the subject of each of the verbs. The first one is easy—air accumulates; the subject is "air." The third one is also simple—an egg stands up; the subject is "an egg." But what is the subject of "is"? That's not such an easy question with this sentence because its structure changes in the middle. So let's try a different approach.

  What exactly is this sentence trying to say? It's clear that the point of this sentence is to explain why a submerged egg stands up, and we have two clauses: one that tells us that "an egg stands up underwater" and another that tells us that the egg stands up "because air accumulates under the eggshell." Now we just have to put them together in an appropriate way.

▶ Because air accumulates under the eggshell, ~~is why~~ an egg stands up underwater.

Did you notice that this version is almost exactly the same as the original sentence? The main difference is the words "is why"—which turn out not to be necessary. We now have one **INDEPENDENT CLAUSE** (an egg stands up underwater) and one **SUBORDINATE CLAUSE** (because air accumulates under the eggshell), with a comma in between. You can also reverse the order of the clauses, and the meaning stays the same. Note that you should not use a comma with this option.

▶ An egg stands up underwater because air accumulates under the eggshell.

We can use the same approach for a sentence that starts with a prepositional phrase but changes its structure in the middle: figure out what the sentence is trying to say, identify the phrases and clauses, and edit as needed so that you can put them together in an appropriate way.

▶ ~~For parents~~ Parents of children with a peanut allergy depend on rules that prohibit nuts in school.

> Edit

Try editing the following mixed construction in two ways. First, make one sentence that includes all of the information in the example. Next, present the same information in two separate sentences. Which way do you like better? Why?

One or two months before mating, male and female eagles together build their nests can be four or five feet in diameter.

≫ Go to **digital.wwnorton.com/littleseagull4** for additional practice.

E-2   Editing Pronouns

Pronouns are some of the smallest words in the English language, so you might think they should be among the easiest to use. Well, no, they're often not. But the good news is that editing your work to make sure all your pronouns are used appropriately is not too complicated. This chapter will give you tools for editing three common pronoun issues: pronoun reference, pronoun-antecedent agreement, and pronoun case.

First, let's clarify the terms. **PRONOUNS**, as you probably know, are words that refer to other words or phrases (and occasionally even whole clauses). They're very useful precisely because they're small and they do a lot of work representing larger units. The words that they represent are their **ANTECEDENTS**. Most frequently, the antecedent is something or somebody that has already been mentioned, and English has very specific conventions for signaling to readers exactly what that antecedent is so that they won't be confused. We call that **PRONOUN REFERENCE**. Let's suppose this next example is the first sentence in a news report.

▶ The Procurement Committee meets today to review the submitted bids, and she will announce the winner tomorrow.

Wait. "She"? "She" who? It's not clear what "she" refers to, and readers are now lost.

Pronoun **AGREEMENT** is another important convention. Pronouns have to agree with their antecedents in number (I, we) and in some cases gender (he, she, they). "Mr. Klein misplaced her phone again." If Mr. Klein is in the habit of losing a specific woman's phone, then perhaps the sentence makes sense. If it's his own phone that he misplaced again, then "her" doesn't agree with its antecedent, Mr. Klein, and readers will get confused.

PRONOUN CASE is a concept that you may never have encountered, but it's one that you use every day, and what's more, if you're a longtime English speaker, you likely do so appropriately and without giving it any thought. For example, you probably say "I bought ice cream" automatically—and would not likely say "Me bought ice cream" or "Coach wants I to play shortstop." Those two pronouns—"I" and "me"—refer to the same person, but they're not interchangeable. The difference between those two words is a simple matter of case; read on for more about that.

E-2a Pronoun Reference

Unclear pronoun reference occurs when readers can't be certain what a **PRONOUN** refers to. Usually this confusion arises when there are several possibilities in the same sentence (or sometimes in the previous sentence). Here's an example: "The science prize and the history prize were both very competitive this year, but luckily Luz was able to win it." The pronoun "it" could refer to either prize, so which one did Luz win? We don't know.

Checking for unclear pronoun reference

To check for unclear pronoun reference, you need to first identify each pronoun and then make sure that it points very clearly to its ANTE-CEDENT. Often, the meanings of the words provide clues about what the pronoun refers to—but not always. Let's look at three sentences that have very similar structures.

▶ My grandparents ordered pancakes because they weren't very hungry.

First, we identify the pronouns: "my" and "they." "My" clearly refers to the writer, but what about "they"? Although both "pancakes" and "grandparents" are possible antecedents for "they," we know that the pronoun here has to refer to grandparents because pancakes don't get hungry. Now let's look at another sentence:

▶ My grandparents ordered pancakes because they weren't very expensive.

This sentence is almost identical to the first one and has the same pronoun, "they," but this time, the antecedent has to be "pancakes" because there is no price on grandparents. Sorry to say, though, that antecedents aren't always so obvious. For example:

▶ My grandparents like playing cards with their neighbors because they aren't very competitive.

Wait. Who's not very competitive here? The grandparents or the neighbors? Or maybe all of them? We really can't be sure.

Editing unclear pronoun reference

Let's look again at the last example:

▶ My grandparents like playing cards with their neighbors because they aren't very competitive.

To edit this sentence, our best option may be to change the structure, and there are several possibilities:

▶ My grandparents like playing cards with their neighbors, ~~because they~~ *who* aren't very competitive.

This option makes clear that the neighbors are the ones who aren't very competitive.

▶ My grandparents, *who aren't very competitive,* like playing cards with their neighbors, *who are also not too* ~~because they aren't very~~ competitive.

Now we know that everybody mentioned here is noncompetitive. You may not think the sentence sounds as good as the original, but at least the meaning is clear. And of course there are usually other options.

The most important objective is to make clear what word or words each pronoun refers to. You don't want to leave your readers guessing. Here is one more example:

▶ After months of posturing and debate, those planning the expensive new football stadium suspended the project, which students loudly celebrated.

What is the antecedent for "which" in this example? You probably interpret this sentence to say that the students celebrated the suspension of the plans to build the stadium, but in fact, that's not clearly established in the sentence. Another plausible interpretation is that the students celebrated the building of the stadium. Let's reword the sentence and remove "which" in order to make the meaning perfectly clear.

▶ After months of posturing and debate, those planning the expensive new football stadium suspended the project, ~~which~~ *and* students loudly celebrated *the news.*

> Edit

The following sentence uses the words "it" and "which" to refer to . . . well, it's not exactly clear what they refer to.

> A temperature inversion happens when a layer of warmer air is
> positioned above a layer of cooler air, which is not how it usually occurs.

You have several options here that would make this sentence better,
but try this one: rewrite the sentence to eliminate the need for any
pronoun at all.

>> **SEE S-6b** for more on how to edit unclear pronoun references. Go
to **digital.wwnorton.com/littleseagull4** for additional practice.

E-2b Pronoun-Antecedent Agreement

Pronoun-antecedent agreement means that every **PRONOUN** has to
agree with its **ANTECEDENT** in gender (he, she, they) and number
(singular or plural). Some sentences with pronouns that don't agree
with their antecedents are relatively easy to understand, and usually
readers can figure them out if they think about it, but they shouldn't
have to do that extra work. For your academic writing, you need to
make sure that all of your pronouns agree with their antecedents.

Checking for pronoun-antecedent agreement

To check for pronoun-antecedent agreement, you need to first identify the pronouns and their antecedents. Then you need to make sure
each pronoun agrees with its antecedent in gender and number. Let's
look at a couple of examples:

> ▶ Trombones might be very loud, but it was drowned out last night by
> the cheering of the crowd.

This sentence has only one pronoun: "it." "Trombones" is the only
noun that precedes "it," so "trombones" has to be the antecedent. Do
they agree? We don't have to think about gender in this example, but
we do have to think about number. And that's a problem, because
the numbers don't match: "trombones" is plural, but "it" is singular.

> ▶ The table is wobbly because one of her legs is shorter than the others.

In some languages, tables, chairs, and other inanimate objects have
grammatical gender, but in English, they don't. The legs of a table are
never referred to with masculine or feminine gender.

Editing for pronoun-antecedent agreement

In order to fix the trombone sentence, you can change either the antecedent or the pronoun to make them agree in number. In this case, it is clear that the first **CLAUSE** refers to trombones in general, and the second clause refers to a specific trombone at a specific event. Assuming that the more important part is the specific event, and that there was only one trombone, let's change the word "trombones" from plural to singular. We can do that easily in this case without really changing the meaning, although sometimes it might be more difficult to do so.

> ~~Trombones~~ The trombone might be very loud, but it was drowned out last night by the cheering of the crowd.

Both the pronoun and its antecedent are now singular; that is, they agree in number. Now let's consider several examples where gender is a factor. In the example about the table legs, we simply have to replace the feminine pronoun with the inanimate one.

> The table is wobbly because one of ~~her~~ its legs is shorter than the others.

Remember that "he," "him," "his," "she," "her," "hers" are the only English pronouns that specify male or female gender. We can use "they," "them," and "their" to refer to a person of unspecified, unknown, or nonbinary gender (see **L-10** for more on nonbinary pronouns). An inanimate object is always referred to as "it." Some languages have more gender-specific pronouns, and some languages have fewer, but let's just stick to English right now.

> My mom and dad have an arrangement about sausage pizza—
> he picks off the sausage, and she eats it.

This sentence has three pronouns—"he," "she," and "it"—and it's quite evident that "he" refers to "dad," "she" refers to "mom," and "it" refers to "sausage." All the antecedents are clear. But what if we changed the cast of characters in the sentence to two men? It would be confusing to refer to each of them as "he," so we need a different strategy. One possibility is to use "he" to represent one of the men and to refer to the other man by name. Will that work?

> Paul and his brother have an arrangement about sausage pizza—Paul
> picks off the sausage, and he eats it.

Who eats the sausage? Paul or his brother? It's still not clear. In this case, our best option is to eliminate the pronoun and refer to both men explicitly both times.

▶ Paul and his brother have an arrangement about sausage pizza—
Paul picks off the sausage, and ~~he~~ eats it.
_{his brother}

If you'd rather not repeat both phrases, and the arrangement itself is more important than which person eats all the sausage, you can try this option:

▶ Paul and his brother have an arrangement about sausage pizza—
~~Paul~~ picks off the sausage, and ~~he~~ eats it.
_{one of them}   _{the other one}

Now we've got it; everything is clear. As this last edit shows, making pronouns and antecedents agree sometimes requires reworking the structure of a sentence and occasionally even modifying what it says. Pronouns may be small words, but getting them right is hugely important; don't be afraid to make changes in your writing.

Now let's look at some other contexts in which making pronouns agree in gender with their antecedents can be complicated. We'll start with one that's pretty straightforward.

▶ Trey noticed a sunflower growing along the path; he grabbed his phone and took a picture of it.

We know that Trey is a man or a boy—"he," "his"—and the flower, of course, is inanimate—"it." In academic writing, inanimate objects are always referred to as "it," even though in casual speech, we may use gendered pronouns to refer to things such as cars, boats (almost always "she"), and others. What about animals? If you know the sex of an animal, then by all means, refer to it as "he" or "she." If you don't know the sex, or if the sex isn't pertinent, just use "it." And what if you're writing about a person whose sex or gender you don't know? That happens, and that's when writing gets complicated. For example:

▶ Anyone who gets three speeding tickets in a year will lose his license.

What's wrong with this example? Plenty, unless only men have such a license. If what you are writing applies to more than just men, your pronouns should reflect that reality. One of the easiest solutions is to use plural nouns and pronouns because they do not specify gender:

▶ ~~Anyone~~ who ~~gets~~ three speeding tickets in a year will lose ~~his license~~.
   Drivers   get   their licenses

You may need to tinker a bit with the structure, but the message can remain the same. Another option is to revise the sentence altogether. Here's one possibility:

▶ Getting three speeding tickets in a year will result in the driver's license being revoked.

Another solution some people use is to write "his or her":

▶ Anyone who gets three speeding tickets in a year will lose ~~his~~ license.
   his or her

This last solution is still used fairly often, but it isn't the best option because it doesn't include everyone, and if you have many such instances close together, it can be awkward. Another possibility is to employ SINGULAR "THEY," using "they," "them," "their," or "theirs" with a singular antecedent.

▶ Anyone who gets three speeding tickets in a year will lose ~~his~~ license.
   their

Many of us use singular "they" this way in casual speech, and its use is becoming more widely accepted in newspapers, style guides, and other more formal contexts. Singular "they" is a very tidy solution, but even though it's becoming ever more common, it's still not always accepted in academic writing. Check with your instructor to see if singular "they" is acceptable in their class. (Did you notice that we used a singular "they" just now?) Some people also use singular "they" as a personal pronoun in place of "he" or "she"; you should always refer to people by using the pronouns they use for themselves. For more guidance on singular "they," see L-10b .

> Edit

Edit the following sentence in two ways. First, make both the pronoun and its antecedent singular; second, make the pronoun and antecedent plural. Both ways are acceptable, but which way do you prefer?

> Applicants must file the forms before the deadline and make sure that it's filled out correctly.

>> SEE S-6a for more on how to edit for pronoun-antecedent agreement, including advice about how to treat indefinite pronouns such as "everyone" and "anyone" and collective nouns such as "team" and "choir." Go to **digital.wwnorton.com /littleseagull4** for additional practice.

E-2c Pronoun Case

Pronoun CASE refers to the different forms a PRONOUN takes in order to indicate how it functions in a sentence. English pronouns have three cases: subject, object, and possessive. Most of the time, we choose the appropriate pronouns without too much trouble, as in the following sentence:

> I saw her, and she saw me, but we didn't see our bikes anywhere.

This sentence involves two people and six distinct pronouns. "I" and "me" refer to one person (the writer), "she" and "her" refer to the other person, and "we" and "our" refer to both people. Each of the three pronoun pairs has a distinct role in the sentence. "I," "she," and "we" are all subjects; "me" and "her" are objects; and "our" is possessive.

Checking for correct pronoun case

Experienced English speakers would probably never say "Me saw her." In casual speech, though, you might hear (or say) "Me and Bob saw her." However, that sentence would not be acceptable in academic writing. Here is a simple and reliable technique for checking your work for case: check for compound subjects like "me and Bob" and cover up everything in the phrase but the pronoun. Read it out loud.

> Me ~~and Bob~~ saw her.

If you're a longtime user of spoken English, you're likely to know that the example doesn't sound quite right. If you're not sure how it sounds, consult a dictionary, another reference source, or the table in S-6c . What needs to change? Read on.

Editing for pronoun case

To edit for pronoun case, the first step is to identify the pronouns in each sentence. The following example has only one, "us":

▶ Us first-year students are petitioning for a schedule change.

Remember that the way a pronoun functions in a sentence is the key and that there are three possibilities for case. Is "us" functioning as subject, object, or possessive? In order to answer that question, first we need to identify the verb: "are petitioning." The subject tells us who (or what) is petitioning—in this sentence, "us first-year students." If you're not sure if "us" is correct, try it by itself, without "first-year students."

▶ Us are petitioning for a schedule change.
▶ U̶s̶ We are petitioning for a schedule change.

We changed "us" to "we" here because it's the subject of the sentence and thus needs to be in the subject case. For more advice on choosing the correct case, see the table in S-6c . Now let's look at two more examples: "Pat dated Cody longer than me." "Pat dated Cody longer than I." The only difference between the two sentences is the case of a pronoun, but that little word gives the sentences totally different meanings. How can that tiny detail of case make such a difference? It does so because case lets readers know whether the person—"I" or "me"—is the subject or the object of a verb, and that fact can make all the difference in the world.

▶ Pat dated Cody longer than me.

Look carefully. There's only one verb, "dated," and its subject is "Pat." Now notice the pronoun: "me." That's object case, right? So, according to the example, Pat dated both Cody and *me.* Try the next one.

▶ Pat dated Cody longer than I.

Here the pronoun is in subject case: "I." Even though it's not followed by a verb, the pronoun tells us that Pat dated Cody and so did I. See S-6c for more information about pronoun case.

> ### > Edit

Use the technique explained in this section to edit the following sentence for pronoun case.

> Iris was unhappy, but the judges called a tie and gave the award to she and Lu.

>> SEE S-6c for more on how to edit pronoun case. Go to **digital .wwnorton.com/littleseagull4** for additional practice.

E-3 Editing Verbs

Verbs. Are any words more important—or hardworking? Besides specifying actions (hop, skip, jump) or states of being (be, seem), verbs provide most of the information about *when* (happening now? already happened? might happen? usually happens?), and they also have to link very explicitly to their subjects. That's a lot of work!

Because verbs are so important, verb problems are often easily noticed by readers, and once readers notice a verb problem in your work, they may question your competence as a writer. But if your readers can catch these problems, so can you. This chapter will help you edit your work for two of the most troublesome verb problems: subject-verb agreement and shifts in tense.

E-3a Subject-Verb Agreement

In English, every **VERB** has to agree with its **SUBJECT** in number and person. That may sound complicated, but it's really only third-person singular subjects (runner, shoe, he, she, it) that you have to look out for, and even then, only when the verb is in the simple present tense. Still, the third-person present tense is the most common construction in academic writing, so it matters. Take a look at this example:

▶ First the coach enters, then you enter, and then all of the other players enter.

The verb "enter" occurs three times in that sentence, but notice that when its subject is third-person singular—"coach"—an "-s" follows the **BASE FORM** of the verb, "enter." In the other two cases, the verb has no such ending. What's so complicated about that? Well, there are two kinds of subjects that cause problems: indefinite pronouns, such as "everyone" and "many," which may require a singular or plural verb even if their meaning suggests otherwise; and subjects with more than one word, in which the word that has to agree with the verb may be hidden among other words.

Checking for subject-verb agreement

To check for subject-verb agreement, first identify the subjects and their verbs, paying careful attention to **INDEFINITE PRONOUNS** and subjects with more than one word. Then, check to make sure that every subject matches its verb in number and person.

Editing for subject-verb agreement

Let's look at a few common mistakes and see what we can do about them.

INDEFINITE PRONOUNS

Indefinite pronouns are words like "anyone," "each," "everything," and "nobody." When they're used as a subject, they have to agree with the verb. Sometimes that's tricky. For example:

▶ First the coach enters, then you enter, and then each of the other players enter.

We know that the subject of the first clause is "coach" and the subject of the second clause is "you," but what about the third clause? Is the subject "each"? Or is it "players"? You might be tempted to choose "players" because that's the word closest to the verb "enter," but that's not accurate; the subject is "each," an indefinite pronoun.

▶ First the coach enters, then you enter, and then each of the other
     enters
  players ~~enter~~.
          ^

That "-s" at the end of "enters" is necessary because the **SIMPLE SUBJECT** of the final clause is "each," which is singular. The phrase "of the other players" is additional information. Now see what happens if we change "each" to "all":

                                              all
▶ First the coach enters, then you enter, and then ~~each~~ of the other
                                                    ^
     enter
  players ~~enters~~.
          ^

Even though the two phrases—"each of the other players" and "all of the other players"—have essentially the same meaning, the word "each" is always singular and requires the verb to have the "-s" ending, while "all" is plural here because it refers to a plural noun, "players."

Because "each" refers to the members of a group individually, it is always singular and requires the verb to have the "-s" ending. "All" is plural when it refers to a plural noun, but it's singular when it refers to a singular noun or a **NONCOUNT NOUN**.

▶ All of the strawberries <u>were picked</u> today.

▶ All of the cilantro <u>was picked</u> yesterday.

In the first sentence, "all" refers to the "strawberries" all together, in plural form, while in the second sentence, "all" refers to "cilantro," which requires the singular form of the verb. When a subject is an **INDEFINITE PRONOUN**, check **S-5f** to see whether that particular pronoun should take a singular or plural verb.

SUBJECTS WITH MORE THAN ONE WORD

Sometimes a sentence has a subject with more than one word, so you need to determine which of the words is the one that the verb has to agree with and which words simply provide extra information. To do that, pull the subject apart to find which word is the essential one. Let's practice with this sentence:

▶ The guy with the mirrored sunglasses run in this park every morning.

The **COMPLETE SUBJECT** is "the guy with the mirrored sunglasses," but who is it that does the running? It's the guy, and the fact that he has mirrored sunglasses is simply extra information. You could remove the phrase "with the mirrored sunglasses" and still have a complete sentence—it might not be very informative, but it's not incorrect.

To check for subject-verb agreement when a subject has more than one word, first locate the verb and then the complete subject. Then check each word in the subject until you find the one key word that determines the form of the verb. Since the **SIMPLE SUBJECT** here—"guy"—is in the third-person singular, and the verb is in the present tense, the verb should also be in the third-person singular:

▶ The guy with the mirrored sunglasses ~~run~~ runs in this park every morning.

Let's try one more problem sentence:

▶ The neighbor across the hall from the Fudds always sign for the Fudds' packages.

First, find the verb: "sign." The complete subject is "the neighbor across the hall from the Fudds." What part of that subject indicates who does the signing? "Neighbor." Everything else is extra. Since it's just one neighbor, the subject is singular, and since a third-person singular subject requires a present tense verb to have an "-s" ending, the edited sentence will be:

▶ The neighbor across the hall from the Fudds always ~~sign~~ signs for the Fudds' packages.

> Edit

The sentence below has four subjects and four verbs. One (or more) of the subjects is singular, so its verb should have an "-s" ending. Edit and make any necessary changes.

All of the boxes need to be stacked neatly, and every box need to be labeled; the red box with the taped edges fit on top, and each of the boxes need its own lid.

In casual speech, you may not use the "-s" ending, or it may be hard to hear, so you may not be able to rely on your ear alone to edit this sentence. Think it through, and consult **S-5b** and **S-5f** to help you choose the appropriate verb forms.

>> SEE **S-5** for more on how to edit for subject-verb agreement.
Go to **digital.wwnorton.com/littleseagull4** for additional practice.

E-3b Shifts in Tense

We live in the present moment; our ideas and our feelings are happening right now. Often, though, our present thoughts—and comments—are responses to things that happened in the past or that haven't happened yet. In conversation, we usually shift our verb tenses smoothly and automatically to account for actions that take place at different times, as in the following example of something you might hear or say:

▶ Flor is upset because Justin informed her that he will not be able to come to her graduation.

In writing, however, we need to take extra care to ensure that our tenses are clear, consistent, and appropriate to what we're describing. In contrast to face-to-face conversation—in which tone of voice, facial expressions, and hand gestures help create meaning—writing has to rely on carefully chosen words. Verb tenses work hard to put complex sequences of events into appropriate context. The previous example has three clauses, each in a different tense: Flor is upset (right now); because Justin informed her (in the past); that he will not be able to come (to an event in the future).

Checking for shifts in tense

In academic writing, you'll often need to discuss what other authors have written, and the different disciplines have different conventions and rules for doing that (see **R-4e**). In classes that require you to use MLA style, for example, you'll rely heavily on the simple present tense:

MLA   Morton argues that even though Allende's characters are not realistic, they're believable.

Notice how "argues," "are not," and "they're" all use the simple present tense even though Morton's article and Allende's novel were both written in the past. If you mention the date when something was written, however, the verb should be in the past tense. In contrast, disciplines that follow APA style require that references to published sources and research results be stated in the past tense or present perfect tense:

APA   Azele reported that 59% of the control group subjects showed high gamma levels.

Notice here that the two verbs in the sentence—"reported" and "showed"—are both in the past tense because both Azele's research and the report were done in the past. Be careful, though, because your sources may be writing about current or future conditions. If that's the case, be sure to preserve the tense of the original in your work, as the following example does.

APA   Donnerstag and Jueves predicted that another Jovian moon will soon be discovered.

Regardless of what class you're writing for, however, the most important thing about verb tenses is consistency.

Editing confusing shifts in tense

Much of the editing that you do calls for sentence-by-sentence work, but checking for confusing shifts in tense often requires that you consider several sentences together.

Starting at the beginning of your first sentence, mark every MAIN VERB, along with any HELPING VERBS, in every sentence you wrote (remembering that there may be more than one clause in each sentence). Don't make any changes yet; just mark the verbs. Next, go back to the beginning and notice what tense you used each time. Examine each tense one by one, and when you notice a shift to a different tense, read carefully what you have written and look for a reason for the shift. If you can explain why the shift makes sense, leave it alone. Then move on to the next verb. Is it in the original tense or the new tense? Can you explain why? Continue all the way through your text, examining every verb tense and making sure that any shifts you find can be explained. Let's practice with two examples:

▶ Bates underestimated the public when she writes disparagingly about voters' intelligence.

First, we mark the verbs — "underestimated," "writes" — and we notice that the first is in past tense while the second is in present. Is there a clear explanation for the shift? No, not really. If you are using MLA style, you'll want to put both verbs in the present: "underestimates" and "writes." In APA style, past tense is more appropriate for both: "underestimated" and "wrote." In any case, there is no reason to use two different tenses in the sentence. Here is another example, this time a little more complicated:

▶ All of the guests ate the stew, but only two showed symptoms of food poisoning.

It's true that the events (ate the stew, showed symptoms) in both clauses of the example occurred in the past, but can we be certain that the symptoms were a result of eating the stew? Could the guests have had the symptoms already? The sentence isn't really clear.

▶ All of the guests ~~ate~~ the stew, but only two showed symptoms of food poisoning.
     had eaten
        ^

By changing the verb tense in the first clause to the **PAST PERFECT**, we show clearly that the stew was eaten before the food poisoning occurred. (We may never know what caused the illness, but at least we know the sequence of events.)

> Edit

Edit the following sentence to eliminate any confusing shifts in tense. Assume that the writing has to follow APA format for verb tenses.

Levi (2020) notes that the trade deficit decreases from 2008 to 2018, but he warns that the improvement may be reversed because the new treaty will go into effect in 2024.

≫ **SEE S-4** and **S-9a** for more on how to edit confusing shifts in tense. Go to **digital.wwnorton.com/littleseagull4** for additional practice.

E-4   Editing Quotations

In academic writing, you are required not only to express your own ideas, but also to incorporate the ideas of other authors. In a way, you are engaging in a conversation with your sources, whether you draw from Aristotle, Toni Morrison, or a classmate. Your success as a writer has a lot to do with how well you weave your sources' ideas in with your own without your readers ever having to wonder who said what. Editing your work for citation and documentation issues therefore involves two main tasks:

- incorporating any words of others that you quote into your text so that everything flows smoothly
- making sure the punctuation, capitalization, and other such elements are correct

The conventions for citing and documenting sources in academic writing are very precise—every period, every comma, every quotation mark has its job to do, and they must be in exactly the right place.

E-4a Incorporating Quotations

Whenever we quote something someone else has said or written, we need to structure the sentences that contain the quoted material so that they read as smoothly as any other sentence. As writers, we need to master our use of language in much the same way that musicians have to master their instruments, and in both cases, it's not easy. Just as musicians playing together in an orchestra (or a garage band) have to coordinate with one another in tempo, key, and melody, you have to make sure that your words and those of others that you quote fit together smoothly.

Checking to see that quotations are incorporated smoothly

One good way to begin checking a draft to see how well any quotations have been incorporated is to read it aloud, or better yet, get someone else to read it aloud to you. If the reader (you or someone else) stumbles over a passage and has to go back and read the sentence again, you can be fairly certain that some changes are necessary. We can practice with some sentences that quote the following passage from a 2013 *Atlantic* article about fast food:

> Introduced in 1991, the McLean Deluxe was perhaps the boldest single effort the food industry has ever undertaken to shift the masses to healthier eating.
> —David Freedman, "How Junk Food Can End Obesity"

Assume that you might not want or need to quote the entire passage, so you incorporate just one part of Freedman's sentence into one of your sentences, as follows:

▶ Freedman refers to a failed McDonald's menu item "the McLean Deluxe was perhaps the food industry's boldest single effort to shift the masses to healthier eating."

If you read the sentence aloud, you might be able to notice that it is awkwardly structured and even hard to understand. Also, do you notice that the quoted section doesn't exactly match the author's words? Some of the words from the original are missing and some others have been added. Changing an author's words in a quoted section is allowed only if the original meaning is not altered in any way. Also, you need to indicate to your readers that you've modified the author's words. Let's see how we can go about fixing these things.

Editing sentences that include quotations

There are two ways of smoothly incorporating quoted material. One strategy is to adjust your own words to accommodate the quoted material; another is to lightly modify the quoted material to fit your sentence. Here's one way we might edit our sentence by adjusting our own words:

▶ ~~Freedman refers~~ ^{Referring} to a failed McDonald's menu item, ^{Freedman notes that} "the McLean Deluxe was perhaps the food industry's boldest single effort to shift the masses to healthier eating."

Let's look at what we did. First, we changed the first two words. The meaning didn't change; only the structure did. Then, we added a **SIGNAL PHRASE** (Freedman notes that) to introduce the quoted words.

So far so good. But what about the places where we changed the author's words? If you modify an author's words, you need to signal to your readers what changes you've made, and there are precise conventions for doing that.

Enclose anything you add or change within the quotation itself in square brackets ([ ]), and insert ellipses (. . .) to show where any content from the original has been omitted.

▶ Referring to a failed McDonald's menu item, Freedman notes that "the McLean Deluxe was perhaps the [food industry's] boldest single effort . . . to shift the masses to healthier eating."

With minimal changes, the sentence now has all the necessary parts and reads smoothly. Note the two things we've done to modify the quotation. We've enclosed the words we added—"food industry's"—in square brackets, and we've inserted ellipses in place of the six words that were omitted from Freedman's sentence. It's worth repeating here that it is permissible to add or delete words only if the meaning of the quotation isn't substantially altered.

> Edit

Here is another sentence based on the Freedman passage:

> Freedman talks about an earlier effort the McLean Deluxe
> by McDonald's was perhaps the boldest try to shift the masses
> to healthier eating.

First, you'll have to make a few changes to help the sentence read smoothly. There are several ways to do that, but try to make as few changes as possible. Once the sentence reads smoothly, compare it with the original passage to see where you might need square brackets (for added material) or ellipses (to show where words have been removed). By the way, you don't have to put "McLean Deluxe" in quotation marks because it was not a term coined by Freedman.

>> SEE **E-4b**, **R-4**, and **P-4** for more on how to incorporate quotations. Go to **digital.wwnorton.com/littleseagull4** for additional practice.

E-4b   Punctuating Quotations

Citation conventions exist to help us clearly distinguish our words from the words of our sources, and one way we do that is by punctuating quotations carefully. When you quote someone's exact words, you need to attend to four elements: quotation marks, capitalization, commas, and end punctuation. These elements let your readers know which words are yours and which are the words of someone else. Note that **MLA** requires marking changes in capitalization at the beginning of a quotation, while **APA** does not. We follow MLA in the examples below.

Checking to see how any quoted material is punctuated

Here is another sentence taken from the *Atlantic* article about fast food; let's use it in a variety of ways in order to show how to capitalize and punctuate sentences that quote from this passage.

> A slew of start-ups are trying to find ways of producing fresh, local, unprocessed meals quickly and at lower cost.
> —David Freedman, "How Junk Food Can End Obesity"

You might write a sentence such as this one:

▶ It may one day be possible to get fast food that is healthy and affordable since a slew of start-ups are trying to find ways, according to David Freedman.

Structurally, the sentence is fine, but it includes a direct quotation from Freedman without letting readers know which words are his and which are yours. Even if you used Freedman's exact words accidentally, it would still be **PLAGIARISM**, which may carry a stiff penalty. The sentence needs to be edited.

Editing quotations to indicate who said what

There are numerous ways to edit the above sentence to make clear who said what. Here is one option:

▶ It may one day be possible to get fast food that is healthy and affordable. since a slew of start-ups are trying to find ways. "according to Freedman.

According to David Freedman, "A
~~since~~ slew of start-ups are trying to find ways~~,~~."~~according to Freedman.~~

What changed? First, we added quotation marks to enclose Freedman's exact words. Second, we broke the sentence into two and started the second one with the signal phrase "According to David Freedman," followed by a comma. Third, we capitalized the first letter of the quotation. Since "A" was capitalized in the original quotation, no brackets are necessary. Finally, notice the period. The sentence ends with the quoted material, so the period goes inside the quotation marks. Now let's look at how you might go about editing another sentence.

▶ Freedman asserts that many new businesses are working to develop fresh, local, unprocessed meals quickly and at lower cost.

Check your four elements. First, insert any necessary quotation marks; make sure they enclose Freedman's exact words. Second, is any additional capitalization necessary? If so, capitalize the appropriate word(s). Third, if there's a **SIGNAL PHRASE** before the quoted material, does it need to be followed by a comma? Finally, make sure any end punctuation is in the right place. Try editing the sentence yourself before you look at the revision below.

▶ Freedman asserts that many new businesses are working to develop "fresh, local, unprocessed meals quickly and at lower cost."

The quoted portion is not a complete sentence, and we placed it within our own sentence, so no capitalization was necessary. We didn't insert a comma because his words flow smoothly within the larger sentence. Since the sentence ends with the quoted material, we put the period inside the quotation marks.

While you should always take particular care to mark which words are your own and which words are someone else's, you do have a little wiggle room when it comes to end punctuation, as long as you don't alter the meaning of the original quotation. That is, you may sometimes make "silent" changes to end punctuation, meaning that you don't always need to mark the changes with square brackets. Here is another passage from Freedman's essay:

▶ How long would it take to create the thousands of local farms we'd need in order to provide these shops with fresh, unprocessed ingredients, even in cities?

Let's suppose that you wanted to refer to his question without quoting the whole thing. You might do something like this:

▶ Freedman wonders how much time it might take "to create the thousands of local farms we'd need in order to provide these shops with fresh, unprocessed ingredients, even in cities."

Or something like this:

▶ Freedman questions the feasibility of rapidly establishing "the thousands of local farms we'd need in order to provide these shops with fresh, unprocessed ingredients, even in cities," where distribution networks are more complicated.

In both examples, we've used quotation marks to show which words are Freedman's, but the quotation is no longer a question. In the first example, we changed the end punctuation to a period; in the second example, since we added more to the sentence, we replaced the question mark with a comma. Since the question mark is the only thing we changed in both examples, no square brackets are required.

Depending on the documentation style that you are using, you may need to provide parenthetical information at the end of any sentences that include quoted material. Some styles require that you name the author(s) if you haven't named them earlier in the sentence, along with the page number(s) where their words appeared. Here's how you would do so to follow MLA and APA style requirements.

MLA   Freedman asserts that many new businesses are working to develop "fresh, local, unprocessed meals quickly and at lower cost" (82).

APA   Freedman (2013) asserted that many new businesses are working to develop "fresh, local, unprocessed meals quickly and at lower cost" (p. 82).

One more important point: notice that with parenthetical documentation, the final period of the sentence is no longer inside the quotation marks; it is after the parentheses. Consult the Chicago and CSE chapters to find out what kind of documentation each style requires.

> Edit

The following sentences cite the passage from Freedman's essay; they need to be formatted properly in order to read smoothly and also to show more clearly which words are the writer's and which are Freedman's. Remember the four elements: quotation marks, capitalization, commas, and end punctuation.

> Healthy and affordable fast food may not be a reality yet, but we may not have too long to wait. As Freedman explains a slew of start-ups are trying to find ways to bring such meals to market.

It is possible to edit the sentence using only the four elements and not adding, subtracting, or changing any words. Try it.

» **SEE P-1g**, **P-4**, and **P-8c** for more on how to edit documentation. Go to **digital.wwnorton.com/littleseagull4** for additional practice.

E-5 Editing Commas

Ideas are made out of words, right? So why should we care about commas? Well, here's why—they help those words make more sense. Nobody wants to have to read the same sentence two or three times in order to get it. Well-placed commas can make your sentence clear and easy to read—and can help keep the words (and ideas) correctly grouped together. Read this next sentence out loud:

▶ The boxer exhausted and pounded on wearily left the ring.

So. Did you start off expecting to read about the boxer's opponent who was getting "exhausted and pounded on"? Did you have to go back and start over? Bet you did. Well-placed commas would have immediately pointed us all in the right direction—like this:

▶ The boxer, exhausted and pounded on, wearily left the ring.

There are a lot of ways to err with commas. You might omit one that's necessary or place one where it doesn't belong. Even professional writers sometimes have trouble deciding where (and where not) to put a comma, and it's not always a big deal. This chapter won't make you a comma superstar, but it will show you how to edit your work for two of the comma problems that matter most to instructors and other readers: the commas that set off introductory information and the commas that distinguish between essential and nonessential information.

E-5a Introductory Information

English sentences generally begin with a **SUBJECT**. Without ever really thinking about it, those of us who read and write in English have an expectation that the first thing we read in a sentence will be its subject. Often, however (like right now), we begin a sentence in a different way. In academic writing especially, we might vary the structure of our sentences just to make our writing interesting. One way we vary our sentences is by starting some of them with introductory words, phrases, or even clauses. And usually we use a comma to set off those introductory words. That comma signals to readers that they haven't gotten to the subject yet; what they are seeing is additional information that is important enough to go first. For example:

▶ In Georgia, Lee's book jumped quickly to the top of the best-seller list.

Without the comma, readers might think the author's name was Georgia Lee, and they would get very lost in the sentence. Introductory words don't always cause so much confusion; in fact, some authors omit the comma if the introductory element is very short (one, two, or three words). Still, adding the comma after the introductory information is never wrong and demonstrates the care you take with your work.

Checking for commas after introductory information

▶ Initially the council proposed five miles of new bike paths; they later revised the proposal.

To check for introductory information, you should first identify the **VERB** — in this case, "proposed." OK, now what's the subject? (In other words, who or what proposed?) The subject here is "the council." Everything that goes before the subject is introductory information, so the comma goes between that information and the subject.

▶ Initially, the council proposed five miles of new bike paths; they later revised the proposal.

In the example above, the introductory element is only one word, and the comma could have been omitted, but its presence adds a little extra emphasis to the word "initially," and in fact, that emphasis is probably why the author chose to put that word at the beginning, before the subject. The comma definitely helps. And sometimes, introductory elements can cause confusion:

▶ Tired and discouraged by the unsuccessful search for the fugitive Sgt. Drexler the detective and her squad returned to headquarters.

In this example, the introductory information is much longer, and without an appropriate comma, readers have no way of knowing if

Sgt. Drexler is the name of the fugitive, the name of the detective, or someone else entirely. Let's imagine that Drexler is the fugitive. With one well-placed comma, the sentence is now perfectly clear.

▶ Tired and discouraged by the unsuccessful search for the fugitive Sgt. Drexler, the detective and her squad returned to headquarters.

Editing for commas after introductory information

Let's take a look at a few examples to see how we can figure out where to put commas with introductory elements. The following sentence needs a comma; where should it go?

▶ For the first twenty minutes of the lecture Yunwen struggled to stay awake.

How do you know where to put the comma? Let's follow the steps described in this chapter. First, identify the verb: "struggled." Next, identify the subject—in other words, who or what struggled? The subject here is "Yunwen," and everything that precedes it is introductory information.

▶ For the first twenty minutes of the lecture, Yunwen struggled to stay awake.

Here is one more example. Follow the same procedure to determine where to put the comma.

▶ In the chaotic final episode of season 2 the shocking plot twists left viewers breathless.

In this example, the comma should go after "2"; the verb in the sentence is "left," and the **COMPLETE SUBJECT** is "the shocking plot twists." Everything that goes before the subject is introductory information, so the comma falls between that information and the subject:

▶ In the chaotic final episode of season 2, the shocking plot twists left viewers breathless.

> Edit

Try editing the following sentence by inserting a comma after the introductory information. Remember the technique: first, find the verb; second, find the subject. The comma goes before the subject because everything that precedes it is introductory information.

> Behind the parade marshal and the color guard the sponsors' convertible carrying the Founders' Day Queen will proceed along Cunningham Street.

» **SEE P-1b** for more on how to edit for commas after introductory information. Go to **digital.wwnorton.com/littleseagull4** for additional practice.

E-5b Essential and Nonessential Information

What do we mean by **ESSENTIAL** and **NONESSENTIAL** information? The simplest way to explain the difference is with examples.

▶ My sister Jamilah graduates on Saturday.

If the writer has more than one sister, the name "Jamilah" tells us which one; that's important to know because we don't want to congratulate the wrong sister. Therefore, her name is essential information. When the information is essential, it should not be set off with commas. But if the writer has only one sister, writing her name there is simply extra information; it's not essential. When the information is nonessential, we set it off with commas:

▶ My sister, Jamilah, graduates on Saturday.

Checking for essential and nonessential information

To check your work for these kinds of commas, read over what you've written and identify the **NOUNS**. When a noun (stadium, achievement, amino acids) is followed immediately by additional information about it, ask yourself if the information is essential: does it tell you which stadium, which achievement, which amino acids? If so, it shouldn't be set off with commas. If, however, the information is nonessential, and the sentence would still be fine without that information, it should be set off with a pair of commas. Let's examine two examples:

▶ The neighbors, who complained about parking, called a meeting to discuss the problem.

▶ The neighbors who complained about parking called a meeting to discuss the problem.

In these examples, the noun "neighbors" is followed by additional information. Which sentence talks about a situation in which all of the neighbors complained? Which one describes a situation in which only some of them did? Remember that the commas set off information that is extra and not essential. In the first sentence, the commas indicate that the information "who complained about parking" is extra, nonessential; it doesn't tell us which neighbors, so we can safely conclude that all of the neighbors complained. In the second sentence, the absence of commas lets us know that the information is essential; the clause "who complained about parking" tells us which neighbors called the meeting—only the ones who complained.

Editing commas with essential and nonessential information

Here is an example to practice with:

▶ Vitamins, such as B and C, are water-soluble and easily absorbed by the body; excess amounts are eliminated in the urine.

In order to edit the example, you will need to know if the phrase "such as B and C" is essential or if it's only additional information. In order to save you some research, here's the answer: not all vitamins are water-soluble; some are fat-soluble and are stored in the body rather than quickly eliminated. Now, is the phrase "such as B and C" essential information? And if it is, should this sentence have commas? Here is the edited version:

▶ Vitamins/ such as B and C/ are water-soluble and easily absorbed by the body; excess amounts are eliminated in the urine.

> Edit

The two sentences below are very similar; the difference is that one has essential information about its subject, while the other one's subject has extra information. Put commas in the appropriate places.

> Lizzo who will perform the closing number will do her sound check at 5:30.

> The backup singers who will perform the closing number will do their sound check at 5:30.

>> **SEE P-1d** for more on how to edit for commas with essential and nonessential information. Go to **digital.wwnorton.com /littleseagull4** for additional practice.

E-6 Editing Words That Are Often Confused

English has more than a million words, and any one of them could be used appropriately—or inappropriately—in a variety of ways, so no book could possibly help you edit all of the "wrong words" that might turn up in your writing. A few basic strategies, however, can help you with many of those problems. Chapter **L-4** lists some of the words that are often confused, and this chapter offers tips for identifying a few of those in your own work—and then editing as need be. Although there are countless ways to get a word wrong, many such problems can be traced back to two causes: words that sound like other words (homophones) and apostrophes (which don't have any sound at all). Here's an example:

▶ Joe should of told them to buy there TV there because its cheaper and its screen is bigger.

Read that sentence out loud and it sounds exactly as the writer intended it; the meaning is perfectly clear. But your writing can't just "sound" right—it has to look right, too. In other words, the written words have to be correct. There are three wrong words in that sentence: "of," "there," and "its." Let's look at each one.

"Of" / "Have"

The useful little word "of," which is a **PREPOSITION**, sounds a lot like another very useful and common word, the verb "have," especially in rapid or casual speech. The two are often confused when "have" is used as a **HELPING VERB** with the **MODALS** "can," "could," "may," "might," "must," "should," "will," or "would"—especially in contractions, such as "could've" or "should've." How do you know if the appropriate word is "of" or "have"? Try reframing your sentence as a question. That should tell you very quickly which one is the right choice.

▶ Should Joe of told them?

▶ Should Joe have told them?

You can probably tell that "have" is the better choice. When you're editing, develop the habit of noticing whenever you use a modal, and make sure the words that follow it are appropriate. "Have" can be written out in its full form or combined with the preceding word to form a contraction—"should've," "would've." Try it without the modal. Have you told them? That's good. Of you told them? Not so good. That's because "have" is a helping verb, and "of" is not.

"There" / "Their" / "They're"

"There" is a common and useful word that sounds exactly like another common word, "their," and those two sound the same as a third common word, "they're," the contracted form of "they are." So not only do we have three homophones, but each of the three words is used very frequently in both speech and writing. That leads to a large number of wrong-word problems. For example:

▶ For security screening, passengers must put all cell phones in the trays, and now <u>there</u> required to put <u>there</u> shoes <u>there</u>, too.

You'll notice three instances of "there" in the example, and two of them are "wrong words." The sentence should have one each of "they're," "their," and "there," so let's take a closer look at each use of "there."

"THEY'RE" Let's start with the first one. That part of the sentence is trying to say that the passengers—they—are required to do something, so the appropriate word would be the contraction of "they are": "they're." The word "they're" has only that one meaning, so using it is very simple. Just see if you can substitute "they are" for the word in question and still have the meaning you intended. If not, you'll need to make a change.

"THEIR" Now let's look at the second instance of "there": "there shoes." That part of the sentence is talking about the shoes that belong to the passengers, so the appropriate word would be a possessive: "their." The word "their" has only that one uncomplicated meaning—it always indicates possession, as in the following examples:

▶ Their feet were swollen and their toes were numb, but the hikers were determined to reach Vogelsang before dark.

▶ The birds are squawking because the wind blew their nest down.

▶ Both of the radios still work, but their clocks are wrong.

When you're trying to decide if "their" is the right word, try asking if the word you are using is intended to show possession. In the examples above, "their" is correct because it indicates possession: Whose feet and toes? Their (the hikers') feet and toes. Whose nest? Their (the birds') nest. Whose clocks? Their (the radios') clocks.

"THERE" That leaves us with the final instance of "there" in our example sentence. That "there" is correct. Most of the time, as in our example, "there" simply indicates a place, telling *where* something is: Where's my phone? It's there, on the table. Sometimes, though, "there" is used as an **EXPLETIVE**, introducing information that's provided later in the sentence. For example:

▶ Whenever there was a big snowstorm, the neighbors all helped clear the street.

▶ There are three candidates in the race, but only one has the right experience.

That meaning of "there" simply indicates the existence of some-thing—a big snowstorm, three candidates. Here's an example that uses both meanings:

▶ There is a coatrack behind the door; you can hang your jacket there.

To check whether "there" is the appropriate word, ask whether the word indicates either the existence of something or a place. If the word indicates either of those two things, "there" is the correct choice.

When editing your own work, check each instance of "there," "their," and "they're" to make sure that you've written the one you really mean. That may sound tedious, but here's a handy shortcut: use the Find function (Command + F) in your word-processing program to search for each instance of "there," "their," and "they're." That way, you won't miss any. Do your search one term at a time, in whatever order makes the most sense to you.

Now let's revise our original example sentence. Try it yourself before you look at the edited version below.

▶ For security screening, passengers must put all cell phones in the trays,
            they're   *their*
  and now ~~there~~ required to put ~~there~~ shoes there, too.

"It's" / "Its"

How do you pronounce an apostrophe? You don't: apostrophes have no sound. So when there are two different words with only an apos-trophe to distinguish them, they're going to sound alike. "It's" and "its" make for many "wrong word" problems. Although they're pro-nounced exactly the same, they really are two distinct words with distinct uses: "its" is the possessive form of "it," and "its"/"it's" is a contraction of "it is" or "it has." That difference makes it easy to know which one is appropriate for your sentence. Let's look at one problematic sentence:

▶ When my phone fell, its screen shattered, but luckily, its still working.

There are two instances of "its" in the sentence, but one of them should really be "it's." How can you tell which is which? Just check to see which one can be replaced by "it is" or "it has." Easy, right? The second one—"it is" still working. The one without the apostrophe, "its," is the possessive form of "it": the screen that belongs to it (the phone). So here's how you'd edit this sentence:

▶ When my phone fell, its screen shattered, but luckily, ~~its~~ it's still working.

Wait. Haven't you been told to use an apostrophe to indicate possessives, as in "the judge's robe," "the frog's sticky tongue"? So how can it be that the version *without* the apostrophe is the possessive one? Isn't that confusing? Well, no. "It" is a **PRONOUN**, along with "he," "I," "she," and "you," for example. What are the possessive forms of those pronouns? "His." "My." "Her." "Your." Do you notice that those possessives don't have an apostrophe? Neither does "its."

▶ Carmen used <u>her</u> binoculars to watch a hawk open <u>its</u> wings and glide on the wind.

If you know or suspect that you have problems confusing "it's" and "its" in your work, you can check for them using the Find function of your word processor. Search your text for each of the two words, and make sure that the possessive "its" has no apostrophe and that the contracted form of "it is" or "it has" always appears as "it's."

> ## Edit

Return now to the first problem sentence at the bottom of page 342, and try editing it using all of the techniques discussed above:

> Joe should of told them to buy there TV there because its cheaper and its screen is bigger.

≫ SEE L-4 for more advice and examples on how to identify and edit wrong words. Go to **digital.wwnorton.com/littleseagull4** for additional practice.

S-1 Elements of a Sentence

In casual situations, we often use a kind of shorthand, because we know our audience will fill in the gaps. When we say "Coffee?" to dinner guests, they know we mean, "Would you like some coffee?" When we text "7 @ Starbucks?" to a friend, it's understood that we're asking, "Should we meet at 7:00 at Starbucks?" In more formal writing or speaking situations, though, our audience may not share the same context; to be sure we're understood, we usually need to present our ideas in complete sentences. This chapter reviews the parts of a sentence.

S-1a Subjects and Predicates

EX. S-1a
1 / P. 460
2 / P. 461

A sentence contains a subject and a predicate. The subject, which usually includes a **NOUN** or **PRONOUN**, names the topic of the sentence; the predicate, which always includes a **VERB**, says what the subject is or does.

▶ Birds fly.

▶ Birds are feathered vertebrates.

Sometimes the subject and the predicate contain only one word. Usually, however, both contain more than one word.

▶ Birds of many kinds fly south in the fall.

▶ Flying in a V formation is characteristic of geese.

▶ One of the flock leads the others.

A sentence may contain more than one subject or verb.

▶ Birds and butterflies fly south in the fall.

      s **v**   **v**

▶ Birds fly south in the fall and return north in the spring.

At times, the subject comes after the verb.

         v   ┌—**s**—┐

▶ Here comes the sun.

            v ┌————**s**————┐

▶ In the attic were old photographs and toys.

............EX. S-1a
3 / P. 462
Expressing subjects explicitly

English requires an explicit subject in every **CLAUSE**, even if all of the clauses in a sentence are about the same subject.

                                  it

▶ Although the dinner cost too much, ᪲impressed my guests.
                                      ^

The only exception is commands, in which the subject is understood to be "you."

▶ Drink plenty of water on hot days.

In informal conversation, speakers sometimes emphasize a noun subject by repeating it as a pronoun: My friend Jing she changed her name to Jane. In academic writing, though, don't repeat a subject this way.

▶ The visiting students ~~they~~ were detained at the airport.

Sentences beginning with "there" or "it." In some cases where the subject comes after the verb, an **EXPLETIVE**—"there" or "it"—is required before the verb.

   There is
▶ ~~Is~~ no place like home.
   ^

   It is
▶ ~~Is~~ both instructive and rewarding to work with young children.
   ^

You can often rephrase the sentence to avoid using the expletive.

   Working with young children
▶ ~~It~~ is both instructive and rewarding. ~~to work with young children.~~
   ^   ^

S-1b Clauses

EX. S-1b
P. 463
EX. S-1b–c
P. 465

A clause is a group of words containing a subject and a predicate. An independent clause can function alone as a sentence: Birds fly. A subordinate clause begins with a **SUBORDINATING WORD** such as "because," "as," or "which" and cannot stand alone as a sentence: because birds fly. (See p. 351 for a list of common subordinating words.)

```
  ┌─ INDEPENDENT CLAUSE ─┐ ┌────────── SUBORDINATE CLAUSE ──────────┐
```
▶ My yard is now quiet because most of the birds flew south.

```
  ┌─────────── SUBORDINATE CLAUSE ───────────┐ ┌───────── INDEPENDENT CLAUSE ─────────┐
```
▶ Although they travel really far, the birds always find their way back.

S-1c Phrases

EX. S-1c
P. 464
EX. S-1b–c
P. 465

A phrase is a word group that makes sense but lacks a subject, a verb, or both and thus cannot stand alone as a sentence. Some common ones are prepositional, appositive, participial, gerund, and infinitive phrases.

A prepositional phrase starts with a **PREPOSITION** such as "at," "from," "of," or "in" and usually ends with a noun or pronoun: at school, from home, in bed. It usually functions as an adjective or adverb.

▶ *During Diwali,* the neighbors *on my street* decorate their houses *with lights.*

An appositive phrase follows and gives additional information about a noun or pronoun. It functions as a noun.

▶ We all know that computers and their spawn, *the smartphone and cellphone,* have created a very different world from several decades ago.   —Alina Tugend,
                    "Multitasking Can Make You Lose . . . Um . . . Focus"

A participial phrase contains the **PRESENT PARTICIPLE** or **PAST PARTICIPLE** of a verb plus any **OBJECTS**, **MODIFIERS**, and **COMPLEMENTS**. It functions as an adjective.

▶ *Brimming with optimism,* I headed over to the neighborhood watering hole and waited.   —Hal Niedzviecki, "Facebook in a Crowd"

▶ A study from Princeton *issued at the same time as the Duke study* showed that women in the sciences reported less satisfaction in their jobs and less of a sense of belonging than their male counterparts.
—Anna Quindlen, "Still Needing the F Word"

A gerund phrase includes the "-ing" form of a verb plus any objects, modifiers, and complements. It functions as a noun.

▶ *Asking for candy on Halloween* was called trick-or-treating, but *asking for candy on November first* was called begging.
—David Sedaris, "Us and Them"

An infinitive phrase includes an infinitive ("to" plus the base form of a verb: to read, to write) and any objects, modifiers, and complements. It functions as a noun, an adjective, or an adverb.

▶ The plan *to add more bike parking racks* requires the dean's approval.

▶ The point of encouraging bike use is *to reduce auto congestion on campus.*

S-2   Sentence Fragments

Sentence fragments often show up in advertising: "Got milk?" "Good to the last drop." "Not bad for something that tastes good too." We use them in informal speech and text messages as well. In other kinds of writing, though, some readers consider fragments too informal, and in many academic writing situations, it's better to avoid them altogether. This chapter helps you identify and edit out fragments.

EX. S-2a
P. 466

S-2a   Identifying Fragments

A sentence fragment is a group of words that is capitalized and punctuated as a sentence but is not a sentence. A sentence needs at least one **INDEPENDENT CLAUSE**, which contains a **SUBJECT** and a **VERB** and does not start with a **SUBORDINATING WORD**.

NO SUBJECT	The catcher batted fifth. Fouled out, ending the inning.
	Who fouled out?
NO VERB	The first two batters walked. Manny Machado again.
	What did Machado do again?
SUBORDINATING WORD	Although the Yankees loaded the bases.
	There is a subject ("Yankees") and a verb ("loaded"), but "although" is a subordinating word. What happened after the Yankees loaded the bases?

SOME SUBORDINATING WORDS

after	because	so that	until	which
although	before	that	when	while
as	if	though	where	who
as if	since	unless	whether	why

S-2b Editing Fragments

EX. S-2b
P. 467

Since some readers regard fragments as errors, it's generally better to write complete sentences. Here are four ways to make fragments into sentences.

Add a subject

▶ The catcher batted fifth. ~~Fouled out,~~ ending the inning.
He fouled out,

Add a verb

▶ The first two batters walked. Manny Machado again.
walked

Sometimes, a fragment contains a verb form, such as a present participle or past participle, that cannot function as the main verb of a sentence. In these cases, you can either substitute an appropriate verb form or add a **HELPING VERB**.

▶ As the game went on, the fans started to lose interest. The pitcher's arm ~~weakening,~~ and the fielders ~~making~~ a number of errors.
weakened,   *made*

▶ The media influence the election process. Political commercials _∧ *are*
appearing on television more frequently than in years past.

Remove the subordinating word

▶ I'm thinking about moving to a large city. ~~Because~~ I dislike the lack of
privacy in my country town of three thousand residents.

Attach the fragment to a nearby sentence

▶ Some candidates spread nasty stories/ ~~About~~ *about* their opponents.

▶ These negative stories can deal with many topics/ ~~Such~~ *such* as marital
infidelity, sources of campaign funds, and drug use.

▶ Put off by negative campaigning/ ~~Some~~ *some* people decide not to vote at all.

Note that using a semicolon to attach a fragment to a nearby sentence
isn't a good solution. See **P–2** for tips on using semicolons.

S-2c Intentional Fragments

Writers sometimes use fragments intentionally.

FOR EMPHASIS	Throughout my elementary and middle school years, I was a strong student, always on the honor roll. I never had a GPA below 3.0. I was smart, and I knew it. *That is, until I got the results of the proficiency test.*
	—Shannon Nichols, " 'Proficiency' "
TO BE INFORMAL	The SAT writing test predicts how successful a student will be in college. *Since when?*
TO LIST SEVERAL EXAMPLES	The small details stand out. *The bathrooms with green stalls and mirrors with painted Ducks slugging conference foes. The extra-large furniture tested to withstand 500 pounds. The elevators decorated with famous plays in Oregon football history, the actual plays, drawn up in Xs and Os by a coach. The room for professional scouts to watch footage of Oregon players. The ticker running sports scores.*
	—Greg Bishop, "We Are the University of Nike."

Though fragments are common in informal contexts, they are often considered errors in academic writing.

S-3   Comma Splices, Fused Sentences

You'll sometimes see a comma splice in ads or literary works: "He dropped the bucket, the paint spilled on his feet." Or the comma may be omitted, forming a fused sentence: "He dropped the bucket the paint spilled on his feet." A comma splice or a fused sentence is generally regarded as an error in academic writing. This chapter shows how to recognize comma splices and fused sentences and edit them out of your writing.

S-3a Identifying Comma Splices and Fused Sentences

EX. S-3a
P. 468

A comma splice occurs when two or more **INDEPENDENT CLAUSES** follow one another with only a comma between them.

COMMA   T. S. Eliot is best known for his poetry, he also wrote
SPLICE   several plays.

A fused sentence occurs when two or more independent clauses follow one another with no punctuation in between.

FUSED   The school board debated the issue for three days they
SENTENCE   were unable to reach an agreement.

S-3b Editing Comma Splices and Fused Sentences

EX. S-3b
P. 469

There are several ways to edit out comma splices and fused sentences.

Make the clauses two sentences

▶ T. S. Eliot is best known for his poetry. He also wrote several plays.

Use a comma and a COORDINATING CONJUNCTION

▶ The school board debated the issue for three days, but they were unable to reach an agreement.

Use a semicolon

If the relationship between the two clauses is clear without a coordinating conjunction, you can simply join them with a semicolon.

▶ Psychologists study individuals' behavior; sociologists focus on group-level dynamics.

When clauses are linked by a TRANSITION such as "therefore" or "as a result," the transition needs to be preceded by a semicolon and should generally be followed by a comma.

▶ The hill towns experienced heavy spring and summer rain; therefore, the fall foliage fell far short of expectations.

Recast one clause as a subordinate clause

Add a SUBORDINATING WORD to clarify the relationship between the two clauses.

▶ Although initial critical responses to *The Waste Land* were mixed, the poem has been extensively anthologized, read, and written about.

S-3c Intentional Comma Splices

Writers sometimes use only a comma between clauses that are very brief or closely parallel in structure, as in proverbs like "Marry in haste, repent at leisure." In academic writing, though, such sentences may be seen as mistakes.

S-4   Verbs

Verbs are the engines of sentences, giving energy, action, and life to writing. "I googled it" is much more vivid than "I found it on the internet"—and the difference is the verb. Sometimes, however, our use of verbs can obscure our meaning, as when a politician avoids taking responsibility by saying, "Mistakes were made." Our choice of verbs shapes our writing in important ways, and this chapter reviews ways of using verbs appropriately and effectively.

S-4a Verb Tenses

EX. S-4a
P. 470

To express time, English verbs have three simple tenses—present, past, and future. In addition, each of these verb tenses has perfect and progressive forms that indicate more complex time frames. The present perfect, for example, can be used to indicate an action that began in the past but is continuing into the present. The lists that follow show each of these tenses for the regular verb "talk" and the irregular verb "write."

Simple tenses

PRESENT	PAST	FUTURE
I talk	I talked	I will talk
I write	I wrote	I will write

Use the simple present to indicate actions that take place in the present or that occur habitually. Use the simple past to indicate actions that were completed in the past. Use the simple future to indicate actions that will take place in the future.

▶ Most wealthy industrialized countries *operate* national health-insurance systems.

▶ In 2010, Congress *approved* the Affordable Care Act.

▶ Prohibiting English *will do* for the language what Prohibition *did* for liquor.   —Dennis Baron, "Don't Make English Official—Ban It Instead"

Use the present tense to express a scientific fact or a general truth even when the rest of the sentence is in the past tense.

▶ The security study showed that taxis and planes are the top places
where people ~~lost~~ *lose* their phones.

In general, use the present tense to write about literature.

▶ In the first book of the series, Rowling *introduces* us to eleven-year-old Harry Potter; in the seventh and final volume, Harry *enters* full adulthood.

In APA style, use the past tense or the present perfect to report results of an experiment and the present tense to give your own insights into or conclusions about the results.

▶ The bulk of the data collected in this study *validated* the research of Neal Miller; the subjects *appeared* to undergo operant conditioning of their smooth muscles in order to relax their frontalis muscles and increase their skin temperatures. Subjects 3 and 6 each *failed* to do this in one session; subject 7 *failed* to do this several times. This finding *is* difficult to explain precisely.

> —Sarah Thomas, "The Effect of Biofeedback Training
> on Muscle Tension and Skin Temperature"

Perfect tenses

PRESENT PERFECT	PAST PERFECT	FUTURE PERFECT
I have talked	I had talked	I will have talked
I have written	I had written	I will have written

Use the present perfect to indicate actions that took place at unspecified times in the past or that began in the past and continue into the present (or have relevance in the present).

▶ Many teachers and parents *have resisted* the increasing pressure for more standardized testing of students.

Use the past perfect for an action that was completed before another past action began.

▶ By the time I was born, the Gulf War *had* already ended.
The war ended before the writer was born.

Use the future perfect to indicate actions that will be completed at a specific time in the future.

▶ By this time next year, you *will have graduated.*

Progressive tenses

PRESENT PROGRESSIVE	PAST PROGRESSIVE	FUTURE PROGRESSIVE
I am talking	I was talking	I will be talking
I am writing	I was writing	I will be writing

PRESENT PERFECT PROGRESSIVE	PAST PERFECT PROGRESSIVE	FUTURE PERFECT PROGRESSIVE
I have been talking	I had been talking	I will have been talking
I have been writing	I had been writing	I will have been writing

Use progressive tenses to indicate continuing action.

▶ The Lakers *are having* a great year, but the Bucks *are leading* the league.

▶ We *were watching* TV when the doorbell rang.

▶ During the World Cup, soccer fans around the world *will be watching* on TV or online.

▶ Willa joined the robotics club when she was ten, and she *has been building* robots ever since.

S-4b   Verb Forms

EX. S-4b
1 / P. 471

There are four forms of a verb: the base form, the past, the past participle, and the present participle. Samples of each appear in the lists below. All of the various tenses are generated with these four forms.

The past tense and past participle of all regular verbs are formed by adding "-ed" or "-d" to the base form (talked, lived). Irregular verbs are not as predictable; see the list of some common ones below. The present participle consists of the base form plus "-ing" (talking, living).

BASE FORM   On Thursdays, we *visit* a museum.

PAST TENSE   Last week, we *visited* the Museum of Modern Art.

| PAST PARTICIPLE | I have also *visited* the Metropolitan Museum, but I've not yet *been* to the Cloisters. |

| PRESENT PARTICIPLE | We will be *visiting* the Cooper-Hewitt Museum tomorrow to see the cutlery exhibit. |

EX. S-4b
2 / P. 472

Some common irregular verbs

BASE FORM	PAST TENSE	PAST PARTICIPLE	PRESENT PARTICIPLE
be	was/were	been	being
bring	brought	brought	bringing
choose	chose	chosen	choosing
come	came	come	coming
do	did	done	doing
eat	ate	eaten	eating
find	found	found	finding
fly	flew	flown	flying
give	gave	given	giving
go	went	gone	going
hang (suspend)	hung	hung	hanging
have	had	had	having
know	knew	known	knowing
make	made	made	making
prove	proved	proved, proven	proving
rise	rose	risen	rising
set	set	set	setting
sit	sat	sat	sitting
teach	taught	taught	teaching
write	wrote	written	writing

It's easy to get confused about when to use the past tense and when to use a past participle. One simple guideline is to use the past tense if there is no helping verb and to use a past participle if there is one.

▶ For vacation last summer, my family ~~gone~~ *went* to Door County.

▶ After a week at the beach, we had ~~ate~~ *eaten* a lot of seafood.

EX. S-4b
3 / P. 473

Gerunds and infinitives

A gerund is a verb form ending in "-ing" that functions as a noun: hopping, skipping, jumping.

▶ Although many people like *driving*, some prefer *walking*.

An infinitive is a verb form made up of "to" plus the base form of a verb: to hop, to skip, to jump.

▶ Although many people like *to drive*, some prefer *to walk*.

Often, infinitives express intentions or desires and gerunds express plain facts.

▶ We planned *to visit* Hollywood, and we also wanted ~~seeing~~ the Grand Canyon.
  to see

▶ Unfortunately, we ran out of time, so we postponed ~~to see~~ the Grand Canyon.
  seeing

However, there are many exceptions to this pattern, so you may need to consult a dictionary in order to make the appropriate choice.

Some verbs—"begin," "continue," "like," "prefer," and a few others—can be followed by either a gerund or an infinitive with little if any difference in meaning. But with several verbs—"forget," "remember," "stop," and a few others—the choice of an infinitive or a gerund changes the meaning.

▶ I stopped *to eat* lunch.

  In other words, I took a break so that I could eat lunch.

▶ I stopped *eating* lunch.

  In other words, I no longer ate lunch.

Always use a gerund after a **PREPOSITION** or a **PHRASAL VERB**.

▶ The water is too cold for ~~to swim.~~
  swimming.

▶ We ended up ~~to spend~~ our whole trip in San Francisco.
  spending

S-4c Helping Verbs

"Do," "have," "be," and **MODALS** such as "can" and "may" all function as helping verbs that are used with **MAIN VERBS** to form certain **TENSES** and **MOODS**. "Do," "have," and "be" change form to indicate different tenses; modals do not.

FORMS OF "DO"	do, does, did
FORMS OF "HAVE"	have, has, had
FORMS OF "BE"	be, am, is, are, was, were, been
MODALS	can, could, may, might, must, ought to, shall, should, will, would

"Do," "does," and "did" require the base form of the main verb.

▶ That professor *did take* class participation into account when calculating grades.

▶ Sometimes even the most prepared students *do* not *like* to answer questions out loud in class.

"Have," "has," and "had" require the past participle of the main verb.

▶ I *have joined* the First Gen club to meet other first-generation students on campus.

▶ When all of the visitors *had gone*, the security guards locked the building for the night.

Forms of "be" are used with a present participle to express a continuing action or with a past participle to express the **PASSIVE VOICE**.

CONTINUING ACTION

▶ The university *is considering* a change in its policy on legacy admissions.

▶ I *was studying* my notes from last week as I walked to class.

PASSIVE VOICE

▶ Six classes per semester *is considered* a heavy course load.

▶ Ancient Greek *was studied* by many university students in the early twentieth century, but it is not a popular major today.

Modals

EX. S-4c
P. 474

"Can," "could," "may," "might," "must," "ought to," "shall," "should," "will," and "would": these are modals, a kind of helping verb used with the base form of a **MAIN VERB** to express whether an action is likely, possible, permitted, or various other conditions. Modals don't take the third-person "-s" or the "-ed" or "-ing" endings that ordinary verbs do.

Likelihood will, could, ought to, may, might

▶ The Mavericks *will* win tomorrow. [*very certain*]

▶ The Nuggets *could* defeat the Nets. [*somewhat certain*]

▶ It *ought to* be a very close series between the Clippers and the Sixers. [*moderately certain*]

▶ The Cavaliers *may* win their game tonight. [*less certain*]

▶ The Knicks *might* make the playoffs someday. [*much less certain*]

Assumption must

▶ The dog just started barking; he *must* hear our guests arriving.

Expectation should, ought to

▶ Two large onions *should* be enough for this recipe.

▶ The potatoes *ought to* be ready in twenty minutes.

Ability can, could

▶ Mick Jagger *can* still put on quite a performance, but years ago he *could* sing and throw himself around the stage more dramatically. How much longer *will* he *be able to* keep rocking?

Necessity or obligation must, should, ought to

▶ Travelers *must* have a passport for foreign travel.

▶ We *should* leave early tomorrow because of the holiday traffic.

▶ You *ought to* get to the airport at least two hours before your scheduled departure.

Permission and requests may, can, could, would, will

▶ People traveling with small children *may* board the plane first.

▶ The hotel's check-in time is 4:00 PM, but travelers *can* often check in earlier.

▶ *Would* someone help me put my suitcase in the overhead rack?

▶ *Will* you please turn off your phone?

Advice should, ought to

▶ You *should* never text while driving.

▶ You *ought to* be careful about using wi-fi networks in public places.

Intention will, shall

▶ Aunt Najwa *will* prepare her famous *atayef* for Eid.

▶ We *shall* overcome.

EX. S-4d
P. 475

S-4d Active and Passive Voice

Verbs can sometimes be active or passive. In the active voice, the subject performs the action of the verb (Becky solved the problem). In the passive voice, the subject receives the action (the problem was solved by Becky).

ACTIVE   One year ago, almost to the day, I *asked* my hairdresser to cut off 16 inches of my hair.
                                        —Suleika Jaouad, "Finding My Cancer Style"

PASSIVE As a teenager I *was instructed* on how to behave as a proper señorita.   —Judith Ortiz Cofer, "The Myth of the Latin Woman"

Active verbs tend to be more direct and easier to understand, but the passive voice can be useful when you specifically want to emphasize the recipient of the action.

▶ In a sense, little girls *are urged* to please adults with a kind of coquettishness, while boys *are enjoined* to behave like monkeys toward each other.   —Paul Theroux, "Being a Man"

The passive voice is also appropriate in scientific writing when you want to emphasize the research itself, not the researchers.

▶ The treatment order was random for each subject, and it *was reversed* for his or her second treatment.
> —Sarah Thomas, "The Effect of Biofeedback Training
> on Muscle Tension and Skin Temperature"

S-4e Mood

EX. S-4e
1 / P. 475

English verbs have three moods: indicative, imperative, and subjunctive. The indicative is used to state facts, opinions, or questions.

▶ Habitat for Humanity *has built* twelve houses in the region this year.

▶ What other volunteer opportunities *does* Habitat *offer*?

The imperative is used to give commands or directions.

▶ *Sit* up straight, and *do* your work.

The subjunctive is used to indicate unlikely or hypothetical conditions or to express wishes, requests, or requirements.

▶ We would be happier if we *had* less pressure at work.

▶ My mother wishes my brother *were* more responsible with his money.

▶ Most colleges require that each applicant *write* an essay.

The subjunctive has two types—one that is the same form as the past tense and one that is the same as the base form.

Conditional sentences

EX. S-4e
2 / P. 476

The subjunctive is used most often in conditional sentences, ones that include a clause beginning with "if" or another word that states a condition. Use the indicative in the "if" clause to show that you are confident the condition is possible; use the subjunctive to show that it's doubtful or impossible.

If it's a fact or a possibility. When there's no doubt that the condition in the "if" clause is true or possible, use the indicative in both clauses.

▶ If an earthquake *strikes* that region, forecasters *expect* a tsunami.

▶ A century ago, if a hurricane *struck*, residents *had* very little warning.

▶ If you *follow* that diet for two weeks, you *will lose* about ten pounds.

If it's unlikely, impossible, or hypothetical. When the condition in the "if" clause is not likely or possible, use the subjunctive (same as the past form) in the "if" clause and "would" (or "could" or "might") + the base form of a verb in the other clause. For "be," use "were" in the "if" clause, not "was."

▶ If I *won* the lottery, I *could pay off* my student loans.

▶ If Shirley Chisholm *were* alive, she *would* likely express disappointment that no woman has yet been elected US president.

Because the subjunctive can sound rather formal, it's often not used in informal contexts. In formal and most academic writing, however, it's best to do so.

INFORMAL   I *wish* I *was* in Paris.

ACADEMIC   In *The Three Sisters,* Masha *wishes* she *were living* in Moscow.

When the "if" clause is about an event in the past that never happened, use the past perfect in the "if" clause and "would have" (or "could have" or "might have") + a past participle in the other clause.

▶ If the police officer *had separated* the witnesses, their evidence *would have been* admissible in court.

Requests, recommendations, and demands

In "that" clauses following verbs such as "ask," "insist," or "suggest," use the subjunctive to express a request, a recommendation, or a demand. Use the base form of the verb in the "that" clause.

▶ I recommended that Rivka *take* a class to get her pilot's license.

▶ The CEO will insist that you *be* at your desk before nine each morning.

S-4f **Phrasal Verbs**

EX. S-4f
P. 477

"Act up." "Back down." "Carry on." These are all phrasal verbs, composed of more than one word—usually a verb and a preposition. You know what "act" means. You know what "up" means. If English is not your primary language, however, you may need to check a dictionary to find out that "act up" means to "misbehave" (or to say that using another phrasal verb, you may need to look it up). With phrasal verbs, knowing the meaning of each part does not always help you to know what the phrasal verb itself means.

Phrasal verbs can be divided into two categories, separable and inseparable. With separable verbs, the parts can be separated by an **OBJECT**; with inseparable ones, the parts can never be separated.

SEPARABLE   I used to *look up* words in a dictionary; now I *look* them *up* on my phone.

INSEPARABLE   Didi has decided to *run for* mayor next year.

With separable phrasal verbs, you have a choice: you can put the object between the parts, or after the complete phrasal verb.

▶ With a hurricane forming nearby, NASA *called off* tomorrow's lunar launch.

▶ Darn! They *called* the launch *off*?

When the object is a long phrase, however, it almost always follows the complete verb.

▶ NASA engineers called the launch of the lunar mission scheduled for tomorrow ~~off~~.
  ^off^

The personal pronouns "me," "you," "him," "her," "it," "us," and "them" are almost always placed between the parts.

▶ The launch was scheduled for yesterday, but NASA called off ~~it~~ because of the weather.
  ^it^

Some phrasal verbs never take an object—for example, "come over" (meaning to "visit") and "catch on" (meaning to "become popular").

▶ Why don't you *come over* and see us sometime?

▶ Even the developers of *Pinterest* were astonished by how quickly it *caught on.*

With some phrasal verbs, the meaning changes depending on whether or not there is an object. To "look something up," for instance, means to "find information"; without an object, to "look up" means to "get better."

▶ When in doubt, *look up* phrasal verbs in a dictionary.

▶ The sun's out and the roses are in bloom; things are *looking up!*

Go to **digital.wwnorton.com/littleseagull4** for a glossary of phrasal verbs.

Some common phrasal verbs

SEPARABLE

back up   means to "support": Dodson's hypothesis is well stated, but the data do not back it up.

break down   means to "divide into smaller parts": Their analysis might be clearer if it broke the data down state by state.

carry out   means to "fulfill" or "complete": We plan to carry out a survey on what the students in our dorm are reading.

find out   means to "learn" or "get information": Some parents decide not to find out the sex before their baby is born because they want to be surprised; others just want to annoy relatives.

point out   means to "call attention to": The lizards blend in with the leaves so well that they were hard to see until the guide pointed them out.

INSEPARABLE

call for   means to "require" or "deserve": Our current economic situation calls for bold and innovative thinking.

get over   means to "recover": Grandma always insisted that the best way to get over a cold was to eat chicken soup.

look into   means to "investigate": GAO investigators are looking into allegations of fraud by some college recruiters.

settle on   means to "decide on" or "choose": We considered Elizabeth, Margaret, Jane, and many other names for our baby, but finally we settled on Susanna.

touch on   means to "mention briefly": The *Wall Street Journal* article focused on productivity and barely touched on issues of worker safety.

DO NOT TAKE AN OBJECT

come about   means to "happen" or "occur": How did the dispute come about in the first place?

get by   means to "survive" or "manage," usually with few resources: Many retired workers can't get by on just their pensions; they have to find part-time work as well.

give in   means to "yield" or "agree": After much discussion, members of the union voted not to give in to management's demands for a reduction in benefits.

show up   means to "arrive": Did everyone show up for the rehearsal?

take off   means to "leave the ground": The JetBlue flight took off an hour late because of thunderstorms in the Midwest. It also means to "make great progress": Sales of *Where the Crawdads Sing* took off in 2018, after it was recommended by Reese Witherspoon.

S-5   Subject-Verb Agreement

EX. S-5
1 / P. 478
2 / P. 479

Subjects and verbs should agree: if the subject is in the third-person singular, the verb should be in the third-person singular—"Dinner is on the table." Yet sometimes context affects subject-verb agreement, as when we say that "macaroni and cheese *make* a great combination" but that "macaroni and cheese is our family's favorite comfort food." This chapter focuses on subject-verb agreement.

S-5a Agreement in Number and Person

Subjects and verbs should agree with each other in number (singular or plural) and person (first, second, or third). To make a present-tense verb agree with a third-person singular subject, add "-s" or "-es" to the base form.

▶ A 1922 *ad* for Resinol soap *urges* women to "make that dream come true" by using Resinol.   —Doug Lantry, "'Stay Sweet as You Are'"

To make a present-tense verb agree with any other subject, simply use the base form without any ending.

▶ *I listen* to NPR every morning while *I brush* my teeth.

▶ *Drunk drivers cause* thousands of preventable deaths each year.

"Be" and "have" have irregular forms (shown on p. 358) and so do not follow the "-s"/"-es" rule.

▶ The test of all knowledge *is* experiment.
                              —Richard Feynman, "Atoms in Motion"

▶ The scientist *has* a lot of experience with ignorance and doubt and uncertainty, and this experience *is* of great importance.
                         —Richard Feynman, "The Value of Science"

In questions, a helping verb is often necessary. The subject, which generally goes between the helping verb and the main verb, should agree with the helping verb.

▶ How long *does an air filter last* on average?

▶ *Have the 10 ml pipettes arrived* yet?

S-5b Subjects and Verbs Separated

A verb should agree with its subject, not with another word that falls in between.

► In the backyard, the *leaves* of the apple tree *rattle* across the lawn.
—Gary Soto, "The Guardian Angel"

fluctuates
► The *price* of soybeans fluctuate according to demand.

S-5c Compound Subjects

Two or more subjects joined by "and" are generally plural.

► Swiss cheese and shrimp *are* both high in vitamin B12.

However, if the parts of the subject form a single unit, they take a singular verb.

is
► Forty acres and a mule are what General William T. Sherman promised each freed slave.

If the subjects are joined by "or" or "nor," the verb should agree with the closer subject.

is
► Either you or she are mistaken.

were
► Neither the teacher nor his students was able to solve the equation.

S-5d Subjects That Follow the Verb

English verbs usually follow their subjects. Be sure the verb agrees with the subject even when the subject follows the verb, such as when the sentence begins with "there is" or "there are."

▶ There ~~is~~ *are* too many unresolved problems for the project to begin.

▶ In the middle of the room ~~was~~ *were* a desk and a floor lamp.

S-5e Collective Nouns

Collective nouns such as "group," "team," "audience," or "family" can take singular or plural verbs, depending on whether the noun refers to the group as a single unit or to the individual members of the group.

▶ Our klezmer band ~~perform~~ *performs* for the whole campus every year in March, around Purim.

▶ Gregor's family *keep* reassuring themselves that things will be just fine again.   —Scott Russell Sanders, "Under the Influence"
The word "themselves" shows that "family" refers to its individual members.

S-5f "Everyone" and Other Indefinite Pronouns

Most **INDEFINITE PRONOUNS**, such as "anyone," "anything," "each," "either," "everyone," "everything," "neither," "nobody," "no one," "one," "somebody," "someone," and "something," take a singular verb, even if they seem plural or refer to plural nouns.

▶ Everyone in our dorm *has* already *signed* the petition.

▶ Each of the candidates ~~agree~~ *agrees* with the president.

"Both," "few," "many," "others," and "several" are always plural.

▶ Although there are many great actors working today, few *are* as versatile as Meryl Streep.

"All," "any," "enough," "more," "most," "none," and "some" are singular when they refer to a singular noun, but they are plural when they refer to a plural noun.

▶ Don't assume that all of the members of a family ~~votes~~ *vote* the same way.

▶ Most of the music we heard last night ~~come~~ *comes* from the baroque period.

S-5g "Who," "That," "Which"

The **RELATIVE PRONOUNS** "who," "that," and "which" take a singular verb when they refer to a singular noun and a plural verb when they refer to a plural noun.

▶ In these songs, Lady Gaga draws on a tradition of camp that *extends* from drag queen cabaret to Broadway and disco.
>   —Jody Rosen, review of *Born This Way*

▶ Bowman, having nearly been sent to a deep-space death by the malfunctioning machine, is calmly, coldly disconnecting the memory circuits that *control* its artificial brain.
>   —Nicholas Carr, "Is Google Making Us Stupid?"

"One of the" is always followed by a plural noun, and when the noun is followed by "who" or "that," the verb should be plural.

▶ Jaime is one of the speakers who ~~asks~~ provocative questions.
    ask

Several speakers ask provocative questions. Jaime is one. "Who" refers to "speakers," so the verb is plural.

If the phrase begins with "the only one," however, the verb should be singular.

▶ Jaime is the only one of the speakers who ~~ask~~ provocative questions.
    asks

Only one speaker asks provocative questions: Jaime. "Who" thus refers to "one," so the verb is singular.

S-5h Words Such as "News" and "Physics"

Words like "news," "athletics," and "physics" seem plural but are usually singular in meaning and take singular verb forms.

▶ The *news* of widespread layoffs *alarms* everyone in the company.

Some of these words, such as "economics," "mathematics," "politics," and "statistics," have plural meanings in some uses and take plural verbs.

▶ For my roommate, mathematics *is* an endlessly stimulating field.

▶ The complex mathematics involved in this proof *are* beyond the scope of this lecture.

S-5i Titles and Words Used as Words

Titles and words that are discussed as words are singular.

▶ *The Royal Tenenbaums* ~~depict~~ ^{depicts} three talented siblings who are loosely based on characters created by J. D. Salinger.

▶ "Man-caused disasters" ~~are~~ ^{is} a term favored by some political analysts as a substitute for the term "terrorist attacks."

S-6 Pronouns

We use pronouns to take the place of nouns so that we don't have to write or say the same word or name over and over. Imagine how repetitive our writing would be without pronouns: Little Miss Muffet sat on a tuffet eating Little Miss Muffet's curds and whey. Luckily, we have pronouns, and this chapter demonstrates how to use them clearly.

EX. S-6a
P. 480

S-6a Pronoun-Antecedent Agreement

Antecedents are the words that pronouns refer to. A pronoun must agree with its antecedent in gender and number.

IN GENDER   *Grandma* took *her* pie out of the oven.

IN NUMBER   *My grandparents* spent weekends at *their* cabin on White Bear Lake.

Generic nouns

Generic nouns refer to a type or category of person or thing (a farmer, a shower cap). You'll often see or hear a plural pronoun used to refer to a singular generic noun, especially if the noun refers to a type of person. In conversation and increasingly in academic writing as well, this usage is becoming more and more acceptable.

▶ *Every lab technician* should always wear goggles to protect *their* eyes while working with chemicals.

In some contexts, you may want to stay with more traditional usage; in those cases, you can make the noun plural.

Lab technicians
▶ ~~Every lab technician~~ should always wear goggles to protect *their* eyes
  ^
while working with chemicals.

Indefinite pronouns like "everyone" and "each"

INDEFINITE PRONOUNS such as "anyone," "each," "everyone," and "someone" are considered singular even if they seem to be plural because they may refer to plural nouns.

▶ All items on that table will have their prices marked down.

                        its
▶ Everything on that table will have ~~their~~ price marked down.
                        ^

Both sentences have the same meaning, and even though "everything" clearly refers to all of the things (plural), the word "everything" is considered singular.

As with generic nouns, in conversation and increasingly in writing as well, "they," "them," and "their" are often used to refer to grammatically singular indefinite pronouns that refer to people. See **L-10b** for more on this usage.

▶ Everyone in the class did their best.

If you want to stay with more traditional usage, you can change the indefinite pronoun to a genuine plural.

All of the students
▶ ~~Everyone~~ in the class did their best.
  ^

Collective nouns like "audience" and "team"

Collective nouns such as "audience," "committee," and "team" take a singular pronoun when they refer to the group as a whole and a plural pronoun when they refer to members of the group as individuals.

▶ Our softball team won ~~their~~ its first championship ever.

▶ Our softball team threw ~~its~~ their gloves in the air in celebration.

The championship belongs to the team as a unit, so the appropriate pronoun is "its." The gloves were thrown in the air by the individual players, so the appropriate pronoun is "their." These two examples are clear, but collective nouns can often be ambiguous. Sometimes, singular and plural pronouns might both be acceptable. In those cases, you can choose whichever one you think works best, as long as you're consistent.

▶ Her family has their reunion in Charlotte every August.

▶ Her family has its reunion in Charlotte every August.

"He," "his," and other masculine pronouns

To avoid **SEXIST LANGUAGE**, use "he," "him," "his," or "himself" only when you know that the antecedent identifies as male.

▶ When meeting a new doctor, it's useful to bring a list of questions ~~for him~~.

Another possibility is to use "him or her."

▶ Before meeting a new doctor, many people worry about not liking him/ or her.

However, not all people identify as either male or female, so this solution doesn't include everyone. Instead, many writers use "they," "them," and "their" to refer to a person whose gender is unknown or not relevant to the context.

▶ Someone in my building is selling ~~his~~ their laptop; ~~he~~ they put up a sign by the mailboxes.

This usage, known as **SINGULAR "THEY,"** is becoming more and more accepted. It has been endorsed by Merriam-Webster's dictionary and many other major publications. Ask your instructor if it's OK to use it in your class writing. In addition, some people use "they" rather than "he" or "she" when being referred to in the third-person singular. Always refer to people by using the pronouns they designate for themselves.

S-6b Pronoun Reference

EX. S-6b
P. 481

A pronoun usually needs a clear antecedent, a specific word to which it refers.

▶ *My grandmother* spent a lot of time reading to me. *She* mostly read the standards, like *The Little Engine That Could.*

  —Richard Bullock, "How I Learned about the Power of Writing"

Ambiguous reference

If there is more than one word that a pronoun could refer to, rewrite the sentence to clarify which one is the antecedent.

▶ After I plugged the printer into the computer, ~~it~~ sputtered and died.
  the printer

  What sputtered and died—the computer or the printer? The edit makes the reference clear.

Implied reference

If a pronoun does not refer clearly to a specific word, rewrite the sentence to omit the pronoun or insert an antecedent.

Unclear reference of "this," "that," and "which." These three pronouns must refer to specific antecedents.

▶ Ultimately, the Justice Department did not insist on the breakup of Microsoft, ~~which~~ set the tone for a liberal merger policy.
  an oversight that

Indefinite use of "they," "it," and "you." Except in expressions like "it is raining" or "it seems that," "they" and "it" should be used only to refer to people or things that have been specifically mentioned. "You" should be used only to address your reader.

▶ ~~In many~~ European countries/~~they~~ don't allow civilians to carry handguns.
  Many

▶ The
~~On the~~ Weather Channel/~~it~~ said that storms would hit Key West today.

▶ Many doctors argue that age should not be an impediment to
physical exercise for people who ~~if you~~ have always been active.

Both in conversation and in writing, antecedents are often left unstated if the audience will easily grasp the meaning. For academic writing, however, it's better not to use implied or indefinite antecedents.

EX. S-6c
1 / P. 482
2 / P. 483

S-6c Pronoun Case

Pronouns change case according to how they function in a sentence. There are three cases: subject, object, and possessive. Pronouns functioning as subjects or subject **COMPLEMENTS** are in the subject case; those functioning as **OBJECTS** are in the object case; those functioning as possessives are in the possessive case.

SUBJECT   *We* lived in a rented house three blocks from the school.

OBJECT   I went to my room and shut the door behind *me*.

POSSESSIVE   All *my* life chocolate has made me ill.

—David Sedaris, "Us and Them"

SUBJECT	OBJECT	POSSESSIVE
I	me	my / mine
we	us	our / ours
you	you	your / yours
he / she / it	him / her / it	his / her / hers / its
they	them	their / theirs
who / whoever	whom / whomever	whose

In subject complements

Use the subject case for pronouns that follow **LINKING VERBS** such as "be," "seem," "become," and "feel."

▶ In fact, Li was not the one who broke the code; it was ~~me.~~ I.
If "It was I" sounds awkward, revise the sentence further: "I broke it."

In compound structures

When a pronoun is part of a compound subject, it should be in the subject case. When it's part of a compound object, it should be in the object case.

▶ On our vacations, my grandfather and ~~me~~ ^I^ went fishing together.

▶ There were never any secrets between ~~he~~ ^him^ and ~~I~~ ^me.^

After "than" or "as"

Often comparisons with "than" or "as" leave some words out. When such comparisons include pronouns, your intended meaning determines the case of the pronoun.

▶ You help Lalo more than *me*.

   This sentence means "You help Lalo more than you help me."

▶ You help Lalo more than *I*.

   This sentence means "You help Lalo more than I help him."

Before or after infinitives

Pronouns that come before or after an **INFINITIVE** are usually in the object case.

▶ The choreographer asked Ravi and ~~I~~ ^me^ to show ~~she~~ ^her^ and the troupe our new steps.

Before gerunds

Pronouns that come before a **GERUND** are usually in the possessive case.

▶ Savion's fans loved ~~him~~ ^his^ tap dancing to classical music.

With "who" or "whom"

EX. S-6c
2 / P. 483

There's strong evidence that "whom" is disappearing from use in both formal and informal contexts, but some instructors may expect you to use it. Use "who" (and "whoever") where you would use "he" or "she," and use "whom" (and "whomever") where you would use "him" or "her." These words appear most often in questions and in **SUBORDINATE CLAUSES**.

In questions. It can be confusing when one of these words begins a question. To figure out which case to use, try answering the question using "she" or "her." If "she" works, use "who"; if "her" works, use "whom."

▶ ~~Who~~ **Whom** do the critics admire most?

They admire her, so change "who" to "whom."

▶ ~~Whom~~ **Who** will begin the discussion on this thorny topic?

She will begin the discussion, so change "whom" to "who."

In subordinate clauses. To figure out whether to use "who" or "whom" in a subordinate clause, you need to determine how it functions in the clause. If it functions as a subject, use "who"; if it functions as an object, use "whom."

▶ You may invite ~~whoever~~ **whomever** you like.

"Whomever" is the object of "you like."

▶ I will invite ~~whomever~~ **whoever** is free that night.

"Whoever" is the subject of "is free that night." The clause "whoever is free that night" is the object of the whole sentence.

When "we" or "us" precedes a noun

If you don't know whether to use "we" or "us" before a noun, choose the pronoun that you would use if the noun were omitted.

▶ *We* students object to the recent tuition increases.

Without "students," you would say "We object," not "Us object."

▶ The state is solving its budget shortfall by unfairly charging *us* students.

Without "students," you would say "unfairly charging us," not "unfairly charging we."

EX. S-7
P. 484

S-7   Parallelism

"Been there, done that." "Eat, drink, and be merry." "For better or for worse." "Out of sight, out of mind." All of these common sayings are parallel in structure, putting related words in the same grammatical form. Parallel structure emphasizes the connection between the elements and can make your writing rhythmic and easy to read. This chapter offers guidelines for maintaining parallelism in your writing.

S-7a In a Series or List

Use the same grammatical form for all items in a series or list—all nouns, all gerunds, all prepositional phrases, and so on.

▶ The seven deadly sins—*avarice, sloth, envy, lust, gluttony, pride,* and *wrath*—were all committed Sunday during the twice-annual bake sale at St. Mary's of the Immaculate Conception Church.   —*The Onion*

▶ After fifty years of running, biking, swimming, weight lifting, and ~~playing~~ tennis to stay in shape, Aunt Dorothy was unhappy to learn she needed knee surgery.

S-7b With Paired Ideas

One way to emphasize the connection between two ideas is to put them in identical grammatical forms. When you connect ideas with "and," "but," or another **COORDINATING CONJUNCTION** or with "either . . . or" or another **CORRELATIVE CONJUNCTION**, use the same grammatical structure for each idea.

▶ Many rural residents are voting on conservation issues and ~~agree~~ *agreeing* to pay higher taxes to keep community land undeveloped.

▶ General Electric paid millions of dollars to dredge the river and ~~for removing~~ *to remove* carcinogens from backyards.

▶ Sweet potatoes are highly nutritious, providing both dietary fiber and ~~as a good source of~~ vitamins A and C.

▶ Information on local cleanup efforts can be obtained not only from the town government but also ~~by going to~~ *at* the public library.

S-7c On Presentation Slides

PowerPoint and other presentation tools present most information in lists. Entries on these lists should be in parallel grammatical form.

> During the 1946 presidential race, Truman
> - Conducted a whistle-stop campaign
> - Made hundreds of speeches
> - Spoke energetically
> - Connected personally with voters

S-7d On a Résumé

Entries on a résumé should be grammatically and typographically parallel. Each entry in the example below has the date on the left; the job title in bold followed by the company on the first line; the city and state on the second line; and the duties performed on the remaining lines, each starting with a verb.

> 2020–present   **INTERN**, Benedetto, Gartland, and Company
> Miami, FL
> Assist in analyzing data for key accounts.
> Design *PowerPoint* slides and presentations.
>
> 2019, summer   **SALES REPRESENTATIVE**, Vector Marketing Corporation
> Miami, FL
> Sold high-quality cutlery, developing client base.
>
> 2018, summer   **TUTOR**, Grace Church Opportunity Project
> Miami, FL
> Tutored children in math and reading.

S-7e In Headings

When you add headings to a piece of writing, put them in parallel form—all nouns, all prepositional phrases, and so on. Consider, for example, the following three headings in R-4:

Acknowledging Sources

Avoiding Plagiarism

Understanding Documentation Styles

S-7f With All the Necessary Words

Be sure to include all the words necessary to make your meaning clear and your grammar parallel.

▶ Voting gained urgency in cities, ^in^ suburbs, and on farms.

▶ She loved her son more than ^she loved^ her husband.

   The original sentence was ambiguous; it could also mean that she loved her son more than her husband did.

▶ A cat's skeleton is more flexible than ^that of^ a dog.

   The original sentence compared one animal's skeleton to a whole animal rather than to another animal's skeleton.

S-8   Coordination, Subordination

EX. S-8
P. 485

When we combine two or more ideas in one sentence, we can use coordination to give equal weight to each idea or subordination to give more emphasis to one of the ideas. Assume, for example, that you're writing about your Aunt Irene. Aunt Irene made great strawberry jam. She did not win a blue ribbon at the Iowa State Fair.

COORDINATION   Aunt Irene made great strawberry jam, but she did not win a blue ribbon at the Iowa State Fair.

SUBORDINATION   Though Aunt Irene made great strawberry jam, she did not win a blue ribbon at the Iowa State Fair.

S-8a Linking Equal Ideas

To link ideas that you consider equal in importance, use a coordinating conjunction, a pair of correlative conjunctions, or a semicolon.

COORDINATING CONJUNCTIONS

and   but   for   nor   or   so   yet

▶ The line in front of Preservation Hall was very long, *but* a good tenor sax player was wandering up and down the street, *so* I took my place at the end of the line.   —Fred Setterberg, "The Usual Story"

▶ New models of coursework may need to be developed, *and* instructors may need to be hired.
                    —Megan Hopkins, "Training the Next Teachers for America"

Be careful not to overuse "and." Try to use the coordinating conjunction that best expresses your meaning.

▶ Mosquitoes survived the high-tech zapping devices, ~~and~~ *but* bites were a small price for otherwise pleasant evenings in the country.

CORRELATIVE CONJUNCTIONS

either . . . or   just as . . . so   neither . . . nor
not only . . . but also   whether . . . or

▶ *Just as* the summer saw endless rain, *so* the winter brought many snowstorms.

While a semicolon alone can signal equal importance, you might use a **TRANSITION** such as "therefore" or "in fact" to make the relationship between the ideas especially clear.

▶ Snowplows could not get through; trains stopped running.

▶ The 1996 film *Space Jam* stars Bugs Bunny and Michael Jordan, an unlikely pairing; *however,* the two are well matched in heroic status and mythic strengths.

S-8b Emphasizing One Idea over Others

EX. S-8b
P. 485

To emphasize one idea over others, put the most important one in an **INDEPENDENT CLAUSE** and the less important ones in **SUBORDINATE CLAUSES** or **PHRASES**.

▶ ⎣——PHRASE——⎦ Wanting to walk to work, LeShawn rented a somewhat expensive apartment downtown.

▶ His monthly expenses were actually lower ⎣——SUBORDINATE CLAUSE——⎦ because he saved so much money in transportation costs.

S-9 Shifts

EX. S-9
P. 487

You're watching the news when your brother grabs the remote and changes the channel to a cartoon. The road you're driving on suddenly changes from asphalt to gravel. These shifts are jarring and sometimes disorienting. Similarly, shifts in writing—from one tense to another, for example—can confuse your readers. This chapter explains how to keep your writing consistent in verb tense, point of view, and number.

S-9a Shifts in Tense

Only when you want to emphasize that actions take place at different times should you shift verb **TENSE**.

▶ My plane *will arrive* in Albuquerque two hours after it *leaves* Portland.

Otherwise, keep tenses consistent.

▶ As the concert ended, several people ~~are~~ *were* already on their way up the aisle, causing a distraction.

In writing about literary works, use the present tense. Be careful not to shift to the past tense.

▶ The two fugitives start down the river together, Huck fleeing his
abusive father and Jim escaping slavery. As they ~~traveled,~~ *travel,*
they ~~met~~ *meet* with many colorful characters, including the Duke and King,
two actors and con artists who involve Huck and Jim in their
schemes.

S-9b Shifts in Point of View

Do not shift between first person (I, we), second person (you), and
third person (he, she, it, they, one).

▶ When ~~one has~~ *you have* a cold, you should stay home to avoid infecting others.

S-9c Shifts in Number

Unnecessary shifts between singular and plural subjects can confuse
readers.

▶ Because of late frosts, oranges have risen dramatically in price. But
since ~~the orange is~~ *oranges are* such a staple, they continue to sell.

L-1   Appropriate Words

"Cool." "Sweet." "Excellent." These three words can mean the same
thing, but each has a different level of formality. We usually use informal language when we're talking with friends, and we use slang and
abbreviations when we send text messages, but we choose words that
are more formal for most of our academic and professional writing.
Just as we wouldn't wear an old T-shirt to most job interviews, we
wouldn't write in a college essay that *Beloved* is "an awesome book."

This chapter offers you help in choosing words that are appropriate for different audiences and purposes.

L-1a Formal and Informal Words

EX. L-1a–b
P. 488

Whether you use formal or informal language depends on your **PURPOSE** and **AUDIENCE**.

FORMAL   Four score and seven years ago our fathers brought forth on this continent, a new nation, conceived in Liberty, and dedicated to the proposition that all men are created equal.
    —Abraham Lincoln, Gettysburg Address

INFORMAL   Our family, like most, had its ups and downs.
    —Judy Davis, "Ours Was a Dad"

The first, more formal sentence was delivered in 1863 to twenty thousand people, including many officials and prominent citizens. The second, less formal sentence was spoken in 2004 to a small gathering of family and friends at a funeral.

Colloquial language (What's up? No clue) and slang (A-list, S'up?) are not appropriate for formal speech and most academic and professional writing.

▶ A lot of high school ~~kids~~ have so little time for lunch that they end up
  Many   students
  ~~gobbling down their food~~ as they race to class.
  eating

L-1b Pretentious Language

EX. L-1a–b
P. 488

Long or complicated words might seem to lend authority to your writing, but often they make it sound pretentious and stuffy. Use such words sparingly and only when they best capture your meaning and suit your **WRITING CONTEXT**.

▶ ~~Subsequent to~~ adopting the new system, managers ~~averred~~ that their
  After   claimed
  staff worked ~~synergistically in a way that exceeded parameters.~~
                together   better than expected.

EX. L-1c–d
P. 489

L-1c Jargon

Jargon is a specialized vocabulary of a profession, trade, or field and should be used only when you know your audience will understand what you are saying. A lawyer might easily understand the following sentences from a Supreme Court decision, but most readers would not be familiar with legal terms like "res judicata," "facial relief," and "claim preclusion."

▶ Res judicata neither bars petitioners' challenges to the admitting-privileges requirement nor prevents the Court from awarding facial relief. The fact that several petitioners had previously brought the unsuccessful facial challenge in *Abbott* does not mean that claim preclusion, the relevant aspect of res judicata, applies.

—Supreme Court of the United States,
Whole Woman's Health v. Hellerstedt

When you are writing for an audience of nonspecialists, resist the temptation to use overly technical language.

▶ The ~~mini-sternotomy~~ **small incision** at the lower end of the ~~sternum resulted in~~ **breastbone preserved** her appearance. ~~satisfactory cosmesis.~~

EX. L-1c–d
P. 489

L-1d Clichés

Steer clear of clichés, expressions so familiar that they have become trite (white as snow, the grass is always greener). Editors and writing instructors in the United States (and much of the English-speaking world) prefer fresh and unique combinations of words rather than familiar and possibly overused phrases.

▶ The company needs a recruiter who thinks ~~outside the box.~~ **unconventionally.**

▶ After canoeing all day, we all slept ~~like logs.~~ **soundly.**

▶ Nita ~~is a team player,~~ **collaborates well,** so we hope she will be assigned to the project.

L-2   Precise Words

"Serena Overpowers Sloane." "Mariano Finishes Off the Sox." In each case, the writer could have simply used the word "beats." But at least to sports fans, these newspaper headlines are a bit more precise and informative as a result of the words chosen. This chapter offers guidelines for editing your own writing to make it as precise as it needs to be.

L-2a "Be" and "Do"

EX. L-2a
P. 490

Try not to rely too much on "be" or "do." Check your writing to see where you can replace forms of these words with more precise verbs.

▶ David Sedaris's essay "Us and Them" ~~is about~~ his love/hate relationship with his family.
   focuses on

▶ Some doctors no longer believe that ~~doing~~ crossword puzzles can delay the onset of senility or Alzheimer's disease.
   solving

Sometimes using a form of "be" or "do" is the right choice, when, for example, you are describing something or someone.

▶ Most critics agree that *Citizen Kane, Casablanca,* and *The Shawshank Redemption* are some of the finest movies ever made.

L-2b Abstract and Concrete Words

Abstract words refer to general qualities or ideas (truth, beauty), whereas concrete words refer to specific things that can be perceived with our senses (books, lipstick). You'll often need to use words that are general or abstract, but remember that specific, concrete words can make your writing more precise and more vivid—and can make an abstract concept easier to understand.

▶ In Joan Didion's work, there has always been a fascination with what she once called "the unspeakable peril of the everyday"—the coyotes by the interstate, the snakes in the playpen, the fires and Santa Ana winds of California.

—Michiko Kakutani, "The End of Life as She Knew It"

The concrete words "coyotes," "snakes," "fires," and "winds" help explain the abstract phrase "peril of the everyday."

L-2c Figurative Language

Figures of speech such as SIMILES and METAPHORS are words used imaginatively rather than literally. They can help readers understand an abstract point by comparing it to something they are familiar with or can easily imagine.

SIMILE His body is in almost constant motion—rolling those cigarettes, rubbing an elbow, reaching for a glass—but the rhythm is tranquil and fluid, *like a cat licking its paw*.
—Sean Smith, "Johnny Depp: Unlikely Superstar"

METAPHOR And so, before the professor had even finished his little story, *I had become a furnace of rage*.
—Shelby Steele, "On Being Black and Middle Class"

EX. L-3
P. 491

L-3 Idioms

"A piece of cake." "Walking on air." "Cute as a button." These are just three of the thousands of English idioms and idiomatic expressions that are used every day. Most idioms are phrases (and sometimes whole sentences) whose meaning cannot be understood by knowing the meanings of the individual words. We use idioms because they give a lot of information in few words and add color and texture to what we say or write. If you're learning English, a well-chosen idiom also demonstrates your fluency in the language. Some idioms appear more often in conversation than in formal writing, but many will be useful to you in your academic work.

L-3a Recognizing Idioms

When you read or hear a phrase that seems totally unrelated to the topic, you have probably encountered an idiom.

▶ Influencing Hollywood is a little *like herding cats.*
                              —Jane Alexander, *Command Performance*

Cats are notoriously independent and indifferent to following directions; thus a difficult, maybe impossible task is said to be "like herding cats."

▶ As the economy contracts, we Americans are likely to find that we have been living too *high on the hog.*   —*Los Angeles Times*

Ham, ribs, bacon, and other meats that are considered the most tasty and desirable are from the upper parts of the hog. People who live extravagantly or luxuriously are sometimes said to be living "high on the hog."

▶ This internship is not just about class credit. This is about really getting *a leg up* for when you graduate.
                              —Morgan to Chelsea, *Days of Our Lives*

When a rider is mounting a horse, another person often supports the rider's left leg while the right one swings over the horse's back. Having "a leg up" means you've been given extra help or certain advantages.

▶ I love to see a young girl go out and *grab* the world *by the lapels.*
                              —Maya Angelou

Grabbing the front of a jacket, or "grabbing someone by the lapels," is a firm and aggressive move that aims to take charge of a situation.

L-3b Understanding Idioms

Idioms may seem peculiar or even nonsensical if you think about their literal meanings, but knowing where they originated can help you figure out what they mean. Many idioms, for example, originate in sports, music, and animal contexts, where their meanings are literal. Used in other contexts, their meanings are similar, if not exactly literal.

▶ When the senator introduced the bill, she thought passage would be a *slam dunk* since public opinion was strongly favorable.

In basketball, a player scores a "slam dunk" by shoving the ball through the basket in a dramatic way. As an idiom, a "slam dunk" refers to a victory gained easily or emphatically.

▶ George Saunders's commencement speech really *struck a chord* with the Syracuse graduates.

A chord is a group of musical notes that harmonize; to "strike a chord" with an audience means to make a connection by bringing up something interesting or relevant to them.

▶ Some members of Congress think that limiting food stamps will get more Americans back to work; I think they're *barking up the wrong tree*.

This idiom refers to a dog in pursuit of an animal that has disappeared into a group of trees; the dog is barking at one tree, but its prey has climbed up another. To "bark up the wrong tree" means to pursue the wrong course of action.

You can sometimes figure out the meaning of an idiom based on its context; but if you're not sure what it means or how to use it properly, look it up online—go to **digital.wwnorton.com/littleseagull4** for links to some good sources. The *Cambridge Dictionary of American Idioms* is a good print source.

L-3c Common Idiomatic Expressions in Academic and Professional Writing

Idiomatic expressions are words that go together like peanut butter and jelly—you often find them together. You've probably encountered expressions such as "with respect to," "insofar as," or "as a matter of fact" in academic or professional writing. Many of these expressions function as **TRANSITIONS**, helping readers follow your reasoning and understand how your ideas relate to one another. You're expected to signal the connections among your ideas explicitly in academic writing, and the following idiomatic expressions can help you do so.

To shift to a narrower focus

with respect to, with regard to   indicate the precise topic you are addressing: "The global economic situation is much more complicated with respect to certain nations' high levels of debt."

insofar as   sets a limit or scope for a statement: "Despite her short stature, Bates is the team leader insofar as direction and determination are concerned."

in particular   points to something especially true within a generalization: "Cosmetic surgery procedures for men have increased tremendously in the last decade; liposuction and eyelid surgery, in particular, showed dramatic increases."

To give examples

a case in point   frames an example that illustrates a point: "Recent business activity shows a clear trend toward consolidation. The merger of two airlines last year is a case in point."

for instance   indicates an example that illustrates an idea: "Green vegetables are highly nutritious; one serving of kale, for instance, provides the full daily recommended value of vitamins A and C."

To add information

in addition   introduces a new but related point: "Locally grown tomatoes are available nearly everywhere; in addition, they are rich in vitamin C."

along the same lines   connects two similar ideas: "Many cities are developing parking meter plans along the same lines as the system in Chicago."

by the same token   signals a point that follows the logic of the previous point: "Insider trading has damaged the reputation of the financial industry in general; by the same token, high-profile embezzlers like Bernie Madoff have eroded the public's confidence in many investment advisers."

as a matter of fact, in fact   signal a statement that explains or contrasts with a previous point: "Wind power is an increasingly common energy source; as a matter of fact, wind energy generation tripled between 2009 and 2019."

To emphasize something

of course   emphasizes a point that is (or should be) obvious: "Fresh foods are preferable to processed foods, of course, but fresh foods are not always available."

in any case, in any event   introduce something that is true regardless of other conditions: "The city has introduced new precautions to ensure the election goes smoothly; the results will be closely scrutinized in any event."

To signal alternatives or conflicting ideas

on the one hand . . . on the other hand   introduces contrasting ideas or conditions: "On the one hand, some critics have loudly rejected reality television; on the other hand, unscripted shows are often received well by the public."

up to a point   signals acceptance of part but not all of an argument or idea: "The senator's statement is correct up to a point, but her conclusions are misguided."

have it both ways   to benefit from two conflicting positions: "Tech companies want to have it both ways, asking the government to be more transparent about its use of user data while not disclosing that they are using these data for their own commercial purposes."

of two minds   signals ambivalence, validates conflicting ideas: "On the question of whether organic food is worth the extra cost, I am of two minds: I like knowing that the food is grown without chemicals, but I'm still skeptical because some studies suggest that the health benefits are questionable."

in contrast   signals a change in direction or a different idea on the same subject: "Large birds such as crows can live for more than ten years; in contrast, tiny hummingbirds generally live less than three years."

on the contrary signals an opposite idea or opposing position: "Some bankers claim that the proposed mortgage regulations would harm the economy; on the contrary, the new rules would be the most effective means of reinvigorating it."

in fact, as a matter of fact signal a statement that challenges or refutes a previous statement: "Nicholas Carr suggests that *Google* is making us stupid; in fact, some argue that by giving us access to more information, it's making us better informed."

To summarize or restate something

in brief, in short introduce a short summary of points already established: "In brief, the accident was caused by a combination of carelessness and high winds."

in other words signals a restatement or explanation of the preceding idea: "Our opposition to the proposal is firm and unequivocal; in other words, we emphatically decline."

in conclusion, in sum signal the final statement or section of a text: "In conclusion, the evidence points to a clear and simple solution to the problem."

Sports idioms in business writing. You'll encounter and use many idioms in business writing, especially ones that come from sports—probably because the competitiveness of the business world makes it easily comparable to sports. Following are some idioms that often come up in business contexts.

a team player someone who acts in the interest of a whole team or group rather than for individual gain: "The best managers are team players, making sure that the credit for a success is shared among everyone who contributed to the effort."

to cover all the bases an expression that comes from baseball, where the fielders must protect all four bases against the other team's runners; as an idiom, it means to be thorough—to deal with all aspects of a situation and consider all possibilities: "Her report was well executed; it covered all the bases and anticipated all possible counterproposals."

across the board   a large board at a racetrack displays the names of all the horses in a race; to place an equal bet on every horse is to bet "across the board," so the idiom refers to something affecting all items in a group equally: "Proponents of the new health-care policy insist that it will reduce costs across the board, from doctor visits to medical procedures to prescription medicines."

Considering context. Many idiomatic expressions are quite informal. These can be used effectively in casual conversation or social media, but they are rarely appropriate in academic or professional writing. As with all writing, you need to consider your **AUDIENCE** and **PURPOSE** when you use idiomatic expressions.

In a conversation with a friend or family member,   you might say "let's cut to the chase"; with a business colleague, however, it may be more appropriate to suggest that you "get right to the point" or "focus on what's most important."

In a text to a friend,   you might say something sounds "like a piece of cake"; with your boss, it would be more appropriate to say it sounds "doable" or "easy to do."

On Instagram,   you might describe an improv show as "over the top"; in a review for a class, it would be more appropriate to say it was "excessive" or "outrageous."

EX. L-4
1 / P. 491
2 / P. 492
3 / P. 493

L-4   Words Often Confused

When you're tired, do you "lay" down or "lie" down? After dinner, do you eat "desert" or "dessert"? This chapter's dual purpose is to alert you to everyday words that can trip you up and to help you understand the differences between certain words that people tend to confuse.

accept, except "Accept" means "to receive willingly" (accept an award). "Except" as a preposition means "excluding" (all languages except English).

adapt, adopt "Adapt" means "to adjust" (adapt the recipe to be dairy free). "Adopt" means "to take as one's own" (adopt a pet from a shelter).

advice, advise "Advice" means "recommendation" (a lawyer's advice). "Advise" means "to give advice" (We advise you to learn your rights.).

affect, effect "Affect" is usually a verb that means "to produce a change in" (Stress can affect health.). "Effect" is a noun that means "result" (The effects of smoking are well known.). As a verb, it means "to cause" (A mediator works to effect a compromise.).

all right, alright "All right" is the preferred spelling.

allusion, illusion "Allusion" means "indirect reference" (an allusion to *Beowulf*). "Illusion" means "false appearance" (an optical illusion).

a lot Always two words, "a lot" means "a large number or amount" or "to a great extent" (a lot of voters; miss her a lot). The phrase is too informal for most academic writing.

among, between Traditionally, "among" is used for three or more items (among the fifty states), while "between" is used with two items (between you and me). In some contexts, however, "between" may be clearer and less awkward (the three-way trade between the Grizzlies, Suns, and Wizards).

amount, number Use "amount" for things you can measure but not count (a large amount of water). Use "number" for things you can count (a number of books).

as, as if, like "Like" introduces a noun or **NOUN PHRASE** (It feels like silk.). To begin a subordinate clause, use "as" or "as if" (Do as I say, not as I do. It seemed as if he had not prepared at all for the briefing.).

bad, badly Use "bad" as an adjective following a linking verb (I feel bad.). Use "badly" as an adverb following an action verb (I play piano badly.).

capital, capitol A "capital" is a city where the government of a state, province, or country is located (Kingston was the first state capital of New York.). A "capitol" is a government building (the dome of the capitol).

cite, sight, site   "Cite" means "to give information from a source by quoting, paraphrasing, or summarizing" (cite your sources). "Sight" is the act of seeing or something that is seen (an appalling sight). A "site" is a place (the site of a famous battle).

compose, comprise   The parts "compose" the whole (Fifty states compose the Union.). The whole "comprises" the parts (The Union comprises fifty states.).

could of   In writing, use "could have" or "could've."

council, counsel   "Council" refers to a body of people (the council's vote). "Counsel" means "advice" or "to advise" (her wise counsel; counsel victims of domestic abuse).

criteria, criterion   "Criteria" is the plural of "criterion" and takes a plural verb (Certain criteria have been established.).

data   "Data," the plural of "datum," technically should take a plural verb (The data arrive from many sources.), but some writers treat it as singular (The data is persuasive.).

desert, dessert   "Desert" as a noun means "arid region" (Mojave Desert). As a verb it means "to abandon" (He deserted his post.). "Dessert" is a sweet served toward the end of a meal.

disinterested, uninterested   "Disinterested" means "fair" or "unbiased" (a disinterested jury). "Uninterested" means "bored" or "indifferent" (uninterested in election results).

emigrate (from), immigrate (to)   "Emigrate" means "to leave one's country" (emigrate from Slovakia). "Immigrate" means "to move to another country" (immigrate to Canada).

etc.   The abbreviation "etc." is short for the Latin *et cetera*, "and other things." "Etc." is fine in notes and bibliographies, but avoid using it in your writing in general. Substitute "and so on" if necessary.

everyday, every day   "Everyday" is an adjective meaning "ordinary" (After the holidays, we go back to our everyday routine.). "Every day" means "on a daily basis" (Eat three or more servings of fruit every day.).

fewer, less   In general, use "fewer" when you refer to things that can be counted (fewer calories). Use "less" when you refer to an amount of something that cannot be counted (less fat).

good, well   "Good" is an adjective (a good book; She looks good in that color.). "Well" can be an adjective indicating physical health after a linking verb (She looks well despite her recent surgery.) or an adverb following an action verb (He speaks Spanish well.).

hopefully   In academic writing, avoid "hopefully" to mean "it is hoped that"; use it only to mean "with hope" (to make a wish hopefully).

imply, infer   "Imply" means "to suggest" (What do you mean to imply?). "Infer" means "to conclude" (We infer that you did not enjoy the trip.).

its, it's   "Its" is a possessive pronoun (The movie is rated R because of its language.). "It's" is a contraction of "it is" or "it has" (It's an action film.).

lay, lie   "Lay," meaning "to put" or "to place," always takes a direct object (She lays the blanket down.). "Lie," meaning "to recline" or "to be positioned," never takes a direct object (She lies on the blanket.).

lead, led   The verb "lead" (rhymes with "bead") means "to guide" (I will lead the way.). "Led" is the past tense and past participle of "lead" (Yesterday I led the way.). The noun "lead" (rhymes with "head") is a type of metal (Use copper pipes instead of lead pipes.).

literally   Use "literally" only when you want to stress that you don't mean "figuratively" (While sitting in the grass, he realized that he literally had ants in his pants.).

loose, lose   "Loose" means "not fastened securely" or "not fitting tightly" (a pair of loose pants). "Lose" means "to misplace" or "to not win" (lose an earring; lose the race).

man, mankind   Use "people," "humans," "humanity," or "human-kind" instead.

many, much   Use "many" when you refer to things that can be counted (many books). Use "much" to refer to something that cannot be counted (much knowledge).

may of, might of, must of   In writing, use "may have," "might have," or "must have."

media   "Media," a plural noun, takes a plural verb (Many political scientists believe that the media have a huge effect on voting behavior.). The singular form is "medium" (TV is a popular medium for advertising.).

percent, percentage   Use "percent" after a number (80 percent). Use "percentage" after an adjective or article (an impressive percentage; The percentage was impressive.).

principal, principle   As a noun, "principal" means "a chief official" or "a sum of money" (in the principal's office; raising the principal for a down payment). As an adjective, it means "most important" (the principal cause of death). "Principle" means "a rule by which one lives" or "a basic truth or doctrine" (against her principles; the principles of life, liberty, and the pursuit of happiness).

raise, rise   Meaning "to grow" or "to cause to move upward," "raise" always takes a direct object (He raised his hand.). Meaning "to get up," "rise" never takes a direct object (The sun rises at dawn.).

the reason . . . is because   Use "because" or "the reason . . . is (that)," but not both (The reason for the price increase was a poor growing season. Prices increased because of a poor growing season.).

reason why   Instead of this redundant phrase, use "the reason" or "the reason that" (Psychologists debate the reasons that some people develop depression and others do not.).

respectfully, respectively   "Respectfully" means "in a way that shows respect" (Speak to your elders respectfully.). "Respectively" means "in the order given" (George H. W. Bush and George W. Bush were the forty-first president and the forty-third president, respectively.).

sensual, sensuous   "Sensual" suggests sexuality (a sensual caress). "Sensuous" involves pleasing the senses through art, music, and nature (the violin's sensuous solo).

set, sit   "Set," meaning "to put" or "to place," takes a direct object (Please set the vase on the table.). "Sit," meaning "to take a seat," does not take a direct object (She sits on the bench.).

should of   In writing, use "should have" or "should've."

stationary, stationery   "Stationary" means "staying put" (a stationary lab table). "Stationery" means "writing paper" (the college's official stationery).

than, then   "Than" is a conjunction used for comparing (She is taller than her mother.). "Then" is an adverb used to indicate a sequence (Finish your work, and then reward yourself.).

that, which   Use "that" to add information that is essential for identifying something (The wild horses that live on this island are endangered.). Use "which" to give additional but nonessential information (Abaco Barb horses, which live on an island in the Bahamas, are endangered.).

their, there, they're   "Their" signifies possession (their canoe). "There" tells where (Put it there.). "They're" is a contraction of "they are" (They're busy.).

to, too, two   "To" is either a preposition that tells direction (Give it to me.) or part of an infinitive (To err is human.). "Too" means "also" or "excessively" (The younger children wanted to help, too. It's too cold to sit outside.). "Two" is a number (tea for two).

unique   Because "unique" suggests that something is the only one of its kind, avoid adding comparatives or superlatives ("more," "most," "less," "least"), intensifiers (such as "very"), or qualifiers (such as "somewhat").

weather, whether   "Weather" refers to atmospheric conditions (dreary weather). "Whether" refers to a choice between options (whether to stay home or go out).

who's, whose   "Who's" is a contraction for "who is" or "who has" (Who's the best candidate for the job? Who's already eaten?). "Whose" refers to ownership (Whose keys are these? Tom, whose keys were on the table, had left.).

would of   In writing, use "would have" or "would've."

your, you're   "Your" signifies possession (your diploma). "You're" is a contraction for "you are" (You're welcome.).

EX. L-5
P. 494

L-5   Prepositions

A great session with your favorite video game. You've finally reached the cave of the dying wise man who will tell you the location of the key that you need. He points a long, bony finger toward a table and struggles to rasp out one word, "jar." You're down to your last life. You only have one chance. Is the key *in* the jar? *under* it? *behind* it? Oh, that one little preposition makes all the difference!

Real life is seldom this dramatic, but accurate prepositions do make a difference. Prepositions are words like "at," "from," "in," and "with" that describe relationships, often in time and space: "at work, in an hour," "with your mom." English has a large number of prepositions compared to other languages, and sometimes it's difficult to choose the right one.

Prepositions are always followed by noun or pronoun **OBJECTS**. (You can't just "write about"; you have to write about something.) Together a preposition and its object form a prepositional phrase. In the following examples, the prepositions are underlined and the prepositional phrases are italicized.

▶ This is a book *about writing.*

▶ We're *in the midst of a literacy revolution.* —Andrea Lunsford

▶ Research is formalized curiosity. It is poking and prying *with a purpose.*

—Zora Neale Hurston

▶ *In the years between 1969 and 1978,* I lived, worked, and played *with the children and their families in Roadville and Trackton.*

—Shirley Brice Heath

The table and lists that follow summarize the basic differences in the ways to use three common prepositions—"at," "on," and "in."

AT	a specific point	●	at home at the gym at noon
ON	a line	——————	on the avenue on the table on a specific day
IN	a shape or enclosure	⬭	in a container in the park in two hours

Prepositions of place

AT   a specific address or business: *at* 33 Parkwood Street, *at* McDonald's
a public building or unnamed business: *at* the library, *at* the gym
a general place: *at* home, *at* work

ON   a surface: *on* the floor, *on* the grass, *on* the wall
a street: *on* Ninth Street, *on* Western Avenue
an electronic medium: *on* the radio, *on* the web
public transportation: *on* the bus, *on* an airplane

IN   a container, room, or area: *in* the jar, *in* my office, *in* the woods
a geographic location: *in* San Diego, *in* the Midwest
a printed work: *in* the newspaper, *in* Chapter 3

Prepositions of time

AT   a specific time: *at* 4:30 PM, *at* sunset, *at* lunchtime

ON   a day of the week: *on* Friday
an exact date: *on* September 12
a holiday: *on* Thanksgiving, *on* Veterans Day

IN   a defined time period: *in* an hour, *in* three years
a month, season, or year: *in* June, *in* the fall, *in* 2022
a part of the day: *in* the morning, *in* the evening

EX. L-6
P. 495

L-6   Unnecessary Words

"At this point in time." "Really unique." "In a manner of speaking." Each of these phrases includes words that are unnecessary or says something that could be expressed more concisely. This chapter shows you how to edit your own writing to make every word count.

L-6a "Really," "Very," and Other Empty Words

Intensifiers such as "really" and "very" are used to strengthen what we say. Qualifiers such as "apparently," "possibly," "seem," or "tend to" are a way to soften what we say. It's fine to use words like these when they are necessary. Sometimes, however, they are not. You shouldn't say that something is "very unique," because things either are unique or they're not; there's no need to add the intensifier. And why say that someone is "really smart" when you could say that they are "brilliant"?

▶   Accepted by five colleges, Jackson ~~seems to be facing an apparently~~ _{is facing a} ~~very~~ difficult decision.

EX. L-6b
P. 496

L-6b "There Is," "It Is"

EXPLETIVE constructions like "there is" and "it is" can be useful ways to introduce and emphasize an idea, but sometimes they only add unnecessary words. Eliminating them in such cases can make the sentence more concise and also make its verb stronger.

▶   ~~It is necessary for~~ Americans today ~~to~~ _{must} learn to speak more than one language.

▶   _{Four} ~~There are four~~ large moons and more than thirty small ones ~~that~~ orbit Jupiter.

In certain contexts, however, expletives can be the best choices. Imagine the ending of *The Wizard of Oz* if Dorothy had said "No place is like home" instead of the more emphatic—and sentimental—"There's no place like home."

L-6c Wordy Phrases

Many common phrases use several words when a single word will do. Editing out such wordy phrases will make your writing more concise and easier to read.

WORDY	CONCISE
as far as . . . is concerned	concerning
at the time that	when
at this point in time	now
in spite of the fact that	although, though
in the event that	if
in view of the fact that	because, since

Because
▶ ~~Due to the fact that~~ Professor Lee retired, the animal sciences
department now lacks a neurology specialist.

L-6d Redundancies

Eliminate words and phrases that are unnecessary for your meaning.

▶ Painting the house purple ~~in color~~ will make it stand out from the many white houses in town.

▶ Dashing ~~quickly~~ into the street to retrieve the ball, the young girl was almost hit by a car.

▶ Campers should know how much wood is ~~sufficient~~ enough for a fire to burn all night.

L-7 Adjectives and Adverbs

Adjectives and adverbs are words that describe other words, adding important information and detail. When Dave Barry writes that the Beatles "were the *coolest* thing you had ever seen" and that "they were *smart*; they were *funny*; they didn't take themselves *seriously*," the adjectives and adverbs (italicized here) make clear why he "wanted *desperately* to be a Beatle." This chapter will help you use adjectives and adverbs in your own writing.

EX. L-7a
P. 497

L-7a Choosing between Adjectives and Adverbs

Adjectives are words used to modify **NOUNS** and **PRONOUNS**. They usually answer one of these questions: Which? What kind? How many?

▶ *Two* rows of *ancient oak* trees lined the *narrow* driveway.

▶ *Many* years of testing will be needed to determine whether the *newest* theories are *correct*.

▶ If you are craving something *sweet,* have a piece of fruit.

Adverbs are words used to modify **VERBS**, adjectives, and other adverbs. They usually answer one of these questions: How? When? Where? Why? Under what conditions? To what degree? Although many adverbs end in "-ly" (tentatively, immediately), many do not (now, so, soon, then, very).

▶ Emergency personnel must respond *quickly* when an ambulance arrives.

▶ Environmentalists are *increasingly* worried about Americans' consumption of fossil fuels.

▶ If the governor had known that the news cameras were on, she would not have responded *so angrily*.

"Well" and "good"

Use "well" as an adjective to describe physical health; use "good" to describe emotional health or appearance.

▶ Some herbs can keep you feeling ~~good~~ well when everyone else has the flu.

▶ Staying healthy can make you feel *good* about yourself.

"Good" should not be used as an adverb; use "well."

▶ Because both Williams sisters play tennis so ~~good,~~ well, they've frequently competed against each other in major tournaments.

"Bad" and "badly"

Use the adjective "bad" after a **LINKING VERB** to describe an emotional state or feeling. In such cases, the adjective describes the subject.

▶ Arguing with your parents can make you feel *bad*.

Use the adverb "badly" to describe an **ACTION VERB**.

▶ Arguing with your parents late at night can make you sleep *badly*.

L-7b Using Comparatives and Superlatives

EX. L-7b
P. 498

Most adjectives and adverbs have three forms: the positive, the comparative, and the superlative. The comparative is used to compare two things, and the superlative is used to compare three or more things.

COMPARATIVE   Who was the *better* quarterback, Eli Manning or his brother?

SUPERLATIVE   Many Colts fans still consider Peyton Manning the *best* quarterback ever.

The comparative and superlative of most adjectives are formed by adding the endings "-er" and "-est": "slow," "slower," "slowest." Longer adjectives and most adverbs use "more" and "most" (or "less" and "least"): "clearly," "more clearly," "most clearly." If you add "-er" or "-est" to an adjective or adverb, do not also use "more" or "most" (or "less" and "least").

▶ The ~~most~~ lowest point in the United States is in Death Valley.

A few adjectives and adverbs have irregular comparatives and superlatives.

	COMPARATIVE	SUPERLATIVE
good, well	better	best
bad, badly	worse	worst
far (distance)	farther	farthest
far (time or amount)	further	furthest
little (amount)	less	least
many, much, some	more	most

EX. L-7c
P. 499

L-7c Placing Modifiers Carefully

Place adjectives, adverbs, and other **MODIFIERS** as close as possible to the word or words they modify so that readers clearly understand the connection.

▶ The doctor _at the seminar_ explained advances in cancer treatment to the families of patients. ~~at the seminar.~~

The doctor, not the patients, is at the seminar.

▶ _Before the anesthesiologist arrived, the_ ~~The~~ surgeons assured the patient that they intended to make only two small incisions. ~~before the anesthesiologist arrived.~~

The original sentence suggests that the incisions will be made without anesthesia, surely not the case.

To avoid ambiguity, position limiting modifiers such as "almost," "even," "just," "merely," and "only" next to the word or phrase they modify—and be careful that your meaning is clear. See how the placement of "only" can result in two completely different meanings.

▶ A triple-threat athlete, Martha ~~only~~ played soccer _only_ in college.

▶ A triple-threat athlete, Martha ~~only~~ played _only_ soccer in college.

Be careful that your placement of "not" doesn't result in a meaning you don't intend.

▶ When I attended college, _not_ every student was ~~not~~ using a laptop.

Dangling modifiers

Modifiers are said to be dangling when they do not clearly modify any particular word in the sentence. You can usually fix a dangling modifier by adding a **SUBJECT** that the modifier clearly refers to, either in the rest of the sentence or in the modifier itself.

▶ Speaking simply and respectfully, _the doctor comforted_ many people ~~felt comforted by the~~ _with her_ ~~doctor's~~ presentation.

The doctor was speaking, not the other people.

>   _{I was}
> While running to catch the bus, the shoulder strap on my bag broke.
>   ^

Split infinitives

When you place a modifier between "to" and the base form of the verb in an INFINITIVE, you create a split infinitive: to deliberately avoid. When a split infinitive is awkward or makes a sentence difficult to follow, put the modifier elsewhere in the sentence.

>   _{rigorously}
> Professional soccer players are expected to ~~rigorously~~ train every day.
>   ^

Sometimes, however, a split infinitive is easier to follow.

> One famous split infinitive appears in the opening sequence of *Star Trek*: "to boldly go where no man has gone before."

L-8   Articles

"A," "an," and "the" are articles, words used before a noun to indicate whether something is general or specific. Use "a" or "an" with nouns whose specific identity is not known to your audience: I'm reading a great book. Use "the" with nouns whose specific identity is known to your audience, whether the noun describes something specific: the new book by Colson Whitehead—or is something you've mentioned: Beverly is almost finished writing her book; the book will be published next year. Sometimes no article is needed: Books are now available in print and online.

L-8a When to Use "A" or "An"

EX. L-8a,c
P. 501

Use "a" or "an" before singular count nouns referring to something that's not specific or that you're mentioning to your audience for the first time. Count nouns name things that can be counted: one book, two books. Use "a" before consonant sounds: a tangerine, a university; use "an" before vowel sounds: an orange, an hour.

▶ *An apartment* near campus might be rather expensive.

   Any apartment near campus would be expensive, not just a specific one.

▶ I put *a carrot*, some tomatoes, and a little parsley in the salad.

   This carrot is being mentioned for the first time.

Do not use "a" or "an" before a noncount noun. Noncount nouns name abstract items (respect, curiosity) and liquids and masses that cannot be measured with numbers (milk, sand, rice).

▶ Our team could use *some encouragement* from the coach.

▶ The last thing Portland needs this week is *more rain.*

EX. L-8b–c
P. 502

L-8b When to Use "The"

Use "the" before any nouns whose identity is clear to your audience and before superlatives.

▶ Mando ordered a cheeseburger and french fries and asked for *the burger* to be well done.

   The article "the" is used because it refers to a cheeseburger that's already been mentioned: the one that Mando ordered.

▶ His friends had raved about *the fries* at this restaurant.

   The specific fries are identified: they are the ones at this restaurant.

▶ His friends were right; these were *the best fries* he'd ever eaten.

   "The" is used before a superlative: these were the best fries ever.

Use "the" with most plural PROPER NOUNS (the Adirondack Mountains, the Philippines, the Dallas Cowboys) and with singular proper nouns in the following categories.

LARGE BODIES OF WATER   the Arctic Ocean, the Mississippi River

GOVERNMENT BODIES   the US Congress, the Canadian Parliament

HISTORICAL PERIODS   the Renaissance, the Tang Dynasty

LANDMARKS   the Empire State Building, the Taj Mahal

REGIONS   the East Coast, the Middle East, the Mojave Desert

RELIGIOUS ENTITIES, TEXTS, AND LEADERS   the Roman Catholic Church, the Qur'an, the Dalai Lama

L-8c When No Article Is Needed

EX. L-8a,c
P. 501
EX. L-8b–c
P. 502

No article is needed before noncount nouns (salt, imagination, happiness) and plural count nouns (ideas, puppies) when they refer to something "in general."

▶ *Milk* and *eggs* are on sale this week.

▶ *Information* wants to be free.   —Stewart Brand, *Whole Earth Review*

▶ Be less curious about people and more curious about *ideas.*
    —Marie Curie

Brand and Curie refer to information and ideas in general, not a specific kind of information or specific ideas.

No article is needed with most singular **PROPER NOUNS** : Barack Obama, Lake Titicaca, Yosemite.

L-9   Respectful and Inclusive Language

A nurse objects to being called one of "the girls." The head of the English department finds the title "chairman" offensive. Why? The nurse is a man, the department head is a woman, and those terms don't include them. We can build common ground with others—or not—through the words we choose, by including others or leaving them out. This chapter offers tips for using language that is positive, respectful, and inclusive and that will build common ground with those we wish to reach.

EX. L-9a
P. 503

L-9a Avoiding Stereotypes

Stereotypes are generalizations about groups of people and as such can offend because they presume that all members of a group are the same. The writer Geeta Kothari explains how she reacts to a seemingly neutral assumption about Indians: "Indians eat lentils. I understand this as an absolute, a decree from an unidentifiable authority that watches and judges me."

We're all familiar with stereotypes based on sex or race, but stereotypes exist about other characteristics as well: age, body type, education, income, gender identity, occupation, physical ability, political affiliation, region, religion, sexual orientation, and more. Be careful not to make any broad generalizations about any group—even neutral or seemingly positive ones (that Asian students work especially hard, for example, or that Republicans are particularly patriotic).

Also be careful not to call attention to a person's group affiliation if that information is not relevant.

▶ The ~~gay~~ physical therapist who worked the morning shift knew when to let patients rest and when to push them.

EX. L-9b
P. 504

L-9b Using Preferred Terms

When you are writing about a group of people, use terms that members of that group prefer. This advice is sometimes easier said than done, because language changes—and words that were commonly used ten years ago may not be in wide use today. Americans of African ancestry, for example, were referred to many years ago as "colored" or "Negro." Today, "Black" is the most widely used term, generally, and "African American" is also used. When writing, we recommend that "Black" be capitalized, as we've done here. See **P-8** for more information on capitalizing the names of races and ethnicities.

When you are referring to ethnicities, especially of individuals, it's usually best to be as specific as possible. Instead of saying that someone is Latina, Latino, Latinx, or Hispanic, for instance, say that they are Puerto Rican or Dominican or Mexican, as appropriate. The same is true of religions; specify a denomination or branch of religion when you can (a Sunni Muslim, an Episcopalian, an Orthodox Jew). When referring to Indigenous peoples of the United States, "Native American" is acceptable as a general term, but it's often better to refer to a particular tribal nation (Dakota, Chippewa). The same goes for Indigenous peoples elsewhere in the world—"Indigenous" is acceptable, but if possible, use the name of the specific group (Māori, Maya).

If a person you are writing about has a disability, mention it only if it's relevant to what you are saying. When you do write about disabilities, don't use terms that focus on the limitations.

▶ Coach Banks will arrive by the east door, where the ramp is; she's
   a wheelchair user
   ~~wheelchair-bound~~.
   ^

There are two general approaches to describing a person with a disability: person first and identity first. **PERSON-FIRST** descriptions focus on the individual; this orientation avoids reducing a whole person to simply a medical condition.

                                    students with epilepsy
▶ All-night study sessions aren't recommended for ~~epileptics~~, since lack
                                                    ^
   of sleep is a common trigger for seizures.

IDENTITY-FIRST descriptions focus on the condition or disability— "an amputee," for example, rather than "a person with an amputation." Some individuals and some disability communities may prefer identity-first terms.

▶ Elliot got many compliments last night at the autism meetup for his
   new "Aspie Power" T-shirt.

Regardless of which approach you take to describe someone's disability, use the terms and descriptions that they prefer. (Don't be afraid to ask them.) Unless someone indicates a preference for identity-first terms, use person-first descriptions wherever possible. Guide your word choice by respect for that person and for how they want their disability to be described; that's your priority. For more examples and help with this topic, see **digital.wwnorton.com/littleseagull4**.

It is becoming more common for people to specify (or ask one another about) their pronouns. It may not be accurate to automatically refer to someone as "he" or "she" on the basis of their appearance. Some individuals opt to be referred to as "they," a usage that transforms "they" from its conventional usage as plural to a singular pronoun of unspecified gender. Always refer to people by using the pronouns they designate for themselves. Also note that you should avoid using the term "preferred pronouns," because a person's pronouns are often integral to their identity. See S-6a and L-10 for more information about pronouns.

EX. L-9c
1 / P. 505
2 / P. 505

L-9c Editing Out Sexist Language

Sexist language is language that stereotypes or ignores women, men, or other gender identities—or that unnecessarily calls attention to someone's gender. You should eliminate such language from your writing. In particular, avoid nouns that include "man" when you're referring to people who may not be men.

INSTEAD OF	USE
man, mankind	humankind, humanity, humans, people
salesman	salesperson
fireman	firefighter
congressman	representative, member of Congress
male nurse	nurse
woman truck driver	truck driver

L-10   Pronouns and Gender

"I like key lime pie." Anyone can make that statement. It may or may not be true, but that first-person pronoun "I" always works, regardless of the gender of the speaker. The same is true for "You are amazing!" That "you" could apply to anyone; the second-person pronouns in English don't indicate gender in any way. Ditto the third-person plural. You could say, "We never saw them play," and the "them" could refer to the Chicago Cubs, the Boston Philharmonic, or the Williams sisters at Wimbledon. Gender wouldn't matter a bit. The only place it matters in English is with third-person singular pronouns: "he," "she," and now, "they." The words are few, but their importance is enormous. This chapter will help you with pronouns and gender in your academic work.

L-10a "He," "She," "They"

Writers once used "he," "him," and other masculine pronouns as a default to refer to people whose sex was unknown to them. Today such usage is not accepted—and it is no way to build common ground. Here are some alternatives.

Replace a singular noun or pronoun with a plural noun

▶ Before ~~anyone~~ travelers can leave the country, ~~he~~ they must have a passport or some other official documentation.

Eliminate the pronoun altogether

▶ Before ~~anyone can leave~~ leaving the country, ~~he~~ a traveler must have a passport or some other official documentation.

Use singular "they"

Increasingly, **SINGULAR "THEY"** is being used to refer to a person whose gender is unknown or not relevant to the context. This usage is becoming more and more accepted in academic writing; check with your instructor about whether it's appropriate in your writing.

▶ Someone left ~~her~~ their clothes in the washing machine overnight.

Use "he or she"

Some people use "he or she" or other masculine and feminine pronouns joined by "or." However, since not everyone identifies as either a "he" or a "she," this is not the most inclusive option. Also, using it repeatedly may become awkward.

▶ Before anyone can leave the country, he or she must have a passport or some other official documentation.

EX. L-10b
P. 506

L-10b Singular "They"

There are two ways to use singular "they": generic and specific. The generic singular "they" has been used for a long time—centuries, really, and even by such prominent authors as Shakespeare and Jane Austen—to refer to someone whose gender is unknown or not relevant to the context. This usage is becoming more and more accepted in academic writing.

▶ Everyone drops <u>their</u> phone sometimes.

The other way of using singular "they" is specific; that is, to refer to *someone* specific. Some people who are nonbinary, trans, gender-nonconforming, or identify as neither exclusively female nor exclusively male designate "they" as their third-person singular pronoun. (See L-10c for more on nonbinary pronouns.) You've no doubt heard or read some objections to either or both of these applications; it's not easy to change routines or habits, especially language habits. Many of the objections focus on confusion, forgetting that some confusion is already an everyday part of English.

Consider this: a friend asks, "Would you like to come over for dinner on Thursday?" An ordinary and straightforward question, perhaps, but the invitee may be left wondering. Is the invitation meant just for me? Is my spouse included? Kids, too? The conversation leading up to the invitation—the context—might make it clear, or it might not. The dual use of the pronoun "you" for both singular and plural reference is something English users take in stride, even though it occasionally causes confusion.

Confusion in conversation can be cleared up easily—we just ask. Writing, however, requires more attention to clarity since readers can't just ask. The two uses of singular "they" present particular challenges for writers, and this section offers some strategies for clearly distinguishing between singular and plural "they" in your academic writing. Context, as always, will do a lot of the work.

Here are a few examples from a March 2020 *Time* magazine article profiling various couples touched by the early circumstances of the COVID-19 pandemic. These examples are describing the couple Rowan and Emily Tekampe:

▶ When Rowan Tekampe found out they may have been exposed to COVID-19, their fever, cough, shortness of breath and body aches suddenly seemed more serious.

A possible interpretation at first glance is that Rowan found out about the exposure of some other people, but the symptoms described here very clearly belong to just one person. A bit later, the article details a painful conversation between Rowan and Emily:

▶ They sat down with their wife Emily . . . and told her she needed to leave the apartment and stay with her dad.

No confusion there. Rowan and Emily are spouses; Rowan's pronoun is "they," and Emily's is "she." Let's look at one more example two paragraphs later:

▶ They've been apart for weeks now, but Emily makes Rowan text her their temperature every hour.

The first instance of "they" in the sentence clearly refers to both spouses. How do we know? We rely on our understanding of the word "apart," which wouldn't make sense applied to one single person. The second instance, the possessive case "their," refers to Rowan's temperature. We are already familiar with Rowan's pronoun from previous context, and we're not surprised that Emily would want frequent updates from Rowan. Another clue is that "temperature" is singular.

Just as we are accustomed to "you" having both a singular and plural application, we will become accustomed in time to the extended applications of "they" in all of its forms.

Themself, Themselves

The account of Rowan and Emily doesn't mention this detail, but it could have: Emily would have liked to accompany Rowan to the clinic, but they had to go by themself. "Themself"? Not "themselves"? In fact, at this formative stage in the acceptable use of singular "they," both forms are in use, and logical arguments exist for each option. The style guides of MLA, APA, and Chicago list both forms as acceptable, as do the *Oxford English Dictionary* and merriam-webster .com. Here are a few examples from other sources:

▶ It's all about letting someone be <u>themself.</u>   —*Cambridge Dictionary*

▶ There's just something that feels really good about buying your produce from someone who grows it <u>themselves</u>.

—Emily Boyes, *The Hub @TTU,* November 2019

As this book goes to press, the singular form "themself" may be slightly more common, but only time and usage will determine which form will gain more acceptance and become the preferred word. In other words, it's really up to all of us to choose.

L-10c "Ze," "Hir," and Other Coined Pronouns

In addition to singular "they," some people who are nonbinary, trans, gender-nonconforming, or don't identify as exclusively male or female use coined or invented pronouns, such as "ze" and "hir" and "xe," when being referred to in the third person. Coined pronouns aren't as widely used as singular "they," but there are people who use them, and in fact, such pronouns have been around for centuries. A few of the more common ones are "ze," "hir," "hir"/"hirs" and "xe," "xem," "xyr"/"xyrs," but there are many others.

▶ Jackie brought <u>hir</u> sweater to dinner because <u>ze</u> wanted to eat outside.

L-10d What's Your Pronoun?

"What's your pronoun?" has become a common question. In fact, many people include their pronouns in their email signatures, résumés, and social media bios. It's a reasonable question to ask of anybody, not just those you think may be trans or nonbinary. Regardless of your personal opinions about others' pronouns, respectful communication requires that we all make every effort to refer to people by the pronouns they indicate for themselves. Are you sometimes unsure which pronoun to use when you refer to someone? You're not alone. When language or grammar rules are uncertain, let courtesy and sensitivity guide you. If you don't know what pronouns someone uses and you're in a situation in which pronouns are relevant, the best thing to do is ask. Keep in mind, though, that not everyone may be comfortable sharing their pronouns or their gender identity. If you feel comfortable sharing your own pronouns, volunteering them can help make others feel at ease. If you don't know a person's pronouns, and you can't or don't think you should ask, best to use singular "they."

L-11   Englishes

EX. L-11
P. 507

"English? Who needs that? I'm never going to England," declares Homer in an early episode of *The Simpsons*. Sorry, Homer. Anyone using this book does need English. In fact, most of us need a variety of Englishes—the academic English we're expected to use at school, the specialized English we use in particular academic and professional fields, and the colloquial English we use in various other communities we belong to.

In fact, you probably speak several other Englishes—and other languages, too—in your everyday life, each with its own set of varieties. In academic writing, as in everyday conversation, you may sometimes add a word, phrase, or more from another variety or language. The practices of code switching, shifting from one language or variety to another, and code meshing, weaving together different languages or varieties, can be powerful tools for adding emphasis, connecting with an audience, or illustrating a point. This chapter offers some guidance in using different varieties of English effectively and appropriately in your academic writing. For example, you can probably say "that doesn't matter to me" in at least half a dozen different ways, but how do you choose which way would work best at any particular moment? In conversation, you make that choice so quickly that you rarely even notice you're doing it. You consider the context of the conversation, the purpose of your statement, and your relationship with the person you're talking with. For academic writing, your decision to mix languages and varieties is made in the same way: thinking about your **PURPOSE** and **AUDIENCE** first.

L-11a Edited Academic English

This is the variety used—and expected—in most academic and professional contexts. "Academic" means scholarly, precise, somewhat formal in manner, and suitable for use in college classes and publications. As you'll see in this chapter, other styles may be used in some academic contexts for specific reasons, but the overall tone of academic writing is factual, straightforward, and undramatic. "Edited" means that it is carefully written and polished. And "English"—well, you already know what that is.

L-11b Formal and Informal English

Some of the variation in English comes from levels of formality. Academic writing is usually formal. The tone is serious; information is stated directly. These characteristics display your competence and authority. The most informal language, on the other hand, tends to be found in the ways we talk with our close friends and relatives; those conversations are full of **IDIOMS**, slang, and personal code that's specific to the people talking.

Words with the same basic meaning can convey very different messages when they have different levels of formality—and so the words you choose should always be guided by what's appropriate to your **AUDIENCE**, **TOPIC**, and the larger **RHETORICAL CONTEXT**.

See, for example, two headlines that appeared in two different newspapers after quarterback Andrew Luck announced his retirement from the NFL:

▶ Colts Quarterback Andrew Luck Retires from NFL —*Wall Street Journal*

▶ LUCK RUNS OUT: Colts QB Shocks Football World, Retires at 29
—New York Post

The first headline is from the *Wall Street Journal*, a newspaper dedicated to business news, with an audience of corporate and government executives. Its tone is professional and businesslike, and its English is formal. The second is from the *New York Post*, a daily tabloid newspaper known for its sensationalist headlines; its English is informal, going for laughs and making a play on words with Andrew Luck's last name.

In the cartoon below, the adult understands quite well what the child is saying; she's merely suggesting a more formal and polite—and appropriate—way to express his judgment of the painting.

"Instead of 'It sucks' you could say, 'It doesn't speak to me.'"

Mixing formal and informal

Occasionally mixing in an informal element—a playful image, an unexpected bit of slang—can enliven formal writing. For example, in a book about the alimentary canal, science writer Mary Roach gives detailed, well-researched descriptions of all aspects of digestion, including the anatomy of the digestive system. Although her topic is serious, she stirs in some irreverent **METAPHORS** and surprising comparisons along the way, as this description of the esophagus shows.

▶ The esophagus is a thin, pink stretchable membrane, a biological bubble gum. —Mary Roach, *Gulp: Adventures on the Alimentary Canal*

Such everyday imagery makes a potentially dry subject come to life. What's more, the information is easier to remember. Quick: what color is your esophagus? You remembered, didn't you?

L-11c English across Fields

If you've ever listened in on a group of nurses, software engineers, lawyers, or taxi drivers, you probably heard words you didn't understand, jokes you didn't think were funny. All professional fields have their own specialized language.

Restaurant staff, for example, have shorthand for relaying food orders and seating information. In this example from an essay about blue-collar work, UCLA professor Mike Rose describes a restaurant where his mother was a waitress:

▶ *Fry four on two,* my mother would say as she clipped a check onto the metal wheel. Her tables were *deuces, four-tops,* or *six-tops* according to their size; seating areas also were nicknamed. The *racetrack,* for instance, was the fast-turnover front section. Lingo conferred authority and signaled know-how.   —Mike Rose, "Blue-Collar Brilliance"

You might not know what "deuces" or "four-tops" are (or maybe you do), but it's language Rose's mother knew her colleagues would understand. On the one hand, specialized language allows professionals to do their work with greater ease and efficiency; on the other hand, it marks and helps construct a community around a certain field of work.

L-11d English across Regions

Have you ever wished that British TV shows had subtitles? The characters are definitely speaking English, but you may have a hard time understanding them. Every region has its own accent, of course, but there may also be words and expressions that are unfamiliar or mean something different to those who don't live there. In Australia (and parts of Wisconsin), for example, a "bubbler" is a drinking fountain. In India, the "hall" is the part of the house known in the United States as the living room.

In the US South, "y'all" is the way many folks say "you all." Country singer Miranda Lambert, a native of Texas, uses "y'all" frequently in her *Twitter* feed, such as in this tweet to pump up interest in one of her albums:

▶ I've got something up my sleeve for y'all this week
                —Miranda Lambert, @mirandalambert, August 12, 2019

In choosing to use "y'all" rather than the more standard "you," Lambert emphasizes her southern heritage and establishes a friendly, down-home tone.

Other regions as well have their own forms of the second person plural. In Chicago and New York you might hear "youse," and in Pittsburgh it's "yinz." Such local language is widely understood in the regions where it is used, though it may sound strange to people from other places. Using regional language in your writing can be a good way to evoke a place—and, as in Lambert's, can demonstrate pride in your own regional roots. If you aren't familiar with the regional language of the place you're writing about, though, you should do careful research to be sure you're getting it right.

L-11e Englishes across Cultures and Communities

Some varieties of English are associated with a particular social, ethnic, or other community. Black or African American English is perhaps the best-known of these Englishes. Not all Black people in the United States use it, and those who do may not use it exclusively. Not all of its users are Black themselves. All of its users, however, follow the conventions and rules that make this variety of English consistent and recognizable.

Linguist Geneva Smitherman has written extensively on this variety of English, often using the language itself to support her points. See how she uses both "academic" English and Black English to establish her authority as an insider and drive home her point with a stylistic punch.

▶ Think of black speech as having two dimensions: language and style. . . . Consider [this example]. Nina Simone sing: "It bees dat way sometime." Here the language aspect is the use of the verb *be* to indicate a recurrent event or habitual condition, rather than a one-time-only occurrence. But the total expression—"It bees dat way sometime"—also reflects Black English style, for the statement suggests a point of view, a way of looking at life, and a method of adapting to life's realities. To live by the philosophy of "It bees dat way sometime" is to come to grips with the changes that life bees puttin us through, and to accept the changes and bad times as a constant, ever-present reality.
—Geneva Smitherman, *Talkin and Testifyin: The Language of Black America*

You'll notice that the use of the verb "be," as Smitherman explains, allows the word to carry a nuanced meaning that is simply absent from other varieties of English. People unfamiliar with that usage or Black English in general may dismiss it as "incorrect"—negative opinions that contribute to the stigma that varieties of English often face. As readers, we would do well to develop flexibility in our judgments about English, a language used by 1.5 billion people all around the world.

Many other communities have developed their own Englishes as well. Ethnic communities often use an English that includes words from another language. Men and women often speak differently, as Deborah Tannen and other linguists have shown. Even young people use an English that might sound very strange coming from a gray-haired elder.

The differences can be subtle but sometimes a single word can make someone sound young, or old, or Texan, or Canadian—and can establish credibility with an audience. See how a simple "FOMO" in the headline of a Bloomberg News article about stock market investing signals a youth-oriented appeal. Bloomberg News is a news agency dedicated to business and financial information—an area more traditionally associated with persons of middle age and up.

▶ FOMO Grows as Investors Scurry to Catch Stock Market Boom
—Bloomberg

FOMO, an acronym for "fear of missing out," is likely very familiar to *Twitter* and *Instagram* users. The term began to appear on social media in 2004, making it a recent addition to the language. Bloomberg, a relatively new media company that prides itself on "a culture of disruption," made a strategic move in putting "FOMO" in the headline of an article on investment strategies. The acronym is sure to grab some eyeballs of a prized demographic—young investors.

L-11f Mixing Languages and Varieties

As a writer, you can use different varieties of English or different languages for various purposes. If you use Black English or any other variety of English in your daily life and want to include it in your academic work, first consider your **PURPOSE** and **AUDIENCE**. What message are you trying to communicate and how will mixing language varieties contribute to that message? Will it help you connect with your audience? illustrate a point? evoke a specific place, person, or community? draw attention?

For example, in a lab report, where precise, straightforward terms are expected so that others can replicate an experiment exactly, you should probably stick with edited Academic English—another language variety likely wouldn't be appropriate. When you do mix languages, mark your switches in some way so that your audience can tell what you're doing—for example, by adding a **SIGNAL PHRASE** or using text effects such as italics. You want readers to know that you are making deliberate language choices.

We recognize that it can be risky to use your home language or language variety in your academic writing. Our best advice is to keep your focus on your audience, context, and purpose—just as you do with all your writing, all the time. And while you might be eager to try some of these techniques in your writing, be careful, sensitive, and genuine; cultural appropriation can be offensive and insulting. If a language variety is not part of your everyday life and culture—even if you understand it well and appreciate it enormously—don't try using it in your own writing without the guidance of an insider.

Here are some more suggestions and examples for mixing languages effectively and appropriately.

To evoke a person or represent speech

When you are describing people, you may want to quote their words, to let readers "hear" them talk—and to let them speak for themselves. Some multilingual authors mix their English writing with words or phrases from another language to give readers an authentic sense of someone's words or thoughts. See, for example, how Sandra Cisneros mixes English and Spanish in relating an exchange between her parents as they bicker about a trip to visit relatives. Using two languages in the dialogue adds realism, and the context makes the meaning clear even for readers who don't speak Spanish.

▶ "Zoila, why do you insist on being so stubborn?" Father shouts into the mirror, clouding the glass. "*Ya verás.* You'll see, *vieja,* it'll be fun." "And stop calling me *vieja,*" Mother shouts back. "I hate that word! Your mother's old; I'm not old."   —Sandra Cisneros, *Caramelo*

When writing dialogue, you may sometimes want to use nonstandard spelling to mimic dialect or sound, as Flannery O'Connor does with the speech of a young boy questioning an outlaw.

▶ "What you got that gun for?" John Wesley asked. "Whatcha gonna do with that gun?"   —Flannery O'Connor, "A Good Man Is Hard to Find"

If you choose to use a nonstandard spelling to evoke a specific person or manner of speaking, your purpose for doing so should be consistent with your overall purpose, and your intention should be respectful and not derogatory or belittling. Also, make sure that your variant is accurate; will a reader be able to "hear" the pronunciation you've represented? Many nonstandard spellings, such as "gonna" or "c'mon," have been conventionalized, so you should try typing your word into *Google* to make sure you've got it right.

To evoke a place or an event

In certain settings or situations—sports, auctions, math class—you will hear language you wouldn't hear anywhere else. In some cases, the topics require specialized words. There's no way to talk about golf without mentioning "par" or "putting" or "a hole in one," or to teach math without words like "variable" or "function." In other cases, people tend to use a certain kind of language. Think about the conversations you'd hear in a board meeting, or a sports bar.

Such language can be used to evoke a place or an event, as in this summary of a 2019 NBA playoff series between the Golden State Warriors and the Portland Trail Blazers.

▶ Curry torched the Portland Trail Blazers in the screen game in the West finals, running over 31 picks per contest while yielding a ridiculous 1.23 points per chance.   —Kirk Goldsberry, *ESPN*

The writer can assume that his readers are familiar with the language he uses; in fact, many readers probably followed the series and just read the summary in order to relive it. His use of basketball JARGON helps put them back in the action. But for an audience unfamiliar with the game, he'd need to explain terms like "screen" and "picks," ordinary words that have specific meanings in a basketball context.

To build common ground with an audience

Language is one good way to establish CREDIBILITY and build common ground with readers. For example, in a feature article about how letters to the editor are chosen for publication in the daily newspaper of a city in Minnesota, the writer included the word "uff-da," a purely local touch:

▶ We don't publish mass produced letters. There are people in these United States who like to send letters to every newspaper in the country on a weekly basis. *Uff-da!* These are easy to catch. There are also some lobbying organizations who provide forms for supporters where writers don't actually pen their own thoughts.

—Tim Engstrom, *Albert Lea Tribune*

"Uff-da" is a Norwegian expression that is widely used in the region. It means "wow" or "no kidding" or even "OMG!" depending on the situation. The writer doesn't need it to convey his meaning, but using it demonstrates a sense of local knowledge and pride—and helps build common ground with his readers.

Think carefully, however, before using words from a language or variety of language that you don't speak yourself; you may offend some readers. And if by chance you use words incorrectly, you could even damage your credibility.

P-1   Commas

Commas matter. Consider the title of the best-selling book *Eats, Shoots & Leaves*. The cover shows two pandas, one with a gun in its paw, one whitewashing the comma. Is the book about a panda that dines, then fires a gun and exits? Or about the panda's customary diet? In fact, it's a book about punctuation; the ambiguity of its title illustrates how commas affect meaning. This chapter shows when and where to use commas in your writing.

P-1a To Join Independent Clauses with "And," "But," and Other Coordinating Conjunctions

EX. P-1a-b
P. 509

Put a comma before the **COORDINATING CONJUNCTIONS** "and," "but," "for," "nor," "or," "so," and "yet" when they connect two **INDEPENDENT CLAUSES**. The comma signals that one idea is ending and another is beginning.

▶ I do not love Shakespeare, but I still have those books.
—Rick Bragg, *All Over But the Shoutin'*

▶ Most people think the avocado is a vegetable, yet it is actually a fruit.

▶ The blue ribbon went to Susanna, and Sarah got the red ribbon.

Without the comma, readers might first think both girls got blue ribbons.

Although some writers omit the comma, especially with short independent clauses, you'll never be wrong to include it.

▶ I was smart, and I knew it.   —Shannon Nichols, "'Proficiency'"

No comma is needed between the verbs when a single subject performs two actions.

▶ Many fast-food restaurants now give calorie counts on menus and offer a variety of healthy meal options.

▶ Augustine wrote extensively about his mother/ but mentioned his father only briefly.

P-1b To Set Off Introductory Words

EX. P-1a-b
P. 509

Use a comma after an introductory word, **PHRASE**, or **CLAUSE** to mark the end of the introduction and the start of the main part of the sentence.

▶ Typically, a girl has a best friend with whom she sits and talks, frequently telling secrets.
—Deborah Tannen, "Gender in the Classroom"

▶ In terms of wealth rather than income, the top 1 percent control 40 percent.   —Joseph E. Stiglitz, "Of the 1%, by the 1%, for the 1%"

▶ Even ignoring the extreme poles of the economic spectrum, we find enormous class differences in the life-styles among the haves, the have-nots, and the have-littles.

—Gregory Mantsios, "Class in America—2003"

▶ When Miss Emily Grierson died, our whole town went to her funeral.
—William Faulkner, "A Rose for Emily"

Some writers don't use a comma after a short introductory word, phrase, or clause, but it's never wrong to include one.

EX. P-1c
P. 510 **P-1c To Separate Items in a Series**

Use a comma to separate the items in a series. The items may be words, **PHRASES**, or **CLAUSES**.

▶ I spend a great deal of time thinking about the power of language— the way it can evoke an emotion, a visual image, a complex idea, or a simple truth.   —Amy Tan, "Mother Tongue"

Though some writers leave out the comma between the final two items in a series, this omission can confuse readers. It's never wrong to include the final comma.

▶ Nadia held a large platter of sandwiches—egg salad, peanut butter, ham, and cheese.

Without the last comma, it's not clear whether there are three or four kinds of sandwiches on the platter.

EX. P-1d
P. 511 **P-1d To Set Off Nonessential Elements**

A nonessential (or nonrestrictive) element is one that could be deleted without changing the basic meaning of the sentence; it should be set off with commas. An essential (or restrictive) element is one that is needed to understand the sentence; therefore, it should not be set off with commas.

NONESSENTIAL

▶ Spanish**,** which is a Romance language**,** is one of six official languages at the United Nations.

The detail about being a Romance language adds information, but it is not essential to the meaning of the sentence and so is set off with commas.

ESSENTIAL

▶ Navajo is the Athabaskan language that is spoken in the Southwest by the Navajo people.

The detail about where Navajo is spoken is essential: Navajo is not the only Athabaskan language; it is the Athabaskan language that is spoken in the Southwest.

Note that the meaning of a sentence can change depending on whether or not an element is set off with commas.

▶ My sister**,** Trinh**,** just auditioned for Cirque du Soleil.

The writer has only one sister.

▶ My sister Trinh just auditioned for Cirque du Soleil.

The writer has more than one sister; the one named Trinh just auditioned for Cirque du Soleil.

Essential and nonessential elements can be clauses, phrases, or words.

CLAUSES

▶ He always drove Chryslers**,** which are made in America.

▶ He always drove cars that were made in America.

PHRASES

▶ I fumble in the dark**,** trying to open the mosquito netting around my bed.

▶ I see my mother clutching my baby sister.

—Chanrithy Him, "When Broken Glass Floats"

WORDS

▶ At 8:59, Flight 175 passenger Brian David Sweeney tried to call his wife**,** Julie.

> At 9:00, Lee Hanson received a second call from his son Peter.
> —The 9/11 Commission, "The Hijacking of United 175"

Sweeney had only one wife, so her name provides extra but nonessential information. Hanson presumably had more than one son, so it is essential to specify which son called.

EX. P-1e–i
P. 512

P-1e To Set Off Parenthetical Information

Information that interrupts the flow of a sentence needs to be set off with commas.

> Bob's conduct, most of us will immediately respond, was gravely wrong.   —Peter Singer, "The Singer Solution to World Poverty"

> With as little as two servings of vegetables a day, it seems to me, you can improve your eating habits.

EX. P-1e–i
P. 512

P-1f To Set Off Transitional Expressions

TRANSITIONS such as "thus," "nevertheless," "for example," and "in fact" help connect sentences or parts of sentences. They are usually set off with commas.

> The real world, *however,* is run by money.
> —Joanna MacKay, "Organ Sales Will Save Lives"

When a transition connects two **INDEPENDENT CLAUSES** in the same sentence, it is preceded by a semicolon and is followed by a comma.

> There are few among the poor who speak of themselves as lower class; *instead,* they refer to their race, ethnic group, or geographic location.
> —Gregory Mantsios, "Class in America—2003"

EX. P-1e–i
P. 512

P-1g To Set Off Direct Quotations

Use commas to set off quoted words from the speaker or source.

> Pa shouts back, "I just want to know where the gunfire is coming from."   —Chanrithy Him, "When Broken Glass Floats"

▶ "You put a slick and a con man together," she said, "and you have predatory lenders."

    —Peter Boyer, "Eviction: The Day They Came for Addie Polk's House"

▶ "Death and life are in the power of the tongue," says the proverb.
                                            ^

P-1h To Set Off Direct Address, "Yes" or "No," Interjections, and Tag Questions

EX. P-1e–i
P. 512

DIRECT ADDRESS "Well, Virginia, I'm glad we cleared that up."

"YES" OR "NO" No, you cannot replace the battery on your iPhone.
               ^

INTERJECTION Oh, a PS4. How long did you have to wait to get it?
               ^

TAG QUESTION That wasn't so hard, was it?
                    ^

P-1i With Addresses, Place Names, and Dates

EX. P-1e–i
P. 512

▶ Send contributions to Human Rights Campaign, 1640 Rhode Island Ave., Washington, DC 20036.

▶ Athens, Georgia, is famous for its thriving music scene.

▶ Amelia Earhart disappeared over the Pacific Ocean on July 2, 1937, while trying to make the first round-the-world flight at the equator.

Omit the commas, however, if you invert the date (on 2 July 1937) or if you give only the month and year (in July 1937).

P-1j Checking for Unnecessary Commas

EX. P-1j
P. 513

Commas have so many uses that it's easy to add them unnecessarily. Here are some situations when you should not use a comma.

Between a subject and a verb

▶ What the organizers of the 1969 Woodstock concert did not anticipate/was the turnout.

▶ The event's promoters/turned down John Lennon's offer to play with his Plastic Ono Band.

Between a verb and its object or complement

▶ Pollsters wondered/how they had so poorly predicted the winner of the 1948 presidential election.

▶ Virtually every prediction indicated/that Thomas Dewey would defeat Harry Truman.

▶ The *Chicago Tribune*'s famous wrong headline was/an embarrassment to the newspaper.

After a coordinating conjunction

▶ The College Board reported a decline in SAT scores and/attributed the decline to changes in "student test-taking patterns."

▶ The SAT was created to provide an objective measure of academic potential, but/studies in the 1980s found racial and socioeconomic biases in some test questions.

After "like" or "such as"

▶ Many American-born authors, such as/Henry James, Ezra Pound, and F. Scott Fitzgerald, lived as expatriates in Europe.

After a question mark or an exclamation point

▶ Why would any nation have a monarch in an era of democracy?/you might ask yourself.

▶ "O, be some other name!/" exclaims Juliet.

P-2 Semicolons

EX. P-2
P. 514

Semicolons offer one way to connect two closely related thoughts. Look, for example, at Martha Stewart's advice about how to tell if fruit is ripe: "A perfectly ripened fruit exudes a subtle but sweet fragrance from the stem end, appears plump, and has deeply colored skin; avoid those that have wrinkles, bruises, or tan spots." Stewart could have used a period, but the semicolon shows the connection between what to look for and what to avoid when buying peaches or plums.

P-2a Between Independent Clauses

Closely related independent clauses are most often joined with a comma plus "and" or another **COORDINATING CONJUNCTION**. If the two clauses are closely related and don't need a conjunction to signal the relationship, they may be linked with a semicolon.

▶ The silence deepened; the room chilled.
                        —Wayson Choy, "The Ten Thousand Things"

▶ The life had not flowed out of her; it had been seized.
                        —Valerie Steiker, "Our Mother's Face"

A period would work in either of these examples, but the semicolon suggests a stronger connection between the two independent clauses.

Another option is to use a semicolon with a **TRANSITION** that clarifies the relationship between the two independent clauses. Put a comma after the transition.

▶ There are no secret economies that nourish the poor; on the contrary, there are a host of special costs.   —Barbara Ehrenreich,
                        Nickel and Dimed: On (Not) Getting By in America

P-2b In a Series with Commas

Use semicolons to separate items in a series when one or more of the items contain commas.

▶ There are images of a few students: Erwin Petschaur, a muscular German boy with a strong accent; Dave Sanchez, who was good at math; and Sheila Wilkes, everyone's curly-haired heartthrob.
                                        —Mike Rose, "Potato Chips and Stars"

P-2c Checking for Mistakes with Semicolons

Use a comma, not a semicolon, to set off an introductory clause.

▶ When the sun finally sets;, everyone gathers at the lake to watch the fireworks.

Use a colon, not a semicolon, to introduce a list.

▶ Every American high school student should know that the US Constitution contains three sections;: preamble, articles, and amendments.

EX. P-3
P. 515

P-3 End Punctuation

"She married him." "She married him?" "She married him!" In each of these three sentences, the words are the same, but the end punctuation completely changes the meaning—from a simple statement to a bemused question to an emphatic exclamation. This chapter will help you use periods, question marks, and exclamation points in your writing.

P-3a Periods

Use a period to end a sentence that makes a statement.

▶ Rose Emily Meraglio came to the United States from southern Italy as a little girl in the early 1920s and settled with her family in Altoona, Pennsylvania.   —Mike Rose, "The Working Life of a Waitress"

An indirect question, which reports something that someone else has asked, ends with a period, not a question mark.

▶ Presidential candidates are often asked how they will expand the economy and create jobs~~?~~.

When a sentence ends with an abbreviation that has its own period, do not add another period.

▶ The Rat Pack included Frank Sinatra and Sammy Davis Jr.~~/~~

See **P-10** for more on periods with abbreviations.

P-3b Question Marks

Use a question mark to end a direct question.

▶ Did I think that because I was a minority student jobs would just come looking for me**?** What was I thinking**?**
                              —Richard Rodriguez, "None of This Is Fair"

Use a period rather than a question mark to end an indirect question.

▶ Aunt Vivian often asked what Jesus would do~~?~~.

P-3c Exclamation Points

Use an exclamation point to express strong emotion or add emphasis to a statement or command. Exclamation points should be used sparingly, however, or they may undercut your credibility.

▶ "Keith," we shrieked as the car drove away, "Keith, we love you**!**"
                              —Susan Jane Gilman, "Mick Jagger Wants Me"

When the words themselves are emotional, an exclamation point is often unnecessary, and a period is sufficient.

▶ It was so close, so low, so huge and fast, so intent on its target that I swear to you, I swear to you, I felt the vengeance and rage emanating from the plane.   —Debra Fontaine, "Witnessing"

P-4   Quotation Marks

"Girls Just Want to Have Fun." "Two thumbs up!" "Frankly, my dear, I don't give a damn." These are just some of the ways that quotation marks are used—to indicate a song title, to cite praise for a movie, to set off dialogue. In college writing, you will use quotation marks frequently to acknowledge when you've taken words from others. This chapter will show you how to use quotation marks correctly and appropriately.

EX. P-4a–b
P. 516

P-4a Direct Quotations

Use quotation marks to enclose words spoken or written by others.

▶ "Nothing against Tom, but Johnny may be the bigger star now," says director John Waters. —Sean Smith, "Johnny Depp: Unlikely Superstar"

▶ Newt Gingrich and Jesse Jackson have both pounded nails and raised funds for Habitat for Humanity. This is what Millard Fuller calls the "theology of the hammer."

—Diana George, "Changing the Face of Poverty"

When you introduce quoted words with "he said," "she claimed," or another such **SIGNAL PHRASE**, put a comma after the verb and capitalize the first word of the quote if it's a complete sentence. When you follow a quote with such an expression, use a comma before the closing quotation mark (unless the quote is a question or an exclamation).

▶ When my mother reported that Mr. Tomkey did not believe in television, my father said, "Well, good for him. I don't know that I believe in it either."
   "That's exactly how I feel," my mother said, and then my parents watched the news, and whatever came on after the news.

—David Sedaris, "Us and Them"

You do not need any punctuation between "that" and a quotation, nor do you need to capitalize the first word of the quote.

▶ We were assigned to write one essay agreeing or disagreeing with George Orwell's statement that "the slovenliness of our language makes it easier for us to have foolish thoughts."

In dialogue, insert a new paragraph and a new pair of quotation marks to signal each change of speaker.

▶   "What's this?" the hospital janitor said to me as he stumbled over my right shoe.
        "My shoes," I said.
        "That's not a shoe, brother," he replied, holding it to the light.
"That's a brick."   —Henry Louis Gates Jr., "A Giant Step"

See P–8c for help with capitalization in a direct quotation.

P-4b Long Quotations

EX. P-4a–b
P. 516

Long quotations should be set off without quotation marks as **BLOCK QUOTATIONS** . Each documentation style has distinct guidelines for the length and formatting of block quotations; you'll find more on long quotations in MLA-d, APA-d, CMS-c, and CSE-c. The following example uses MLA style, which calls for setting off quotations of more than four typed lines of prose by indenting them five spaces (or half an inch) from the left margin. Note that in the following example, the period precedes the parenthetical documentation.

> Biographer David McCullough describes Truman's railroad campaign as follows:
>> No president in history had ever gone so far in quest of support from the people, or with less cause for the effort, to judge by informed opinion. . . . As a test of his skills and judgment as a professional politician, not to say his stamina and disposition at age sixty-four, it would be like no other experience in his long, often difficult career, as he himself understood perfectly. (655)

P-4c Titles of Short Works

EX. P-4c
P. 517

Use quotation marks to enclose the titles of articles, chapters, essays, short stories, poems, songs, and episodes of television series. Titles of books, films, newspapers, and other longer works should be in italics (or underlined) rather than enclosed in quotation marks.

► In **"**Unfriendly Skies Are No Match for El Al,**"** Vivienne Walt, a writer for *USA Today*, describes her experience flying with this airline.
                                    —Andie McDonie, "Airport Security"

Note that the title of the newspaper is italicized, whereas the newspaper article title takes quotation marks.

► With every page of Edgar Allan Poe's story **"**The Tell-Tale Heart,**"** my own heart beat faster.

► Rita Dove's poem **"**Dawn Revisited**"** contains vivid images that appeal to the senses of sight, sound, smell, and taste.

P-4d Single Quotation Marks

When you quote a passage that already contains quotation marks, whether they enclose a quotation or a title, change the inner ones to single quotation marks.

► Debra Johnson notes that according to Marilyn J. Adams, "effective reading instruction is based on **'**direct instruction in phonics, focusing on the orthographic regularities of English.**'** "

► Certain essays are so good (or so popular) that they are included in almost every anthology. *The Norton Reader* notes, "Some essays—Martin Luther King Jr.'s **'**Letter from Birmingham Jail**'** and Jonathan Swift's **'**A Modest Proposal,**'** for example—are constant favorites" (xxiii).

EX. P-4e
P. 518
P-4e With Other Punctuation

When other punctuation follows material in quotation marks, it should go inside the closing quotation mark in some cases and outside in others. The following guidelines are those that are conventional in the United States; they differ from those in many other countries.

Commas and periods

Put commas and periods inside closing quotation marks.

► "On the newsstand, the cover is acting as a poster, an ad for what's inside**,"** she said. "The loyal reader is looking for what makes the magazine exceptional**."**
                                    —Katharine Q. Seelye, "Lurid Numbers on Glossy Pages!"

Semicolons and colons

Put semicolons and colons outside closing quotation marks.

▶ No elder stands behind our young to say, "Folks have fought and died for your right to pierce your face, so do it right"; no community exists that can model for a young person the responsible use of the "right"; for the right, even if called self-expression, comes from no source other than desire.   —Stephen L. Carter, "Just Be Nice"

▶ According to James Garbarino, author of *Lost Boys: Why Our Sons Turn Violent and How We Can Save Them*, it makes no sense to talk about violent media as a direct cause of youth violence. Rather, he says, "it depends": Media violence is a risk factor that, working in concert with others, can exacerbate bad behavior.
                    —Maggie Cutler, "Whodunit—The Media?"

Question marks and exclamation points

Put question marks and exclamation points inside closing quotation marks if they are part of the quotation but outside if they apply to the whole sentence.

▶ Then she began to talk more loudly. "What he want, I come to New York tell him front of his boss, you cheating me?"
                    —Amy Tan, "Mother Tongue"

▶ How many people know the words to "Louie, Louie"?

P-4f With Parenthetical Documentation

When you provide parenthetical **DOCUMENTATION** for a quotation, put the documentation after the closing quotation mark, and put any end punctuation that's part of your sentence after the parentheses.

▶ An avid baseball fan, Tallulah Bankhead once said, "There have been only two geniuses in the world: Willie Mays and Willie Shakespeare" (183).

P-4g Words Discussed as Words

Use quotation marks around a word you are discussing as a word. The same practice applies to letters, phrases, and sentences.

▶ In the mayor's speech, you will hear the word "ventilator" eight times.

▶ Most American dictionaries call for one "t" in the word "benefited."

▶ The phrase "once in a blue moon" refers to something that happens very rarely.

▶ The teacher asked her students to write "All work is my own." at the top of every assignment.

Some writers use italics rather than quotation marks to signal words discussed as words. We recommend quotation marks because they are more legible and accessible than italicized text for many readers. When referring to a number as a numeral, don't italicize or enclose it in quotation marks.

▶ All computer codes consist of some combination of 0s and 1s.

EX. P-4h
P. 519

P-4h Checking for Mistakes with Quotation Marks

Avoid using quotation marks to identify slang or to emphasize a word. Remove the quotation marks, or substitute a better word.

SLANG   Appearing hip is important to many parents in New York.

EMPHASIS   The woman explained that she is ⫽only⫽ the manager, not the owner, of the health club.

Do not put quotation marks around indirect quotations, those that do not quote someone's exact words.

▶ Grandmother always said that ⫽meat that was any good didn't need seasoning.⫽

P-5 Apostrophes

"McDonald's: 'I'm lovin' it'" proclaims an ad, demonstrating two common uses of the apostrophe: to show ownership (McDonald's) and to mark missing letters (I'm, lovin'). This chapter offers guidelines on these and other common uses for apostrophes.

P-5a Possessives

EX. P-5a
P. 520

Use an apostrophe to make a word possessive: Daniel Craig's eyes, someone else's problem, the children's playground.

Singular nouns

To make most singular nouns possessive, add an apostrophe and "-s."

▶ The challenge now will be filling the park**'s** seats.
                    —Michael Kimmelman, "A Ballpark Louder Than Its Fans"

▶ In Plato**'s** *Phaedrus*, Socrates bemoaned the development of writing.
                    —Nicholas Carr, "Is Google Making Us Stupid?"

▶ Bill Gates**'s** philanthropic efforts focus on health care and education.

If adding "-'s" makes pronunciation awkward, some writers use only an apostrophe with singular nouns that end in "-s": Euripedes' play, George Saunders' jacket.

Plural nouns

To form the possessive of a plural noun not ending in "-s," add an apostrophe and "-s." For plural nouns that end in "-s," add only an apostrophe.

▶ Are women**'s** minds different from men**'s** minds?
                    —Evelyn Fox Keller, "Women in Science"

▶ The neighbors**'** complaints about noise led the club owner to install soundproof insulation.

▶ Did you hear that Laurence Strauss is getting married? The reception will be at the Strausses' home.

Personal pronouns

Personal pronouns such as "we," "she," and "you" have their own possessive forms, which never take an apostrophe. See S-6c for a complete list.

▶ The graduates let out a cheer as they tossed *their* hats in the air—and later got a good chuckle when the valedictorian accidentally stepped on *hers*.

"Something," "everyone," and other indefinite pronouns

To form the possessive of an INDEFINITE PRONOUN, add an apostrophe and "-s."

▶ Spaghetti was everyone's favorite lunch.

Joint possession

To show that two or more individuals possess something together, use the possessive form for the last noun only.

▶ Castillo and Medina's book is an introduction to Latinx writers for English-speaking adolescents.

To show individual possession, make each noun possessive.

▶ Jan's and Bo's lung transplants inspired me to quit smoking.

Compound nouns

For nouns made up of more than one word, make the last word possessive.

▶ The surgeon general's report persuaded many people to start flossing.

P-5b Contractions

An apostrophe in a contraction indicates where letters have been omitted.

▶ **I've** learned that sometimes friends and business don**'t** mix.

—Iliana Roman, "First Job"

"I've" is a contraction of "I have"; *"don't"* is a contraction of "do not."

P-5c **Plurals**

You'll often see apostrophes used to pluralize numbers and abbreviations, and letters or words discussed as words when they're in italics: 7's, NGO's, C's, *thank you*'s. Usage is changing, however, and you should leave out the apostrophe in your own writing. If you use quotation marks for words discussed as words, you shouldn't add an apostrophe for the plural: "thank you"s. Same goes for letters: "C"s.

Plural of numbers

▶ The winning hand had three 8**s**.

▶ We never knew that Aunt Beulah won baking contests in the 1950**s**.

Plural of letters

▶ Mrs. Duchovny always reminded us to dot our "i"s and cross our "t"s.

▶ The admissions officers spoke enthusiastically about the college's no-grades option—and then said we'd need mostly "A"s to get in.

Plural of abbreviations and words discussed as words

▶ How many TV**s** does the average American family have in its home?

▶ The resolution passed when there were more "aye"**s** than "nay"**s**.

See that words discussed as words are in quotation marks but the "-s" ending is not.

P-5d **Checking for Mistakes with Apostrophes**

EX. P-5d
P. 521

Do not use an apostrophe in the following situations.

With plural nouns that are not possessive

▶ Both ~~cellist's~~ *cellists* played encores.

With "his," "hers," "ours," "yours," and "theirs"

▶ Look at all the lettuce. ~~Our's~~ *Ours* is organic. Is ~~your's?~~ *yours?*

With the possessive "its"

▶ It's an unusual building; ~~it's~~ *its* style has been described as postmodern, but it fits beautifully with the Gothic buildings on our campus.

"It's" is a contraction meaning "it is" or "it has"; "its" is the possessive form of "it."

P-6   Other Punctuation

Some carpenters can do their jobs using only a hammer and a saw, but most rely on additional tools. The same is true of writers: you can get along with just a few punctuation marks, but having some others in your toolbox—colons, dashes, parentheses, brackets, ellipses, and slashes—can help you say what you want to more precisely and can help readers follow what you write more easily. This chapter can help you use these other punctuation marks effectively.

EX. P-6a
P. 522

P-6a   Colons

Colons are used to direct attention to words that follow the colon: an explanation or elaboration, a list, a quotation, and so on.

▶ What I remember best, strangely enough, are the two things I couldn't understand and over the years grew to hate: grammar lessons and mathematics.
                                    —Mike Rose, "Potato Chips and Stars"

▶ I sized him up as fast as possible: tight black velvet pants pulled over his boots, black jacket, a red-green-yellow scarf slashed around his neck.   —Susan Jane Gilman, "Mick Jagger Wants Me"

▶ She also voices some common concerns: "The product should be safe, it should be easily accessible, and it should be low-priced."
                                        —Dara Mayers, "Our Bodies, Our Lives"

▶ Fifteen years after the release of the Carnegie report, College Board surveys reveal data are no different: test scores still correlate strongly with family income.   —Gregory Mantsios, "Class in America—2003"

Colons are also used after the salutation in a business letter, in ratios, between titles and subtitles, between chapter and verse in biblical references, and between numbers that indicate hours, minutes, and seconds.

▶ Dear President Michaels:

▶ For best results, add water to the powder in a 3:1 ratio.

▶ *The Last Campaign: How Harry Truman Won the 1948 Election*

▶ "And God said, 'Let there be light,' and there was light" (Genesis 1:3).

▶ The morning shuttle departs at 6:52 AM.

P-6b Dashes

EX. P-6b,c,f
P. 523

You can create a dash by typing two hyphens (--) with no spaces before or after or by selecting the em dash from the symbol menu of your word-processing program.

Use dashes to set off material you want to emphasize. Unlike colons, dashes can appear not only after an independent clause but also at other points in a sentence. To set off material at the end of a sentence, place a dash before it; to set off material in the middle of the sentence, place a dash before and after the words you want to emphasize.

▶ After that, the roller coaster rises and falls, slowing down and speeding up—all on its own.
                    —Cathi Eastman and Becky Burrell, "The Science of Screams"

▶ It did not occur to me—possibly because I am an American—that there could be people anywhere who had never seen a Negro.
                                    —James Baldwin, "Stranger in the Village"

Dashes are often used to signal a shift in tone or thought.

▶ The best way to keep children home is to make the home atmosphere pleasant—and let the air out of the tires.   —Dorothy Parker

Keep in mind that dashes are most effective if they are used only when material needs particular emphasis. Too many dashes can interfere with the flow and clarity of your writing.

EX. P-6b,c,f
P. 523

P-6c Parentheses

Use parentheses to enclose supplemental details and digressions.

▶ When I was a child, attending grade school in Washington, DC, we took classroom time to study manners. Not only the magic words "please" and "thank you" but more complicated etiquette questions, like how to answer the telephone ("Carter residence, Stephen speaking") and how to set the table (we were quizzed on whether knife blades point in or out).   —Stephen L. Carter, "Just Be Nice"

▶ But even companies with a market cap of over $970 billion (Google's parent company, Alphabet) or over $614 billion (Facebook) aren't immune to the punches of potential talent.
                    —Emma Goldberg, "'Techlash' Hits College Campuses"

▶ To control the appliance, you select a heat mode (like bake, roast, or broil), turn a knob to set the temperature and then wait for the oven to heat up.
                        —Brian X. Chen, "Gadget of the Year: The Toaster Oven"

P-6d Brackets

Put brackets around words that you insert in a **QUOTATION**.

▶ As Senator Reid explained, "She [Nancy Pelosi] realizes that you cannot make everyone happy."

If you are quoting a source that contains an error, put the Latin word "sic" in brackets after the error to indicate that the mistake is in the original source.

▶ Warehouse has been around for 30 years and has 263 stores, suggesting a large fan base. The chain sums up its appeal thus: "styley [*sic*], confident, sexy, glamorous, edgy, clean and individual, with it's [*sic*] finger on the fashion pulse."

—Anne Ashworth, "Chain Reaction: Warehouse"

P-6e Ellipses

Ellipses are three spaced dots that indicate an omission or a pause. Use ellipses to show that you have omitted words within a QUOTATION. If you omit a complete sentence or more in the middle of a quoted passage, add the three dots after the period.

ORIGINAL

▶ The Lux ad's visual content, like Resinol's, supports its verbal message. Several demure views of Irene Dunne emphasize her "pearly-smooth skin," the top one framed by a large heart shape. In all the photos, Dunne wears a feathery, feminine collar, giving her a birdlike appearance: she is a bird of paradise or an ornament. At the bottom of the ad, we see a happy Dunne being cuddled and admired by a man.

—Doug Lantry, "'Stay Sweet as You Are'"

WITH ELLIPSES

▶ The Lux ad's visual content . . . supports its verbal message. Several demure views of Irene Dunne emphasize her "pearly-smooth skin," the top one framed by a large heart shape. . . . At the bottom of the ad, we see a happy Dunne being cuddled and admired by a man.

If you use a quote as a full sentence and the quote doesn't include the end of the original sentence, MLA requires you to add an ellipsis at the end of the quotation; APA does not. If you use parenthetical documentation after quoted material, place ellipses *before* the parentheses to indicate the deletion of words, but put the end punctuation *after* the parentheses, as in the following example using MLA style.

▶ According to Kathleen Welch, "One can turn one's gaze away from television, but one cannot turn one's ears from it without leaving the area . . . " (102).

EX. P-6b,c,f
P. 523

P-6f Slashes

When you quote two or three lines of poetry and run them in with the rest of your text, use slashes to show where one line ends and the next begins. Put a space before and after each slash.

▶ In the opening lines of the poem, he warns the reader to "Lift not the painted veil which those who live / Call Life" (1-2).
　　　　　—Stephanie Huff, "Metaphor and Society in Shelley's 'Sonnet'"

EX. P-7
P. 524

P-7　Hyphens

If your mother gives you much needed advice, has she given you a great deal of advice that you needed, or advice that you needed badly? What about a psychiatry experiment that used thirty five year old subjects? Were there thirty-five subjects who were a year old? thirty subjects who were five years old? or an unspecified number of thirty-five-year-old subjects? Hyphens could clear up the confusion. This chapter provides tips for when to use hyphens and when to omit them.

P-7a Compound Words

Compound words can be two words (ground zero), a hyphenated word (self-esteem), or one word (outsource). Check a dictionary, and if a compound is not there, assume that it is two words.

Compound adjectives

A compound adjective is made up of two or more words. Most compound adjectives take a hyphen before a noun.

▶ a little-known trombonist

▶ a foul-smelling river

Do not use a hyphen to connect an "-ly" adverb and an adjective.

▶ a carefully executed plan

A compound adjective after a noun is usually easy to read without a hyphen; add a hyphen only if the compound is unclear without it.

▶ The river has become foul smelling in recent years.

Prefixes and suffixes

A hyphen usually isn't needed after a prefix or before a suffix (preschool, antislavery, counterattack, catlike, citywide). However, hyphens are necessary in the following situations.

WITH "GREAT-," "SELF-," "-ELECT"   great-aunt, self-hatred, president-elect

WITH CAPITAL LETTERS   anti-American, post-Soviet literature

WITH NUMBERS   post-9/11, the mid-1960s

TO AVOID DOUBLE AND TRIPLE LETTERS   anti-intellectualism, ball-like

FOR CLARITY   re-cover (cover again) *but* recover (get well)

Numbers

Hyphenate fractions and compound numbers from twenty-one to ninety-nine.

▶ three-quarters of their income

▶ thirty-five subjects

P-7b At the End of a Line

Use a hyphen to divide a multisyllabic word that does not fit on one line. (A one-syllable word is never hyphenated.) Divide words between syllables as shown in a dictionary, after a prefix, or before a suffix. Divide compound words between the parts of the compound, if possible. Do not leave only one letter at the end or the beginning of a line.

op-er-a-tion   knot-ty   main-stream

Dividing internet addresses

Do not insert a hyphen in a URL or DOI that you break at the end of a line. It's standard practice to break URLs or DOIs that won't fit on a line after a double slash or before any other punctuation mark. See the chapters on APA, Chicago, MLA, and CSE for more specific advice on how to divide internet addresses in each of those styles.

EX. P-8
P. 525

P-8   Capitalization

Capital letters are an important signal, either that a new sentence is beginning or that a specific person, place, or brand is being discussed. Capitalize "Carol," and it's clear that you're referring to a person; write "carol," and readers will know you're writing about a song sung at a holiday. This chapter offers guidelines to help you know what to capitalize and when.

P-8a Proper Nouns and Common Nouns

Capitalize proper nouns, those naming specific people, places, and things. All other nouns are common nouns and should not be capitalized.

PROPER NOUNS	COMMON NOUNS
Sanjay Gupta	a doctor
Senator Feinstein	a senator
Uncle Daniel	my uncle
France	a republic
the Mississippi River	a river
the West Coast	a coast
Christianity	a religion
Allah	a god

the Torah	a sacred text
Central Intelligence Agency	an agency
US Congress	the US government
Kansas State University	a university
Composition 101	a writing course
World War II	a war
July	summer
the Middle Ages	the fourteenth century
Kleenex	tissues

Adjectives derived from proper nouns, especially the names of people and places, are usually capitalized: Shakespearean, Swedish, Chicagoan. There are exceptions to this rule, however, such as "french fries," "roman numeral," and "congressional." Consult a dictionary if you are unsure whether an adjective should be capitalized.

All languages change, and the guidelines for appropriate use sprint along to keep up. As we go to press, the capitalization of the names of some social categories is up for debate. Specifically, in the discussion of racism, race, and related topics, academic and journalistic style guides are now unanimous in calling for the capitalization of "Black" when referring to groups, individuals, and cultures or cultural artifacts. With the word "white," however, opinions are more varied. In this book, we capitalize both "Black" and "White," following APA style.

▶ My high school classmates and I were almost all Black and Mexican, but all our teachers were White.

Other style guides and influential sources, such as the *New York Times*, AP, and notable authors are not capitalizing the word "white." The issue is complicated, with arguments from diverse angles, and usage is not likely to be widely settled anytime soon. We suggest that you think, learn, and participate in the discussion yourself. (It's your language, too!) For your academic writing, follow the style guide you're using for your course and/or consult your instructor. Appropriate and respectful usage is your priority; see **L-9b** for more on using preferred names.

P-8b Titles before a Person's Name

A professional title is capitalized when it appears immediately before a person's name but not when it appears after a proper noun or alone.

> Senator (*or* Sen.) Elizabeth Warren   Elizabeth Warren, the senator

P-8c The First Word of a Sentence

Capitalize the first word of a sentence. The first word of a quoted sentence should be capitalized, but not the first word of a quoted phrase.

- ▶ Speaking about acting, Clint Eastwood notes, "You can show a lot with a look.... It's punctuation."

- ▶ Sherry Turkle argues that we're living in "techno-enthusiastic times" and that we're inclined "to celebrate our gadgets."

Interrupted quotations

Capitalize the second part of an interrupted quotation only if it begins a new sentence.

- ▶ "It was just as nice," she sobbed, "as I hoped and dreamed it would be."   —Joan Didion, "Marrying Absurd"

- ▶ "On the newsstand, the cover is acting as a poster, an ad for what's inside," she said. "The loyal reader is looking for what makes the magazine exceptional."
           —Katharine Q. Seelye, "Lurid Numbers on Glossy Pages!"

P-8d Titles and Subtitles

Capitalize the first and last words and all other important words of a title and subtitle. Do not capitalize less important words such as ARTICLES, COORDINATING CONJUNCTIONS, and PREPOSITIONS.

"Give Peace a Chance"
Pride and Prejudice
The Shallows: What the Internet Is Doing to Our Brains

Each documentation style has guidelines for formatting titles in notes and bibliographies. You'll find more on titles and subtitles in **MLA-c**, **APA-c**, **CMS-b**, and **CSE-b**.

P-9   Italics

EX. P-9
P. 526

Italic type tells us to read words a certain way. Think of the difference between the office and *The Office*, or between time and *Time*. In each case, the italicized version tells us it's a specific television show or magazine. This chapter provides guidelines on using italics in your writing.

P-9a Titles of Long Works

Titles and subtitles of long works should appear in italics (or underlined). Notable exceptions are sacred writing such as the Qur'an or the Old Testament and historical documents such as the Declaration of Independence.

BOOKS   *War and Peace*; *The Hobbit*; *The Brief Wondrous Life of Oscar Wao*

PERIODICALS   *The Atlantic*; *Teen Vogue*; *College English*

NEWSPAPERS   *Los Angeles Times*

PLAYS   *Medea*; *Six Degrees of Separation*

LONG POEMS   *The Odyssey*; *Paradise Lost*

FILMS AND VIDEOS   *Selma*; *Inside Out*; *The Wizard of Oz*

MUSICAL WORKS OR ALBUMS   *The Four Seasons*; *Rubber Soul*

RADIO AND TV SERIES   *Fresh Air*; *Modern Family*; *Game of Thrones*

PAINTINGS, SCULPTURES   the *Mona Lisa*; Michelangelo's *David*

DANCES BY A CHOREOGRAPHER   Mark Morris's *Gloria*

SOFTWARE   *Adobe Acrobat XI Standard*

SHIPS, SPACECRAFT   *Queen Mary*; *Challenger*

WEBSITES   *Salon*; *Etsy*; *IMDb*

A short work, such as a short story, an article, an episode of a series, or a song, takes quotation marks.

P-9b Non-English Words

Use italics for an occasional unfamiliar word or phrase in a language other than English. Do not italicize proper nouns.

▶ *Verstehen*, a concept often associated with Max Weber, is the sociologist's attempt to understand human actions from the actor's point of view.

If the word or phrase has become part of everyday English or has an entry in English-language dictionaries, it does not need italics.

▶ An ad hoc committee should be formed to assess the university's use of fossil fuels and ways to incorporate alternative energy sources.

▶ The plot of *Jane Eyre* follows the conventions of a bildungsroman, or a coming-of-age story.

See L-11f for more on mixing languages.

P-9c For Emphasis

You can use italics occasionally to lend emphasis to a word or phrase, but do not overuse them.

▶ It is, perhaps, as much what Shakespeare did *not* write as what he did that seems to indicate something seriously wrong with his marriage.
              —Stephen Greenblatt, "Shakespeare on Marriage"

▶ Despite a physical beauty that had . . . hordes of teenage girls (and a few boys) dreaming of touching his hair *just once*, Depp escaped from the Hollywood star machine.

> —Sean Smith, "Johnny Depp: Unlikely Superstar"

P-10   Abbreviations

EX. P-10
P. 527

HBO. USA. OC. DNA. fwiw. DIY. These are some common abbreviations, shortcuts to longer words and phrases. You can use common abbreviations if you are sure your readers will recognize them. If not, spell out the full term with the abbreviation in parentheses the first time it appears. After that, you can use the abbreviation alone.

▶ In a recent press release, officials from the international organization Médecins Sans Frontières (MSF) stressed the need for more effective tuberculosis drugs.

Periods are generally used in abbreviations of personal titles that precede a name and in Latin abbreviations such as "e.g." or "etc." They are not needed for state abbreviations such as "CA," "NY," or "TX," or for most abbreviations made up of initials, like "AP" or "YMCA." In some cases, periods are optional ("BCE" or "B.C.E."). Be sure to use them or omit them consistently. If you're not sure about periods for a particular abbreviation, check a dictionary.

P-10a With Names

Most titles are abbreviated when they come before or after a name.

Mr. Ed Stanford   Ed Stanford Jr.

Dr. Ralph Lopez   Ralph Lopez, MD

Prof. Susan Miller   Susan Miller, PhD

Judge Laquanda Evans   Laquanda Evans, JD

Do not abbreviate job titles that are not attached to a name.

▶ The ~~RN~~ who worked with trauma victims specialized in cardiac care.
     nurse

P-10b With Numbers

The following abbreviations can be used with numbers.

632 BC ("before Christ")

344 BCE ("before the common era")

AD 800 ("*anno Domini*")

800 CE ("common era")

10:30 AM (*or* a.m.)

7:00 PM (*or* p.m.)

Notice that "BC," "BCE," and "CE" follow the date, while "AD" precedes the date. Remember that the abbreviations in the list cannot be used without a date or time.

▶ By early ~~p.m.,~~ all prospective subjects for the experiment had checked in.
          afternoon,

P-10c In Notes and Documentation

With only a few exceptions, the names of months, days of the week, colleges and universities, cities, states, and countries should not be abbreviated in the body of an essay. But they often are abbreviated in footnotes and bibliographies; follow the rules of whichever documentation system you are using.

The same applies to Latin abbreviations like "ibid.," "op. cit.," and "et al.": while you may use them in notes and documentation, they're not appropriate in the body of your text. Use equivalent English expressions (such as "and others" for "et al.") instead.

▶ Being left-handed presents some challenges for writers—~~e.g.,~~ it hurts
                                         for example,
   to write in spiral notebooks, and ink smears across the page and the side of your hand.

P-11   Numbers

EX. P-11
P. 528

Numbers may be written with numerals (97) or words (ninety-seven). Spell out numbers and fractions that you can write in one or two words (thirteen, thirty-seven, thirty thousand, two-thirds). Use numerals otherwise (578; 5,788). Spell out any number that begins a sentence. Be aware, however, that the conventions for writing numbers vary across disciplines.

MLA recommends spelling out numbers you can write in one or two words (seventy-seven) and using numerals for other numbers (532). Chicago recommends spelling out whole numbers up to one hundred (twenty-five) and any numbers followed by "hundred," "thousand," or "hundred thousand" (fifty-three thousand), but using numerals for specific numbers above one hundred (101).

▶ In a survey of *two hundred* students, *135* said they spent more than two hours each day writing.

In the social sciences, APA generally recommends spelling out numbers zero through nine and using numerals for numbers above ten.

▶ We conducted *nine 40*-minute interviews of subjects in *three* categories.

In the sciences, CSE recommends using numerals in almost any situation, but spelling out zero and one to avoid confusion with "l" and "O."

▶ The physician recommended *one* dose of *200* mg per day for *8* days.

In most business writing, spell out numbers one through ten and use numerals for all numbers over ten (ten goals, 11 strategies).

▶ We received *35* applications and identified *five* strong candidates, who we'll interview this week.

For very large numbers that include a fraction or decimal, use a combination of numerals and words.

▶ One retailer sold more than *4.5 million* of its basic T-shirts last year.

In addition, numerals are generally used in the following situations.

ADDRESSES   500 Broadway; 107 175th Street

DATES   December 26, 2019; 632 BCE; the 1990s

MONEY IN EXACT AMOUNTS $3.75; $375,000; a deficit of $3.75 trillion

PARTS OF WRITTEN WORKS   volume 2; Chapter 5; page 82; act 3, scene 3

PERCENTAGES   66 percent (*or* 66%)

RATIOS   16:1 (*or* 16 to 1)

STATISTICS   a median age of 32

TIMES OF DAY   6:20 AM (*or* a.m.)

WHOLE NUMBERS WITH DECIMALS OR FRACTIONS   66.7; 66 2/3; 59½

Exercise

My secret is practice.

—David Beckham

S-1 Elements of a Sentence

S-1a Subjects and Predicates

EXERCISE 1/Identifying Subjects. Circle the letter that indicates the
SUBJECT of the sentence.

> **EXAMPLE**
>
> The term "fast food" first appeared in American English dictionaries in
> the 1950s. (A) (B)

1. Prepared and served more quickly than food in a regular restaurant, (A)
   fast food usually can be either taken out of the restaurant or eaten (B)
   there.

2. There is debate over whether the term applies to hot dogs, falafel, (A) (B)
   noodles, and tacos when they are sold at stands or kiosks.

3. Characteristics of fast-food restaurants include franchising, preparing (A) (B)
   food at a central facility and shipping it to outlets, and serving food
   in cartons, bags, or plastic wrap.

4. One of the earliest American fast-food restaurants was White Castle, (A) (B)
   which began serving hamburgers in 1921.

5. Sometimes, fast food is referred to as convenience food. (A) (B)

6. It is indeed convenient to rely on fast food. (A) (B)

7. Eating fast food may not save consumers money, however, according (A)
   to some reports. (B)

8. In addition, both individuals and groups have long criticized fast-food (A) (B)
   chains.

Note: Answers to even-numbered items can be found at the back of the book.

460

9. Among the accusations are harm to consumers' health, exploitation
   of workers, and mistreatment of animals.

10. McDonald's, perhaps the chain most synonymous with fast food, has
    made changes to reduce calories, fat, and sodium in its Happy
    Meals.

EXERCISE 2/Identifying Predicates. Circle the letter that indicates
the PREDICATE of the sentence.

EXAMPLE

American Sign Language (ASL) is the dominant face-to-face
communication system of deaf Americans.

1. ASL is not just actions and gestures without words.

2. ASL users employ their hands—both shaping and moving them—
   to generate words and sentences soundlessly.

3. For example, a user signs "mother" by opening the hand and placing
   the thumb against the chin.

4. Not limiting themselves to their hands, ASL users also involve other
   parts of the body in their communication.

5. Among the facial expressions used in ASL is mouthing, or moving the
   mouth to form, but not speak, words.

6. The explanation for the sign "mother" comes from Bill Vicars.

7. Vicars, who teaches ASL at California State University–Sacramento,
   created and manages *Lifeprint.com*, a website about ASL.

8. Supplementing the vocabulary of signs is a finger alphabet for
   spelling out names and concepts lacking signs.

9. As with spoken English, there are regional accents and dialects of ASL.

10. It is not unusual to teach ASL to babies before they can speak.

EXERCISE 3 / Adding or Deleting Subjects. Edit the following sentences to add needed **SUBJECTS** or **EXPLETIVES** and to delete any repeated subjects. Write "correct" after any sentences that don't contain errors.

> **EXAMPLE**
>
> While the tomato is one of the most popular vegetables today, ^it^ hasn't always been so popular.
>
> Tomatoes ~~they~~ used to be considered poisonous.

1. Many rich people ate from plates made with lead, and the acid in tomatoes interacted with the lead to release poisonous ions.

2. Was the lead that was poisonous, not the tomatoes.

3. Since poor people ate from wooden plates, didn't have any problem with tomatoes.

4. The tomato it is native to the Western Hemisphere, and it was the Spanish explorer Cortés who brought it back to Europe.

5. Cortés he found tomatoes growing in what is now Mexico.

6. The English word "tomato" comes from the Nahuatl language; the Italian name is *pomodoro*, which means "golden apple."

7. Although tomatoes are usually classified as vegetables, are really fruits.

8. Tomatoes were at the center of a US Supreme Court case in 1893, when an import company sued New York State to recover the duty charged on a shipment of tomatoes from the West Indies.

9. The importer it claimed that tomatoes are fruits, not vegetables, and therefore the duty on vegetables should not apply.

10. Was decided by the Court that tomatoes are prepared and eaten like vegetables, not like fruits, and that therefore the vegetable duty had been charged correctly.

Note: Answers to even-numbered items can be found at the back of the book.

S-1b Clauses

Underline the SUBORDINATE CLAUSES, and circle the SUBORDINATING WORDS in each of the following sentences.

> **EXAMPLE**
> Some authors use pseudonyms, or pen names, to protect their reputation (when) they switch to a different kind of writing.

1. For example, when the mathematician Charles Lutwidge Dodgson published *Alice's Adventures in Wonderland*, he used the name Lewis Carroll.

2. In the past, some authors used pseudonyms because they couldn't get published under their real names.

3. Three such authors were the sisters Anne, Charlotte, and Emily Brontë, who were originally published under the names Acton, Currer, and Ellis Bell.

4. Mary Ann Evans opted for the male pseudonym George Eliot, which appeared on her novels such as *Middlemarch* and *Silas Marner*.

5. So that he could have credibility as a writer of books for girls, L. Frank Baum, the male author of the Oz books, took a female pseudonym, Edith Van Dyne.

6. Other authors, like some actors, take pseudonyms simply to have a name that is catchy or easy to spell or pronounce.

7. That was the motivation for Ford Madox Ford and Joseph Conrad, whose original names were Ford Herman Hueffer and Józef Teodor Konrad Korzeniowski.

8. Yet another reason to assume a pseudonym is to disguise the fact that the author is actually two people.

9. When cousins Manfred Lee and Frederic Dannay decided to collaborate on detective novels, they took the name Ellery Queen.

10. Two name changers who won the Nobel Prize for Literature are the poet Pablo Neruda (Neftalí Ricardo Reyes Basoalto) and the novelist Toni Morrison (Chloe Anthony Wofford).

S-1c Phrases

Combine each of the following pairs of sentences into a single sentence by using a participial, gerund, appositive, or infinitive **PHRASE**.

> **EXAMPLE**
>
> The 1925 novel *The Great Gatsby* features the American Dream, romantic love, and violence. F. Scott Fitzgerald wrote the novel.
>
> *The 1925 novel The Great Gatsby, written by F. Scott Fitzgerald, features the American Dream, romantic love, and violence.*

1. Fitzgerald wrote the novel in the 1920s about the 1920s. The novel has been called a timeless classic.

2. The book has been criticized for its morally despicable characters. This criticism is not as common as it once was.

3. Nick Carraway is the first-person narrator. He introduces us to the main characters.

4. The mysterious, wealthy Jay Gatsby is obsessed with a goal. He is determined to win back Daisy, who married another man.

5. Millions of copies of the book have been sold, but its early sales were unimpressive. The sales were low between 1925 and 1940.

6. A 2012 stage production of the novel included every word of the text. That production ran seven hours.

7. Critics called the 2000 TV version of *Gatsby* dreary and the 1974 film version lifeless. Robert Redford starred in the latter.

8. Some critics of the 2013 film of *Gatsby* questioned the director's decision. The director replaced 1920s jazz with contemporary hip-hop.

9. Charles McGrath writes for the *New York Times*. He calls the novel "unfilmable because its real power comes not from the plot but the prose."

10. Yet critics did not entirely dismiss the 2013 movie. They acknowledged its appeal for a new audience unfamiliar with the novel.

Note: Answers to even-numbered items can be found at the back of the book.

S-1b–c **Clauses and Phrases**

Indicate whether the underlined words in each sentence are a <mark>CLAUSE</mark> or a <mark>PHRASE</mark>.

> **EXAMPLE**
>
> The term "martial arts" now refers to unarmed combat and self-defense <u>practiced as sport rather than as fighting</u>, its original purpose. *phrase*
>
> In Olympic competition today, <u>athletes practice two martial arts</u>, judo and taekwondo. *clause*

1. Aikido, judo, and karate incorporate methods <u>of jujitsu</u>.
2. <u>Developed among samurai warriors in Japan in the seventeenth century</u>, jujitsu declined in the mid-nineteenth century.
3. Aikido, <u>a Japanese art of self-defense</u>, neutralizes an opponent using their own momentum.
4. One way that a contestant can win in judo is <u>by pinning an opponent to the ground for twenty seconds</u>.
5. First practiced by monks and priests in Asia, <u>karate uses punches, kicks, chops, and various open-hand techniques</u>.
6. Kung fu goes back at least to 1111 BCE, <u>when the Shang dynasty of China was in power</u>.
7. <u>Many kung fu moves imitate animals</u> fighting with one another.
8. Taekwondo, <u>which originated in Korea</u>, uses more than a dozen kicking techniques.
9. The Chinese form of exercise known as t'ai chi was designed <u>to relax the body</u> while conditioning it.
10. <u>Flowing slowly from one deliberate move to another</u>, practitioners of t'ai chi attract spectators in parks throughout the world.

S-2 Sentence Fragments

S-2a Identifying Fragments

Underline all the SENTENCE FRAGMENTS . If an item doesn't include any fragments, write "no fragment."

> **EXAMPLES**
>
> Man is the only animal who blushes. Or needs to.   —Mark Twain
>
> Courage is resistance to fear, mastery of fear—not absence of fear. no fragment
>   —Mark Twain

1. What made something precious? Losing it and finding it. —Celeste Ng

2. I'm nobody! Who are you?   —Emily Dickinson

3. We made powwows because we needed a place to be together. Something intertribal, something old, something to make us money, something we could work toward, for our jewelry, our songs, our dances, our drum.   —Tommy Orange

4. Books, books, books. It was not that I read so much. I read and reread the same ones. But all of them were necessary to me. Their presence, their smell, the letters of their titles, and the texture of their leather bindings.   —Colette

5. What's a book? Everything or nothing. The eye that sees it is all.
                                            —Ralph Waldo Emerson

6. A bad review is like baking a cake with all the best ingredients and having someone sit on it.   —Danielle Steel

7. *Admiration.* Our polite recognition of another's resemblance to ourselves.   —Ambrose Bierce

8. Action is the antidote to fear.   —Joan Baez

9. Definitions belong to the definers, not the defined.   —Toni Morrison

10. The one thing that doesn't abide by majority rule is a person's conscience.   —Harper Lee

---

Note: Answers to even-numbered items can be found at the back of the book.

S-2b Editing Fragments

Edit each of the **SENTENCE FRAGMENTS** in the following paragraphs by attaching it to a nearby sentence or revising it as a complete sentence.

EXAMPLE

What is the condition of Civil War battlefields today? *National Geographic* magazine addresses that question. And gives a distressing answer.

> The *National Geographic* writer reports how disturbing it was to find. That some Civil War battlefields were next to convenience stores. For example, part of the land involved in the 1863 Battle of Chancellorsville rested under a Hardee's. Also under a Chick-fil-A and a grocery store. Yet other parts of the Chancellorsville battlefield look much the same. As they did in 1863. The writer explains that in many cases Congress does not provide sufficient money to buy a whole battlefield for historic preservation. As a result, commercial development occurring on land once considered sacred.

> *National Geographic* not the first to sound the alarm. The Civil War Sites Advisory Commission reported in 1993 on 384 principal Civil War battlefields. At the time, the commissioners concluded that more than a third of the 384 were already lost to modern development or close to being lost. In fact, predicted that the number lost might soon grow to two-thirds. Although private organizations are trying to preserve what remains. Raising enough money and public awareness remains a challenging task.

> Several projects are under way to use technology to increase tourism to some battlefields and other Civil War sites. More public interest in the Civil War because of the 150th anniversary of the events. There are now a number of podcasts about Civil War battles and battlefields. Downloadable for free on many podcast platforms.

S-3 Comma Splices, Fused Sentences

S-3a Identifying Comma Splices

Write "cs" after each item that contains a **COMMA SPLICE** and "no cs" after those that do not.

> **EXAMPLE**
>
> It's not a lie, it's a terminological inexactitude. *cs*   —Alexander Haig
>
> The truth is balance, but the opposite of truth, which is unbalance, may not be a lie. *no cs*   —Susan Sontag

1. Nobody is healthy in London, nobody can be.   —Jane Austen
2. Don't get mad, get even.   —Joseph P. Kennedy
3. Your story is what you have, what you will always have.
                                                        —Michelle Obama
4. Martyrdom does not end something, it is only a beginning.
                                                        —Indira Gandhi
5. They'd like to think I have melted in the pot. But I haven't, we haven't.   —Gloria Anzaldúa
6. We are all in the gutter, but some of us are looking at the stars.
                                                        —Oscar Wilde
7. Writers from a minority, write as if you are the majority.
                                                     —Viet Thanh Nguyen
8. Procrastinate now, don't put it off.   —Ellen DeGeneres
9. I love my past. I love my present. I'm not ashamed of what I've had, and I'm not sad because I have it no longer.   —Colette
10. I did not have three thousand pairs of shoes, I had one thousand and sixty.   —Imelda Marcos

---

Note: Answers to even-numbered items can be found at the back of the book.

S-3b Editing Comma Splices, Fused Sentences

Revise the following passage to make all the COMMA SPLICES and FUSED SENTENCES into correctly punctuated sentences.

EXAMPLE

A human disease from almost seven hundred years ago
made headlines again recently. in 2011, scientists reported
                              In
reconstructing the DNA of the bacterium responsible for the Black
Death of 1347–1351. By 1400, at least five additional outbreaks
had followed; about 25 million people, roughly a third of Europe's
population at the time, had died from the Black Death.

Also called the plague, the Black Death traveled from Asia to the area around the Mediterranean Sea, then, it spread to the rest of Europe. The symptoms of the Black Death gave the disease its name. One form of it was marked by swellings that caused black stains from bleeding under the skin, another form caused fever. Those who got the first form died within five days victims of the second form died even faster. The Black Death was so terrifying that parents and children abandoned each other, priests refused to visit the sick to hear last confessions. Some towns tried to keep out the disease by banning any outsiders from entering, meanwhile, many rich people fled to the countryside to try to escape.

To study the original bacterium, scientists extracted material from the teeth of four victims of the Black Death, these victims, buried in a London cemetery at some point after 1348, were exhumed in the 1980s. The bacterium is known as *Yersinia pestis* a modern-day strain of it exists in small rodents in eastern Asia.

Scientists planned to look at the differences between the old and the new *Y. pestis.* Each contained millions of DNA units however fewer than a hundred of the new units were different from the old units. Would scientists find that one or more of the DNA differences made the old bacterium much more deadly than today's *Y. pestis* would they confirm that the poor living conditions of the fourteenth century explain the microbe's drastic effect on Europe at that time? After all, that era did not have antibiotics and vaccines such tools would have minimized danger to humans from the medieval *Y. pestis.*

S-4   Verbs

S-4a   Verb Tenses

Edit the following sentences to correct problems with **VERB TENSE**.
Write "correct" after any sentences that don't contain errors.

> **EXAMPLE**
> American film studios ~~have produced~~ *produce* new movies every year.

1. The first film studios were in New York, but Hollywood, California, has soon become the preferred location because of its good weather and plentiful land.

2. By the 1930s, each studio became known for a specialty—for example, Warner Brothers created gritty crime dramas on tight budgets.

3. To combat complaints about racy content, Hollywood enforces a set of rules known as the Motion Picture Production Code from 1934 to 1968.

4. One of the rules limits the length of an onscreen kiss to three seconds.

5. Alfred Hitchcock worked around this requirement in *To Catch a Thief* by interrupting a lengthy kiss between Cary Grant and Grace Kelly with shots of exploding fireworks.

6. In 1947, some members of Congress argued that communism influences film topics and dialogue; many writers, directors, and performers were blacklisted from film work for decades as a result of these accusations.

7. Critics today see *High Noon*, a 1952 western about a town that turns against its sheriff, as an allegory about the hysteria surrounding the communist scare.

8. World War II influences American film as it did every other part of American life.

9. Soldiers who fought overseas had higher expectations about accuracy in settings, so movies began to be filmed outside of the United States.

10. Julie Andrews and Christopher Plummer starred in the 1965 film *The Sound of Music*, based on a 1959 Broadway hit.

Note: Answers to even-numbered items can be found at the back of the book.

S-4b Verb Forms

EXERCISE 1/Regular Verbs. Fill in each blank with the correct form of the **VERB(S)** given in brackets.

> **EXAMPLE**
>
> Since 1947, the American Theatre Wing has *presented* Tony Awards to Broadway shows and actors. [present]

1. In 1949, Arthur Miller's *Death of a Salesman* earned the award for best play, but its lead _____ to win the award for best actor. [fail]
2. In 1960, *The Miracle Worker* _____ the awards for both best play and best actress. [gain]
3. In 1969, James Earl Jones _____ the best actor title for his role in *The Great White Hope*, which also _____ the Tony for best play. [receive; earn]
4. Eighteen years later, Jones again _____ the honor for best actor, this time for his work in *Fences*. [accept]
5. Glenn Close _____ to win best actress twice—first for *The Real Thing* in 1984 and then for *Death and the Maiden* in 1992. [manage]
6. The Tonys have always _____ musicals separately from other plays. [rate]
7. In 2015, *Fun Home* _____ many by being the first Tony Award–winning musical based on a graphic novel. [surprise]
8. When it was first published, the graphic novel *Fun Home* _____ a fair amount of controversy. [generate]
9. The musical *Hamilton* has _____ a new generation of listeners with the story of the founding of the United States. [engage]
10. *Hamilton*, which combines rap elements with meticulous attention to historical detail, _____ eleven Tony Awards. [receive]

EXERCISE 2/Irregular Verbs. Fill in each blank with the correct form of the IRREGULAR VERB given in brackets after the sentence.

EXAMPLE

The PBS program *Frontline* and the ESPN program *Outside the Lines* _undertook_ a joint project to investigate the effect of concussions on football players. [undertake]

1. The episode, called "League of Denial," _____ in fall 2013, at about the time two ESPN reporters published a book of the same title. [run]

2. The show claimed that concussions in football players _____ to brain damage and sometimes to degenerative brain disease and death. [lead]

3. The league in question is the National Football League (NFL), which allegedly _____ about the effect of concussions but did not share the data. [know]

4. In fact, the NFL _____ disability benefits to some players who suffered brain damage but kept the payouts secret. [pay]

5. According to the show, Dr. Bennet Omalu _____ disease in the brain of Steelers legend Mike Webster. [see]

6. Later, other doctors _____ disease in dozens of deceased players who had suffered concussions. [find]

7. In August 2013, the NFL _____ to a $765 million settlement with injured players who had sued. [come]

8. At the time, NFL Commissioner Roger Goodell _____ media, "There was no admission of guilt." [tell]

9. Players sometimes suffer concussions when a force _____ their heads straight on or from one side. [strike]

10. Although NFL players _____ helmets, scientists have explained that helmets can protect only against skull fractures, not against concussions. [wear]

_____

Note: Answers to even-numbered items can be found at the back of the book.

EXERCISE 3 / Gerunds and Infinitives. Fill in each blank with either the **GERUND** or the **INFINITIVE** form of the verb given in brackets after the sentence.

EXAMPLE

The International Union for Conservation of Nature decided _to add_ almost 2,000 species to its 2012 Red List of endangered species. [add]

1. Failure to enforce laws against _____ is devastating many species in Africa. [poach]

2. The western black rhinoceros became extinct because of illegal _____ . [hunt]

3. Poachers expect _____ a handsome price for rhinoceros horn, which has long been considered an aphrodisiac. [receive]

4. Few poachers end up _____ any significant punishment for their crimes. [receive]

5. Conservationists cannot stop _____ about endangered species. [think]

6. Poachers seem _____ a lucrative living from preying on animals. [earn]

7. Some conservationists have started _____ the eastern black rhino. [breed]

8. Other rhino populations—for example, the southern white rhino—are also facing danger from _____ . [poach]

9. Why do so few poachers want _____ with conservation efforts? [cooperate]

10. Authorities who enforce antipoaching laws risk _____ targets themselves. [become]

S-4c Helping Verbs

Most of the sentences below contain an error involving the use of **MODALS**. Find the errors, and edit to fix them. Write "correct" after the sentences with no error.

> **EXAMPLE**
>
> Wild mushrooms can makes̶ a wonderful addition to soup and stew.
>
> You must t̶o̶ be very careful in picking wild mushrooms, however, because some varieties are highly poisonous.

1. Consuming even a small amount of certain poisonous mushrooms might could result in serious illness or even death.

2. Still, many wild varieties are very distinctive and not similar to any dangerous variety, so it is unlikely that anyone would makes an error in picking them.

3. Some of the tastiest varieties can to grow from the trunks of trees, and no poisonous mushrooms ever grow on tree trunks.

4. You may not find any mushrooms the first time you go hunting, but don't give up.

5. If you go out in the morning after a good, drenching rain, you may could find a surprising number.

6. Before eating any wild mushroom, you should be certain that you have identified it correctly.

7. Although a few experts may disagree, wild mushrooms ought to be eaten cooked, not raw.

8. You can sauté wild mushrooms in olive oil or butter, and you may want to add a little garlic.

9. The so-called chicken mushroom is well named; if you had tasted it without knowing what it was, you would sworn that you had eaten chicken.

10. The morel mushroom is so delicious that it must to be eaten to be believed.

Note: Answers to even-numbered items can be found at the back of the book.

S-4d Active and Passive Voice

Rewrite each of the following quotations by changing at least one verb from the **ACTIVE VOICE** to the **PASSIVE VOICE**, or vice versa. Be prepared to explain whether the original or your revision sounds better—and why.

> **EXAMPLE**
>
> If you have never been hated by your child, you have never been a parent.   —Bette Davis
>
> If your child has never hated you, you have never been a parent.

1. The most ferocious animals are disarmed by their young.
                                                            —Victor Hugo
2. If you bungle raising your children, I don't think whatever else you do well matters very much.   —Jacqueline Kennedy Onassis
3. Children must be taught how to think, not what to think.
                                                            —Margaret Mead
4. Pretty much all the honest truth telling there is in the world is done by children.   —Oliver Wendell Holmes Sr.
5. My children weary me. I can only see them as defective adults.
                                                            —Evelyn Waugh

S-4e Mood

EXERCISE 1 / Indicative and Subjunctive. Edit the following sentences to use the indicative or subjunctive **MOOD** correctly. If a sentence is correct, write "correct" after it.

> **EXAMPLE**
>
> Specialists in sleep disorders usually recommend that a patient who is
>   sleep
> suspected of having sleep apnea ~~sleeps~~ in a lab overnight.
>   ^

1. If people do not get enough sleep, they often feel tired or have trouble concentrating during the day.

2. If a patient complains to a doctor about insomnia, the doctor generally does a physical exam and asks about the patient's medications, narcotics use, and medical history.

3. If watching television makes people sleepy, they wouldn't need to buy sleep medications.

4. If a person is short on sleep, their immune system might not fight infections effectively.

5. If caffeine was banned on college campuses, more assignments would be turned in late.

6. Many doctors recommend that a person with insomnia avoids late-afternoon naps.

7. Sleep therapists insist that a person with insomnia is consistent about bedtime.

8. Some researchers suggest that a person with insomnia stays away from the hormone melatonin, which is not regulated by the Food and Drug Administration.

9. Some people wish that every over-the-counter sleep aid was banned.

10. However, the night before exams some students probably wish that any prescription sleep aid was available over the counter.

EXERCISE 2 / Conditional Sentences; Requests, Recommendations, and Demands. Each of the following sentences contains errors in one or more verbs. Revise the **VERB(S)** in each sentence as necessary.

EXAMPLE

                    had
If someone put together key pieces of information better, the 9/11
          ^
hijackers might have failed in their mission.

1. If John Wilkes Booth's assassination attempt failed, would Abraham Lincoln have eventually run for a third term as president?

2. Some scholars argue that if a Serbian nationalist had not assassinated Archduke Franz Ferdinand of Austria in 1914, World War I would not take place.

3. If the United States did not bomb Hiroshima and Nagasaki in 1945, World War II might continue longer.

Note: Answers to even-numbered items can be found at the back of the book.

4. If the Boston Red Sox did not trade Babe Ruth to the New York Yankees in 1920, would the Red Sox have had more success?

5. If Anne Frank was alive today, how old would she be?

6. In developing Apple products, Steve Jobs insisted that design received the highest priority.

7. *The 9/11 Commission Report* recommended that the organization of the government changes significantly.

8. If the emergency response to Hurricane Katrina in 2005 was smoother, the politicians involved would have fared better in public opinion.

9. If a flu vaccine would have existed in 1918, most of the people who died in the flu epidemic that year could have survived.

10. Even with flu shots available today, health professionals strongly suggest that everyone washes their hands frequently.

S-4f Phrasal Verbs

Edit the following sentences to correct any errors with **PHRASAL VERBS**. Write "correct" after any sentence with no error.

EXAMPLE

When journalists want to do an investigative article, they must start
               into
by looking ˄the background of the situation ~~into~~.

1. Good investigative reporting calls for open-mindedness, curiosity, and persistence.

2. Previous articles are a good place to start, so journalists usually look up them.

3. A sharp journalist will notice a suspicious remark in an interview and will think over it for more clues.

4. When someone refuses a request for an interview, the journalist must get the disappointment over quickly and move on.

5. The subject of an investigation may try to persuade a reporter to call off it.

6. Despite setbacks and discouragement, good journalists keep at their work.

7. Some journalists may face personal risks to complete an investigation, but the most dedicated ones see it through.

8. Juicy details may come out in an interview, but the finished article needs facts and evidence to back up it.

9. With a complete article in hand, the job is still not done; once the writer turns in it, an editor may ask for additional information or evidence.

10. Given how little most investigative journalists are paid, few can live on what they earn.

S-5 Subject-Verb Agreement

EXERCISE 1 / Making Verbs and Subjects Agree. Underline the **VERB** in brackets that agrees with the subject of the sentence.

EXAMPLE
Ringo Starr of the Beatles still [*has* / *have*] millions of fans.

1. The oldest musical instrument and the most popular one in the world [*is* / *are*] the drum.

2. Rhythmical drumming by monkeys and other primates [*goes* / *go*] far back in time.

3. Motivating troops, setting a marching pace, and relaying commands [*has* / *have*] been common roles for drums through the ages.

4. A drum that has two heads with a set of wires across one or both heads [*is* / *are*] known as a snare drum.

5. Worldwide, there [*is* / *are*] so many kinds of drums that it's hard to keep track of them.

6. A jazz drummer and a rock drummer [*needs* / *need*] different kinds of drums.

7. A hand and a stick [*serves* / *serve*] as basic drum-playing tools.

Note: Answers to even-numbered items can be found at the back of the book.

8. Either a mallet or a brush also [*comes / come*] in handy.

9. The connection between rhythm and healing [*explains / explain*] the growing popularity of drumming circles.

10. At the heart of many musical groups [*is / are*] the drummers, sometimes relied on as the time keepers.

EXERCISE 2 / Editing to Make Verbs and Subjects Agree. Edit the following sentences to correct any problems with subject-verb **AGREE-MENT**. Write "correct" after any sentences without errors.

EXAMPLE

In many orchestral works, everyone await̂ the entrance of the kettle drums.

1. Often, the term "drums" refer to a drum kit—that is, a set of drums incorporating cymbals.

2. One of the best-known rock percussionists, still going strong, are drummer and musicologist Mickey Hart of the Grateful Dead.

3. Nigeria is one of the countries that have influenced Hart's approach to drumming.

4. Hart is surely the only one of the world's drummers who have collaborated with a winner of the Nobel Prize in Physics.

5. *Rhythms of the Universe* are the result of that collaboration.

6. The physics of drums are of interest to some music fans.

7. A community drum circle include people of many ages and backgrounds playing drums—usually, hand drums.

8. Drums of every kind has been played for centuries all over the world.

9. Drum songs are those that are famous for their amazing drum parts.

10. There are many great drum songs, but none is better than Led Zeppelin's "Moby Dick."

S-6   Pronouns

S-6a Pronoun-Antecedent Agreement

In the passage below, fill in each blank with a **PRONOUN** that agrees in number, person, and gender with the **ANTECEDENT** .

> **EXAMPLE**
> The popularity of artist Frida Kahlo reached new heights in the 1990s, and a feature film about _____*her*_____ was released in 2002.

Frida Kahlo, the daughter of a Spanish and Mexican Indian mother and a German father, gained fame in Mexico and around the world for _____1_____ vividly colored paintings. _____2_____ have been called intense and bizarre, surrealist and realist.

Kahlo contracted polio when she was six years old. Then at age eighteen, she was seriously hurt in a bus accident, eventually undergoing thirty-five operations. While recovering, Kahlo taught _____3_____ how to paint. Anyone who devotes _____4_____ attention to the many self-portraits by Kahlo can see the enormous physical and psychic pain she endured.

In addition to a distinctive artistic style, Kahlo cultivated a striking personal style. For example, _____5_____ favored Mexican Indian clothing over American and European dress, and she allowed her eyebrows to run into each other across the bridge of _____6_____ nose.

Kahlo and the muralist Diego Rivera married in 1929, divorced in 1939, and later remarried. The couple helped each other with _____7_____ work, but the relationship was a tumultuous one. Kahlo's *The Two Fridas* (1939) captures the ups and downs of her emotions by showing on one side of the canvas a content Frida, when Rivera loved _____8_____ , and on the other side a distraught Frida, after the couple divorced.

PBS set up an interactive website to accompany _____9_____ 2005 documentary about Kahlo. When someone clicks paintings on the site, _____10_____ can read in depth about the work.

Note: Answers to even-numbered items can be found at the back of the book.

S-6b Pronoun Reference

Edit the following sentences as necessary to make all **PRONOUNS** refer clearly to a specific **ANTECEDENT**.

> **EXAMPLE**   *reputation*
> Yosemite National Park is famous for its spectacular cliffs, and that
> makes it a destination for rock climbers from all over the world. ^

1. El Capitan is a vertical rock formation in Yosemite Valley, which has been made famous by the photographer Ansel Adams.

2. In a guidebook to the park, it says that *El Capitan* is a Spanish translation of the original Native American name *To-to-kon oo-lah*, meaning "the chief."

3. Its smooth vertical faces make El Capitan a favorite challenge for rock climbers. The most popular climbing route follows the projecting ridge between the two faces; climbers call it the Nose.

4. In 1958, Warren Harding, Wayne Merry, and George Whitmore became the first to climb the Nose successfully. This took them forty-seven days.

5. The team used ropes attached to metal holds called pitons, driving them into the rock to construct a climbing course.

6. In 1993, Lynn Hill became the first person to climb the Nose without ropes and pitons, which was especially extraordinary because she reached the top in just four days.

7. El Capitan remains one of the most difficult climbs in the world. In the news, they often report on the deaths of climbers whose attempts fail.

8. This makes climbers think twice before taking on El Capitan.

9. Climbers sleep in hanging tents anchored into the cliff; that sounds even scarier than the climb itself.

10. At night, you can see lights from these hanging campsites dotting the rock.

S-6c Pronoun Case

EXERCISE 1/Editing Sentences for Pronoun Case. Edit the following sentences to correct any errors in PRONOUN case. If an item does not have an error in pronoun case, write "correct" after it.

> **EXAMPLE**
> Matthew Weiner developed the idea for the TV show *Mad Men,* for
> which ~~him~~ and his team have won many Emmy awards.
>   he

1. Don Draper, the lead character in *Mad Men*, has a mysterious past. In fact, there's no other character in the series as mysterious as him.

2. Set in an advertising agency on New York City's Madison Avenue, the show traces conflicts among Draper and his colleagues as well as between he and various women.

3. Comparing *Mad Men* with *The Sopranos*, *The Wire*, and *Friday Night Lights*, some critics felt it wasn't as good as them.

4. Even many fans of those other shows, however, enjoyed *Mad Men* more than they.

5. In the first season, viewers were startled by the characters' use of cigarettes and alcohol, but a series set in the 1960s would have looked unrealistic without them smoking and drinking.

6. The creator of *Mad Men* so admired Alfred Hitchcock that he made the show's opening title sequence an homage to him.

7. The executive producer of the show is Matthew Weiner, and the head writer is he as well.

8. Though Don's stay-at-home wife, Betty, seemed outdated compared with "career girl" Peggy Olson, one report found that women viewers identified more with Betty than she.

9. Years later, when Don marries Megan, he feels threatened by her career, and there's constant tension between he and Megan.

10. Although Weiner has been praised for the show's visual style and authentic period details, him and his writers have been criticized for not addressing gender and race issues more directly.

Note: Answers to even-numbered items can be found at the back of the book.

EXERCISE 2 / "Who" / "Whom," "We" / "Us." Underline the correct PRO-NOUN in each of the following sentences.

> **EXAMPLE**
> Are psychics as useful to the real police [*who* / *whom*] search for missing persons as they are fascinating to fans of TV cop shows?

1. The answer given by people [*who* / *whom*] have studied the effectiveness of psychics is "No."

2. Dozens of studies show that psychics are no more accurate in making predictions than [*we* / *us*] nonpsychics are.

3. One FBI agent, though, became convinced of the power of a psychic [*who* / *whom*] had predicted the 1981 shooting of President Ronald Reagan.

4. Some police departments agree to call in a psychic [*who* / *whom*] the family of a missing person recommends.

5. Interestingly, the mere threat of bringing a psychic onto a case can force a suspect [*who* / *whom*] police consider superstitious to confess.

6. Sometimes people [*who* / *whom*] psychics have declared dead then show up alive.

7. How do family members react when a psychic [*who* / *whom*] they've trusted turns out to be wrong?

8. Self-proclaimed psychics [*who* / *whom*] seek the spotlight are usually unwilling to admit their bad calls.

9. [*Whoever* / *Whomever*] consults a psychic about the sex of a baby might also consider amniocentesis or other medical tests instead.

10. To what extent do [*we* / *us*] human beings just believe [*whoever* / *whomever*] we want to believe?

S-7   Parallelism

Edit the following items to correct any errors in **PARALLELISM**. Write "correct" after any sentences with no errors.

> **EXAMPLE**
> Many American writers held other jobs either before they became
> writers or while ~~writing.~~ *they wrote.*

1. Between 1891 and 1894, Jack London spent his time as a sailor, a waterfront loafer, and sometimes was a hobo.

2. In addition to writing poems, Carl Sandburg sang folk songs and was collecting old ballads.

3. Robert Frost not only wrote poems but also an instructor of poetry.

4. Before the age of thirty, Samuel Clemens
   - worked as a printer
   - piloted boats on the Mississippi
   - newspaper reporter in Virginia City and San Francisco

5. Before *Little Women* was published, its author, Louisa May Alcott, nursed Union soldiers and edited a magazine for children.

6. Katherine Anne Porter enjoyed reporting for a newspaper and taught at several colleges in addition to writing novels and short stories.

7. As a girl, Eudora Welty enjoyed golfing, baseball, and bicycling; as an adult, after working for a radio station and a newspaper, she started to write fiction and taking photographs.

8. Flannery O'Connor, confined to the family farm by chronic illness for most of her adult life, disciplined herself to sit down at her desk every day and working there for two hours whether she felt inspired or not.

9. Edith Wharton, whose upper-class background relieved her from ever having to worry about money, is admired for her novels about New York society as well as for writing *Ethan Frome*, a brief novel set in New England.

10. Poet Edna St. Vincent Millay lived as a young woman in New York City, where she found freedom to voice her opinions, set her own rules, and concentrate on her writing career.

Note: Answers to even-numbered items can be found at the back of the book.

S-8   Coordination, Subordination

Adding Ideas Using Coordination and Subordination. Expand each of the following sentences by adding a second idea using <mark>COORDINATION</mark> or <mark>SUBORDINATION</mark>.

EXAMPLE

Twitter was launched in 2006.

Twitter was launched in 2006, but I didn't sign up until 2011.

1. A tweet can be no more than 280 characters.
2. At first, *Twitter* was criticized as a new way to waste time.
3. Using hashtags (#), you can group tweets by topic.
4. Some users tweet to stay in touch with friends.
5. Celebrities and politicians often use ghost tweeters.
6. Users can choose to make their accounts private.
7. In 2019, *Twitter* reported more than 300 million monthly active users.
8. *Twitter* claims to connect users to the latest information.
9. *Twitter* promises companies "an engaged audience."
10. In 2013, *Twitter* sold shares and became a public company.

S-8b   Emphasizing One Idea over Others

Rewrite the sentences below to subordinate one of the ideas where appropriate. For sentences where both ideas seem equal, write "correct."

EXAMPLE

Toms shoes are made by a company in Santa Monica, California, and they're based on the *alpargata* shoes worn by Argentine farmers.

Made by a company in Santa Monica, California, Toms shoes are based on the alpargata shoes worn by Argentine farmers.

1. A *Life* magazine photographer took pictures of the footwear of famous people, and the resulting portfolio contains pictures of John Lennon's black boots, Elvis Presley's blue patent-leather loafers, and Dave Eggers's brown lace-ups.

2. Viewers of the portfolio smile at Katy Perry's white platforms with candy dots; another crowd pleaser is Bozo's oversized clown shoes.

3. Derek Jeter of the New York Yankees got his three thousandth hit on July 9, 2011, and the *Life* photographer took a picture of Jeter's cleats that day.

4. The portfolio shows red shoes belonging to Marilyn Monroe and to Madonna; except for color, the shoes were dramatically different—plain leather stiletto pumps for Monroe but ankle-strap heels with metallic dots for Madonna.

5. *Complex* lists the "30 most influential sneakers of all time," and the list includes the Air Jordan XI, the adidas Stan Smith, the Puma Suede, and twenty-seven others.

6. One website claims that college students need five kinds of footwear, but maybe the site is more interested in selling products than in reporting trends.

7. According to the same website, female students need rain boots, running shoes, cold weather boots, high heels, and flip-flops; male students should have flip-flops, boat shoes, tennis shoes, formal shoes, and work boots.

8. Run-DMC's "My Adidas" may have been the first song about athletic shoes; two decades later came Mac Miller's "Nikes on My Feet."

9. People expressed both outrage and disbelief at reports of Imelda Marcos's 3,000 pairs of shoes, but the final tally was only 1,600.

10. The most beloved American shoes of all time may be the ruby slippers worn by Dorothy in *The Wizard of Oz*, and one pair of them sold at auction for $666,000.

Note: Answers to even-numbered items can be found at the back of the book.

S-9 Shifts

Edit each sentence that contains an inappropriate shift in **TENSE**, **POINT OF VIEW**, or number. If a sentence does not contain an inappropriate shift, write "correct" after it.

> **EXAMPLE**
>
> If you take a liking to stories about the afterlife, ~~one has~~ *you have* a limited collection of TV shows to work through.

1. In the first episode of *The Good Place*, Eleanor Shellstrop was told that she is dead.

2. Viewers may be relieved to learn that Eleanor is in the part of the afterlife reserved for good people, although you must wonder what happens to people who led bad lives.

3. Michael, the architect in charge of Eleanor's neighborhood, explained that Eleanor gets to live in paradise for eternity.

4. In the show, architects create different neighborhoods in the afterlife; an architect is responsible for creating neighborhoods that are perfectly tailored to their residents.

5. Some viewers have applauded the show for its deep exploration of morality; others have criticized it for its irreverence.

6. The show's creator, Michael Schur, decided early on that he would end the show after four seasons, and he sticks to that plan.

7. Many of the show's writers have said that they loved working on *The Good Place*; they also say that they learned a lot from Michael Schur.

8. People who like the show tend to enjoy its exploration of moral philosophy, while a person who doesn't like the show tends to think that moral philosophy is not a good subject for television.

9. One might not think that a show about moral philosophy would be interesting, but you would be wrong.

10. Part of what is so compelling about the show was the characters' ability to grow and change in the afterlife.

L-1 Appropriate Words

L-1a–b Formal, Informal, and Pretentious Words

The following memo from a resident of a town to the town's elected officials contains nine words and phrases that are too **INFORMAL** or pretentious. Edit the passage to replace these words with more appropriate language.

> **EXAMPLE**
> Since August of this year, I have ~~thrice~~ written to Torreytown's elected officials about the proposed municipal solar energy system.   *three times*

    We should commission an analysis of the financial consequences of owning (as opposed to leasing) the proposed municipal solar energy system. At this point, we know only that the lease as promulgated will reduce the current annual cost of $400,000 for municipal electric needs by 50 percent. Several officials enunciated interest in my suggestion. Nan Byrnes, the consultant who guided the town through the negotiation process with the energy company, confirmed at the September meeting that the town can request from West Side Electric a price for purchasing the system from the get-go. (Such a price will be substantially lower, Nan has communicated to me, than the later purchase price that West Side offers if we commence our relationship by leasing.)

    If the accounts in the *Torrey Times* are accurate, the town is not exploring its options responsibly and fully. Today's *Times* article quotes official Donna Penner as saying that leasing beats owning because the town cannot procure the tax credits that a private developer gets. This statement offers zip financial comparison of where the town will be subsequent to twenty years of owning as opposed to twenty years of leasing.

Note: Answers to even-numbered items can be found at the back of the book.

L-1c–d Jargon and Clichés

Edit the following sentences to replace any **JARGON** and **CLICHÉS** with more appropriate language for a general audience.

> **EXAMPLE**
>
> Perhaps to show that the glass ceiling had shattered, the *New York Times* printed a photo of Sheryl Sandberg, not Mark Zuckerberg, when *Facebook* announced its IPO.
>
> *Perhaps to show that women executives could attain top jobs, the New York Times printed a photo of Sheryl Sandberg, not Mark Zuckerberg, when Facebook announced its public stock offering.*

1. Thieves who planned a major cyberattack on banks in 2013 struck while the iron was hot.
2. Job applicants need to highlight what they bring to the table.
3. As soon as a director blocks a scene, some actors want to rehearse wearing the shoes that are part of their costumes.
4. Employers might want to incentivize employees to reach beyond the low-hanging fruit.
5. University of Michigan students illustrated how to improve housing projects on Manhattan's Lower East Side with infill.
6. As an alternative to fracking, some countries are studying the environmental advantages of using methane hydrate—what *Atlantic* writer Charles C. Mann refers to as "ice you can set on fire."
7. Most dentists have experience in treating a wide range of problems, yet some limit their practice to prosthodontics or periodontics.
8. Advertisements for biologic dentistry have become more common recently in community newspapers.
9. The jury is still out on whether the US healthcare system will change the way elderly patients are cared for at the end of their lives.
10. In our fast-paced world, we want those who tell us stories or jokes to cut to the chase.

L-2   Precise Words

L-2a "Be" and "Do"

Each of the following sentences uses one or more forms of "be" or "do." Edit the sentences to replace these verbs with more precise ones. Restructure sentences if necessary.

EXAMPLE

Steph Curry is a point guard for the Golden State Warriors of the NBA.

Steph Curry plays point guard for the Golden State Warriors of the NBA.

1. Curry is the first NBA player ever to be unanimously voted MVP.
2. Curry is also the 2015 winner of the BET Sportsman of the Year Award.
3. According to Larry Bird, Kevin Durant, and other NBA stars, Curry is one of the all-time greatest shooters in the game.
4. Steph Curry is the son of former NBA player Dell Curry.
5. San Francisco, California, home to Curry's Golden State Warriors, is also home to an NFL team and an MLB team.
6. A nickname for Curry and teammate Klay Thompson is the Splash Brothers because of their astonishing combined record for three-point baskets.
7. As part of a United Nations program to combat malaria, Curry is the donor of three insecticide-treated mosquito nets for every three-point basket he makes.
8. Curry was not a member of the 2016 US Olympic basketball team.
9. In the 2015–16 regular season, the Golden State Warriors did a record-breaking 73 wins.
10. The Warriors is Curry's only team since he entered the league in 2009.

Note: Answers to even-numbered items can be found at the back of the book.

L-3   Idioms

Use each of the idioms listed below in a sentence that would be appropriate in some ACADEMIC CONTEXT —in a paper, in class discussion, and so on.

EXAMPLE

strike a chord

The company is hoping that its new commercials will strike a chord with the target demographic of college-age women.

1. have it both ways
2. with respect to
3. a case in point
4. across the board

5. a leg up
6. a team player
7. slam dunk
8. cover all the bases

L-4   Words Often Confused

EXERCISE 1/Using Commonly Confused Words. Underline the word in brackets that makes sense in each of the following sentences.

EXAMPLE

The Baroque period, which lasted from about 1600 to about 1750, [*sets* / *sits*] between the Renaissance and the Classical periods.

1. Most reference works about music say or [*imply* / *infer*] that Johann Sebastian Bach was the greatest composer of the Baroque period.
2. Bach's music [*lays* / *lies*] at a kind of intersection of the northern German contrapuntal style and the lively Italian style.
3. Bach's works were almost forgotten after his death, but [*than* / *then*] in the nineteenth century his reputation grew.

4. Bach [*lead* / *led*] other composers to create harpsichord concertos, a genre he invented.

5. Bach's full body of work also [*composes* / *comprises*] church and secular cantatas, a mass, preludes, fugues, sonatas, and suites.

6. Compared with the heavy texture of Baroque music, the Classical style became known for [*its* / *it's*] lightness and simplicity.

7. The [*principal* / *principle*] composers of the Classical period were Franz Joseph Haydn, Wolfgang Amadeus Mozart, and Ludwig van Beethoven.

8. Their genius produced [*sensual* / *sensuous*] string quartets, symphonies, and operas.

9. The piano [*raised* / *rose*] to prominence over the harpsichord and clavichord in the Classical period.

10. [*As* / *Like*] the aristocracy had once enjoyed music in the courts of mighty rulers, the growing middle class in the Classical period experienced it at public concerts.

EXERCISE 2 / Using Commonly Confused Words. Underline the word in brackets that makes sense in each of the following sentences.

EXAMPLE
During the Romantic period, the expression of emotion became a new [*criteria* / <u>*criterion*</u>] for judging music.

1. Beethoven's Ninth Symphony is longer by a significant [*percent* / *percentage*] than his earlier symphonies.

2. In general, Romantic music is more complex [*than* / *then*] earlier music.

3. Two new forms of music during the Romantic period were program music, [*that* / *which*] is music connected to a visual or to a narrative text, and lieder, [*that* / *which*] is music based on poetry.

4. Operas [*to* / *too*] became longer and more majestic during the Romantic period.

5. A large [*amount* / *number*] of new styles and forms developed in Western music after the Romantic period.

6. Beginning in the late 1800s, Western society in general and music in particular saw a shift toward more expression of individual personality and [*fewer* / *less*] limits on experimentation.

Note: Answers to even-numbered items can be found at the back of the book.

7. By the twenty-first century, opera fans could decide [*weather /
   whether*] to attend operas by Philip Glass and John Adams that
   included multimedia elements.

8. Meanwhile, the operetta of the Romantic period evolved into musical
   theater such as *West Side Story*, which makes many [*allusions /
   illusions*] to Shakespeare's *Romeo and Juliet*.

9. "Popular music" refers to the tunes the average person listens to
   [*everyday / every day*].

10. Music historians have analyzed the relationships [*among / between*]
    the many genres of popular music.

EXERCISE 3 / Editing Commonly Confused Words. Edit the following
sentences as necessary to make them appropriate in ACADEMIC CON-
TEXTS . Write "correct" if everything in the sentence is appropriate.

> **EXAMPLE**
>   that
> One reason ~~why~~ Jelly Roll Morton gained new fame in the 1990s was
> the Broadway production of *Jelly's Last Jam*.

1. Some say that only the United States could of given birth to jazz.

2. New Orleans jazz, swing, big band jazz, bebop, cool jazz, hard bop,
   etc., are subcategories of jazz.

3. Hopefully, new performers will come along to revive the fusion of
   jazz and rock that was popular in the 1960s and 1970s.

4. The reason for the falling off of fusion in the 1980s and beyond is
   because of a revived interest in traditional, or pure, jazz at that time.

5. Smooth jazz has its detractors, but supporters call it very unique—
   a very easy-to-listen-to jazz.

6. A lot of people learned about jazz through Ken Burns's 2001
   documentary series for PBS.

7. Jazz fans say that recordings are alright, but there's no substitute for
   a live performance, when the musicians may try something new.

8. The internet is by far the top media for accessing all kinds of
   popular music.

9. People have always listened to music because it literally transports them to where they'd rather be.

10. Some of us now think we should have taken a course on jazz.

L-5   Prepositions

Fill in the blanks with "at," "on," or "in." Use one of those three PREPO-SITIONS even if another one makes sense.

> **EXAMPLE**
>
> Niagara Falls, ___*on*___ the US–Canadian border, was known to many tribes of Native Americans before Europeans settled ___*in*___ North America.

1. Old Faithful, _____ Yellowstone National Park, erupts _____ intervals of about seventy minutes _____ all seasons.

2. Washington State's Grand Coulee Dam, completed _____ 1942, sits _____ the Columbia River _____ the junction of Douglas, Okanogan, and Lincoln counties.

3. Noted _____ maps, El Morro is a national monument _____ western New Mexico; it consists of ruins of ancient sandstone pueblos with inscriptions made _____ the seventeenth and eighteenth centuries.

4. Another national monument, the Statue of Liberty, stands _____ Liberty Island _____ New York City's harbor; it is lit _____ night.

5. Guilford Courthouse National Military Park, established as a park _____ 1917, marks the site of a Revolutionary War battle _____ March 15, 1781, when Americans ended British power _____ the Carolinas.

6. Visitors to Acadia National Park _____ Mount Desert Island _____ Maine generally prefer to visit _____ the summer.

7. _____ the campus of the University of Virginia _____ Charlottesville, visitors can see the architecture of Thomas Jefferson; they can continue to take in his design _____ Monticello, his home nearby.

8. The Gettysburg Address was delivered _____ the military cemetery _____ Gettysburg, Pennsylvania, _____ November 19, 1863.

Note: Answers to even-numbered items can be found at the back of the book.

9. Companies offering tours of the Grand Canyon _____ airplanes operate almost every day but not _____ Christmas. Tourists can inquire online and get an answer _____ a few hours.

10. Information about the landmarks and other places mentioned _____ this exercise was found _____ printed reference works as well as _____ the internet.

L-6   Unnecessary Words

Editing Out Unnecessary Words. Edit the following sentences to eliminate any empty words, wordiness, or redundancy.

EXAMPLE

The spring and summer months mean tornado season for many who live in the ~~middle areas of the country farther from the coasts.~~ central United States.

1. Tornado Alley is the nickname given to the area around northern Texas, Oklahoma, Kansas, and Nebraska, where tornados tend to occur more often than in other parts of the country.

2. There has been a pattern over the last few years in the United States of seeing more than a thousand tornados a year, the majority of which touch down in Tornado Alley.

3. It used to be the case that residents of Tornado Alley got little notice or warning in the event that a storm was on its way.

4. When they saw a low cloud that was large in size, grayish-yellow in color, and shaped like a funnel, they knew they had to race quickly to a storm shelter.

5. Gary England, chief meteorologist at Oklahoma City's Channel 9 and the area's most famous TV weather personality, has dedicated his work and career to tracking tornados and predicting their course.

6. He is a hero among the local residents living in that area.

7. Prior to the time when England persuaded Channel 9 to invest in Doppler radar, people had less than a minute's warning of a tornado; now, they have more than twenty.

8. At the time that a tornado hits, England and his team of meteorologists hunker down in the station office around their multicolored radar screens, while the rest of Oklahoma City watches them.

9. According to Oklahomans, you're able to guess that a storm is apparently going to be very bad when Gary England removes his jacket.

10. Some scientists believe that tornados at this point in time are more severe and are causing more damage than in the past due to the existence of climate change.

L-6b "There Is," "It Is"

Rewrite each of the following sentences so that it no longer begins with an **EXPLETIVE**. Begin each rewrite with the words in brackets.

EXAMPLE

There was civilization in Mesopotamia between 4000 and 3000 BCE, long before it developed in the Americas. [Civilization developed]

Civilization developed in Mesopotamia between 4000 and 3000 BCE, long before it developed in the Americas.

---

1. It was 2500 BCE when Neolithic cultures in Mexico began to grow squash, beans, chilies, and corn. [Neolithic cultures in Mexico]

2. It was the growth of such crops that enabled the Neolithic cultures to settle in villages. [The growth of such crops]

3. Then there arose the Olmec, the earliest civilization in the Americas. [Then the Olmec]

4. Traditionally, there were two conditions required for a culture to earn the label "civilization." [Traditionally, two conditions]

5. First, it was necessary for the culture to form settled agricultural communities. [First, the culture]

6. Second, there had to develop urban centers with religious and social power structures made up of literate leaders. [Second, urban centers]

7. It was the Zapotec people who overtook the Olmec around 400 BCE. [The Zapotec people]

Note: Answers to even-numbered items can be found at the back of the book.

8. About the same time but farther south, there was the beginning of the great civilization of the Maya. [About the same time but farther south, the great civilization of the Maya]

9. There developed out of Olmec, Zapotec, and Maya contributions Mesoamerican civilization, noted for its monumental buildings, calendars, ritual ballgames, and systems of counting and writing. [Mesoamerican civilization]

10. It is also noteworthy that Mesoamericans sacrificed humans to their corn goddess and other deities. [Notably, Mesoamericans]

L-7   Adjectives and Adverbs

L-7a Editing Adjectives and Adverbs

Edit the following sentences to correct any errors with **ADJECTIVES** or **ADVERBS**. Write "correct" after sentences without any errors.

> **EXAMPLE**
> Michael Lewis's book *Moneyball* tells how the Oakland A's baseball
> team learned new ways to predict which prospects would play ~~good~~ well in
> the years ahead.

1. *Moneyball* looks close at the Oakland A's and their general manager, Billy Beane.

2. By choosing prospects more careful, the A's became competitive with the New York Yankees, who had much more money to spend.

3. Beane succeeded with players who had been playing bad by such traditional standards as batting average, runs batted in, and stolen bases—and so weren't highly valued by other teams.

4. When he was a young player, Beane himself had been widely hailed by scouts but went on not to do so good.

5. Beane and those scouts may have felt badly about his lackluster performance after such high expectations.

6. As a manager with a small budget, Beane knew that his team's odds of success seemed bad. Looking for a better way to pick players, he turned to a kind of statistics called "sabermetrics."

7. A sabermetrics statistician showed him that players who hadn't been highly valued by traditional standards actually looked good when measured by other criteria.

8. The undervalued players scored well on many measures that scouts and managers had not taken as serious as the traditional ones.

9. After *Moneyball* was published, other teams hired sabermetric statisticians as quick as they could.

10. Both copies of the book and tickets to the movie version sold well.

L-7b Comparatives and Superlatives

Fill in the blank in each of the following sentences with the appropriate comparative or superlative form of the word in brackets.

> **EXAMPLE**
> Many people are fascinated by dinosaurs, perhaps because researchers know _less_ about them than about modern-day animals. [little]

1. Researchers believe that the _____ dinosaurs lived roughly 243 million years ago. [early]

2. One of the _____ dinosaurs that we know of is the *Nyasasaurus parringtoni*, whose bones were discovered in the 1930s. [ancient]

3. With its neck extended, the *Sauroposeidon proteles* would have reached roughly 59 feet, which is _____ than the Hollywood sign. [high]

4. The *Stegosaurus stenops*, a plant eater with a spiked tail and distinctive bones on its back, is one of the _____ dinosaurs. [famous]

5. The _____ dinosaur fossil is from a *Tyrannosaurus rex* named Sue; it sold for $8.3 million at auction. [costly]

6. The neck of a sauropod dinosaur could extend _____ than the neck of any other animal. [far]

Note: Answers to even-numbered items can be found at the back of the book.

7. Birds are the only living dinosaurs; their _____ relatives are members of the order Crocodilia, which includes crocodiles and alligators. [close]

8. The world's _____ bird, the bee hummingbird, weighs about the same as a penny. [small]

9. The dinosaur that many kids like _____ is the *Tyrannosaurus rex*, or T-Rex. [good]

10. It was probably _____ to be an *Apatosaurus* than a *Tyrannosaurus*, because the *Apatosaurus* dinosaurs had longer life spans. [good]

L-7c Placing Modifiers Carefully

Edit the passage below to correct any **MODIFIERS** that are misplaced, ambiguous, or dangling, or that split an **INFINITIVE** awkwardly.

EXAMPLE

The Revolutionary War saw each side trying to ~~once and for all~~ win an
advantage/ but for years first one side and then the other gained the
upper hand.

The colonists protested in 1764 and 1765 against taxes that Britain had placed on imports of sugar and printed matter using the slogan "No taxation without representation." In 1766, the British agreed to repeal the taxes when the colonists stopped buying all British products. In 1767, however, the British placed other taxes on the colonists, who proceeded to again boycott imports from Britain. Sending four thousand soldiers to Boston in response to the boycott, the stage was set for violence, and indeed nervous British soldiers shot and killed protesting colonists in what became known as the Boston Massacre.

After the 1767 taxes were repealed and the British troops withdrawn, relative peace resumed in Boston until 1773. In December of that year, protesting the British monopoly on importing tea into Boston and its delivery only to merchants loyal to Britain, three ships in Boston Harbor were boarded by colonists and all cases of tea thrown overboard. This so-called Boston Tea Party was soon followed by anti-British tea parties in other colonies. Though not amounting to acts of war, the Boston Tea

Party's inspirational effect led many colonists to begin preparing for armed resistance to the British, who they expected would soon attack them. In April 1775, Paul Revere and colleagues alerted Boston-area residents on horseback that British troops would soon enter the towns of Lexington and Concord. The British killed eight Minutemen in Lexington, battles followed in Concord, and the British suffered significant losses.

In January 1776, Thomas Paine wrote, printed, and distributed *Common Sense,* an argument in defense of independence for the colonies. Half a million copies sold quickly, and public opinion began to shift significantly. Still, every colonist was not supporting the revolution; historians estimate that about a third of the population favored separation from Britain, with another third opposed and the rest not caring much either way. Meanwhile, hostilities continued between the rebels and British troops. In June 1776, the Second Continental Congress, with delegates representing all thirteen colonies, appointed a committee to as quickly as possible prepare a document announcing independence from Britain. Congress formally adopted the Declaration of Independence on July 4, 1776.

While fighting the British for five more years, the French and Prussians aided the new nation. Finally, in October 1781, the British general Charles Cornwallis said that after a twenty-one-day siege by the Americans and French in Yorktown, Virginia, he would surrender. This event ended the American Revolution on the battlefield.

Note: Answers to even-numbered items can be found at the back of the book.

L-8   Articles

L-8a, c Using "A," "An," or No Article

Insert the ARTICLE "a" or "an" as appropriate in the following sentences. If an article is not required, write "no article" after the sentence.

> **EXAMPLE**
> Chef, caterer, cooking instructor, and cookbook author Amy Cotler says that __*a*__ locavore is "anyone who seeks out and savors foods grown, raised, or produced close to home."

1. The main principle of the locavore movement is to eat only fresh, in-season, local foods. _____ additional principle is to dry, ferment, pickle, or can part of the harvest for later consumption.

2. Even if it is grown in an environmentally friendly way, local food is not necessarily _____ organic food.

3. When you bite into an heirloom apple grown locally and it tastes the same today as it would have sixty years earlier, you can say that you are having _____ historic experience.

4. Restaurants catering to locavores see themselves as providing _____ unique and valuable (if sometimes expensive) dining option.

5. Most locavores in New England won't eat _____ corn or tomatoes before August.

6. While some people may think that eating fresh corn every day for a month sounds like _____ one-note diet, locavores savor corn during the peak of its season.

7. They may even have _____ ear of corn for breakfast.

8. Locavores consider it _____ honor to shop at a nearby farm.

9. They also try to persuade supermarkets and even big-box stores to feature locally produced or at least locally processed foods—for example, _____ milk or coffee beans.

10. For both _____ overview of and plenty of details about eating local, see the website *FoodPrint*.

L-8b–c Using "The" or No Article

In each of the following sentences, write "the" in any blank where it is required. If "the" is not required, write "no article" after the sentence.

EXAMPLE
Most people know that corn is associated with Kansas but that it grows in many other states as well and in countries throughout _the_ world.

1. Europeans did not know about corn, a crop native to the Americas, until _____ Age of Exploration, which began in the fifteenth century.

2. Native Americans explain the origin of corn in a variety of myths, but some of _____ myths tell about a god or goddess who dies and then makes corn available forever.

3. Today, corn is used as _____ livestock feed, human food, and raw material.

4. People often insist that their local corn is _____ best in the country.

5. Companies such as _____ Kellogg's have long manufactured and sold corn flakes and other cereals.

6. Two brothers, _____ Kelloggs, contributed to the original product, which came about by accident.

7. _____ other brands of cereal include Post and General Mills.

8. Erewhon is _____ one, but not the only, brand of organic corn flakes.

9. In the United States, corn is especially associated with _____ Midwest.

10. Corn is considered _____ most important crop in the United States, but it does not have as much nutritional value as other cereal grains do.

Note: Answers to even-numbered items can be found at the back of the book.

L-9   Respectful and Inclusive Language

L-9a Avoiding Stereotypes

Edit the following sentences to eliminate any stereotypes or unnecessary references to a person's group affiliation—and explain how you came to your decision. If the sentence doesn't contain any problematic language, write "no problematic language."

> **EXAMPLE**
> The ~~asexual~~ painter whose work was featured at the gallery last month has focused on landscapes his entire career.
>
> *The fact that the painter is asexual isn't relevant in the context of this sentence.*

1. The Jewish bank on 3rd Street is uniquely adept at handling its clients' assets and has been a fixture of the community for over 30 years.

2. The local food bank, which is run by the town's aging mayor, is organizing a holiday drive.

3. Despite being Asian, Ted excelled in the humanities and struggled with math.

4. Ben, who is open about his family's financial insecurity, says the short notice that the university gave students to vacate the dorms displayed a lack of understanding for students whose financial situations make moving home difficult.

5. The blonde head cheerleader wasn't allowed to participate in her sophomore year because of her failing grades.

6. Surprisingly enough, the obese receptionist who worked the afternoon shift ate mostly salad for lunch.

7. An anonymous billionaire has pledged a million dollars over the next ten years to combat urban homelessness.

8. The trans ophthalmologist who specialized in macular degeneration could predict how well a treatment would work on a particular patient.

9. None of the people on the city council went to college, but most of them are actually pretty smart.

10. Rashida, who wrote a new play about LGBTQ+ youth in a small town, told the local reporter that she identifies as bisexual and that it was important to her to include bisexual characters in her play.

L-9b   Using Preferred Terms

Edit the following sentences to include only the terms people use for themselves and to eliminate any unnecessary references to identity or disability. If necessary, revise so that each sentence uses **PERSON-FIRST LANGUAGE**. Write "correct" after any sentence in which no changes are needed.

> **EXAMPLE**
> Tables will be spaced far enough apart to allow ample paths for ~~wheelchair-bound~~ guests *using wheelchairs.*

1. The fund-raising committee's meeting began tensely when Abigail referred to Belle with the wrong pronoun ("he" instead of "they"); however, Belle tactfully corrected her, Abigail apologized to him, and the meeting ended up being productive.
2. The board of directors, whose president is a disabled biracial woman, notified staff that the fund-raising committee should reflect the ethnic and gender-identity diversity of the community as a whole.
3. While the guests are mingling and enjoying wine and appetizers, local rap artists The Carat Sisters will perform.
4. The committee plans to kick off the evening's formal program with a Land Acknowledgment Statement delivered by a member of a local Indian group.
5. For the annual fund-raising dinner, Elvira Patel, the asthmatic chef, has designed a menu that accommodates the dietary restrictions of as many guests as possible.
6. Many local residents pledged to support Black-owned businesses, including the recently opened Ethiopian café on River Street.
7. The dessert menu will include sugar-free options for the diabetics on our guest list.
8. All speeches will be interpreted in ASL by Leroy Bishop, whose work in the Deaf community has earned him much respect and recognition.

Note: Answers to even-numbered items can be found at the back of the book.

L-9c **Editing Out Sexist Language**

EXERCISE 1 / Editing Out Sexist Language. Edit the following sentences to eliminate any **SEXIST LANGUAGE**. Write "no sexist language" after any sentence that contains appropriate sex or gender references.

EXAMPLE
Someone may join the Marines to serve our country but then realize
that the leadership training is what will change ~~his~~ ^their^ life forever.

1. In general, a nurse values her role in the healing process.
2. Seeing someone regain his smile again after a few days in the hospital satisfies a nurse's need for positive feedback.
3. A policeman's job often consists of long stretches of tedium interrupted by brief periods of high stress.
4. Health-care workers today explain to a person who tests positive for HIV that he has a much better chance for long-term survival than an HIV-positive person did in the 1980s.
5. Many news reports saw the healthcare professionals who treated COVID-19 patients as a brotherhood of rescue workers.
6. Before applying to the Air Force Academy, a student should ask himself if he is prepared mentally and physically to meet the demands of the school and of service to his country.
7. Esther Duflo, a French economist currently teaching at MIT, won the 2002 Elaine Bennett Research Prize, which is awarded by the American Economic Association to a woman economist under the age of forty.
8. Jared Flood is a male knitter and knitwear designer who writes the blog *Brooklyn Tweed*.
9. Psychologists claim that at times a baby studies his parents' mouths to learn how to make a sound that is new to him.
10. As you are doing in this exercise, a feminist tries to eliminate sexist terms from her speaking and writing.

EXERCISE 2 / Revising Sexist Sentences. For each of the following mottoes, proverbs, and quotations, suggest an alternative wording that expresses the same meaning but eliminates **SEXIST LANGUAGE**.

EXAMPLE

Let ~~each~~ become all ~~he is~~ capable of being.

(us) ... *(we are)*

—Original Motto of the State University of New York

1. From each according to his ability, to each according to his needs.

   —Karl Marx

2. He who dies with the most toys wins.   —Malcolm Forbes

3. He who does things for others does things for himself.

   —Motto of Perse School, England

4. Everyone must row with the oars he has.   —English proverb

5. The best surgeon is he that hath been hacked himself.

   —English proverb

L-10   Pronouns and Gender

L-10b Singular "They"

In the following exercise, seven college friends are organizing a party. Take note of each organizer's respective pronoun (*they*: Reese, Blake; *she*: Jazmine, Donna, Lin; *he*: Jimmy, Aziz). For each set of sentences below, identify the option with the clearest pronoun references.

EXAMPLE

A. For the music, Lin and Jimmy propose hiring a DJ, but Reese wants to hire Ornery Shoelace, their brother's band, to play, and they spend an hour arguing about the choice.

B. For the music, Lin and Jimmy propose hiring a DJ, but Reese wants to hire Ornery Shoelace, their brother's band, to play, and the three organizers spend an hour arguing about the choice.

Option B. Since we know that Reese's pronoun is "they," we can safely interpret that Ornery Shoelace is the band of Reese's brother. Sentence A, however, has an unclear pronoun reference for who is doing the arguing; sentence B uses the phrase "the three organizers" to clarify.

Note: Answers to even-numbered items can be found at the back of the book.

1. A. Blake and Donna offered to contact a DJ who lives on the block and ask how much she would charge the group for a three-hour daytime gig.
   B. Blake and Donna offered to contact a DJ who lives on the block and ask how much she would charge them for a three-hour daytime gig.
2. A. Aziz and Jazmine agree with Reese about preferring live music to a DJ, but they don't want the performers to be Ornery Shoelace.
   B. Aziz and Jazmine agree with Reese about preferring live music to a DJ, but unlike Reese, they don't want the performers to be Ornery Shoelace.
3. A. When Reese found out that Aziz and Jazmine don't really like Ornery Shoelace, their feelings were hurt.
   B. Reese's feelings were hurt when they found out that Jazmine and Donna don't really like Ornery Shoelace.
4. A. By a vote of 5 to 2, the group decided to hire the DJ who lives on the block, but Reese was such a good sport that the group offered to ask Ornery Shoelace to donate the use of a pair of speakers for the event.
   B. By a vote of 5 to 2, the group decided to hire the DJ who lives on the block, but Reese was such a good sport that they offered to ask Ornery Shoelace to donate the use of their speakers for the event.

L-11   Englishes

Each of the following passages is from a classic novel. Choose one and rewrite it in edited academic English. Which version do you prefer, and why?

From *The Adventures of Huckleberry Finn*, by Mark Twain

Huck has just set out in the canoe that he had hidden in the bushes until the time was right for his escape.

I got out amongst the driftwood, and then laid down in the bottom of the canoe and let her float. I laid there, and had a good rest and a smoke out of my pipe, looking away into the sky; not a cloud in it. The sky looks ever so deep when you lay down on your back in the moonshine; I never knowed it before. And how far a body can hear on the water such nights! I heard people talking at the ferry landing. I heard what they said, too—every word of it. One man said it was getting towards the long days and the short nights now. T'other one said this warn't one of the short ones, he reckoned—and then they laughed, and he said it over again, and they laughed again; then they waked up another fellow and told him, and laughed, but he didn't laugh; he ripped out something brisk, and said let him alone. The first fellow said he 'lowed to tell it to his old woman—she would think it was pretty good; but he said that warn't nothing to some things he had said in his time. I heard one man say it was nearly three o'clock, and he hoped daylight wouldn't wait more than about a week longer. After that the talk got further and further away, and I couldn't make out the words any more; but I could hear the mumble, and now and then a laugh, too, but it seemed a long ways off.

From *Pride and Prejudice,* by Jane Austen

Elizabeth Bennet has just refused a marriage proposal. Her mother, Mrs. Bennet, insists that she accept it and goes to her husband's study to ask him to back her up. She is astonished that he does not.

"My dear," replied her husband, "I have two small favours to request. First, that you will allow me the free use of my understanding on the present occasion; and secondly, of my room. I shall be glad to have the library to myself as soon as may be."

Not yet, however, in spite of her disappointment in her husband, did Mrs. Bennet give up the point. She talked to Elizabeth again and again; coaxed and threatened her by turns. She endeavoured to secure Jane in her interest; but Jane, with all possible mildness, declined interfering; and Elizabeth, sometimes with real earnestness, and sometimes with playful gaiety, replied to her attacks. Though her manner varied, however, her determination never did.

Note: Answers to even-numbered items can be found at the back of the book.

P-1   Commas

P-1a–b With Coordinating Conjunctions and Introductory Words

Insert commas wherever they are needed between INDEPENDENT CLAUSES or after introductory words. If a sentence is correct as given, write "correct."

> **EXAMPLE**
> Christine Ohlman sang for a long time with the Saturday Night Live Band, but she eventually moved on to a band named Rebel Montez.

1. Known as the Beehive Queen Ohlman performs music influenced by the blues and other styles.
2. Nick Zammuto composed the music for the film *Achantè* and formed a four-piece band.
3. Catherine Russell may sing old blues and jazz songs but she makes them sound brand-new.
4. Morgan Taylor created the animated character Gustafer Yellowgold and claims that the character came from the sun.
5. A dragon lives in Gustafer's fireplace and Gustafer has a pet eel.
6. Under the direction of Anouk Van Dijk the Australian dance group Chunky Move receives rave reviews.
7. In a different vein Darrah Carr Dance blends Irish step and modern dance.
8. Jeff and Jane Hudson issued the album *Flesh* in the 1980s so thirty years later it was time to reissue it.
9. As their fans know the Hudsons were pioneers in electronic music.
10. Incidentally all seven acts mentioned in this exercise have performed at the Massachusetts Museum of Contemporary Art.

P-1c To Separate Items in a Series

Insert commas as needed to separate items in a series. If a sentence is correct as given, write "correct."

EXAMPLE

"A Scandal in Bohemia," "The Red-Headed League," and "A Case of Identity" are the first Sherlock Holmes stories written by Arthur Conan Doyle.

1. *The Girl with the Dragon Tattoo The Girl Who Played with Fire* and *The Girl Who Kicked the Hornets' Nest* make up a popular series of novels.

2. Which of the following titles was published first: *Harry Potter and the Half-Blood Prince Harry Potter and the Deathly Hallows Harry Potter and the Goblet of Fire* or *Harry Potter and the Order of the Phoenix*?

3. "Long," "complicated," and "engrossing" are three words that some readers say describe the Harry Potter novels.

4. Paula Fox's novel *The Slave Dancer* conveys the horrors of capturing transporting and selling Africans to become slaves.

5. As a young man, Ralph Ellison was advised to read great authors—for example, Joseph Conrad and Fyodor Dostoyevsky.

6. J. R. R. Tolkien earned a graduate degree in the study of languages worked on the *Oxford English Dictionary* and became a professor at Oxford University before he wrote *The Hobbit*.

7. After *The Hobbit*, Tolkien created the Lord of the Rings trilogy, made up of *The Fellowship of the Ring The Two Towers* and *The Return of the King*.

8. Mark Twain's novel *The Adventures of Huckleberry Finn* shows the best and the worst qualities of American society examines Huck's moral struggle over helping Jim to escape and explores issues of race and identity.

9. *The Color Purple*, by Alice Walker, won a Pulitzer Prize and an American Book Award and was made into a film.

10. The first trilogy by Jane Yolen consists of *Dragon's Blood Heart's Blood* and *A Sending of Dragons*.

Note: Answers to even-numbered items can be found at the back of the book.

P-1d To Set Off Nonessential Elements

Add or delete commas as necessary in each of the following sentences. If a sentence is correct as given, write "correct."

> **EXAMPLES**
>
> Quarterback Tim Tebow, who went from the University of Florida to the National Football League, attracted attention for praying on the football field.
>
> "Tebowing," a new word formed from a proper noun (like "Googling"), referred to his signature kneel after a touchdown. *correct*

1. Former New England star Tom Brady has called Joe Montana who played for San Francisco in the 1980s and 1990s inspiring.

2. Brady and Montana are the only National Football League players, who have been named most valuable player more than once in both the league and the Super Bowl.

3. The first quarterback in NFL history who led a team to ten division titles was Tom Brady.

4. New Orleans quarterback Drew Brees who was born in Dallas was named after Dallas Cowboy wide receiver Drew Pearson.

5. Brees was the first quarterback in NFL history to score more than four hundred yards passing in three consecutive postseason games, which he played in 2010 and 2011.

6. Quarterback Cam Newton became the third player in NFL history to do all these things in the same year: (1) win a national championship, (2) be the first pick in the NFL draft, and (3) receive the Heisman Trophy which goes to the best college football player.

7. Newton, who was the first NFL rookie to throw for four hundred yards in his debut game, led the Panthers to the Super Bowl in 2016.

8. In late 2013, Green Bay quarterback Aaron Rodgers led the NFL in his passer rating, 104.9.

9. Passer rating is based on a formula, that uses a passer's completion percentage, passing yardage, touchdowns, and interceptions.

10. In fact, at that point, Rodgers was the only passer whose career passer rating exceeded 100.0.

P-1e–i Commas Used for Other Purposes

Insert commas wherever necessary in the following sentences. If a sentence is correct as given, write "correct."

EXAMPLE

When Tina Fey joined the writing team on *Saturday Night Live*, you may be surprised to know, she was the only woman on the team.

1. Tina Fey was born on May 18 1970 in Upper Darby Pennsylvania.

2. After years of training in comedy at Chicago's Second City theater company, Fey was hired in 1997 as a writer for *Saturday Night Live*.

3. October 11 2006 was another important date in Fey's life: the pilot aired on NBC for the situation comedy *30 Rock*.

4. The characters and plot lines of *30 Rock* as most of the show's fans know grew out of Fey's experiences at *Saturday Night Live*.

5. The title of the show of course is the nickname for the GE Building, home to NBC Studios in New York City. NBC's complete address is 30 Rockefeller Plaza New York NY 10112.

6. Episodes of *30 Rock* were shot however at Silvercup Studios in Long Island City New York, in the borough of Queens.

7. When *Vanity Fair* magazine asked Fey for her motto in May 2011, she answered "Stop reaching for the stars!" At the time, Fey had been writing, acting, producing, and caring for her first child. Her answer suggests that she was tired doesn't it?

8. In a typical line on *30 Rock*, Liz Lemon says "Check this out Jack. Tile samples. First I redo the bathroom, then I redo the whole apartment, and then the world." Jack responds "I'm impressed Lemon. You're talking like a winner."

9. On the topic of her resemblance to Sarah Palin, Fey said "I was resistant to acknowledge there was a resemblance. But my kid saw her and said 'That's Mommy,' so I thought 'Oh great.'"

10. Is "Tina" short for "Christina"? No Tina Fey's full name is Elizabeth Stamatina Fey, reflecting her partly Greek ancestry. Furthermore she has given Greek middle names to her daughters.

Note: Answers to even-numbered items can be found at the back of the book.

P-1j Unnecessary Commas

Edit the following sentences to delete any unnecessary commas. If the sentence is correct as given, write "correct."

EXAMPLE
The Mark Twain Prize for American Humor goes back to 1998, when Richard Pryor won it. Recent winners have been stars such as/Will Ferrell, Tina Fey, and Ellen DeGeneres.

1. Will Ferrell, the 2011 prize winner, was born in Irvine, California. He earned a degree in sports journalism and, went on to work as a sportscaster on a weekly television show for a while.

2. Ferrell's impersonations go back to high school, where he made, public address announcements in disguised voices.

3. Even earlier, Ferrell had shown, that his humor could entertain his elementary school classmates.

4. What Tina Fey got in 2010, was more than the Mark Twain Prize itself. In addition, she had the satisfaction of knowing that she was the youngest winner ever.

5. "Well deserved!," commented one of Fey's fans on the website of the Kennedy Center, which administers the Mark Twain Prize.

6. A comic who's considered one of the most influential performers of the twentieth century, accepted the Mark Twain Prize in 2012. The 2012 winner, Ellen DeGeneres, has been praised as a writer, an actor, and a humanitarian.

7. DeGeneres once said, "Never follow anyone else's path, unless you're in the woods and you're lost."

8. On June 22, 2008, the winner of the 2008 prize, George Carlin, died of heart failure. The award ceremony that fall at the Kennedy Center, celebrated his long and influential career.

9. "Why is the humor prize named for Mark Twain?," one might ask.

10. Twain once said, "Against the assault of laughter nothing can stand," and the recipients of the prize named for him, have proved him right.

P-2   Semicolons

Edit each of the following sentences to replace commas with semi-colons as necessary.

> **EXAMPLE**
> Most major sports organizations ban steroids/; still, some athletes rely on them.

1. Steroids are performance-enhancing drugs, indeed, they build muscle mass and strength, which lead to better results in competition.

2. Steroids are synthetic forms of the hormone testosterone, megadoses of steroids give users an unfair advantage.

3. Males in good health usually produce less than ten milligrams of testosterone a day, athletes on steroids swallow or inject hundreds of milligrams a day.

4. In adults, steroids cause rapid weight gain, problems with blood clotting, and heart attacks, in adolescents they can shut down bone growth.

5. Signs of steroid use are jaundice, or yellow skin, sudden combative behavior, excessive vomiting that lasts more than a few days, and swollen feet.

6. Athletes who later admitted steroid use include Mark McGwire and Barry Bonds, the baseball players, Marion Jones, the track and field athlete, and Lance Armstrong, the cyclist.

7. McGwire surpassed Roger Maris's season home-run record of sixty, Bonds beat McGwire's number and set the record for most career home runs as well.

8. In 2013, Alex Rodriguez was suspended for 211 games for allegedly using steroids, thirteen other major-league baseball players were also suspended, but A-Rod was the only one to appeal his suspension.

9. A 2012 report by the Associated Press claimed college football players use steroids, it suggested that colleges knowingly look the other way.

10. Books about steroid use in athletics include *Game of Shadows,* 2007, *Bases Loaded,* 2009, and *Steroids: A New Look,* 2011.

Note: Answers to even-numbered items can be found at the back of the book.

P-3   End Punctuation

Add a period, a question mark, or an exclamation point as appropriate at the end of each of the following items.

> **EXAMPLE**
> Why do journalists seem so obsessed with writing about dogs?

1. In one week, a small-town paper offered articles about why dog obesity is increasing, whether dogs love their people, and what tail wagging means

2. The Association for Pet Obesity Prevention asked in 2012 how many dogs in America are overweight or obese

3. The startling answer was 52.5 percent

4. As with people, weighing too much can cause dogs to develop joint pain and diabetes

5. No wonder today's dogs are overweight: instead of working, as in past eras, domesticated dogs may sleep twenty-three hours a day

6. What motivates dogs more—food or love

7. The brain region that lights up when people expect pleasure lights up in dogs when they see a signal for a treat or sniff the scent of those who feed them

8. A positive event raises activity in the left side of a dog's brain, causing its tail to wag more to the right; a negative event causes wagging to the left

9. In a scientific experiment, dogs watching videos of right waggers stayed calm, but dogs watching left waggers acted anxious

10. What practical use can tail-wagging studies serve

P-4   Quotation Marks

P-4a–b With Direct Quotations, Long Quotations

Edit each of the items below, inserting any quotation marks that are necessary and removing those that do not belong. In some cases, you'll need to add or delete commas as well.

EXAMPLE

The film *12 Years a Slave* tells of Solomon Northup, a "free Black man," who was enslaved in Louisiana in 1841. It is, to quote a respected magazine, a "soberly powerful, beautiful film."

---

1. After reading Solomon Northup's 1853 autobiography, the director said, "The book reads like Anne Frank's diary but written ninety-seven years before.

2. The film was endorsed by Sean "Diddy" Combs, who called it very painful but very honest.

3. He continued, I beg all of you to take your kids, everybody, to see it.

4. "Stark, visceral and unrelenting, *12 Years a Slave* is not just a great film, said one British newspaper, but a necessary one."

5. Along the same lines, the *Rotten Tomatoes* consensus was, to quote the website, brilliant—and quite possibly essential—cinema.

6. Northup's book was republished in 1968 by a university press, which was quoted as calling him a shrewd observer of people and events.

7. In two consecutive sentences from the film's script, Northup (played by Chiwetel Ejiofor) says, "I do not want to survive." "I want to live."

8. The better-known 1855 autobiography of Frederick Douglass, an escaped slave, includes the following passage about his early years:
   > "I remember [my mother] only in her visits to me at Col. Lloyd's plantation, and in the kitchen of my old master. Her visits to me there were few in number, brief in duration, and mostly made in the night. The pains she took, and the toil she endured, to see me, tells me that a true mother's heart was hers, and that slavery had difficulty in paralyzing it with unmotherly indifference." (152)

Note: Answers to even-numbered items can be found at the back of the book.

9. The Library of America, which reissued Douglass's books in 1994, said on the dust jacket that "His autobiographical narratives stunned the world."

10. In one stunning scene, sixteen-year-old Douglass fights back when his master, Covey, strikes him. Covey asks, Are you going to resist, you scoundrel?

   Yes, sir, replies Douglass, steadily gazing Covey in the eye.

P-4c With Titles of Short Works

Add quotation marks as needed in the following sentences.

> **EXAMPLE**
> The final scene of the *Homeland* episode called "Game On" surprised viewers by showing that Carrie and Saul had been in cahoots.

1. Fritters, Fools, and Other Fruit Favorites is the title of one chapter in a cookbook devoted to early American desserts.

2. In another book, the brief essay Mint Snowball by Naomi Shihab Nye describes a mixture of shaved ice, mint syrup, and vanilla ice cream.

3. A Headstrong Boy is among the poems collected by Nye in the book *This Same Sky*.

4. In the *National Geographic* book *Complete Photography*, People & Pets is surely the most-read chapter.

5. After ten years spent sea kayaking around the world, an explorer wrote the article Alone in the Aleutians, recalling his experience traveling in Alaska.

6. A 2010 publication titled *Rolling Stone: The Beatles' 100 Greatest Songs* ranks I Want to Hold Your Hand as number 2.

7. In the *Mayo Clinic Family Health Book*, Complementary and Alternative Medicine is the title of the final chapter.

8. The 2009 book review Abraham Lincoln: Misery's Child tells of Lincoln's miserable early life.

9. The Tell-Tale Heart is one of the most famous American short stories.

10. The Raven and the Crow is one part of the long ancient poem called *Metamorphoses*.

P-4e **With Other Punctuation**

Edit each of the following sentences to put the punctuation mark given in brackets where it belongs.

EXAMPLE

John Lennon said that he'd received much praise for "Yesterday," but then he quickly added, "That is Paul's song, of course, and ^ Paul's baby." [comma]

---

1. Looking up at the balcony, John Lennon said, "For those in the cheap seats, I'd like ya to clap your hands to this one" then he went on to say, "The rest of you can just rattle your jewelry." [semicolon]

2. "We all looked up to John," Paul once said. "He was the quickest wit and the smartest" [period]

3. Lennon and Yoko Ono once held up a sign that said, "Don't hate what you don't understand" [exclamation point]

4. In 1970, Lennon was asked, "What do you think rock and roll will become?" He replied, "Whatever we make it" [period]

5. Asked why the Beatles' music was so infectious, Lennon said, "We didn't sound like everybody else" [period]

6. When did Lennon say, "If everyone demanded peace instead of another television set, then there'd be peace" [question mark]

7. "I don't believe in killing," Lennon once said, "whatever the reason" [period]

8. When asked how he would describe "Beatle music," Lennon responded with a question: "*Which* Beatle music do you mean" [question mark]

9. Consider the stylistic range in just three examples of "Beatle music" "I Want to Hold Your Hand," "Hey Jude," and "We Can Work It Out." [colon]

10. About "Give Peace a Chance," Lennon said, "In my secret heart, I wanted to write something that would take over 'We Shall Overcome'" [period]

Note: Answers to even-numbered items can be found at the back of the book.

P-4h Common Mistakes with Quotation Marks

Delete any unnecessary quotation marks in the following items. Write "correct" after any item in which the quotation marks are necessary.

> **EXAMPLE**
>
> In the 1980 election campaign, President Jimmy Carter and Vice President Walter Mondale used ⁄"attack politics⁄" against Carter's Republican challenger, Ronald Reagan. They lost.

1. President Ronald Reagan reportedly made fun of himself when he said, "The day after I was elected, I had my high school grades classified Top Secret."

2. "Back in the day," President Reagan was popular with many voters outside his political party.

3. "There you go again" was a notable Reagan response in a debate with Jimmy Carter during the 1980 campaign.

4. Reagan's reelection in 1984 was considered a "landslide."

5. The economic policies of the Reagan administration were based on a theory called "supply-side economics."

6. Many commentators acknowledged that Reagan succeeded in achieving the goal he described as "making the American people believe in themselves again."

7. Supposedly, after he was wounded in an assassination attempt, Reagan told the doctors who were about to operate on him that "he hoped they were all Republicans."

8. In a 1983 speech, Reagan called the Soviet Union "the evil empire," an attack that drew both praise and criticism.

9. One slogan associated with Reagan's foreign policy was "peace through strength."

10. Although the Iran-Contra "affair" blemished his record, Reagan remained a popular president.

P-5   Apostrophes

P-5a With Possessives

Edit each of the following items to correct any apostrophe errors. If a sentence is correct as given, write "correct."

EXAMPLE
The nation's health-care industry has frustrated many Americans for a long time now.

1. The attorney general of more than one state sued to block the 2010 federal law that requires individuals to have health insurance. But the attorney general's suit was unsuccessful.
2. Congress's own pre-2014 health-insurance system offered good benefits for representatives and senators.
3. Each representative and senator's premium for health insurance was paid in part by the government.
4. Does "paid in part by the government" mean at taxpayer's expense?
5. Some Americans think that everyone's medical insurance should be as generous as that available to members of Congress before 2014.
6. Others argue that every Americans' coverage should follow the model of Medicare.
7. Medicares' current beneficiaries include most people over sixty-five and those with long-term disabilities.
8. In the United States, unlike in some other countries, the typical doctors' employer is not the government.
9. Running a private medical practice these days, like that of Dr. Melanie Levitan and Dr. Michael Kaplan, means more than just diagnosing and treating people's illnesses.
10. Levitan's and Kaplan's practice, like many others, has merged with a firm that handles the business side of things so that the doctors have more time for their patients.

Note: Answers to even-numbered items can be found at the back of the book.

P-5d Common Mistakes with Apostrophes

Edit out any errors related to apostrophes.

EXAMPLE
The video game *Angry Bird's* was first released in 2009.
(Birds)

1. The game became popular because its addictive, witty, and cheap.
2. *Angry Birds* appeals to teenager's, adult's, and even four-year-old's.
3. It was first sold on Apples App Store.
4. Both the free limited version and the full-featured paid version have been downloaded million's of times.
5. The birds are angry at pigs that have stolen many bird's eggs.
6. So what are players to do? Their's is a straightforward mission.
7. Its up to each player to wipe out the pigs by launching birds directly at them and at structures that collapse on and kill the pigs.
8. *The Angry Birds Movie* debuted in May 2016 after nine month's of marketing.
9. Critic's had mixed reactions to the film.
10. The movie has a notable cast, including voicing by such actor's as Sean Penn, Maya Rudolph, and Peter Dinklage.

P-6   Other Punctuation

P-6a Colons

Insert a colon where needed in each of the numbered items below.

> **EXAMPLE**
>
> Singer-songwriter Justin Townes Earle lists the following influences, calling them his "short list": Woody Guthrie, Tom Waits, Elvis Costello, Patti Smith, Merle Haggard, Ray Charles, Doc Watson, Etta James, Johnny Cash, Lucinda Williams, and Elliot Smith.

1. Of the musicians Earle mentions, only three are women Patti Smith, Etta James, and Lucinda Williams.

2. The Rock and Roll Hall of Fame describes Patti Smith as follows "a bohemian New York poet and punk-rock artiste."

3. When she won Sweden's top music prize, Smith received this tribute "Patti Smith has demonstrated how much rock 'n' roll there is in poetry and how much poetry there is in rock 'n' roll."

4. Smith's accomplishments are wide-ranging beyond singing and song writing, she has lectured on poetry, won the National Book Award, and exhibited her own photographs.

5. Accepting the National Book Award for *Just Kids*, a memoir about her friendship with photographer Robert Mapplethorpe, Smith admitted that she'd always wanted to be an author "When I was a clerk at Scribner's bookstore, I always dreamed of writing a book of my own."

6. In his review of *Just Kids*, Edmund White notes that it's "full of memorable sentences," including this one "We were both praying for Robert's soul, he to sell it and I to save it."

7. The Rock and Roll Hall of Fame offers packages for visits by Girl Scouts or Boy Scouts, with free admission for their scout leaders in a ratio of 10 1.

8. Many visitors buy the book *The Rock and Roll Hall of Fame The First 25 Years*.

9. During the summer, the Rock and Roll Hall of Fame is open until 900 PM on Wednesdays and Saturdays.

Note: Answers to even-numbered items can be found at the back of the book.

10. The Hall of Fame offers educational programs for all ages toddlers, preteens, teenagers, and adults.

P-6b,c,f Dashes, Parentheses, Slashes

Edit each of the following sentences to insert dashes, parentheses, or slashes, where necessary.

EXAMPLE

In 2020, Daylight Saving Time in the United States started the second Sunday in March and ended the first Sunday in November—totaling almost eight months.

1. Because of the tilt of Earth on its axis, the length of daylight changes seasonally more hours in summer, fewer in winter across most of the planet.
2. You can guess the last word of this stanza of R. L. Stevenson's poem: "In winter I get up at night And dress by yellow candle-light. In summer quite the other way . . ."
3. When Daylight Saving Time starts in the spring, those who work during the daytime gain an hour of light after work.
4. Areas that use Daylight Saving Time also called Daylight Savings Time put clocks forward in the spring and then backward in the fall.
5. Modern Daylight Saving Time DST was first proposed in 1895 by an entomologist.
6. George Vernon Hudson 1867–1946 wanted more daylight in which to collect insects after he finished his day job.
7. The idea was not implemented until World War I, when Germany and Austria-Hungary adopted DST *Sommerzeit* in German in 1916 to save energy.
8. The United States first used DST in 1918. Today, not all of the country does so notably, Hawaii and part of Arizona do not.
9. Near the equator where the sun rises and sets at about the same time all year long nations generally do not use DST.
10. That DST is used by only a small number of people is obvious when you learn one fact Asian and African countries generally do not adopt it.

P-7   Hyphens

Edit the following sentences to correct any errors in hyphenation. If a sentence has no errors, write "correct" after it. Check a dictionary if necessary.

EXAMPLES

Before *The Daily Show with Jon Stewart* and *The Colbert Report,* Stephen Colbert worked with Amy Sedaris and Paul Dinello on *Exit 57,* a half-hour TV comedy series.

Some consider Colbert an achingly funny actor; others do not.

1. *The Colbert Report,* a spinoff of *The Daily Show,* launched in late 2005 and ended in 2014.
2. Stephen Colbert played a caricature of a conservative host of a talk-show.
3. Colbert was forty one years old when he launched his own show.
4. On *The Daily Show,* Colbert created the role of a self-important correspondent.
5. Most of the humor on *The Colbert Report* was political, but not all: a recurring joke was about Colbert's deepseated fear of bears.
6. The program's No Fact Zone promoted nonfacts.
7. Colbert had a one man crusade against the Supreme Court's decision that corporations have the same rights as people when contributing to political campaigns.
8. Colbert is still a highly-prized performer; he now hosts *The Late Show* on CBS.
9. He is also well known as a devout Roman Catholic who teaches Sunday school.
10. The show had a nine year run on Comedy Central.

Note: Answers to even-numbered items can be found at the back of the book.

P-8   Capitalization

Edit the following sentences to correct any errors in capitalization. If a sentence has no errors, write "correct" after it.

EXAMPLE

How does it feel to achieve business success at such a young age as
~~mark zuckerberg~~, the ~~Cofounder~~ of ~~facebook~~, did?
Mark Zuckerberg   cofounder   Facebook

1. As of april 2020, the social network site, which got its start at Harvard university, had 2.5 billion monthly active users, over 190 million of them in the united states.

2. In 2012, Free Press published a book by Lori Andrews, a professor at Chicago-kent college of law, about the social network giant.

3. The American bar association calls Andrews "A lawyer with a literary bent."

4. The book by professor Andrews is titled *I know who you are and I saw what you did: social networks and the death of privacy*.

5. The first sentence of the book reads, "when David Cameron became Britain's prime minister, he made an appointment to talk to another head of state—Mark Zuckerberg."

6. Sheryl K. Sandberg is chief operating officer of facebook; previously, she worked for google.

7. Sandberg was also Chief of Staff for Lawrence Summers when he was Secretary of the Treasury.

8. She is famous for encouraging women to take on big challenges, and her book *Lean in* offers advice for how to do so.

9. Some critics question Sandberg's focus on "women running the world as is," wishing she would instead look at "women doing our part to change the world."

10. Sandberg was born in Washington, DC, but had a floridian childhood before she headed north to Harvard.

P-9   Italics

In each of the following sentences, underline any words that require italics. If none of the words in a sentence require italics, write "correct" after that sentence.

> **EXAMPLE**
> In the Wall Street Journal, Joe Morgenstern called the movie about Facebook "contentious."

1. The Social Network, a film released in 2010, combines fact and fiction about an idea of Harvard student Mark Zuckerberg that he and some of his classmates turned into a succès fou.
2. The screenplay was adapted from The Accidental Billionaires, a 2009 book by Ben Mezrich.
3. While The Social Network lost out to The King's Speech for the Academy Award for best picture, the former won Oscars for best adapted screenplay, original score, and film editing.
4. Many critics, including Peter Travers in Rolling Stone magazine, praised the Facebook film, while Zuckerberg pointed out its inaccuracies.
5. Two earlier versions of the Facebook site were called Facemash and Thefacebook.
6. Harvard has not allowed filming on its campus since Love Story, a 1970 release, so The Social Network was filmed elsewhere.
7. The movie about building Facebook is hardly the first time Hollywood has woven fiction into real-life events; the 1912 sinking of the ocean liner Titanic is another story that was changed in a film.
8. Not everyone loves Facebook; some people consider it the antisocial network.

Note: Answers to even-numbered items can be found at the back of the book.

P-10   Abbreviations

Edit the following sentences to abbreviate or spell out words and phrases according to the conventions of **ACADEMIC WRITING**.

EXAMPLE
Martin Luther King Jr. was born in Atlanta, ~~Ga.~~ *Georgia.*

1. Martin Luther King Junior Day is celebrated in January.
2. The civil rights leader is the only person not a president to have a monument in his honor on the Mall in DC.
3. Doctor King was born in Jan. 1929 and was assassinated in Apr. 1968.
4. King received his doctorate from BU in Mass. in 1955.
5. King's book *Where Do We Go from Here: Chaos or Community?* was published in NY in 1967.
6. Many lines from his speeches and other writing have become classic American phrases, e.g., "Free at last!" and "I have a dream."
7. King did not hesitate to challenge presidents—whether JFK on civil rights or LBJ on the Vietnam War—and his activism earned him many enemies.
8. The Federal Bureau of Investigation kept an extensive file on King.
9. His father, Martin Luther King Senior, gave the invocation at the 1976 Democratic National Convention, which nominated Gov. Jimmy Carter of Georgia for president.
10. King's widow, Coretta, and his children did not always agree on their attitudes toward other civil rights causes of recent decades, such as the campaign for equality for lesbian, gay, bisexual, transgender, and queer people.

P-11   Numbers

Edit the following sentences according to the style used in this book to correct any errors in the way numbers are presented. If all the numbers in a sentence are already correctly expressed, write "correct."

EXAMPLE

Before James Cameron began work on *Avatar,* his mother dreamed about a blue-skinned woman ~~12~~ twelve feet tall.

1. *Avatar*, the epic science-fiction motion-capture film released in 2009, takes place in the twenty-second century.

2. James Cameron, the writer and director, estimates that sixty percent of the film consists of computer-generated elements.

3. The theatrical release runs for 162 minutes.

4. Nominated for 9 Oscars, the film won 3.

5. A linguist created a language of about 1,000 words for the Na'vi characters to speak. Cameron added 30 more words.

6. Back in 1994, Cameron prepared an 80-page plan for the movie, but he had to wait for film technology to catch up with his vision.

7. Four-fifths of professional critics gave *Avatar* a positive review.

8. The average rating by a critic was 7.4 out of 10.

9. On the seventh of January 2010, the *New York Times* political columnist David Brooks turned film critic for a day and called *Avatar*'s "white Messiah fable" offensive.

10. In response, three hundred readers left comments on his newspaper's website.

Note: Answers to even-numbered items can be found at the back of the book.

Answers to Even-Numbered Exercises

S-1a EXERCISE 1, p. 460

| 2. B | 4. A | 6. B | 8. A | 10. A |

S-1a EXERCISE 2, p. 461

| 2. B | 4. B | 6. B | 8. A | 10. A |

S-1a EXERCISE 3 (possible answers), p. 462

2. It was the lead that was poisonous, not the tomatoes.

4. The tomato it is native to the Western Hemisphere, and it was the Spanish explorer Cortés who brought it back to Europe.

6. *correct*

8. *correct*

10. It was decided by the Court that tomatoes are prepared and eaten like vegetables, not like fruits, and that therefore the vegetable duty had been charged correctly.

S-1b, p. 463

2. In the past, some authors used pseudonyms because they couldn't get published under their real names.

4. Mary Ann Evans opted for the male pseudonym George Eliot, which appeared on her novels such as *Middlemarch* and *Silas Marner*.

6. Other authors, like some actors, take pseudonyms simply to have a name that is catchy or easy to spell or pronounce.

8. Yet another reason to assume a pseudonym is to disguise the fact that the author is actually two people.

10. Two name changers who won the Nobel Prize for Literature are the poet Pablo Neruda (Neftalí Ricardo Reyes Basoalto) and the novelist Toni Morrison (Chloe Anthony Wofford).

S-1c (possible answers), p. 464

2. Criticizing the book for its morally despicable characters is not as common as it once was.

4. The mysterious, wealthy Jay Gatsby is obsessed with a goal: winning back Daisy, who married another man.

6. Running seven hours, a 2012 stage production of the novel included every word of the text.

8. Some critics of the 2013 film of *Gatsby* questioned the director's decision to replace 1920s jazz with contemporary hip-hop.

10. Not entirely dismissing the 2013 release, critics acknowledged its appeal for a new audience unfamiliar with the novel.

S-1b–c, p. 465

2. phrase   4. phrase   6. clause   8. clause   10. phrase

S-2a, p. 466

2. no fragment

4. Books, books, books. Their . . . bindings.

6. no fragment

8. no fragment

10. no fragment

S-2b (possible answers, first paragraph), p. 467

The *National Geographic* writer reports how disturbing it was to find that some Civil War battlefields were next to convenience stores. For example, part of the land involved in the 1863 Battle of Chancellorsville rested under a Hardee's, a Chick-fil-A, and a grocery store. Yet other parts of the Chancellorsville battlefield look much the same as they did in 1863. The writer explains that in many cases Congress does not provide sufficient money to buy a whole battlefield for historic preservation. As a result, commercial development has been occurring on land once considered sacred.

S-3a, p. 468

2. cs   4. cs   6. no cs   8. cs   10. cs

S-3b (possible answers, first paragraph), p. 469

Also called the plague, the Black Death traveled from Asia to the area around the Mediterranean Sea. Then, it spread to the rest of Europe. The symptoms of the Black Death gave the disease its name. One form of it was marked by swellings that cause black stains from bleeding under the skin, and another form caused fever. Those who got the first form died within five days, while victims of the second form died even faster. The Black Death was so terrifying that parents and children abandoned each other, and priests refused to visit the sick to hear last confessions. Some towns tried to keep out the disease by banning any outsiders from entering; meanwhile, many rich people fled to the countryside to try to escape.

S-4a, p. 470

2. had become	8. influenced
4. limited	10. correct
6. had influenced	

S-4b EXERCISE 1, p. 471

2. gained	8. generated
4. accepted	10. received
6. rated	

S-4b EXERCISE 2, p. 472

2. led	8. told
4. paid	10. wear
6. found	

S-4b EXERCISE 3, p. 473

2. hunting	8. poaching
4. receiving	10. becoming
6. to earn	

S-4c, p. 474

2. Still, many wild varieties are very distinctive and not similar to any dangerous variety, so it is unlikely that anyone would make an error in picking them.

4. *correct*

6. *correct*

8. *correct*

10. The morel mushroom is so delicious that it must ~~to~~ be eaten to be believed.

S-4d (possible answers), p. 475

2. If raising your children is bungled by you, I don't think whatever else is done well by you matters very much.

4. Children do pretty much all the honest truth telling there is in the world.

S-4e EXERCISE 1, p. 475

2. *correct*

4. *correct*

6. Many doctors recommend that a person with insomnia *avoid* late-afternoon naps.

8. Some researchers suggest that a person with insomnia *stay* away from the hormone melatonin, which is not regulated by the Food and Drug Administration.

10. However, the night before exams some students probably wish that any prescription sleep aid *were* available over the counter.

S-4e EXERCISE 2, p. 476

2. Some scholars argue that if a Serbian nationalist had not assassinated Archduke Franz Ferdinand of Austria in 1914, World War I would not *have taken* place.

4. If the Boston Red Sox *had not traded* Babe Ruth to the New York Yankees in 1920, would the Red Sox have had more success?

6. In developing Apple products, Steve Jobs insisted that design *receive* the highest priority.

8. If the emergency response to Hurricane Katrina in 2005 *had been* smoother, the politicians involved would have fared better in public opinion.

10. Even with flu shots available today, health professionals strongly suggest that everyone *wash* their hands frequently.

S-4f, p. 477

2. Previous articles are a good place to start, so journalists usually *look them up.*

4. When someone refuses a request for an interview, the journalist must *get over the disappointment* quickly and move on.

6. *correct*

8. Juicy details may come out in an interview, but the finished article needs facts and evidence to *back it up.*

10. *correct*

S-5 EXERCISE 1, p. 478

2. goes   4. is   6. need   8. comes   10. are

S-5 EXERCISE 2, p. 479

2. One of the best-known rock percussionists, still going strong, *is* drummer and musicologist Mickey Hart of the Grateful Dead.

4. Hart is surely the only one of the world's drummers who *has* collaborated with a winner of the Nobel Prize in Physics.

6. *correct*

8. Drums of every kind *have* been played for centuries all over the world.

10. *correct*

S-6a, p. 480

2. They   8. her
4. their *or* his or her   10. they *or* he or she
6. her

S-6b (possible answers), p. 481

2. ~~A~~ guidebook to the park ~~it~~ says that *El Capitan* is a Spanish translation of the original Native American name *To-to-kon oo-lah*, meaning "the chief."

4. In 1958, Warren Harding, Wayne Merry, and George Whitmore became the first to climb the Nose successfully. The climb took them forty-seven days.

6. In 1993, Lynn Hill became the first person to climb the Nose without ropes and pitons, a feat that was especially extraordinary because she reached the top in just four days.

8. This reputation makes climbers think twice before taking on El Capitan.

10. At night, ~~you can see~~ lights from these hanging campsites can be seen dotting the rock.

S-6c EXERCISE 1, p. 482

2. Set in an advertising agency on New York City's Madison Avenue, the show traces conflicts among Draper and his colleagues as well as between him and various women.

4. Even many fans of those other shows, however, enjoyed *Mad Men* more than them.

6. correct

8. Though Don's stay-at-home wife, Betty, seemed outdated compared with "career girl" Peggy Olson, one report found that women viewers identified more with Betty than her.

10. Although Weiner has been praised for the show's visual style and authentic period details, he and his writers have been criticized for not addressing gender and race issues more directly.

S-6c EXERCISE 2, p. 483

2. we
4. whom
6. whom

8. who
10. we; whomever

S-7 (possible answers), p. 484

2. In addition to writing poems, Carl Sandburg sang folk songs and collected old ballads.

4. Before the age of thirty, Samuel Clemens
   • worked as a printer

- piloted boats on the Mississippi
- reported for newspapers in Virginia City and San Francisco

6. Katherine Anne Porter enjoyed reporting for a newspaper and teaching at several colleges in addition to writing novels and short stories.

8. Flannery O'Connor, confined to the family farm by chronic illness for most of her adult life, disciplined herself to sit down at her desk every day and to work there for two hours whether she felt inspired or not.

10. correct

S-8 (possible answers), p. 485

2. At first, *Twitter* was criticized as a new way to waste time, but it gained respect in 2009 by helping Iranians share protest information.

4. Some users tweet to stay in touch with friends, but others want to follow famous and powerful people.

6. Users can choose to make their accounts private, or they can allow anyone to see their tweets.

8. *Twitter* claims to connect users to the latest information that they care about.

10. In 2013, seven years after it had launched, *Twitter* sold shares and became a public company.

S-8b (possible answers), p. 485

2. correct

4. The original sentence unnecessarily uses the first independent clause merely to say that Monroe's and Madonna's shoes show up in the collection. The revision puts that information in a subordinate position, giving more prominence to the contrast between the two pairs of shoes and, in particular, to Madonna's pair: Whereas a photo of plain red leather stiletto pumps represents Marilyn Monroe, a shot of red ankle-strap heels with metallic dots represents Madonna.

6. correct

8. correct

10. The original sentence gives equal weight to a claim that the ruby slippers may be "the most beloved American shoes of all time" and to a piece of evidence for this claim. The revision puts the emphasis on the more important idea—the claim itself—and subordinates the evidence: The most beloved American shoes of all time may be the ruby slippers worn by Dorothy in The Wizard of Oz, one pair of which sold at auction for $666,000.

S-9, p. 487

2. Viewers may be relieved to learn that Eleanor is in the part of the afterlife reserved for good people, although they must wonder what happens to people who led bad lives.

4. In the show, architects create different neighborhoods in the afterlife; architects are responsible for creating neighborhoods that are perfectly tailored to their residents.

6. The show's creator, Michael Schur, decided early on that he would end the show after four seasons, and he stuck to that plan.

8. People who like the show tend to enjoy its exploration of moral philosophy, while people who don't like the show tend to think that moral philosophy is not a good subject for television.

10. Part of what is so compelling about the show is the characters' ability to grow and change in the afterlife.

L-1a–b (possible answers, first paragraph), p. 488

We should commission an analysis of the financial consequences of owning (as opposed to leasing) the proposed municipal solar energy system. At this point, we know only that the lease as submitted will reduce the current annual cost of $400,000 for municipal electric needs by 50 percent. Several officials expressed interest in my suggestion. Nan Byrnes, the consultant who guided the town through the negotiation process with the energy company, confirmed at the September meeting that the town can request from West Side Electric a price for purchasing the system from the outset. (Such a price will be substantially lower, Nan has told me, than the later purchase price that West Side offers if we begin our relationship by leasing.)

L-1c–d (possible answers), p. 489

2. Job applicants need to highlight what they *have to offer to the employer*.

4. Employers might want to *motivate* employees *to work for goals higher than easy or obvious ones*.

6. As an alternative *to opening wells of oil and natural gas by fracturing rock under high pressure, a common method known as fracking that could potentially have harmful side effects,* some countries are studying the environmental advantages of *producing natural gas from* methane hydrate *(natural gas in its crystal form)*—what *Atlantic* writer Charles C. Mann refers to as "ice you can set on fire."

8. Advertisements for *dental treatment that emphasize the effects of oral health on the entire body* have become more common recently in community newspapers.

10. In our fast-paced world, we want those who tell us stories or jokes to *get to the point quickly.*

L-2a (possible answers), p. 490

2. Curry also won the BET Sportsman of the Year Award in 2015.

4. Steph Curry's father, Dell Curry, also played in the NBA.

6. Fans and announcers call Curry and teammate Klay Thompson the Splash Brothers because of their astonishing combined record for three-point baskets.

8. Curry did not play on the 2016 US Olympic basketball team.

10. Since he entered the league in 2009, Curry has only played for the Warriors.

L-3 (possible answers), p. 491

2. The candidate said that she had no comment with respect to the scandal.

4. The new manager made changes across the board, firing or transferring almost half the staff of each department.

6. John thought his colleagues' proposal was uninspired, but he went along with it in order to be a team player.

8. Carlos tried to cover all the bases in his search for a place to live, asking friends, family members, and co-workers for leads as well as posting an ad on *Craigslist*.

L-4 EXERCISE 1, p. 491

2. lies
4. led
6. its

8. sensuous
10. As

L-4 EXERCISE 2, p. 492

2. than
4. too
6. fewer

8. allusions
10. among

L-4 EXERCISE 3, p. 493

2. New Orleans jazz, swing, big band jazz, bebop, cool jazz, and hard bop, etc., are among the subcategories of jazz.

4. The reason for the falling off of fusion in the 1980s and beyond is because of a revived interest in traditional, or pure, jazz at that time.

6. Many people learned about jazz through Ken Burns's 2001 documentary series for PBS.

8. The internet is by far the top medium for accessing all kinds of popular music.

10. correct

L-5, p. 494

2. in; on; at
4. on; in; at
6. on; in; in

8. at; in; on
10. in; in; on

L-6 (possible answers), p. 495

2. In the last few years, the United States has seen more than a thousand tornados a year, the majority of them in Tornado Alley.

4. When they saw a low cloud that was large ~~in size~~, grayish-yellow ~~in color~~, and shaped like a funnel, they knew they had to race ~~quickly~~ to a storm shelter.

6. He is a hero among the local residents ~~living in that area~~.

8. *When* a tornado hits, England and his team of meteorologists hunker down in the station office around their multicolored radar screens, while the rest of Oklahoma City watches them.

10. Some scientists believe that tornados ~~at this point in time~~ are more severe ~~and are causing more damage~~ than in the past *because* of climate change.

L-6b (possible answers), p. 496

2. The growth of such crops enabled the Neolithic cultures to settle in villages.

4. Traditionally, two conditions were required for a culture to earn the label "civilization."

6. Second, urban centers had to develop with religious and social power structures made up of literate leaders.

8. About the same time but farther south, the great civilization of the Maya began to take form.

10. Notably, Mesoamericans sacrificed humans to their corn goddess and other deities.

L-7a, p. 497

2. By choosing prospects more *carefully*, the A's became competitive with the New York Yankees, who had much more money to spend.

4. When he was a young player, Beane himself had been widely hailed by scouts but went on not to do so *well*.

6. *correct*

8. The undervalued players scored well on many measures that scouts and managers had not taken as *seriously* as the traditional ones.

10. *correct*

L-7b, p. 498

2. most ancient
4. most famous
6. farther

8. smallest
10. better

L-7c (possible answers, first paragraph), p. 499

Using the slogan "No taxation without representation," the colonists protested in 1764 and 1765 against taxes that Britain had placed on imports of sugar and printed matter~~. using the slogan "No taxation without representation."~~ In 1766, *when the colonists stopped buying all British products,* the British agreed to repeal the taxes~~. when the colonists stopped buying all British products.~~ In 1767, however, the British placed other taxes on the colonists, who proceeded *again* to ~~again~~ boycott imports from Britain. *When* four thousand soldiers *were sent* to Boston in response to the boycott, the stage was set for violence, and indeed nervous British soldiers shot and killed protesting colonists in what became known as the Boston Massacre.

L-8a,c, p. 501

2. *no article*
4. a
6. a
8. an
10. an

L-8b–c, p. 502

2. the
4. the
6. the
8. *no article*
10. the

L-9a (possible answers), p. 503

2. The local food bank, which is run by the town's ~~aging~~ mayor, is organizing a holiday drive.

   There is no need to call attention to the mayor's age in this sentence.

4. no problematic language

   Ben's economic status gives relevant information about his perspective on the university's actions. Also, it is described using respectful, preferred terms and is clearly being shared with Ben's consent.

6. ~~Surprisingly enough, the obese~~ The receptionist who worked the afternoon shift ate mostly salad for lunch.

   The idea that an obese person doesn't eat healthy food is a stereotype.

8. The ~~trans~~ ophthalmologist who specialized in macular degeneration could predict how well a treatment would work on a particular patient.

> There is no need to call attention to the ophthalmologist's gender identity in this sentence.

10. no problematic language

> Rashida's sexual orientation is mentioned in the context of her public statement to the reporter, rather than as a label assigned to her by the writer. Her sexual orientation and those of the play's characters are also important to the point of the sentence itself.

L-9b (possible answers), p. 504

2. The board of directors~~, whose president is a disabled biracial woman,~~ notified staff that the fund-raising committee should reflect the ethnic and gender-identity diversity of the community as a whole.

> In the absence of any contextualizing information, the description of the president's identity is not relevant to this sentence.

4. The committee plans to kick off the evening's formal program with a Land Acknowledgment Statement delivered by a member of ~~a local Indian group~~ the Cheyenne and Arapaho Tribal Nations.

> The specific tribal or nation name should be used instead of the generic word "Indian."

6. *correct*

> The term "Black-owned" is a respectful way to indicate that a business is majority-owned by people who are Black, and it is relevant here to specify which businesses are getting support. To give context for why the café is being supported in this situation, the sentence specifies Ethiopia as the origin of its cuisine and possibly its ownership.

8. *correct*

> Use capital "D" when referring to the "Deaf community." In general, use lowercase "d" when referring to a hearing-loss condition, but ask the person or people you're describing if possible because preferences vary.

L-9c EXERCISE 1 (possible answers), p. 505

2. Seeing someone ~~regain his~~ smile again after a few days in the hospital satisfies a nurse's need for positive feedback.

4. Health-care workers today explain to a person who tests positive for HIV that they have a much better chance for long-term survival than an HIV-positive person did in the 1980s.

6. Before applying to the Air Force Academy, students should ask themselves if they are prepared mentally and physically to meet the demands of the school and of service to their country.

8. Jared Flood is a ~~male~~ knitter and knitwear designer who writes the blog *Brooklyn Tweed.*

10. As you are doing in this exercise, feminists try to eliminate sexist terms from their speaking and writing.

L-9c EXERCISE 2 (possible answers), p. 505

2. Whoever dies with the most toys wins.

4. Everyone must row with the oars they have.

L-10b, p. 506

2. Option B. The phrase "but unlike Reese" clarifies that "they" refers to Aziz and Jazmine.

4. Option A. In sentence B, "they" could refer to either Reese or the group, and "their" could refer to the band or to Reese. Sentence A specifies that "the group" made the offer to Ornery Shoelace and eliminates the possessive pronoun, making the sentence clearer.

L-11, p. 507

Answers will vary.

P-1a–b (possible answers), p. 509

2. correct

4. correct

6. Under the direction of Anouk Van Dijk, the Australian dance group Chunky Move receives rave reviews.

8. Jeff and Jane Hudson issued the album *Flesh* in the 1980s, so thirty years later it was time to reissue it.

10. Incidentally, all seven acts mentioned in this exercise have performed at the Massachusetts Museum of Contemporary Art.

P-1c, p. 510

2. Which of the following titles was published first: *Harry Potter and the Half-Blood Prince*, *Harry Potter and the Deathly Hallows*, *Harry Potter and the Goblet of Fire*, or *Harry Potter and the Order of the Phoenix*?

4. Paula Fox's novel *The Slave Dancer* conveys the horrors of capturing, transporting, and selling Africans to become slaves.

6. J. R. R. Tolkien earned a graduate degree in the study of languages, worked on the *Oxford English Dictionary*, and became a professor at Oxford University before he wrote *The Hobbit*.

8. Mark Twain's novel *The Adventures of Huckleberry Finn* shows the worst and the best qualities of American society, examines Huck's moral struggle over helping Jim to escape, and explores issues of race and identity.

10. The first trilogy by Jane Yolen consists of *Dragon's Blood*, *Heart's Blood*, and *A Sending of Dragons*.

P-1d (possible answers), p. 511

2. Brady and Montana are the only National Football League players/ who have been named most valuable player more than once in both the league and the Super Bowl.

4. New Orleans quarterback Drew Brees, who was born in Dallas, was named after Dallas Cowboy wide receiver Drew Pearson.

6. Quarterback Cam Newton became the third player in NFL history to do all these things in the same year: (1) win a national championship, (2) be the first pick in the NFL draft, and (3) receive the Heisman Trophy, which goes to the best college football player.

8. *correct*

10. *correct*

P-1e–i, p. 512

2. *correct*

4. The characters and plot lines of *30 Rock,* as most of the show's fans know**,** grew out of Fey's experiences at *Saturday Night Live.*

6. Episodes of *30 Rock* were shot**,** however**,** at Silvercup Studios in Long Island City**,** New York, in the borough of Queens.

8. In a typical line on *30 Rock*, Liz Lemon says**,** "Check this out**,** Jack. Tile samples. First I redo the bathroom, then I redo the whole apartment, and then the world." Jack responds**,** "I'm impressed**,** Lemon. You're talking like a winner."

10. Is "Tina" short for "Christina"? No**,** Tina Fey's full name is Elizabeth Stamatina Fey, reflecting her partly Greek ancestry. Furthermore**,** she has given Greek middle names to her daughters.

P-1j (possible answers), p. 513

2. Ferrell's impersonations go back to high school, where he made**/** public address announcements in disguised voices.

4. What Tina Fey got in 2010**/** was more than the Mark Twain Prize itself. In addition, she had the satisfaction of knowing that she was the youngest winner ever.

6. A comic who's considered one of the most influential performers of the twentieth century**/** accepted the Mark Twain Prize in 2012. The 2012 winner, Ellen DeGeneres, has been praised as a writer, an actor, and a humanitarian.

8. On June 22, 2008, the winner of the 2008 prize, George Carlin, died of heart failure. The award ceremony that fall at the Kennedy Center**/** celebrated his long and influential career.

10. Twain once said, "Against the assault of laughter nothing can stand," and the recipients of the prize named for him**/** have proved him right.

P-2, p. 514

2. Steroids are synthetic forms of the hormone testosterone**;** megadoses of steroids give users an unfair advantage.

4. In adults, steroids cause rapid weight gain, problems with blood clotting, and heart attacks; in adolescents, they can shut down bone growth.

6. Athletes who later admitted steroid use include Mark McGwire and Barry Bonds, the baseball players; Marion Jones, the track and field athlete; and Lance Armstrong, the cyclist.

8. In 2013, Alex Rodriguez was suspended for 211 games for allegedly using steroids; thirteen other major-league baseball players were also suspended, but A-Rod was the only one to appeal his suspension.

10. Books about steroid use in athletics include *Game of Shadows,* 2007; *Bases Loaded,* 2009; and *Steroids: A New Look,* 2011.

P-3, p. 515

2. .   4. .   6. ?   8. .   10. ?

P-4a–b, p. 516

2. The film was endorsed by Sean "Diddy" Combs, who called it "very painful but very honest."

4. "Stark, visceral and unrelenting, *12 Years a Slave* is not just a great film," said one British newspaper, "but a necessary one."

6. Northup's book was republished in 1968 by a university press, which was quoted as calling him "a shrewd observer of people and events."

8. The better-known 1855 autobiography of Frederick Douglass, an escaped slave, includes the following passage about his early years:

> "I remember [my mother] only in her visits to me at Col. Lloyd's plantation, and in the kitchen of my old master. Her visits to me there were few in number, brief in duration, and mostly made in the night. The pains she took, and the toil she endured, to see me, tells me that a true mother's heart was hers, and that slavery had difficulty in paralyzing it with unmotherly indifference." (152)

10. In one stunning scene, sixteen-year-old Douglass fights back when his master, Covey, strikes him. Covey asks, "Are you going to resist, you scoundrel?"

> "Yes, sir," replied Douglass, steadily gazing Covey in the eye.

P-4c, p. 517

2. In another book, the brief essay "Mint Snowball" by Naomi Shihab Nye describes a mixture of shaved ice, mint syrup, and vanilla ice cream.

4. In the *National Geographic* book *Complete Photography,* "People & Pets" is surely the most-read chapter.

6. A 2010 publication titled *Rolling Stone: The Beatles' 100 Greatest Songs* ranks "I Want to Hold Your Hand" as number 2.

8. The 2009 book review "Abraham Lincoln: Misery's Child" tells of Lincoln's miserable early life.

10. "The Raven and the Crow" is one part of the long ancient poem called *Metamorphoses.*

P-4e, p. 518

2. "We all looked up to John," Paul once said. "He was the quickest wit and the smartest."

4. In 1970, Lennon was asked, "What do you think rock and roll will become?" He replied, "Whatever we make it."

6. When did Lennon say, "If everyone demanded peace instead of another television set, then there'd be peace"?

8. When asked how he would describe "Beatle music," Lennon responded with a question: "*Which* Beatle music do you mean?"

10. About "Give Peace a Chance," Lennon said, "In my secret heart, I wanted to write something that would take over 'We Shall Overcome.'"

P-4h, p. 519

2. delete   4. delete   6. *correct*   8. *correct*   10. delete

P-5a, p. 520

2. *correct*

4. Does "paid in part by the government" mean at taxpayers' expense?

6. Others argue that every American's coverage should follow the model of Medicare.

8. In the United States, unlike in some other countries, the typical doctor's employer is not the government.

10. Levitan and Kaplan's practice, like many others, has merged with a firm that handles the business side of things so that the doctors have more time for their patients.

P-5d, p. 521

2. *Angry Birds* appeals to teenagers, adults, and even four-year-olds.

4. Both the free limited version and the full-featured paid version have been downloaded millions of times.

6. So what are players to do? Theirs is a straightforward mission.

8. *The Angry Birds Movie* debuted in May 2016 after nine months of marketing.

10. The movie has a notable cast, including voicing by such actors as Sean Penn, Maya Rudolph, and Peter Dinklage.

P-6a, p. 522

2. The Rock and Roll Hall of Fame describes Patti Smith as follows: "a bohemian New York poet and punk-rock artiste."

4. Smith's accomplishments are wide-ranging: beyond singing and song writing, she has lectured on poetry, won the National Book Award, and exhibited her own photographs.

6. In his review of *Just Kids,* Edmund White notes that it's "full of memorable sentences," including this one: "We were both praying for Robert's soul, he to sell it and I to save it."

8. Many visitors buy a copy of the book *The Rock and Roll Hall of Fame: The First 25 Years.*

10. The Hall of Fame offers educational programs for all ages: toddlers, preteens, teenagers, and adults.

P-6b,c,f, p. 523

2. You can guess the last word of this stanza of R. L. Stevenson's poem: "In winter I get up at night / And dress by yellow candle-light. / In summer quite the other way / . . ."

4. Areas that use Daylight Saving Time (also called Daylight Savings Time) put clocks forward in the spring and then backward in the fall.

6. George Vernon Hudson (1867–1946) wanted more daylight in which to collect insects after he finished his day job.

8. The United States first used DST in 1918. Today, not all of the country does so—notably, Hawaii and part of Arizona do not.

10. That DST is used by only a small number of people is obvious when you learn one fact—Asian and African countries generally do not adopt it.

P-7, p. 524

2. Stephen Colbert played a caricature of a conservative host of a talk show.

4. correct

6. correct

8. Colbert is still a highly prized performer; he now hosts *The Late Show* on CBS.

10. The show had a nine-year run on Comedy Central.

P-8, p. 525

2. In 2012, Free Press published a book by Lori Andrews, a professor at Chicago-Kent College of Law, about the social network giant.

4. The book by Professor Andrews is titled *I Know Who You Are and I Saw What You Did: Social Networks and the Death of Privacy.*

6. Sheryl K. Sandberg is chief operating officer of Facebook; previously, she worked for Google.

8. She is famous for encouraging women to take on big challenges, and her book *Lean In* offers advice for how to do so.

10. Sandberg was born in Washington, DC, but had a Floridian childhood before she headed north to Harvard.

P-9, p. 526

2. The screenplay was adapted from The Accidental Billionaires, a 2009 book by Ben Mezrich.

4. Many critics, including Peter Travers in Rolling Stone magazine, praised the Facebook film, while Zuckerberg pointed out its inaccuracies.

6. Harvard has not allowed filming on its campus since <u>Love Story</u>, a 1970 release, so <u>The Social Network</u> was filmed elsewhere.

8. Not everyone loves <u>Facebook</u>; some people consider it the <u>anti</u>social network. [Italicizing the entire word *antisocial* is also acceptable.]

P-10, p. 527

2. The civil rights leader is the only person not a president to have a monument in his honor on the Mall in the District of Columbia. [or Washington, DC.]

4. King received his doctorate from Boston University in Massachusetts in 1955.

6. Many lines from his speeches and other writing have become classic American phrases, for example, "Free at last!" and "I have a dream."

8. The FBI kept an extensive file on King.

10. King's widow, Coretta, and his children did not always agree on their attitudes toward other civil rights causes of recent decades, such as the campaign for equality for LGBTQ+ people.

P-11, p. 528

2. James Cameron, the writer and director, estimates that 60 percent of the film consists of computer-generated elements.

4. Nominated for nine Oscars, the film won three.

6. Back in 1994, Cameron prepared an eighty-page plan for the movie, but he had to wait for film technology to catch up with his vision.

8. correct

10. correct

Credits

Illustrations: p. 15: US Bureau of Census 2013; **p. 16**: US Bureau of Labor Statistics 2014; **p. 44 (top)**: Wachirawit Iemlerkchai/Alamy Stock Photo; **p. 44 (bottom)**: RNGS/RTR/Newscom; **p. 45 (top)**: NASA-JPL/Caltech; **p. 45 (center)**: Figure 1B from "Income Segregation and Intergenerational Mobility across Colleges in the United States" by Raj Chetty, John N. Friedman, Emmanuel Saez, Nicholas Turner, Danny Yagan, *The Quarterly Journal of Economics*, Volume 135, Issue 3, August 2020, Pages 1567–1633, https://doi.org/10.1093/qje/qjaa005 Reprinted by permission of Oxford University Press on behalf of the President and Fellows of Harvard College; **p. 45 (bottom)**: NASA; **p. 51**: Library of Congress, Prints and Photographs Division. LC-USZ62-106327 (b&w film copy neg.); **p. 120**: Nicholas S. Holtzman, Simine Vazire, and Matthias R. Mehl, "Sounds Like a Narcissist: Behavioral Manifestations of Narcissism in Everyday Life." *Journal of Research in Personality,* Volume 44, Issue 4, August 2010, Pages 478–484; **p. 121 (top)**: The Atlantic; **p. 121 (bottom)**: Medium.com; **p. 132 (top)**: Pacific Standard; **p. 132 (center and bottom)**: google.com; **p. 133**: google. com; **p. 168**: Jessamyn Neuhasus "Marge Simpson, Blue-Haired Housewife: Defining Domesticity on *The Simpsons*." *Journal of Popular Culture* 43.4 (2010): 761–81. Print; **p. 169**: Segal, Michael. "The Hit Book That Came from Mars." *Nautilus*. NautilusThink. 8 January 2015. Web. 10 October 2016. Permission by Nautilus; **p. 169 (inset art)**: Matt Taylor; **p. 171**: © 2015 Ebsco Industries, Inc. All rights reserved; **p. 176**: from *Pink Sari Revolution: A Tale of Women and Power in India* by Amana Fontanella-Khan. New York: Norton 2013. Used by permission of W. W. Norton & Company, Inc.; **p. 181**: John McIlwain, Molly Simpson, and Sara Hammerschmidt. "Housing in America: Integrating Housing, Health, and Resilience in a Changing Environment." Urban Land Institute. Urban Land Institute 2014. Web. 17 Sept. 2016; **p. 193**: Bettmann/Getty Images; **p. 217**: Copyright 2013. From *Smart Technology and the Moral Life* by Guthrie, C. F. Reproduced by permission of Taylor & Francis LLC (http://www.tandfonline.com); **p. 219**: Lazette, M. P. (2015, February 25). A hurricane's hit to households. © 2015 Federal Reserve Bank of Cleveland; **p. 220**: From *The Great Divide: Unequal Societies and What We Can Do about Them* by Joseph E. Stiglitz. Copyright © 2015 by Joseph E. Stiglitz. Used by permission of W. W. Norton & Company, Inc.; **p. 244**: Courtesy University of Chicago Press *Knossos and the Prophets of Modernism* by Cathy Gere 2009; **p. 255**: Reprinted with permission from *Current History* magazine December 2009. © 2010 Current History Inc.; **p. 256**: Copyright © 2009 by Harper's Magazine. All rights reserved. Reproduced from the August issue by special permission; **p. 261**: Image published with permission of ProQuest. Further reproduction is prohibited without permission. www.proquest.com; **p. 264**: National Park Service; **p. 282**: from *Einstein's Mistakes: The Human Failings of Genius* by Hans C. Ohanian. New York (NY): W. W. Norton; 2008. Used by permission of W. W. Norton & Company, Inc.; **p. 285**: © 2007, Ecological Society of America. By permission of John Wiley and Sons; **p. 289**: Courtesy of Journal of Nutrition National Institutes of Health; **p. 417**: Matt Groening/20th Century Fox/Kobal/Shutterstock; **p. 419**: Mike Twohy/The New Yorker Collection/The Cartoon Bank.

Text: pp. 59–62: Gavin Reid. "The True Enshrinement of American Ideals: The Electoral College." Copyright © Gavin Reid. Reprinted by permission of the author; **pp. 68–71**: Pierce Rendall. "The Potential of Hip-Hop and the Impact It Creates." Copyright © Pierce Rendall. Reprinted by permission of the author; **pp. 76–79**: Rocio Celeste Mejia Avila. "Cyberloafing: Distraction or Motivation?" Copyright © Rocio Celeste Mejia Avila. Reprinted by permission of the author; **pp. 83–85**: Mohammed Masoom Shah. "One Last Ride." Copyright © Mohammed Masoom Shah. Reprinted by permission of the author; **pp. 92–93**: Jacob MacLeod. "Guns and Cars Are Different." Copyright © Jacob MacLeod. Reprinted by permission of the author; **p. 107**: Kelly Green. "Researching Hunger and Poverty." Copyright © Kelly Green. Reprinted by permission of the author; **pp. 192–200**: Dylan Borchers. "Against the Odds: Harry S. Truman and the Election of 1948." Copyright © Dylan Borchers. Reprinted by permission of the author; **pp. 233–38**: Katryn Sheppard. "Early Word Production: A Study of One Child's Productions." Copyright © Katryn Sheppard. Reprinted by permission of the author; **pp. 273–76**: Erika Graham. "History at Home: Leighton House, Sambourne House, and the Heritage Debate." Copyright © Erika Graham. Reprinted by permission of the author; **pp. 295–97**: Pieter Spealman. "Guppies and Goldilocks: Models and Evidence of Two Types of Speciation." Copyright © Pieter Spealman. Reprinted by permission of the author.

Glossary/Index

553

APA style, 201–38 A system of DOC-UMENTATION used in the social sciences. APA stands for the American Psychological Association.

appendix A section at the end of a written work for supplementary material that would be distracting in the main part of the text.

application letter A letter written to apply for a job or other position. Key Features: succinct indication of qualifications • reasonable and pleasing tone • conventional, businesslike form

argument, 53–62 A writing GENRE and STRATEGY that uses REASONS and EVIDENCE to support a CLAIM or POSITION and, sometimes, to persuade an AUDIENCE to accept that position. Key Features: clear and arguable position • necessary background • good reasons • convincing support for each reason • appeal to readers' values • trustworthy TONE • careful consideration of other positions

article, 407–9 The word "a," "an," or "the" used to indicate that a NOUN

is indefinite (<u>a</u> writer, <u>an</u> author) or
definite (<u>the</u> author).
 capitalizing, in titles, 452–53
 exercises, 501–2
 when to use, 407–9

articles, periodical. *See* periodical
   articles
"as"
 vs. "as if" and "like," 395
 and pronoun use, 377
 as subordinating word, 351
"as a matter of fact," 392, 393
"at," vs. "in," "on," 400–401
atlases, 126

audience, 2–3 Those to whom a text
is directed—the people who read, listen to, or view the text.
 for annotated bibliographies, 108
 appealing to readers' values, 54
 appropriate language and,
  418–19
 arguments and, 56
 building common ground, 425–26
 idioms and, 394
 reading strategy, 12
 research sources and, 129, 136
 rhetorical context and, 8

Audioburst Search, 124
audio material
 online collections of, 124
 in presentations, 50
audio sources, documenting
 APA style, 224–27
 MLA style, 184–89

authorities People or texts that are
cited as support for an ARGUMENT. A

structural engineer may be quoted as
an authority on bridge construction,
for example. "Authority" also refers to
a quality conveyed by writers who are
knowledgeable about their subject.

authors, documenting
 APA style, 204–7, 209–10, 212–14
 Chicago style, 242–43, 244–46, 257,
  286
 CSE style, 280–81, 284
 MLA style, 161–62, 165–67
authors, expertise of, 131, 133

B

"bad," "badly," 395, 405
balance
 argument and, 14
 as a design element, 41

bandwagon appeal A logical FAL-
LACY that argues for thinking or
acting in a certain way just because
others do.

bar graphs, 45

base form, 357 The simplest form of a
verb: eat, have, be, buy. The base form
doesn't indicate tense (ate, had) or
third person in the present (is, buys).

"BC" ("before Christ"), 456
"BCE" ("before the common era"), 456
"be"
 conditional sentences and, 364
 exercise, 490
 as helping verb, 360
 overuse of, 387

brackets, 446–47 Square parentheses ([ ]) used to indicate words inserted in a quotation.

brainstorming, 17 A process for GENERATING IDEAS AND TEXT by writing down everything that comes to mind about a topic, then looking for patterns or connections among the ideas.

C

case, 321–23 The different forms some PRONOUNS can take to indicate how they function in a sentence, for example, as the SUBJECT or OBJECT. "I" and "me" refer to the same person, but they are not interchangeable in a sentence: Joanne offered me one of the puppies, but I am allergic to dogs.

cause and effect, 29–30 A STRATEGY for analyzing why something occurred or speculating about what its consequences will be. Cause and effect can serve as the organizing principle for a paragraph or a whole text.

Chicago style, 239–76 A system of DOCUMENTATION for papers in history and other subject areas in the humanities. "Chicago" is short for *The Chicago Manual of Style*, which is published by the University of Chicago Press.

chronological order, 82 A way of organizing text that proceeds from the
beginning of an event to the end. Reverse chronological order proceeds
in the other direction, from the end
to the beginning.

citation, 138–297 In a text, the act of
giving information from a source. A
citation and its corresponding parenthetical DOCUMENTATION, footnote,
or endnote provide minimal information about the source; complete
bibliographic information appears in
a list of WORKS CITED or REFERENCES at
the end of the text. *See also* APA style;
Chicago style; CSE style; MLA style

claim, 53 A statement that asserts
a belief or position. In an ARGUMENT,
a claim needs to be stated in a THE-
SIS or clearly implied, and it requires
support by REASONS and EVIDENCE.

classification and division, 30 A
STRATEGY that either groups (classi-
fies) numerous individual items by
their similarities (for example, classifying cereal, bread, butter, chicken,
cheese, cream, eggs, and oil as carbohydrates, proteins, and fats) or
breaks (divides) one large category
into small categories (for example,
dividing food into carbohydrates,
proteins, and fats). Classification
and/or division can serve as the organizing principle for a paragraph or
a whole text.

clause, 301, 349 A group of words
that consists of at least a SUBJECT and
a PREDICATE; a clause may be either
INDEPENDENT or SUBORDINATE.

cliché, 386 An expression used so
frequently that it is no longer fresh:
busy as a bee.

coordinating conjunction, 382   One of these words—"and," "but," "or," "nor," "so," "for," or "yet"—used to join two elements in a way that gives equal weight to each one (bacon <u>and</u> eggs; pay up <u>or</u> get out).

correlative conjunction   A pair of words used to connect two equal

elements: either . . . or, neither . . . nor, not only . . . but also, just as . . . so, and whether . . . or.

counterargument, 54, 57   In ARGU-MENT, an alternative POSITION or an objection to the writer's position. The writer of an argument should not only acknowledge counterarguments but also, if at all possible, accept, accommodate, or refute each one.

count noun, 325, 407–8   A word that names something that can be counted: one book, two books.

credibility   The sense of trustworthiness that a writer conveys through text.

organizing principle for a paragraph or a whole text.

definitions, in reports, 73

description, 33 A STRATEGY that tells how something looks, sounds, smells, feels, or tastes. Effective description creates a clear DOMINANT IMPRESSION built from specific details. Description can be *objective*, *subjective*, or both. Description can serve as the organizing principle for a paragraph or a whole text.
    in personal narratives, 80, 81
    in reflections, 103–4
    in rhetorical analysis, 65

descriptive abstracts, 111–12
descriptive annotations, 106, 109
"desert," "dessert," 396

design, 40–47 The way a text is arranged and presented visually. Elements of design include font, color, illustration, layout, and white space.
    accessibility and, 47
    elements
      color, 41, 47, 51
      fonts, 41–42
      headings, 43
      layout, 42
    italics, 42
    lists and, 42
    paragraphs and, 42
    principles of, 40–41
    of reports, 73
    visuals, 43–47

diagrams, 45

dialogue, 80 A STRATEGY for adding people's own words to a text. *See also* quotation

dictionaries, documenting
    APA style, 222
    Chicago style, 250
    MLA style, 157
"did." *See* "do"
digital archives, 125
direct address, 431
direct object. *See* object
direct questions, 435
direct quotations, 430–31, 436–37
discussions, online. *See* online forums, documenting
"disinterested," "uninterested," 396
dissertations, documenting
    APA style, 223–24
    MLA style, 180
division. *See* classification and division
"do"
    exercise, 490
    as helping verb, 360
    overuse of, 387

documentation, 138–297 Publication information about the sources cited in a text. The documentation usually appears in an abbreviated form in parentheses at the point of CITATION or in an endnote or a footnote. Complete documentation usually appears as a BIBLIOGRAPHY, list of WORKS CITED, or REFERENCES at the end of the text. Styles vary by

DOI, 161 A digital object identifier, a stable number identifying the location of a source accessed through a database.

dominant impression The overall effect created through specific details when a writer DESCRIBES something.

draft, 19 To put words on paper or screen. Writers often write several drafts, REVISING each until they achieve their goal and submit a finished final draft.

E

edit, 23–25 To fine-tune a text by examining each word, PHRASE, sentence, and paragraph to be sure that the text is correct and precise and says exactly what the writer intends. *See also* editing errors that matter

edited academic English, 300, 418, 423 The conventions of spelling, grammar, and punctuation standardized and expected in academic discourse, usually more formal than conversational English.

either-or argument A logical FAL-LACY, also known as a false dilemma, that oversimplifies to suggest that only two possible POSITIONS exist on a complex issue.

ellipses, 447–48 Three spaced dots (. . .) that indicate an omission or a pause.

emotional appeal, 54 In ARGUMENT, an appeal to readers' feelings. Emotional appeals should be used carefully in academic writing, where arguments are expected to emphasize logical reasons and evidence more than emotion.

Englishes, 417–26 The plural form recognizes that there are many legitimate varieties of English.

essential element, 428–30 A word, PHRASE, or CLAUSE with information that is necessary for understanding the meaning of a sentence: French is the only language that I can speak.

ethical appeal In ARGUMENT, a way a writer establishes credibility with readers, such as by demonstrating knowledge of the topic; pointing out common ground between the writer's values and those of readers; or incorporating the views of others, including opposing views, into the argument.

evaluation A writing GENRE that makes a judgment about something—a source, poem, film, restaurant, whatever—based on certain CRITERIA. Key Features: description of the subject • clearly defined criteria • knowledgeable discussion of the subject • balanced and fair assessment

evidence, 54, 56 In ARGUMENT, the data you present to support your REASONS. Such data may include statistics, calculations, examples, ANECDOTES, QUOTATIONS, case studies, or anything else that will convince your reader that your reasons are compelling. Evidence should be sufficient (enough to show that the reasons have merit) and relevant (appropriate to the argument you're making).

explanation of a process, 33–34 A STRATEGY for telling how something is done or how to do something. An explanation of a process can serve as the organizing principle for a paragraph or a whole text.

expletive A word such as "it" and "there" used to introduce information provided later in a sentence: It was difficult to drive on the icy road. There is plenty of food in the refrigerator.

F

fact-checking, 131–33 The act of verifying the accuracy of facts and claims presented in a piece of writing, a speech, media such as images or videos, or a social media post.

fallacy, 14 Faulty reasoning that can mislead an AUDIENCE. Fallacies include AD HOMINEM, BANDWAGON

H

hasty generalization A FALLACY that reaches a conclusion based on insufficient or inappropriately qualified EVIDENCE.

helping verb, 360–62 A VERB that works with a main verb to express a TENSE and MOOD. Helping verbs include "do," "have," "be," and MODALS: Elvis <u>has</u> left the building. Pigs <u>can</u> fly.

irregular verb, 358   A VERB that does not form its past TENSE and PAST PARTICIPLE by adding "-ed" or "-d" to the base form (for example, "eat," "ate," "eaten").

J

jargon, 386   A specialized vocabulary of a profession, trade, or field that should be used only when you know your AUDIENCE will understand what you are saying.

K

keyword   A term that a researcher inputs when searching for information electronically.

L

lab report   A writing GENRE that covers the process of conducting an experiment in a controlled setting. Key Features: explicit title • ABSTRACT • PURPOSE • methods • results and discussion • REFERENCES • APPENDIX • appropriate format

layout, 42 The way text is arranged on a page or screen—for example, in paragraphs, in lists, on charts, with headings.

linking verb, 376 A VERB that expresses a state of being: appear, be, feel, seem.

listing, 104 A process for GENERATING IDEAS AND TEXT by making lists while thinking about a topic, finding relationships among the notes, and arranging the notes as an OUTLINE.

literacy portfolio An organized collection of materials showing examples of one writer's progress as a reader and/or writer.

literary analysis, 94–97 A writing GENRE that examines a literary text (most often fiction, poetry, or drama) and argues for a particular INTERPRETATION of the text. Key Features: arguable THESIS • careful attention to the language of the text • attention to patterns or themes • clear interpretation • MLA style

literature Literary works—including fiction, poetry, drama, and some nonfiction; also, the body of written work produced in given field.

logical appeal In ARGUMENT, an appeal to readers based on the use of logical reasoning and of EVIDENCE such as facts, statistics, authorities on the subject, and so on.

looping, 17 A process for GENERAT-ING IDEAS AND TEXT in which a writer writes about a topic quickly for several minutes and then reads the results and writes a one-sentence summary of the most important or interesting idea, which becomes the beginning of another round of writing and summarizing, and so on, until the writer finds a tentative focus for writing.

M

main verb The verb form that presents the action or state. It can stand alone or be combined with one or more HELPING VERBS. My dog might have <u>buried</u> your keys. Leslie Jones <u>is</u> a comedian. Alexa was <u>wearing</u> a gown by Milly. The agent didn't <u>appear</u> old enough to drive.

medium, 5 A way that a text is delivered—for example, in print, with speech, or online.

Memoir A GENRE that focuses on something significant from the writer's past. Key Features: good story • vivid details • clear significance

metaphor, 388 A figure of speech that makes a comparison without using the word "like" or "as": "All the world's a stage / And all the men and women merely players" (Shakespeare, *As You Like It*).

misinformation, 125 False or inaccurate information that may or may not be intended to deceive (lies, on the other hand, are always told deliberately).

mixed construction, 310–13 A sentence that starts out with one structure and ends up with another one: *Although bears can be deadly is not a good reason to avoid camping altogether.*

MLA style, 150–200 A system of DOCUMENTATION used in the humanities. MLA stands for the Modern Language Association.

modal, 360–62 A helping VERB—such as "can," "could," "may," "might," "must," "ought to," "should," "will," or "would"—used with the base form of a verb to express whether an action is likely, possible, permitted, or various other conditions.

modifier, 349 A word, PHRASE, or CLAUSE that describes or specifies something about another word, phrase, or clause (a <u>long</u>, <u>informative</u> speech; the actors spoke <u>in unison</u>; the man <u>who would be king</u>). *See also* adjective; adverb; participial phrase

mood, 363–64 A characteristic of VERBS that indicates a writer's attitude about whether a statement is possible or unlikely. The *indicative mood* is used to state fact or opinion: I'm waiting to buy tickets. The *imper-* *ative mood* is used to give commands or directions: Sit down, and take off your shoes. The *subjunctive mood* is used to express wishes or requests or to indicate unlikely conditions: I wish the ticket line were shorter.

multimedia Using more than one medium of delivery, such as print, speech, or electronic. Often used interchangeably with MULTIMODAL.

multimodal Using more than one mode of expression, such as words, images, sound, links, and so on. Often used interchangeably with MULTIMEDIA.

N

narration, 34 A STRATEGY for presenting information as a story, for telling "what happened." It is a pattern most often associated with fiction, but it shows up in all kinds of writing. When used in an essay, a REPORT, or another academic GENRE, narration is used to support a point—not merely to tell an interesting story for its own sake. It must also present events in some kind of sequence and include only pertinent detail. Narration can serve as the organizing principle for a paragraph or a whole text.

noncount noun, 408 A word that names an abstract item (happiness, curiosity) and liquids and masses (milk, sand, salt) that cannot be measured with numbers.

nonessential element, 428–30 A word, PHRASE, or CLAUSE that gives additional information but that is not necessary for understanding the basic meaning of a sentence: I learned French, <u>which is a Romance language</u>, online. Nonessential elements should be set off with commas.

noun, 347–48 A word that names a person, place, thing, or idea (teacher, Zadie Smith, forest, surgeon general, Amazon River, notebook, democracy). *See also* proper noun; subject-verb agreement

proposal, 98–101 A GENRE that argues for a solution to a problem or suggests some action. Key Features: well-defined problem • recommended solution • answers to anticipated questions • call to action • appropriate TONE

Publication Manual of the American Psychological Association, 201

pull quote, 41 A brief excerpt set off within a text in order to highlight certain information. Pull quotes are often set in a different FONT or color.

purpose, 2 A writer's goal: to explore ideas; to express oneself; to entertain; to demonstrate learning; to inform; to persuade; and so on. Purpose is one element of the RHETORICAL SITUATION.

Q

qualifying word, 6, 18, 56 A word such as "frequently," "often," "generally," "sometimes," or "rarely" that limits a CLAIM in some way.

questioning, 17 A process of GENERATING IDEAS AND TEXT about a topic—asking, for example, "What?," "Who?," "When?," "Where?," "How?," and "Why?" or other questions. *See also* questions

quotation, 138–41 The use of someone else's words exactly as they were spoken or written. Quoting is most effective when wording is worth

R

reason, 53–54, 56 Support for a CLAIM or POSITION. A reason, in turn, requires its own support in the form of EVIDENCE.

references, 209–29, 280–94 The list of sources at the end of a text prepared in APA STYLE or CSE STYLE.

reflection, 102–5 A GENRE of writing that presents a writer's thoughtful, personal exploration of a subject. Key Features: topic intriguing to the writer • some kind of structure • specific details • speculative TONE

relative pronoun, 371 A PRONOUN such as "that," "which," "who," "whoever," "whom," or "whomever" that introduces a SUBORDINATE CLAUSE: The professor <u>who</u> gave the lecture is my adviser.

report, 72–79 A writing GENRE that presents information to readers on a subject. Key Features: tightly focused TOPIC • accurate, well-researched information • various writing STRATEGIES • clear DEFINITIONS • appropriate DESIGN

résumé, 380 A GENRE that summarizes someone's academic and employment history, generally written to submit to potential employers. DESIGN and word choice depend on whether a résumé is submitted as a print document or in an electronic or scannable form. Key Features: organization that suits goals and experience • succinctness • design that highlights key information (for print) or that uses only one typeface (for scannable)

reviews, documenting
    APA style, 216
    Chicago style, 254
    MLA style, 174

revision, 21–23 The process of making substantive changes, including additions and cuts, to a DRAFT so that it contains all the necessary content and presents it in an appropriate organization. During revision, writers generally move from whole-text issues to details with the goals of sharpening their focus and strengthening their position.

rhetorical analysis, 63–71 A writing GENRE in which a writer looks at what a text says and how it says it. Key Features: SUMMARY of the text • attention to context • clear INTERPRETATION or judgment • reasonable support for conclusions
    key elements, 63–64
    sample essay: "Hip-Hop's Potential Impact" (Rendall), 68–71
    tips for writing, 64–67

rhetorical context, 2–5, 49, 418 The rhetorical situation in which writing or other communication takes place, including PURPOSE, AUDIENCE, GENRE, TOPIC, STANCE, TONE, MEDIUM, and DESIGN.
    academic contexts, 6–8
    appropriate language and, 418–19
    audience, 8
    design, 8, 40
    genre, 8
    media, 8
    purpose, 8

rhetorical situation. *See* rhetorical context
"rise," "raise," 398

Rogerian argument, 57 A technique for arguing that aims to solve conflicts by seeking common ground among people who disagree.

run-on sentence. *See* fused sentence

S

sacred texts, documenting
    APA style, 223
    Chicago style, 251
    MLA style, 158, 178
sample paper/pages
    APA style, 76–79, 232–38
    Chicago style, 272–76
    CSE style, 294–97
    MLA style, 59–62, 68–71, 191–200
scholarly vs. popular sources, 119–23
Science.gov, 124

secondary source, 119 An ANALYSIS or INTERPRETATION of a PRIMARY

stance, 4–5 A writer's attitude toward the subject being discussed—
for example, reasonable, neutral,
angry, curious. Stance is conveyed
through TONE and word choice.

strategy, 29–35 A pattern for orga-
nizing text to analyze CAUSE AND EF-
FECT, CLASSIFY AND DIVIDE, COMPARE
AND CONTRAST, DEFINE, DESCRIBE, EX-
PLAIN A PROCESS, give EXAMPLES, and
NARRATE.

style In writing, the arrangement of
sentences, CLAUSES, PHRASES, words,
and punctuation to achieve a desired
effect; also, the rules of capitalization, punctuation, and so on for DOC-
UMENTATION of a source.

subject, 347–48 The NOUN or PRO-
NOUN plus any MODIFIERS that tell
who or what a sentence or CLAUSE
is about. A simple subject is a single
noun or pronoun. A complete subject
is the simple subject plus any modifiers. In the sentence "Ten commuters
waited for the late bus," the complete
subject is "Ten commuters" and
the simple subject is "commuters."
See also subject-verb agreement

thesis, 56   A statement that identifies the TOPIC and main point of a piece of writing, giving readers an idea of what the text will cover.

tone, 4–5   The way a writer's or speaker's STANCE toward the readers and subject is reflected in the text.

topic, 4   The specific subject written about in a text. A topic should be narrow enough to cover, not too broad or general. A topic needs to be developed appropriately for its AUDIENCE and PURPOSE.

topic proposal A statement of intent to examine a topic; also called a proposal ABSTRACT. Some instructors require a topic proposal in order to assess the feasibility of the writing project that a student has in mind. Key Features: concise discussion of the subject • clear statement of the intended focus • rationale for choosing the subject • mention of resources

topic sentence, 27–29 A sentence, often at the beginning of a paragraph, that states the paragraph's main point. The details in the rest of the paragraph should support the topic sentence.

transition, 36–38 A word or PHRASE that helps to connect sentences and paragraphs and to guide readers through a text. Transitions can help to show comparisons (also, similarly); contrasts (but, instead); examples (for instance, in fact); sequence (finally, next); time (at first, meanwhile); and more.

U

working bibliography, 118 A record of all sources consulted during research. Each entry provides all the bibliographic information necessary for correct DOCUMENTATION of each source, including author, title, and publication information. A working bibliography is a useful tool for recording and keeping track of sources.

works-cited list, 160–89 A list at the end of a researched text prepared in MLA STYLE or CHICAGO STYLE that contains full bibliographic information for all the sources cited in the text.

writing portfolio A collection of a writer's work, including a statement assessing the work and explaining what it demonstrates.

writing process, 17–26 In writing, a series of actions that may include

Y

Checklist for Revising and Editing

- How do you appeal to your AUDIENCE? [See W-1b.]

- Think about your PURPOSE. Will your text achieve that purpose? Does it meet the requirements of your assignment? [See W-1a and W-2.]

- What MEDIUM are you using—print? spoken? electronic?—and how does it affect your text? [See W-1f and W-6.]

- What KIND OF WRITING have you been assigned? Does your draft include all the key features of that kind of writing? [See W-8 through W-17.]

- Check any QUOTATIONS, PARAPHRASES, and SUMMARIES to be sure they support your point—and include DOCUMENTATION. [See R-4, E-4, and MLA, APA, CHICAGO, CSE.]

- Check that your SENTENCES are complete and that there are no unintentional fragments, fused sentences, or comma splices. Be sure each verb agrees with its subject, and each pronoun refers to a clear antecedent. [See S-1 through S-6 and E-1 through E-3.]

- Does your LANGUAGE reflect your STANCE? Is it appropriate? precise? inclusive and respectful? [See W-1e, L-1 through L-11, and E-6.]

- Check all PUNCTUATION AND MECHANICS—commas, apostrophes, quotation marks, capitalization, and so on. [See P-1 through P-11 and E-5.]

Revision Symbols

abbr	abbreviation **455**		∧	insert
adj	adjective **403**		*i/p*	interesting point
adv	adverb **403**		*ital*	italics **453**
agr	agreement **367, 372**		*jarg*	jargon **386**
⍌	apostrophe **441**		*lc*	lowercase letter **450**
no ⍌	unnecessary apostrophe **443**		*mm*	misplaced modifier **406**
			nice	well done!
art	article **407**		*num*	number **457**
awk	awkward*		¶	new paragraph
cap	capitalization **450**		//	parallelism **378**
case	pronoun case **376**		*pass*	passive voice **362**
cite	citation needed **138–49**		*ref*	pronoun reference **375**
cliché	cliché **386**		*run-on*	comma splice or fused sentence **353**
⌒	close up space		*sexist*	sexist language **412**
∧	comma needed **426**		*shift*	confusing shift **383**
no ∧	unnecessary comma **431**		*sl*	slang **384**
cs	comma splice **353**		#	insert space
def	define **32**		*sp*	spelling
⌿	delete		*trans*	transition **36**
dm	dangling modifier **406**		∿	transpose
doc	documentation **150–298**		*vb*	verb **355**
emph	emphasis **383**		*wrdy*	wordy **402**
frag	sentence fragment **350**		*ww*	wrong word **394**
fs	fused sentence **353**			
hyph	hyphen **448**			

*****Awk** usually indicates a problem with phrasing that cannot be easily described in a brief marginal comment. If you can't figure out the problem, ask your instructor for clarification.

MLA Documentation Directory

APA Documentation Directory

Chicago Documentation Directory

CSE Documentation Directory

Menu of Exercises

Detailed Menu